In Memory of Howel Williams,

a Guardian of the Buttes

Acknowledgments

A book grows from the sharing and caring of many persons. To my students I owe a debt for helping me to see and for encouraging me to leave a written body to continue my teaching long after I have departed from the Buttes.

To Rebecca I owe thanks beyond measure. It was she who shared the ups and downs of my life; who saw to it that I could translate experience into words; who attended to innumerable details for which she would claim no credit; who designed graphs and tables, drew fine drawings, wrote the chapter "Meadows on the Wing", typed endless drafts; and who, through it all, brought music into my life.

To Thelma Anderson, whose support has been unfailing, I owe more than a son's gratitude.

Then there are the landowners, whose cooperation made possible my intimate relationship with the land. Special thanks go to Pete and Sue Carr, Howard and Frances Cull, Randy and Shirley Schnabel, and Peter Steidlmayer.

For scientific credibility, I am grateful to those whose knowledge was available to me as needed: Lowell Ahart, Dave Cavagnaro, Blair Csuti, John Thomas Howell, Frank Koch, Donald Kowalski, June McCaskill, Jenny Metz, Burt Monroe, Kim Peeples, Tom Rodgers, Pete and Margit Sands, Kingsley Stern, Sue Taylor, John Hunter Thomas, Gene Trapp, Allen Whittemore, and Dave Woodward.

For special favors, I wish to recognize Jim Davison, Len Fulton, Arnie and Betty Hartjen, Lloyd Heidinger, Ira Heinrich, John and Diane Vafis, and others unnamed whose contributions are known and appreciated.

Finally, I salute the Buttes herself, a unique source of power and inspiration. May this book be a tribute to the range and to all who fall beneath her mystical spell.

— Walt Anderson

Foreword

"**W**alk through a Sutter Buttes oak woodland with me," Walt Anderson invites us. "I hope to see you there!"

And indeed you **will** see him, even if you never have the privilege of sharing the eagle's call or the vulture's silence with him there in person, for he comes to us **here** with open heart and mind on every page of this book.

The Sutter Buttes is indeed "a naturalist's view" in the most intimate sense, an invitation to carefully explore and thoroughly appreciate a spectacular volcanic island castle in the vast sea of California's Great Central Valley. You will crawl with Walt under logs and through ponds, wander over meadows blanketed with spring flowers and past cliffs jeweled with brilliant lichens. You will ride updrafts with dragonflies and swallows, burrow through leaf mould with earthworms and millipedes, hunt among crags with Red-tailed Hawks, and hitchhike in sheep wool with the Unicorn Plant.

Walt writes as he teaches; he is direct, warm, personal, knowledgeable, humorous. On any walk with Walt, nature becomes the greatest thing in the world simply because he shows us in such a loving way that nature **is** the world. Read any chapter in this book and you will have **fun** learning, for even complicated lessons are palatable for us common folk.

Unlike the highly restrained academic biologist, Walt often allows himself a pleasure we mere humans can hardly resist — anthropomorphizing nature. Yet he remains throughout a far more faithful and reliable scientist than I have become since I laid down my butterfly net. His cards are always on the table, calling a spade a spade, nudging us to remember that nature does quite well on her own without our interpretations. In fact, she may have done even better without our very presence!

But this book, while primarily a natural history guide to a specific and very tiny spot on this globe, is far more than that. It is a merging of art and philosophy as well as science. It is a living, friendly, human experience.

This special place also in a mysterious way becomes anyplace on Earth. It is Thoreau's Walden, Leopold's Sand County, Krutch's Forgotten Peninsula, Dillard's Tinker Creek, Zwinger's Aspen Grove, your own back yard; for, like each of these great nature writers, Walt shows us the macrocosm in the microcosm and leaves us in the end with the abiding self-confidence that we can each become a naturalist if we allow ourselves to **be** in the world with all our senses tuned.

Besides, it is important to remember that the careful understanding of a place that this book represents has been achieved in only six years. When I first introduced Walt and Rebecca to the Sutter Buttes in 1976, they hardly had an idea even where the Buttes were. By example, they teach us that we can all accomplish something of what they have achieved, if we only cultivate care, attention, and a sense of wonder wherever we are.

What is a naturalist, really? Years ago I nearly starved, spiritually at least, looking for one in the science departments before I flunked out of the university. But when I crossed paths with Walt Anderson, I knew that I had found one — the naturalist of old cast in modern times, the next generation of a proud and ancient lineage.

A naturalist, I think, is first a person of the Earth, a shaman really, one who feels as well as sees, one who simply **knows** with greater breadth and depth than intellect alone can muster. Second, a naturalist is an interpreter, one who can translate the complex language of nature into the vocabulary of the common man, who can reach out to us from the heart of the natural world and lead us in.

A naturalist is a mediator between the Earth and alien Man — those of us at least who have in some ways lost touch with the laws that govern all life and who have forgotten (or never had the good fortune to learn) the symbolic meaning of every sight, sound, smell, process, or feeling that represents those laws. He not only introduces the world to us, sharing with us its ways and its meaning; he also introduces us to the Earth, guiding us to treat this nurturing mother gently, reassuring her that once we are aware again of our rightful place and heritage, we mean her no harm.

This is the way in which Walt teaches, in person as well as in writing, restoring wonder where there has been callousness, trust where there has been suspicion, caring where there has been neglect, unity where there has been separateness, bringing nature and humanity together again as one.

In a very real sense, Walt has helped restore this balance in the Sutter Buttes.

He has succeeded in developing controlled public access and educational land use within an existing pattern of private ownership. Old tensions between ranchers and the public have been eased through this new spirit of constructive cooperation, and a program has been established that is a superb national model.

So, also, does he treat hunters and environmentalists with equal respect in a region where duck clubs and game refuges stand side by side as vital feeding and resting places on the Pacific Flyway. "Despite the polarization that often occurs between hunters and non-hunters," Walt states, "much of the motivation is the same — the experience differs mainly in final punctuation."

I know at least a hundred people who have been with Walt personally in the field — Alaska, Kenya, Baja, Brazil, the Galapagos, and of course, the Sutter Buttes. At a glance I can see how their lives have changed.

Walt has courted the Buttes since 1976 as a naturalist in the largest meaning of the word. "Never has she disappointed me," he writes, "though if truth were known, never has she responded."

Here at last, my dear friend Walt, I will disagree with you. That singular flock of dowitchers that shot past you unexpectedly in the fog, the unusual Green-backed Heron sighting in the interior, the Lazuli Bunting that happens to appear in gleaming brilliance before your astonished class, the perfectly timed call of an eagle, that special little flower that seems almost to walk out of the shadows into a beam of sunlight in order to be seen — these experiences are **given** to you, I propose, by the Buttes herself.

Let the last great pillars of Academe quake when this heretic parsnip farmer speaks an age-old truth — that the Earth is a conscious being — for I believe that the Sutter Buttes has given herself to you, and you to us, that we may all return to her in joy and trust as the Maidu and Wintun peoples did before our own race went astray. You are a vital part of a great healing; **of course,** the Buttes would respond, as all that is alive responds when healed.

— David Cavagnaro

Table of Contents

Figures and Tables

the Sutter Buttes:
a naturalist's view

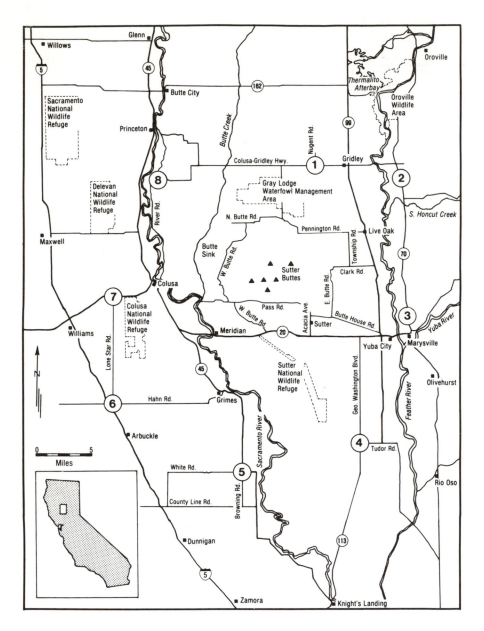

Figure 1. Sutter Buttes Profiles from Various Valley Vantages

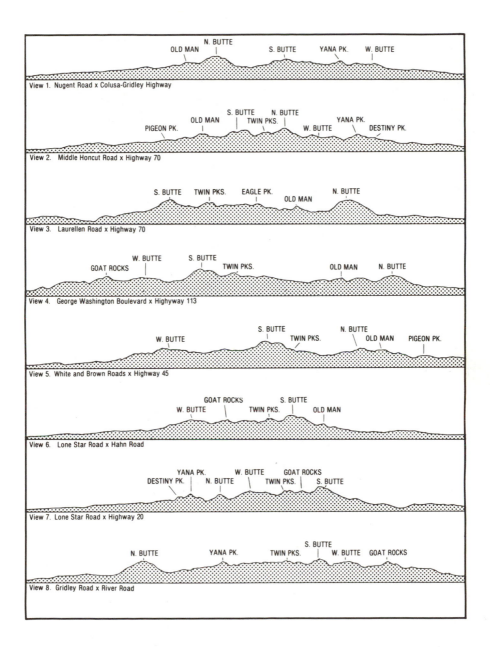

View 1. Nugent Road x Colusa-Gridley Highway

View 2. Middle Honcut Road x Highway 70

View 3. Laurellen Road x Highway 70

View 4. George Washington Boulevard x Highway 113

View 5. White and Brown Roads x Highway 45

View 6. Lone Star Road x Hahn Road

View 7. Lone Star Road x Highway 20

View 8. Gridley Road x River Road

1

A Singular Range

It was August of 1976 when we first saw the Buttes. Our plane came in high over the cloud-wrapped Sierra Nevada and began its descent into the great trough of the Sacramento Valley. Thousands of fields in all shades of green, gold, and brown formed a crazy-quilt pattern of human endeavor. And then we saw it — a surprisingly circular dome of peaks and ridges rising in singular isolation from the flat patchwork: the Sutter Buttes.

In the next few days we entered the range on foot, hiking beneath spreading oaks, through canyon thickets, over grassy ridges, to the summits of rocky peaks. Like the deer and the eagles we saw, at first we experienced the range in immediate terms — we sought shade, refreshing spring water, reasonable paths across the rugged landscape. But unlike the wildlife, our survival was not hitched so intimately to the land. We could look at the plants, the birds, the pinnacles, not simply in relation to physical needs, but as sources of wonder. And wonder we did.

As we sought answers to our questions, two things became apparent. First, information on the Buttes was scarce, sketchy, and subjective. Second, we were not alone in our curiosity and intense interest in the range.

Between the long corridors of the Coast Range and Sierra Nevada, one's eyes may sweep across the broad valley and find but one source of relief — the

Sutter Buttes. Here, as a winter storm begins to dissipate, clouds hang over pinnacles as if reluctant to leave. Here the sun has contours and angularities upon which to cast its rays and form its shadows. Here the migrating waterfowl (and indeed, the human neighbors of the Buttes) can judge the proximity of home.

Rationally considered, a mountain range is as cold and impersonal as the rocks that form it. Animals may recognize it as habitat (good, bad, or mediocre), but only we humans see in a range something more, a spirit or personality perhaps. I am but one of untold numbers of people smitten by the spell of the Sutter Buttes. When I travel around the valley, I am surprised by the strong feelings of proprietary nature that so many people feel, even people who have never been in the Buttes. As I will explain later, it was a high spiritual center to the Indians as well.

Since 1976 the Buttes and I have been close friends. Oh, it's been a one-sided affair, to be sure. I have hiked her canyons, climbed her peaks, drunk her sparkling spring water, and brought all my friends to meet her. I've seen her beneath the baking sun and in torrential rain, as a black silhouette cut out of a field of stars and as a stone monument bathed in cool lunar glow, as fields as green and bright as country-Ireland and as hills as gold as harvest wheat. I have peered in her caves and beneath rocks, as if there I might fathom her secrets. I have studied her intensely with a scientist's eye, as if attention to detail would impress her. Other times I have sought her on an emotional level, striving for a communication based on feelings and sensations alone. Never has she disappointed me, though if truth were known, never has she responded.

You see, this little range is important to so many people for what it symbolizes. The Sutter Buttes stands apart, aloof from its higher neighbors. The big chains define the valley, the small gem gives it class. It is a gem because it contrasts so dramatically with the agricultural fabric upon which it lies. Its softly rounded hills and strong pinnacles are cloaked in grasses, shrubs, and trees in patterns that reflect nature's design, not man's. As our lives grow farther from the land itself, our spirits **need** that kind of contrast. Nature provides a tonic, a spiritual freshening, a point of perspective; the Buttes is the best example of the natural world still left in the valley.

Figure 1 places the Buttes with respect to towns, rivers, roads, and refuges. Since it is roughly circular, a cross-sectional view from almost any point around its periphery will be about ten miles wide. The eight views illustrated in this figure should help the viewer apply names to all the major landmarks visible from any angle. Of course, perspective changes along with viewpoint; a close view is likely to be distorted more quickly as the viewer moves laterally.

Let's take a short drive around the Buttes on public roads, just for an overall view. I'll take you inside the range later for a naturalist's view of the landscape. Consult the features map (Figure 2) to keep from getting lost.

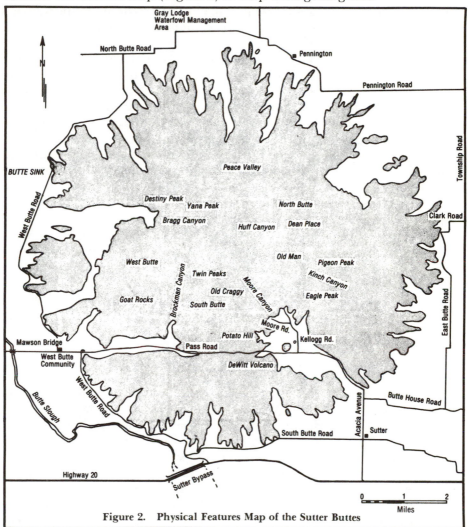

Figure 2.   **Physical Features Map of the Sutter Buttes**

Let's start on Butte House Road in Sutter. Dark evergreens and spreading hardwoods tower over hundreds of grave sites in the big cemetery, with the Buttes looming up to the northwest. Here lie many folks to whom the Buttes was the daily backdrop to their lives. Some left their marks on the Buttes and their genes in the county.

Going west, take a right at Acacia (you can't go any farther west), and head north for the edge of the Buttes. The road, now Pass Road, swings west at the county yards, where a sprinkling of houses stands beneath tall eucalyptus and other planted trees.

A gate on the right marks the road to the Sutter Cross, the site of Easter sunrise services since 1921. The wildflowers that burst forth at that time of year seem to echo the resurrection message.

A bit farther into the valley formed by flanking ridges, you will come to the Fremont Monument, a handy pullout where students from Sutter High drive their highwater pickups for lunch. You and I at any other time can enjoy an impressive view toward the interior and contemplate the historical significance of the 1846 camp that General Fremont and followers used just before the Bear Flag Revolt. The closest peaks to the north still show scars of quarrying operations, but otherwise typify the Buttes interior; here I've seen deer, foxes, coyotes, eagles, and vultures almost beyond counting.

Several of the older houses along this stretch of Pass Road show the craftsmanship and pride of ranching families, both early and late. Immaculate orchards of almonds can add to the peacefulness of the setting, especially when in full bloom in late February.

Proceeding west you reach Kellogg Road, which leads north and bifurcates later with Moore Road. This fertile valley is perhaps the most settled of any area in the Buttes.

On Pass Road just past Kellogg Road, a small rocky volcano juts from the valley floor on the right. A short way further, DeWitt Volcano looms on the left, then Potato Hill (or Hill 777, for its altitude) comes up on the right.

The road is climbing now to the low pass for which it is named. Just past Potato Hill you can get the full impact of the highest peak in the range, South Butte, the one that a service road snakes up toward the towers on top. Keep your eyes open for Golden Eagles. I'll bet you didn't know that this peak apparently has the only California Junipers and Blazing-stars in the Buttes.

Hesitate a moment at the crest of the pass. Parallel rows of large rocks mark the old wagon road or track, dating back to before the road was engineered so well. Here and there you'll see traces of old rock walls, whose manageable boulders have been trucked off for river fill or for landscaping. Mourn their passing if you like, but you'll see plenty of good, intact, history-rich walls when we get back in the interior later.

Look west at the rolling hills with the sharp volcanic dome behind. Those hills and the formations beneath your feet are made of materials laid on the valley floor long before the Buttes arose. Read on with me later as I discuss what the geologists have to say.

Continuing west past the rounded hills, you can look north into Brockman Canyon, which geologists say is a major fault. Don't hold that against it.

You are in sheep country now on both sides of the road. Winter and spring greenery keeps them fat; in the torrid days of summer, they are elsewhere, perhaps in moist bottomlands near Butte Slough or the Sacramento River, perhaps high in the Sierra.

A fenceline to keep sheep in and trespassers out can become a convenient perch for many a bird. Watch along here in winter for such birds as the American Kestrel, Mourning Dove, Horned Lark, Say's Phoebe, Loggerhead Shrike, Mountain Bluebird, Western Meadowlark, Lesser Goldfinch, Lark Sparrow, Savannah Sparrow, and Vesper Sparrow. In summer, a Western Kingbird may sit out in the open sun.

This is gas country too. The wells pump the combustible legacy of ancient plants which lived perhaps 300,000,000 years ago. Never underestimate a plant.

Pass Road soon intercepts West Butte Road coming from the south, where it flanks the Sutter Bypass. Just past this intersection is the old West Butte School, now a home, a remnant of a once bustling community on the main route between Marysville and Colusa.

Turn north to take West Butte Road along the western margin of the Buttes. On your left the entire way will be the famous Butte Sink, a line of trees and winter-flooded waterways that accommodate one of the largest concentrations of migratory waterfowl anywhere in the country. To the right, open grasslands crossed with meandering rock walls lead up to the triangular point of Goat Rocks, just south of the jagged ridge called West Butte. On almost any day you should see the dark shapes of Turkey Vultures cruising on the thermals. Perhaps an eagle will be among them.

Fingers of upland reach down from your right, ending abruptly at the deeper valley soils which support pasture, vineyard, orchard, row crop, or rice field. Watch for Texas longhorns in the rocky grasslands, as well as Rock Wrens and Burrowing Owls amidst the boulders.

About halfway along the west side of the Buttes, a broad valley leads back to become a major canyon — Bragg Canyon — penetrating the interior. Along West Butte Road you will pass remnants of the settlement of Noyesburg. The pioneer cemetery is history-rich and unpretentious. Older tombstones wear colorful patches of lichens, whose acids are slowly dissolving the relief of the letters.

Further north some of the buildings you see are gun clubs; others are hidden among trees in the Butte Sink to the west. High quality hunting comes at a premium these days, for demand certainly exceeds supply. The lodges have their social functions too, plus amenities not available to the weekend hunters who stand in line for access at public refuges. The buildings reflect a long tradition of hunting; their decors celebrate the sportsmen's fondness for good bird dogs and skies filled with whistling wings. With luck, you may catch some of this flavor first hand. In winter, fields along the road often have flocks of geese — Snows, White-fronts, Canadas — and stately Sandhill Cranes. At dusk, the evening flights of hundreds of thousands of ducks may pass over, an always awesome spectacle.

The larger peaks north of Bragg Canyon are Yana and Destiny. Their lower slopes are densely wooded with oaks and bay, where Raccoons, Ringtails, a few Bobcats still hang out.

West Butte Road hits North Butte Road at a T; turn right (left is a private road leading to more gun clubs). After a couple right angle corners, you will see a fine paved road heading south to the Buttes. Don't get your hopes up. Signs and barriers keep the casual explorer out from this former Titan Missile site, now back in private ownership.

North Butte Road continues on through almond orchards and by oak groves that seem almost continuous on the northern flanks of the Buttes. Another small cemetery, the historic Spillman grave site, is visible to the south of the road. Now the dark dome of North Butte on the northeast edge of the Buttes dominates the skyline.

The Almond Orchard or Pennington Road shoots straight north of the Buttes to the Gray Lodge Wildlife Area, a gun club until it was purchased by the state. The refuge accommodates both hunters and non-hunters during waterfowl season; activities of the former encourage thousands of birds to congregate in the unhunted sanctuary area, where the Sutter Buttes forms a most impressive background to the multitudes of birds.

Soon you pass through what remains of the town of Pennington, formerly North Butte. When roads were bad and travel slow, small towns had to be relatively self-sufficient; now community residents are in close touch with Live Oak and Gridley and yet bigger towns beyond.

If you wish to complete the circle of the Buttes, you must proceed toward Live Oak way out to Township Road, head south, and double back on Clark Road. Along East Butte Road you may see signs of early settlement — Camp Bethel, several old houses, the old Union District School.

Finally, as you approach Sutter again on Butte House Road, note the site of the old Butte House, where a cement watering trough built around 1912 remains. An important stop for stage, horseman, and carriage, the trough was a natural place to advertise; its construction costs were defrayed in part by business ads worked into the cement. To me that seems far preferable to modern billboards.

So much for the round-the-Buttes tour. It was pleasant enough — good scenery, a bit of history, wildlife. But it's a bit like trying to hear the whispers in the huddle from the top row of the bleachers in the football stadium! From a car, the Buttes is mere scenery; on foot, or better yet, on hands and knees, the place is **alive,** a feast for all the senses. How much enjoyment can you experience in a restaurant by leaving after you've licked the menu?

The Buttes is a vast library filled with thousands of volumes of autobiographical material. Nature is a peculiar librarian, however, sorting her works by physical and biological laws, shielding important material deep in her vaults, changing the books daily and seasonally. The facts are there, but not neatly catalogued or accessible to the human visitor.

I like to think of a naturalist as a good reference librarian. He or she need not **know** everything, just know where to look to find the answers. This book does provide some answers; it organizes, generalizes, summarizes, and hypothesizes from personal observations and existing data. It mentions published references from which the reader can extract more information. It exposes lists of organisms, an automatic challenge to stimulate the inevitable amendments and additions that must come.

If my desk and mind have not been too far removed from the land and wildlife which motivated me, I hope that facts, ideas, or phrases herein will in some way inspire and motivate others to move a step closer to nature. I hope to see you there!

2

Intellectual Honesty

As a sixteen-year-old merit badge counselor at a scout camp, I maintained a rain barrel with a half dozen or so fine bullfrogs — big specimens varying in color from green to turquoise to brown to black. I used the animals in my teaching — no, not in the coldly analytical way that frogs are dissected and reduced to component parts in biology labs, but in an appreciative and ecological way.

The frogs were popular, great for hands-on teaching, but I worried that kids visiting my rain barrel when I was gone would leave the lid ajar and inadvertently allow the frogs to escape. So in my demonstrations, I warned my naive students that in the barrel, along with plain old ordinary Bullfrogs, was a single specimen of a most-dangerous species, a Deadly Black Poison-spitting Bullfrog. I would carefully lift the lid while shielding my eyes, plunge my hand in, and bring out my black bullfrog, emphasizing that only my finger pressure on certain glands behind the head kept the frog from discharging its toxic defenses. The story worked. Hazardous radiation signs would not have been as effective at keeping people from tampering with my captive collection. At the end of each week when parents came to pick up their sons, I discovered that the adults were equally ready to believe my tale. Their curious questions led me into inventing a most-convincing life history for a most-improbable creature.

Thus at sixteen, I discovered the potential power a naturalist can control, and I have seen that power used by "scientists" in ways little different from those of shamans or witch-doctors in primitive societies. By selectively concealing and revealing facts, by withholding knowledge so that the novice must remain dependent upon the expert, the "authority" can assure that he **remains** one. A teacher can appear altruistic by dispensing information but can assure himself an indefinite sustenance, almost parasitically off his gullible followers.

Now that's an extreme case. In recent years, I believe the trend in natural history teaching has been more honest and responsible. Field guides and books written in simple English have made nature more accessible than when facts were obscured among technical terms in specialist journals. The fact that **volunteers** can acquire and dispense knowledge has made professionals more responsive to information needs. A bluff or outright lie can be found out. There is no monopoly on nature knowledge.

Nature is so downright amazing in the first place, especially the closer we look, that exaggeration and fabrication are totally unnecessary, at least as far as "selling the product". Thus having confessed my youthful indulgence in a bit of nature fakery, I must assert that intentional deceptions have no place in my teaching or in those of other conscientious naturalists whom I know. Nature is an inexhaustible source of knowledge, and I take satisfaction not in imparting a lengthy list of names or facts but in helping to open the doors of self-discovery. Sharing facts and anecdotes is a teaching **tool** only, a way to use vocabulary to arouse investigation. Verbal teasing, punning, tongue-in-cheek allusions all help to make learning fun. And the more that my students learn, the more stimulation and learning I receive myself. That's mutualism, not parasitism.

This book is designed for anyone interested in natural history. The data will be useful to serious naturalists — scientists, if you prefer — and the background information, anecdotes, and touches of philosophy should help the beginner begin. It is about the Sutter Buttes but goes beyond the Sutter Buttes. By grasping the patterns and processes that occur in this range, a well-defined ecosystem, we can relate them to other environments, natural and man-made.

3

Speaking of Names

Ideally, names bring order to what otherwise might be chaos. How can we communicate with one another without some common ground, without handles to handle and labels to stick?

Back in the eighteenth century, a Swede named Karl von Linné (or Carolus Linnaeus, in Latin) attempted to derive a system that would allow biologists anywhere in the world, regardless of native tongue, to communicate sensibly about organisms. Each type was given a two-part name, a binomial. Furthermore, groups of organisms were arranged into what he called classes, united by some features in common, such as number of stamens or absence of flowers.

Later generations of biologists have elaborated upon the Linnean binomial system of names in Latin. They also have assigned higher levels of organization, first based on features in common (naming was well underway before Darwin came on the scene), later based on presumed evolutionary relationships. Each level of the hierarchy is a taxon (plural taxa), and those who organize these names systematically are taxonomists.

Take the widespread bird we call an Osprey or Fish Hawk. The same bird is called *Balbuzard pêcheur* in France, *Visareud* in the Netherlands, *Fischadler* in Germany, *Fiskgjuse* in Sweden, *Aguila pescadora* in Venezuela, *Águia-pesqueira* in Brazil, *Sangual* in Argentina, and *Gavilán pescador* in Mexico.

Yet anywhere in the world, the latin name *Pandion haliaetus* is understood; the scientific name is a common currency internationally.

The scientific name is properly italicized. The genus (plural genera) is capitalized and the species name is not, as in *Pandion haliaetus*. Taxonomists place this one species in a family of its own, the Pandionidae. The next higher taxon is the order, in this case Falconiformes, which the Osprey shares with three other families: the vultures (Cathartidae); the kites, hawks, and eagles (Accipitridae); and the falcons (Falconidae). Above the order comes the class, in this case, Aves (all birds have class). Birds, mammals, reptiles, amphibians, and several classes of fishes are all considered to be in the phylum Chordata. Along with creatures as diverse as Arthropoda (with jointed legs, such as lobsters, spiders, butterflies, etc.) and Mollusca (shellfish), these organisms belong to the kingdom Animalia.

There was a time when living things could be separated without much fuss into two kingdoms, Plant and Animal, but there always were a few borderline cases that defied easy packaging. Many biologists now use five kingdoms, recognizing that these groups are united by common structure, not strictly by common descent.

The kingdom Plantae has the producers, the photosynthetic green things that ordinarily stay rooted in one place while we members of the Animalia, the major consumers of the world, move around as we eat. The kingdom Fungi has the reducers, the saprophytes and parasites that extract rather than manufacture food; in the old days they were thought to be odd, pale plants, but not any more. Single-celled organisms comprise two more kingdoms — the Monerans, bacteria and blue-green algae without nuclei or other typical organelles, and the Protistans, such as other algae, protozoans, and sponges. The slime molds are still a sticky bunch; perhaps their kingdom will come. Viruses are equally enigmatic; biologists debate as to whether or not they are even alive.

Well, if assigning organisms to the proper kingdom is that much effort, then grouping the lower taxa must be challenging at times. Indeed, all taxa from genus to kingdom are artificial categories of convenience. Taxonomists attempt to group according to close relationships but the level of compartmentalization depends on many factors, including how large and unwieldy a taxon is becoming (a family too large to handle easily may be divided into subfamilies, or in the extreme, into several families).

On the other hand, the species is meant to be defined biologically, not arbitrarily. Before the mechanisms of natural selection and heredity were known, species were separated by degree of difference, often by examination of study skins or herbarium specimens. Now biologists look at ecology, behavior, and the like, as well as morphological differences; the species is said to be composed of populations of similar organisms capable of interbreeding successfully with others of their kind, but reproductively isolated from other kinds. The new biological species definition means that superficial similarities or differences upon which classifications were made may have been in error. Hence names change, sometimes faster than we who write about them can keep up!

The Baltimore Oriole, for example, is now a name from the past, a species that suffered nomenclatural extinction. The sad fact is that, though color patterns and voices seem distinct to us upright mammals, the Baltimore and Bullock's Orioles are one and the same biologically. Where their ranges overlapped, they paid little, if any, attention to what we perceive as differences, and the offspring of these liaisons were good orioles fully capable of making more little orioles. To offend neither side (and thus offending both), the august AOU (American Ornithologists' Union) declared Bullock's and Baltimore as no more than mere races or subspecies of a single species, the Northern Oriole. Oh weep, you Baltimore baseball fans!

But the orioles are not alone in falling before the taxonomists' blades. Myrtle and Audubon would not be pleased to learn that **their** warblers are now Yellow-rumped (or "Butterbutts" as some birders describe them). Slate-colored and Oregon Juncos are now Dark-eyed. Our beautiful Red-shafted Flicker joins the Yellow-shafted and the Gilded as the Northern Flicker.

Occasionally a splitting occurs. The little nondescript Traill's Flycatcher was found to be made up of two superficially similar species, now called Willow and Alder Flycatcher. The Red-breasted race of the Yellow-bellied Sapsucker has been elevated to full species status. The Screech-Owl, similarly, has been divided into Western and Eastern species.

Some new names arose to reduce confusion among unlike birds with similar names. The Sparrow Hawk we have long known in this country is very unlike the Sparrow Hawk of Britain and Europe, a bird more like our Cooper's or Sharp-shinned Hawk. Our old Sparrow Hawk, however, is the New World counterpart of the European Kestrel, hence is very appropriately called the American Kestrel. Our former Pigeon Hawk is the same species as the Merlin of the Old World, and Merlin seems far more fitting. Our Robin and the Robin of England are quite different birds, so why not call ours the American Robin? Minor alterations have left us with American Wigeon, Northern Shoveler, Bushtit, and Common Yellowthroat.

The Blue Goose is not only gone as a species; it doesn't even rate the status of a race or subspecies. The genetic basis for the bluish coloration, its "blue genes" so to speak, is apparently a simple case of a dominant character trait.

Both Blue and Snow phases can be found in the same clutch, so the Blue is a Snow.

The present trend among name-calling (-giving?) ornithologists is to lump several very closely related species into a single species. One might expect simplification to be greeted with enthusiasm, but the opposite often occurs. You see, there is something very appealing about collecting lists of species. Real listers tick off on a checklist each bird or mammal or reptile as encountered, then race off to get more. For some, there are day lists, year lists, yard lists, state lists, and most important of all, the life list, the grand total of all species seen within defined North American limits, or sometimes, anywhere in the world. Anyone tampering with life lists, especially by reducing the number of species available, risks the wrath of dedicated birders and other taxa-collectors.

Actually, keeping lists can provide very useful data on changes in populations and unusual occurrences. To be valuable, such lists should include information on date, time, amount of effort expended, habitats, localities, and actual numbers of individuals of each species detected. To aid with such data collection, or simply for the fun of listing, this book gives taxonomic lists of the major groups of fungi, plants and animals. The author would be most pleased to receive copies of well-documented records that will add to the base of knowledge of inhabitants of the Buttes.

It is a basic though frustrating, rule of taxonomy that any published list becomes obsolete immediately. This means that taxonomists have been doing their jobs, little by little working out details of relationships, clearing up confusing names that may differ in several English-speaking countries, and so on.

Recently, the American Ornithologists' Union published the 34th supplement to the checklist of North American birds (July 1982). The numerous changes there make sense to me, but they are well ahead of the field guides and checklists that most of us use. This book follows the newly accepted names and groupings, but older names are indicated in parentheses.

The botanists have been busy too, generating name changes and building botanical reputations simultaneously. New names and their recent precursors are used here, but one should be aware that like a phone book, a plant list will change somewhat every year.

It would be nice if we could look at the suffix of each taxon and immediately recognize its level. To some extent that's possible within a given class, but biologists have tended to work apart in their specialties, and endings are often different for each group.

Animal families end in -idae, such as Felidae (cats), Vireonidae (vireos), Viperidae (pit vipers), Sphingidae (sphinx moths). Plant families end in -aceae, though some long-used names such as Compositae and Umbelliferae are in transition to Asteraceae and Apiaceae respectively. Because they were lumped with plants (and will be still for some conservative botanists), the fungi families end in -aceae.

Orders are less orderly. Birds and fishes have orders ending in -iformes. Most other animal orders end in -a, but that tells us little, and there are exceptions. Many, but not all, insect groups end in -optera, but so do bats in the order Chiroptera (-optera simply refers to wings). Plant orders end in -ales, but that taxonomic level is rarely used, compared to class and division (above class and below kingdom). Hence the checklists in this book reflect commonly used taxonomic levels and are clearly labeled to avoid any confusion that differences among groups might create.

Ornithologists in the U.S. have standardized common names of birds, in order to reduce the problem of varying regional preferences. The American Coot is the accepted name for what locals here and there may call baldface, blue peter, crow-bill, flusterer, ivory-billed mudpecker, meadow hen, mud hen, pond crow, pull-doo, spatterer, shuffler, or water hen.

The bird people have adopted the convention of capitalizing the accepted common (or English) names but not names of groups that may include several species. For example, we would write Mallard, Cinnamon Teal, Redhead, or Ruddy Duck for certain ducks, but we wouldn't write Duck alone. Our doves and pigeons include the Band-tailed Pigeon, Rock Dove, and Mourning Dove.

For sake of consistency, I apply the same conventions to other taxa. Thus our frogs include Bullfrog and Pacific Treefrog, our foxes are the Red Fox and Gray Fox, our poppies are the Tufted Poppy, California Poppy, and Lobb's Poppy.

Geology is a bit different, in that inorganic things cannot be defined by the biological species concept. Rocks may grow through crystallization, but they don't reproduce and may change type through weathering, metamorphosis through heat or pressure, etc. Types are often defined by structural differences or percentages of certain minerals. Rhyolite and dacite differ by degree, and intermediate forms are called rhyodacite. On the other hand, geological formations are often named for a type locality. These specific formations are conventionally capitalized — e.g., Butte Gravels, Kione Sands, Forbes Shale.

Names are the logical starting point in getting to know the natural world. Identifying organisms allows us to compare and contrast, to appreciate diversity, to document the wealth of an ecosystem. Occasionally, dropping the right name may get results impossible otherwise (nothing slows up unwanted development faster than the name of an endangered species in an EIR). But don't stop with the names. Make the effort to step beyond our categories and pigeon-holes to see the cats and pigeons themselves.

4

Castles of Stone: Geology

It's as natural to seek origins as it is to name something. Lacking information, we may invent a good story. Paul Bunyan, so one story goes, finished piling up the Sierra and started across the muddy region to the west to begin his next job, the building of the Coast Range. His blue ox Babe, heavily laden with rock and soil for the next project, became mired in the marshy mucks. Paul had to dump part of the load so Babe could continue. Splat — the Sutter Buttes was born.

Today we often hear the Buttes called "the world's smallest mountain range". Superlatives, even in the negative sense, are greatly satisfying. Easy labels, however, are scarcely edifying. What do respected scientists have to offer us?

Geology is a science of hindsight. The geologist must try to decipher the ancient and modern sagas of creation and destruction from a library of rock. His task is complicated by incomplete access to the collections. Working among the outer shelves, he must deduce indirectly the contents of massive amounts of deeply-buried data. Moreover, the filing system of these archives is often less than orderly. Some volumes are missing, some have been reshelved out of order. All must be translated into forms that can be understood by and communicated to people.

We tend to think of the earth as the essence of stability, perhaps until an earthquake reminds us of the dynamic nature of our planet. Geology, the study of the earth, often seems to be anchored firmly in data-bound concretions. Within the last few decades, however, that science has undergone theoretical upheavals that provide a new framework upon which to interpret existing data. Because of the incredible time scales involved, inferences are somewhat speculative, but they are not wild guesses. The geologist reconstructs the past by linking current theory with observations of present processes. Then comes the great mental leap back across the chasm of time. That story may change as data accumulate and theories evolve, yet change is a strength of the system, a means to increase accuracy.

Back in 1926 a young graduate student, fresh from England, strode into the (then Marysville) Buttes with rock hammer in hand. Howel Williams, later to become dean of American volcanology, mapped, described, and analyzed the rocks and developed theories about the volcanic origin of the Buttes, publishing them in a classic monograph in 1929.

Over the next fifty years, Williams returned often and new tools became available to him. Aerial photographs, drilling of gas wells, radiometric dating of rocks, new geological theories, and experience with other volcanoes throughout the world led to major changes in his theories. The 1929 work, good for its time, was an oversimplification. With charm and self-deprecating wit, the eminent geologist often subtitled his talks on the geology of the Buttes, "Confessions of a Misspent Youth".

Today's standard of authority on the Buttes geology is the 1977 monograph by Williams and Curtis, entitled *The Sutter Buttes of California: a Study of Plio-Pleistocene Volcanism*. Written primarily for the benefit of other geologists, the book updates and corrects Williams' early work and shows new data. Until then, most references to the Buttes (e.g., Alt and Hyndman 1975) referred to the 1929 work and thus gave a misleading view of the origin of the Buttes. New questions and new tools undoubtedly will reveal more, and each new answer seems to pose new questions.

It was my good fortune to get to know the late Dr. Williams, to accompany him in the Buttes and see his never-flagging enthusiasm for the range, his "first American love". Once a group of geologists planning to visit the Buttes under my guidance asked me to have copies of the 1977 monograph ("copies of Williams", they said) available for members of the trip. Unfortunately, the book was then out of print. When the group arrived, I gave them the bad news. Then came the good news: Dr. Williams himself, as my guest, would accompany us all to the field. It was one of "Willy's" last visits to the Buttes, and his presence helped us transcend the obscurities of time to see the range with fresh and appreciative eyes.

Having set the record straight for geologists, Dr. Williams regretted only that the story of the Buttes wasn't more accessible to the general public. In a letter dated January 3, 1979, he wrote: "Alas, my energy has dwindled so much that I see no prospect of ever writing a popular story on the geologic history of the Buttes. I leave it to you, Walt."

So here I am, a non-geologist just a few decades old, grappling with processes spanning millions of years. I am interpreting the data and conclusions of modern experts, yet I'm fully aware that the story may have faults. Although I think my translation is reasonably correct, I advise the volcano-watcher to take it with a grain of basalt. Perhaps an open and healthy skepticism will allow some of us, amateur and expert alike, to unearth new evidence and apply our insight to answering more of the riddles of the formation of the Sutter Buttes.

The Beginnings

A high-altitude aerial view shows the Sutter Buttes to be roughly circular, ten miles in diameter, rising gradually from the 50-foot valley floor elevation to numerous peaks above 1600 feet. Its symmetry is striking. Williams visualized the Buttes as a castle, with an outer *rampart* wall surrounding a narrow valley *moat* within which rises the craggy *castellated core*.

We must look far beyond the castles for clues to their origin. Within the past thirty years, a revolutionary view of the dynamics of our planet's crust has come forth. Earth-building events reasonably well fit the predictions of the theory of plate tectonics (Alt and Hyndman 1975, Flint and Skinner 1974, Francis 1976, Hill 1975). Gigantic plates forty miles thick, about seven major ones across the earth, ride on a layer of "crystal slush" above the mantle. Plate margins can be recognized by patterns of seismic and volcanic activity.

When plates move apart, as in mid-ocean ridges, molten volcanic rock (magma) wells up to close the gap, forming new crust (typically basalt). Gradually these rocks move outward from the trench as new molten rock rises, so sea floor basalt gets progressively older farther from the source.

When plates move together, one may tip and slide at an angle beneath the other forming an ocean trench which will collect sediments from both plates. The descending edge generates earthquakes as it goes, and through frictional heating and melting, causes volcanic activity to occur inland from the trench. The leading edge is thus assimilated back into the "crystal slush". Recent activity at Mt. St. Helens in Washington reflects this type of plate movement.

Two plates can also move alongside one another, creating a transform fault such as the San Andreas presently along the California coast. Neither constructive (creating ocean crust) nor destructive (destroying crust) in the geologic

Table 1. Sutter Buttes Geologic History

Era	Period	Epoch	Years Ago	Formation	Comments
C E N O Z O I C	Quaternary	(recent) Holocene	20,000	Rhyolite Andesite Dacite	Lava flows at Lassen Peak 65 years ago / End of last ice-age advance
		Pleistocene	3 M		Formation of Sutter Buttes 2½-1½ M years ago / Dinohippus teeth 2-5 M years ago
	Tertiary	Pliocene	10 M	Sutter	Volcanic sediments from Sierra Nevada deposited on deltaic fans and on broad floodplains of Sacramento Valley
		Miocene	26 M		Some airborne rhyolitic tuff (Valley Springs, Sierra)
		Oligocene	38 M		Mostly andesite debris and bedrock debris (quartz, quartzite, chert, schist, etc.) from Tertiary Yuba River
		Eocene	54 M	Butte Gravels / Ione Sands / Capay Shales	Coarse gravels from Sierran bedrock / Erode to rounded hills / Fossil-rich sandstone (*Turritella*) / Foraminifera fossils, some inferior coal — Laid down in shallow seas and small lagoons
		Paleocene	65 M	(unconformity)	Evidence missing
M E S O Z O I C	Cretaceous	(upper)	75 M	Kione Sands	White quartz-anauxite sands with lenses of pebbles, cobbles, siltstones, sandstones with *Trigonias* and other fossils / Contain natural gas — Channel-filling deposits laid down in shallow seas and on tidal flats
		(middle)	(100 M)	Forbes Shale	With beds of iron- and mica-rich sandstones, sandy limestones, some conglomerate
		(lower)	135 M		Great Valley first became an isolated arm of the sea about 140 M years ago
	Jurassic		190 M		Granite forms in pre-Sierra (actually metamorphic counterparts of sandstones and shales)
	Triassic		225 M		
PALEOZOIC			500 M		Virtually all "California" beneath the sea

sense, the transform faults nevertheless can scarcely be considered benign (remember the 1906 San Francisco earthquake).

Now let's get specific. A generalized history of the formation of the Sutter Buttes is presented in Table 1. Rock and sediment types are defined more completely in Appendices A and B and geologic formations are mapped in Figure 3.

From 200 to 100 million years ago, melting of the descending edge of the Pacific plate led to rising magmas which rose as early volcanoes or slowly cooled at depth to form the great masses of granite which are exposed in today's Sierra. For more than 100 million years, the rising hot magmas disturbed the existing sediments, changing or metamorphosing some rocks to quartzite, slate, schist, and gneiss (see Appendix A for information on rock types). Fragments of these buried rocks, far in the future, would be eroded and transported westward to lie in beds above the rising Buttes.

Further west, sediments lying atop the conveyer-belt of basalt moving inexorably eastward into the oceanic trench were scraped off, stacked together, and uplifted to form first islands, then the initial Coast Range. By 140 million years ago, the present Great Valley was an isolated arm of the sea. Uplifting of the land east of this sea was accompanied by erosion which stripped much of the cover from the Sierran granite. Rivers carrying these rock fragments into the Great Valley Seaway passed through broad-leaved forests of tropical luxurience.

Then about 20 million or so years ago, volcanoes again became active in the area later to become the Sierra Nevada. Some spewed ash that drifted for thousands of miles. River bottoms became channels for huge volcanic mud flows which swept westward into the developing valley. The gradual uplift by faulting of the northern Sierra Nevada began just 10 million years back. By 3 million years ago the future site of the Buttes was deeply layered with sediments — sands, gravels, volcanic debris.

Far below these sediments, perhaps 120 miles deep within the earth, magma was generated which was destined to become the Buttes. Incredibly high pressures and temperatures melted, squeezed, deformed the "solid" rock. Gradually, fitfully, streamers of magma rose through mantle and crust and finally, perhaps first 2½ million years ago, into the water-soaked sediments of the valley itself. Cooling as they neared the surface, these viscous bodies of rhyolite arched the overlying sediments into a rounded dome perhaps eight miles across and up to 2500 feet above the valley floor (Figure 4).

The strain of the gradual uplift was relieved by great cracks or faults which broke the tilted layers into blocks. Heavy rains during pluvial (exceptionally wet) periods worked at tearing down these hills until after thousands of years, mere hummocks remained.

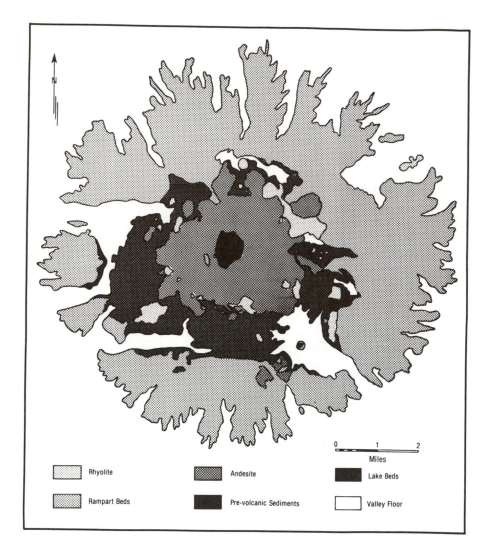

Figure 3. Simplified geologic map of the Sutter Buttes. For more detailed breakdown of rampart
beds and pre-volcanic sediments, see Williams and Curtis (1977:figure 4).

A. Early pre-explosive uplift (omitting erosion).

B. At end of early explosive phase when central lake beds had filled with volcanic debris. Interior had many ash-cones and small volcanic domes whose feeder pipes are omitted. Rampart beds have built up on periphery.

C. Current situation, after young andesitic domes developed.

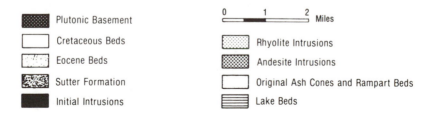

Plutonic Basement

Cretaceous Beds

Eocene Beds

Sutter Formation

Initial Intrusions

0   1   2   Miles

Rhyolite Intrusions

Andesite Intrusions

Original Ash Cones and Rampart Beds

Lake Beds

Figure 4.   Evolution of the Sutter Buttes (after Williams and Curtis 1977).

Roughly 2 million years ago, a burst of volcanic activity resumed. Hot magma thrust up into water-filled sediments and reacted violently, producing dramatic steam explosions which catapulted small rock particles high into the air. Then the gas-rich magma itself reached the surface, either blasting violently enough to shatter its own structure or flowing forth in the patient movement of highly viscous lava and cracking into angular fragments as it cooled.

The rising domes created a lake basin which filled through time with rock particles washed from the flanks of the early andesite and rhyolite peaks. Other volcanic debris was swept outward, sometimes gradually by stream movement, sometimes dramatically fast in floods or mudflows. The perimeter of the Buttes thus built up in the early stages of the rampart's formation.

Eventually the central lake beds with their accumulation of a thousand feet of rock debris and early peaks throughout the range were pushed skyward or broken asunder by rising andesite domes. The lake probably spilled its contents in one or more catastrophic floods that moved tons of rock to the Buttes' margins. Some of the layered sediments of the lake rode rising lava shafts to an incongruous perch high in the center of the range.

Pushed by hotter, more plastic lavas within the tight feeder pipes below, the rigid andesite domes continued to rise, cracking and steaming. The brittle summits, pressured from below, split into vertical slabs and spires, sometimes breaking off to crash in wild avalanches to leave trains of angular boulders spilled out across the erosion-built shoulders nearby. Some of the highest peaks we see today — North, South, and West Buttes, Twin Peaks — were created in this final dramatic episode.

Though the young andesite peaks of this creative burst had their own feeder pipes, the rising domes and lavas merged and united to form a continuous sequence of andesites in the central core. Until rock-dating became practical, geologists assumed the central andesite mass represented a laccolith, a major intrusive body that had risen as a single event. Now they know that the emergence of the peaks, both andesite and rhyolite, was a lengthy and complex series of events occurring in irregular order, ending about 1½ million years ago.

In summary, a million years of volcanic activity — uplifts, explosions, ash falls, lake formation, dome upheaval, erosion — created the Sutter Buttes. All of this has been inferred from geologic evidence — no one was around to chronicle the events. Let's step closer to the Buttes now, examining land forms for the very clues that enable geologists to piece together this fascinating story.

The Evidence

The Rampart

The edge of the Buttes is distinct, easily definable. We don't have to set an arbitrary contour line as the lower limit of the range. We can **feel** it, as we step from soft loams of the valley floor onto rock-based shallow soils of volcanic origin. The grasses and other plants reflect the sharp change in soils. Valley wading birds — herons, egrets, bitterns — look incongruous in short dry grass-land just a few feet from their preferred habitat of marsh or rice field. A few feet, though, may be as far into the Buttes many plants or animals will extend; the rampart edge is a biological barrier as real as the castle allusion suggests.

The rampart formation is the Buttes' great concession to gravity. Volcanic ash and rock were carried downward and outward from the upthrust domes, sometimes picking up sediments that originated many years before in the Sierra. The downslope movements were gradual, through stream erosion (hence sediments sorted or stratified) or sudden, through mudflows or "lahars" (hence jumbled and unsorted). Logically, gravity funneled the flows into then-existing depressions, gullies, channels. If the hardened flows were more erosion-resistant than the sediments flanking them, the gradual removal of the latter would leave elevated ridges or tongues of rampart rocks. Thus over geologic time, valleys became ridges and ridges became valleys.

The story of the rampart is revealed here and there in roadcuts, quarries, natural cliffs, and streambanks. It's a story in three parts which, read from bottom to top (youngest to oldest), can be called the basal, middle, and upper members of the rampart (Figure 5).

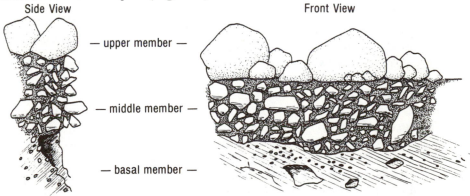

Side View
Front View

— upper member —

— middle member —

— basal member —

Figure 5.   Diagram of a rampart outcrop. Basal member of rhyolitic and dacitic tuffs, middle member of consolidated andesitic debris, upper member of bouldery andesite.

The basal member reflects the early history of explosive activity. It is typically pale-colored, fine-grained volcanic sediments consolidated into soft rock called tuff. Originally much of the material was cast into the air to settle outward from the active cones, settling to depths reflecting wind patterns and particle sizes. The particles were then eroded and reworked downslope by streams and mudflows, away from the active cones, gradually changing in place from a sediment to the volcanic sedimentary rocks, tuff and breccia (Appendices A and B). The particles in this case were both pumiceous (porous, light) and vitric (glassy, heavy) and were composed of rhyolite, andesite, and dacite. In the earliest deposits, rhyolitic debris predominated, reflecting the period of ash-fall associated with eruption of rhyolite domes.

Where the basal member is exposed on cliff faces, it may be crusted with lichens and pitted with distinctive weathering and erosional patterns. A close look may reveal areas where the sediments are arranged in well-defined bands, evidence for deposition by floods or mudflows. It's reasonable to assume that the beds were laid down approximately horizontally. Tipped beds then suggest that a subvolcanic body arose nearby after the beds were formed and consolidated. The basal member contains occasional pieces of older rock picked up by the streams or mudflows crossing the valley sediments at the margins of the domes. Instead of just the younger sediments (2-3 million years old) close to the volcanic rocks in age, we also find rocks from the Cretaceous, more than 70 million years old. We infer that the older strata were exposed at the surface when rising domes tipped the sedimentary layers up on edge, allowing streams to pluck off the long-buried pieces.

Most of the basal beds were buried by later deposits, and some of the beds were completely eroded away so that occasionally the middle and upper member rocks lie directly against older pre-volcanic sedimentary rocks. Outcrops of the basal beds, according to Williams, reach thicknesses of nearly 500 feet near North Butte but are generally well under 200 feet thick.

The middle member clearly dominates the rampart formation. On the inner wall of the rampart it varies in thickness from 250-500 feet, its maximum thickness occurring near North Butte.

Particles in the middle member range from the size of ash and sand to six-foot boulders, but typically are gravel-sized and angular, having been moved relatively short distances so that rubbing and rounding effects are minor.

Darker rocks, primarily andesitic, distinguish the middle member, although lower portions of it contain fragments of rhyolite and dacite. Airfall material is rare in this layer. Streams and mudflows carried the volcanic sediments into place, but thicknesses of remaining beds vary considerably over short distances because of the uneven terrain at the time of deposition and because parts of some beds have been removed by erosion.

The upper member consists of trains of large, uneven blocks of andesite. Originating on the growing domes of the younger volcanoes such as North, West, and South Buttes, these boulders plus finer debris were swept downward and outward in avalanches and torrential mudflows. Later most of the matrix of finer material eroded away to leave the boulder trains we see today.

Williams and Curtis (1977:33) note that the blocks often wear thin, reddish crusts over pale gray cores. They believe the outer layers were "oxidized and reddened by fumarolic gases rising along cracks within the solidified crusts of growing andesite domes". Thus the reddening of these rocks occurred not at great depth but as the domes neared completion of their growth into the valley skies.

The Moat

Biologically, the moat, a valley between the rampart and the craggy castles, is less a barrier to organisms than is the outer rampart. In fact, breaks in the rampart allow continuous connections between the outside valley and several small inner valleys, where orchards and grain crops show the affinity.

Recall that these literary terms — castle, moat, and rampart — are terms of convenience, descriptive tools applicable to the structure of the Sutter Buttes and perhaps nowhere else so appropriate. You could not witness the eruption of a new volcanic range and predict that a moat would develop. The odds against the formation of the striking symmetry of the Buttes are overwhelmingly negative. The feature called the moat would be interesting to a geologist under any name, but those of us with literary appreciation can be grateful that a young and imaginative Englishman, Howel Williams, got there first.

In the Buttes' library of autobiographical material, the moat contains the archives, a cross-section of much of the history of the valley prior to the building of the Buttes themselves. This ancient material consists of the sedimentary beds tipped upward and exposed by rising bodies of andesite and rhyolite. Some of these modern volumes (displacement, after all, implies volume) are scattered throughout the archives, while others remain buried in unsorted stacks near the basement.

Upward tilting of the sedimentary beds resulted in oldest layers closest to the interior (Figure 4). Dating back more than 70 million years to the Cretaceous period are sediments which were laid down in the shallow inland sea, in river deltas and brackish lagoons, and on broad floodplains. Particle sizes and types, as well as fossils of invertebrates, give a reasonable picture of how the future valley floor evolved.

The oldest Cretaceous formation in the Buttes is Forbes Shale. The beds contain shale, mica- and iron-bearing sandstone, sandy limestone, and some conglomerate. Above these beds lie the Kione Sands, originally "channel-filling deposits laid down in shallow seas and on tidal flats" (Williams and Curtis 1977:11). Predominantly whitish sands, the Kione Formation also contains lenses of water-rounded rocks (cherts, quartzite, etc.) derived from Sierran bedrock, plus marine siltstones and sandstones. Fossil mollusks such as *Baculites* and *Pachydiscus,* long-extinct relatives of the squid, link the formation to the marine environment.

Kione Sands and Forbes Shales are of more than casual interest to many geologists. They are associated with significant quantities of natural gas, which has been produced commercially in the Buttes since the early 1930's. The beds have been deformed complexly by rising subvolcanic domes, so an understanding of the structure of these formations can mean a difference between a dry hole and a multi-million dollar bonanza when a gas well is drilled.

Eocene beds overlie the Cretaceous beds and date back to roughly 40-50 million years before present. They represent a time of deposition in shallow seas and minor lagoons. The oldest Eocene rocks are the Capay Shales, which consist of buff-colored sands with iron-rich inclusions, greenish-gray shales with foraminiferan fossils, some mudstones and small amounts of poor-quality coal. Over them lie thin beds of white Ione Sands of Eocene age with numerous fossils of the mollusk *Turritella.*

The youngest and most extensive of the Eocene beds are the Butte Gravels, also formed in shallow seas with delta and rivermouth channeling. They consist of cobbles of quartz, chert, quartzite, greenstone, diorite, and schist derived from pre-Sierra Nevada bedrock. A small amount of gold has been found, demonstrating similarity to the auriferous (gold-bearing) gravels of the Sierra. Although limited because of great distance from its origin, the traces of gold have occasionally stimulated intense interest by would-be prospectors. Limestones and fossil-rich sandstones are interbedded with the gravels.

Butte Gravels erode to gentle, rounded hills. Soils formed tend to be thick, clay-based mixtures of pebbles and cobbles, that commonly are marked by concentric rings of livestock trails etched in the heavy soils.

Oligocene, Miocene, and Pliocene beds in the moat closest to the peripheral rampart range in age from 2 to 30 million years, and are generally lumped as the Sutter Formation. The base of the formation is rhyolite tuff, 20 to 30 million years old, derived from ash fall and erosion of ashy materials in the Sierra to the east. Most of the formation consists of river-transported andesitic debris, again from the mudflows and peak eruptions in the Sierra. Bits and pieces of Sierran bedrock material joined the westward migration of rock and are intermixed with the volcanics. Marine fossils are conspicuously absent in the Sutter Formation (the days of the inland sea had passed). Fossil horse teeth (*Dinohippus*, a near-modern horse of 4 to 5 million years ago) in the upper (youngest) part of the formation clearly indicate the terrestrial habitats of the time.

The moat, then, depicts a nearly 100 million year sequence of sedimentary deposition. The strata, like some gigantic layer cake, have been tipped on edge with the frosting (the rampart cover) removed in places (Figure 4).

The layer cake analogy and Figure 4 itself are but simple models for a much more complex process. The apparent symmetry of the moat around the castles obscures a significant amount of tipping, folding, and fracturing of the Tertiary and Cretaceous beds. Erosion has not been uniform around the ring, and still-buried intrusions have deformed these beds and often raised the rampart layers far above where they were left by erosion.

Initially I was puzzled by the absence of boulders on the rounded hills of the moat along Pass Road. The rampart was littered with boulders, which presumably originated across the moat in the castles of the interior. If mud-flows carried the bouldery debris across the moat, then subsequent erosion should have left some of the hard volcanic boulders standing atop the softer sediments in the middle — or so I reasoned.

As long as one starts with the premise that the mudflows crossed sedimentary beds tipped on edge the way we see them today, one cannot avoid being puzzled by that apparent enigma. My only hope for understanding lay in rejecting the simple model and starting with new assumptions. Imagine the sedimentary beds just partially tilted by early uplifts and covered by a tapering layer of volcanic debris, the pre-rampart. Then subsequent uplifts could tilt a section of sandwiched beds such that the pre-rampart layer was moved outward and that formerly buried strata were now tipped vertically, newly exposed at the surface. Since no mudflow or erosional volcanic debris lay on the secondarily-tipped beds, the absence of boulders is understandable. The rampart rocks, ultimately tuffs and breccias, were in some cases lifted up by other igneous intrusions. Thus the simple rampart-moat-castles appearance requires a far more compli-cated explanation than one would first expect.

The Castles

North, South, and West Buttes, Twin Peaks — the names are roughly descriptive if not imaginative. Old Man, Old Craggy, Destiny Peak, Goat Rocks, Pigeon Peak, Eagle Peak — these names carry an association, even if some details of origin may now be obscure.

Encircled by the moat and rampart, the interior castles of andesite, dacite, and rhyolite are geological monuments to the forces of volcanism. From the beginning of the explosive phase about 2 million years ago to the final eruptions 1½ million years ago, literally dozens of individual intrusions arose. Some burst through the earth's surface, some cooled and solidified beneath, but nearly all pushed and deformed the overlying sediments, the developing rampart, and the earliest volcanic masses.

The central portion of the Buttes is a coalescing mass of andesites, a merging of many extrusions each with feeder pipes. Radiometric dating clearly shows it was not a single laccolith as originally assumed but was formed by a complex and prolonged series of events. Older andesites have been altered by crystal replacement to form propylites, but younger andesites remain fresh.

The immensity of the andesite domes can perhaps be best appreciated by considering the work done against gravity as the bodies of magma pushed up through thousands of feet of sediment and sometimes rose well above the valley floor. A column of andesite six feet high, one foot wide, and one foot deep — a size I can relate to by standing next to it — would weigh close to one thousand pounds. It is not something to be taken for granite.

Rhyolite and dacite domes are exposed most conspicuously within the moat area. They tend to be steep-sided, pale-colored rock masses, though their color is obscured somewhat by heavy covering of crustose lichens.

Distinguishing between rhyolite and andesite is not difficult, though rock classification usually involves assigning arbitrary dividing lines, often based on mineral percentages, on a continuous range of characters. In general, andesites are darker in color with large (5 mm maximum) white crystals of feldspar and smaller (< 1-3 mm) dark crystals of biotite ("black mica") and hornblende. Rhyolites are light-colored, lack obvious feldspar crystals, and often show flow-banding. Dacites are intermediate in percentages of certain minerals but are lumped with rhyolites for superficial mapping.

Let's backtrack from the rocks we see to the magma from which they were derived. Magma is the source of the igneous (literally, "from fire") rocks. Unlike water, a simple liquid that freezes to form the single compound ice, freezing magma forms a variety of minerals which crystallize at different temperatures. If the mixture cools slowly, large crystals may grow (typical of intrusive rocks), or if rapidly, the mixture may solidify with very fine grains (as in extrusive or volcanic rocks). As cooling occurs, some crystals change composition (such as becoming richer in sodium) on a gradual, continuous basis. Others react with the remaining liquid and change in discrete steps (such as from olivine to pyroxene to amphibole to biotite).

Three kinds of magma are common and are distinguished by their silica content. Common glass is made of silica, as are beach sands (in the form of quartz). Igneous rocks are classified by the amount of silica, or silicon dioxide (SiO_2) they contain. Magmas with about fifty percent SiO_2 form gabbro (intrusive) or basalt (extrusive). With about sixty percent SiO_2, magmas solidify to form diorite (intrusive) or andesite (extrusive). Magmas containing more than seventy percent SiO_2 form granite (intrusive) and rhyolite (extrusive).

Although treated as a liquid, magma typically flows slowly and seems in many ways like a solid. The viscosity of a magma, which depends on SiO_2 content and temperature is a measure of its resistance to flow. At high temperatures, reasonably enough, magma is more fluid. Erupted molten lavas flow relatively rapidly until they cool, become more viscous, and eventually solidify. Rocks with high SiO_2 content, such as rhyolite, are more viscous than andesites because silicon and oxygen form an interlocked network that interferes with flow.

Silica content also influences the explosive potential of an eruption. Less viscous lavas such as basalt flow readily but explode rarely. Highly viscous lavas such as rhyolite tend to erupt with fireworks, producing pyroclastic ("fire-broken") particles. Such materials range from ash, when fine, to bombs and blocks, when coarse. A rhyolite dome is steep-sided since its ability to flow is nearly gone when it emerges. That near-rigidity contributed to the gradual deformation of sedimentary beds which is so evident in the Sutter Buttes.

The intermediate magmas of andesite are moderately viscous so the andesite flows have a rough, bouldery surface. Actually the flow is plastic, rather than liquid, with the outer rock surface chilled and solid while the inner, hotter parts are more fluid. Pressure from the rising plastic materials below can cause the brittle exterior to crack into sharp-edged angular blocks and spires.

Andesites in the Buttes formed both strongly vertical domes (e.g., North Butte) and, less commonly, lava flows (e.g., DeWitt Volcano). The latter formed flows up to 100 feet thick that extend outward from the presumed source as far as 400 feet. The flows are similar in composition to the hornblende-biotite andesites of many of the interior domes but differ by being broken into rubble by the cracking action just described. Probably no one but a keen-eyed geologist, in fact, would be able to distinguish the DeWitt Volcano flows from some of the rampart mudflows, which really represent no more than short-range displacement of the same kinds of rocks with the aid of water.

Geologists can look at the now-cold rhyolite and andesite domes and see flow-planes as evidence of the long-ago fluidity of the rocks. The flow-planes themselves contribute to pinnacle production as weathering and erosion occur.

Though no one was present to witness the ascent of the Sutter Buttes, a similar series of events on smaller scale was observed in northern Japan in

1944-45. Recent events at Mt. St. Helens and in other volcanoes around the world can give us a better understanding of the formative processes that created the Sutter Buttes.

Often I am asked by persons who know that the Buttes are volcanic, "Have you been to the crater?" Volcanoes and craters are inevitably linked by many people. Even Williams in 1929 referred to the "central vent" and labeled his geologic map in the center "VT" for "vent tuffs". Now we know that no single central vent exists in the complex, merging cluster of volcanoes of varied ages. The cones and conelets that survived the steam-blast eruptions during the explosive phase have been largely removed by erosion.

The so-called "central vent" does indeed differ from the surrounding aggregate of andesitic peaks but in an unexpected way. Williams and Curtis (1977:35) now define the 1.0 x 0.7 mile area as the "central lake bed". Exposures on the wall of Bragg Canyon suggest that the lake gradually filled with volcanic debris before the youngest peaks even existed and after the Sierran and marine sediments had been eroded away from the site. Material that washed into the lake resembles that in the upper part of the basal member and lower part of the middle member of the rampart formation. Though the lake originally lay in a depression approximately where Bragg Canyon now is, part of it was shouldered roughly upward by intruding domes. The highest part, sculpted and rounded by weathering, is known to us as Raptor Peak, where magnificent birds of prey soar, oblivious to the geologic story of the rocks below.

Deep Reflections on Geology

Another Sutter Buttes hike is over, and I sit miles away picking chips of andesite loose from the Vibram tread of my boots. I too am an agent of erosion, moving rock downward and outward as part of the great leveling process. My role is minor; I could more than compensate for my part by carrying a ten-pound rock from the river banks back up into the interior of the Buttes and leaving it there, perhaps to puzzle some curious geologist in the future.

Gravity, wind, and water work away at exposed rock masses. Last year a twenty-ton (wild guess) chunk of andesite tore loose from the south face of Old Man to crash down among the lichen-crusted boulders below. A dozen or more hillsides this spring exhibited slumping, where water-soaked soils slid in lumpy masses toward the feet of the slopes. Eventually, as has happened here and elsewhere in the past, the Buttes will erode to gently-rounded hills, finally disappearing as a prominent landmark in the valley . . . **maybe** . . . A similar prediction would have seemed in order over 2 million years ago as the once 2500-foot high mound of uplifted sediments eroded nearly to the level of the valley floor. Then began the explosive phase which itself was superceded by the period of andesitic dome formation. It's far easier and **safer** to speak in hindsight about how it was than to project forward as to how it will be.

As a mountain range, the Sutter Buttes is small potatoes. South Butte looms to a modest altitude of 2132 feet (656 meters). Some geologists wouldn't even define it as a mountain, though anyone who has hiked the interior would be willing to argue the point.

Yet apart from a few tourist-traps where social amenities override geological interests, I can think of no comparable acreage in either the nearby northern Coast Range or northern Sierra with the power of attraction, spiritual if not magnetic, to people as the Sutter Buttes. What makes it so unique?

Geologically, the surprising symmetry and resulting castle-moat-rampart appearance are certainly without peer. Many volcanic phenomena are evident, not hopelessly obscured by later geological events, forests, or human developments. No volcanoes known show "stronger or more extensive deformation of overlying beds by rising magmas than can be seen in the Sutter Buttes" (Williams and Curtis 1977:37). A 5000-foot thickness of rock standing vertically is indeed impressive.

Few places in the Great Valley expose the early sedimentary beds so clearly as where they were shouldered upward by the magmatic pillars of the Buttes. Here we see remnants of ancient seas and rivers. Unfortunately, many organisms thriving 50 to 100 million years ago left no remains. Fossil beds have disproportionate representation of hard-shelled little creatures, while the soft-bodied ones have vanished without a trace, though certainly some genes have trickled down from generation to generation.

Take the Capay Formation of Eocene time, for example. Forty to fifty million years ago the inland sea where the Buttes would later form teemed with countless tiny organisms. At least 47 kinds of Foraminifera are represented in the claystone that dates from that period (Olson 1961). These minute protozoans were encased in calcium carbonate shells, the remains of which tell us that there were such fascinating creatures as *Alabamina wilcoxensis, Anomalina umbonata, Ceratobulimina perplexa, Cibicidoides coalingensis, Globigerina triloculinoides, Martinottiella eocenica, Quinqueloculina zequaensis, Vaginulinopsis alticostata,* and more than three dozen other tongue-twisters. At least eleven species of Ostracods, small crustaceans with bivalved shells, contributed their remains to the bottom ooze which later became rock and immortalized their names: *Actinocythereis howei, Munseyella israelskyi,*

Paijenborchella trigona, Trachyleberis paucispinata, and the like. Why is it that these miniscule, seemingly insignificant (what can be more insignificant than being extinct?) creatures rate such polysyllabic appellations?   .

The Buttes cannot be lumped with other mountains and thus be reduced to an outlier of another formation. It stands alone, unrelated to peaks in the Sierra Nevada, Cascades, or Coast Ranges.

Actually, drilling in the valley has discovered some "poor relatives" of the Buttes that never emerged from the thick valley sediments. Most notable are the buried "Colusa Buttes" about four miles west of the Sutter Buttes. The hidden range is nearly oval, about twelve miles long on its north-south axis and three to four miles wide east-west. The highly viscous bodies of rhyolite up-arched the Cretaceous-age beds to heights exceeding 1500 feet, but the bulge that must have been present at the surface has since eroded back to the level of the valley floor. A lot can happen in 2 million years.

Just when I learned that rhyolite and andesite are extrusive igneous rocks, solidifying as they emerge at the surface, I discovered that rock in the "Colusa Buttes" at a depth below the valley floor of 9430 feet is identical to exposed rhyolite in the Sutter Buttes. Reading further in Williams and Curtis' monograph (1977:22), I found that some andesites at 6000 feet below the surface are identical to those above the surface. Clearly my understanding of the rules on intrusive/extrusive rocks can't be adequate here. I would expect to find granite and diorite at those depths.

Not surprisingly, my sense of scale is overwhelmed by geological reality. Geologist Frank Koch reminds me that "6000 feet is not **that deep**", that Sierran granites formed hundreds of thousands of feet deep. Williams and Curtis point out that the speed of cooling is most important in determining whether the resulting rock will be, say, rhyolite or granite. Ordinarily the depth at which cooling occurs is highly related to the speed of cooling so that intrusive rocks (cooling slowly) tend to be coarse-grained and extrusive rocks fine-grained. But certain cooling conditions can create fine-grained rocks even where in general we would predict the opposite. To quote Williams and Curtis (1977:41): "The deep-seated, but fine-grained rhyolites in the 'Colusa Buttes' must have been suddenly and drastically chilled, presumably by injection into cold, water-soaked sediments."

Isolation, symmetry, deformation of sedimentary beds, exposure of fossil strata, complexity without obscurity, unusual conditions of formation — clearly all these do qualify the Sutter Buttes as an extraordinary geological phenomenon. Yet is this why the range is so attractive to people, most of whom have never set foot within those hills? Impossible, I insist. Most people don't know **any** of these geological attributes. Nor can the biological uniqueness be the answer, for most people aren't familiar with that aspect either.

To be truthful, the spell cast by the Sutter Buttes is an indefinable, emotional feeling — not based on data at all. Yet as we learn the facts and perceive the natural patterns in operation, that feeling is enhanced and our sense of awe grows greater.

References

Alt, D.D. and Hyndman, D.W. 1975. *Roadside Geology of Northern California.* Mountain Press Publ. Co., Missoula, Mont.

Flint, R. F. and Skinner, B. J. 1974. *Physical Geology.* John Wiley and Sons, Inc., New York.

Francis, P. 1976. *Volcanoes.* Penguin Books, New York.

Hill, M. 1975. *Geology of the Sierra Nevada.* University of California Press, Berkeley.

Olson, R.E. 1961. Correlation of Eocene strata exposed in Fig Tree Gulch, Sutter County, California. *Geological Society of Sacramento Annual Field Trip Mimeo,* 32-35.

Pough, F.H. 1976. *A Field Guide to Rocks and Minerals.* Houghton Mifflin Co., Boston.

Williams, H. and Curtis, G.H. 1977. *The Sutter Buttes of California: a Study of Plio-Pleistocene Volcanism.* University of California Press, Berkeley.

5

The Little Kingdoms: Monera, Protista, Fungi

Life seemed simpler in the old days. In our guessing games, we could encompass the entire natural world in three categories; animal, vegetable, and mineral. Never mind that the easy divisions seemed to fall apart in total fuzziness among what we, in our Brobdingnabian shortsightedness, would call "simpler" organisms. Who cares that there are some 300 species of single-celled euglenoids that feed by ingestion into a gullet as they swim animallike through the water, yet possess chloroplasts by which they can photosynthesize in sunlight like plants? Why worry about the 500 or so types of slime molds which act like primitive animals as they creep about with amoeboid flowing, engulfing bacteria as food, yet cease movement and develop plantlike reproductive structures when they breed? Well, some biologists **do** care, and they figure the plant-animal dichotomy simply will not do any longer. It makes more sense to have **five** kingdoms (Whittaker 1969), based on cell structure and nutritional modes rather than common descent (for example, plants may have come from four ancestral types, fungi from five). A few problematic groups (e.g., viruses, slime molds) may require yet more changes in the system.

Actually, life **was** much simpler in the old days. **Long** before we overencephalized primates debated how to divide organisms among kingdoms, there was but one kingdom, Monera. In fact, the fossil record suggests that for 2/3 — 5/6 of the history of life on earth, all organisms were Monerans! The Precambrian (from say 3 billion to 600 million years ago) can rightly be called the "Age of Blue-green Algae" (Gould 1977).

Blue-green algae and bacteria, the Monerans, are procaryotes, a formidable title that simply means that their single-celled contents are not organized into packaged organelles such as nuclei (their DNA strands hang loose, so to speak), plastids, mitochondria. They seem ancestral to all members of the four other kingdoms.

The Precambrian blue-green algae flourished in simple monotony for two or three **billion** years. Then, 600 million years ago, life began to diversify at an incredible rate that paleontologists refer to as the Cambrian Explosion (Gould 1977). In just a few million years, an eyeblink geologically, the greatest creative experimentation in evolutionary history took place.

Biologists speculate that the big breakthrough came with the appearance of the first Protistans, the little (in size, if not numbers) members of the second kingdom. Here appeared the first herbivores (or grazers), turned loose in a sea of algal producers. Until then the algal species best able to convert nutrients into growth and reproduction eliminated their potential competitors and kept the system simple. Grazers reduced the populations of the dominant forms, thereby opening niches for other types which would have failed on a competitive basis before.

The Protistans had one other thing going for them — sex. This allowed more rapid production of variety, upon which natural selection could act in forming new species. New species themselves meant new opportunities or niches could be exploited.

Some of the single-celled Protistans, with their more organized structures (real nuclear membranes, mitochondria, plastids) then gave rise to the three multicellular kingdoms: Fungi, Plantae, and Animalia. These differ from one another primarily in nutrition: absorption of food in solution, photosynthesis, and herbivory or carnivory (Stern 1982). The biological blossoming of the Cambrian, roughly 600 million years ago, makes the two million year rocks of the Sutter Buttes seem very young indeed!

Let's look at (or at least think about) some of these surviving monuments to antiquity. Those few types I know by face, I rarely know by name. At best I might recognize a half dozen of the 30,000 species of algae, a few of the 2000 or so bacteria, probably not one of the 500 slime molds, maybe a score of the 40,000 fungi. Even if I started learning a fungus a day, I'd never catch up; mycologists describe a thousand or more species of fungi each year (Baker and

Allen 1971). They are abundant as well as diverse: "their total mass is twenty times greater than that of animal life" (Northen & Northen 1970).

In many ways, the whole pyramid of life (to resurrect an old cliche) stands on the shoulders of these simple organisms, yet we accord them little credit, barely acknowledge the existence of most of them. In contrast, we make an effort to get to know the ferns and the flowering plants; a "new" vascular plant in the Buttes is an occasion to pull our references and tack a name to it.

This is a naturalist's guide, of course, and we tend to be most interested in the things within the reach of our unaided senses. It wouldn't be reasonable to haul microscopes and other sophisticated devices into the field in order to see and identify microorganisms. Still, it would be a gross biological oversight to omit them from our thinking.

Every plant or animal we see, the very air we breathe, and even our own body surfaces which we so righteously consider "clean" are covered or inhabited by incredible numbers and kinds of viral, bacterial, and fungal organisms. If we had microscopic vision, we'd be astonished by the variety and abundance of living things growing, mating, competing, and interacting in innumerable ways down there beyond the normal limits of our senses. Their potential impacts on us can be enormously out of proportion to their physical minuteness.

Some of these organisms attack us and other animals to produce lesser or greater diseases. The "bad actors" among the bacteria have brought us such notables as anthrax, botulism, cholera, diptheria, bacterial dysentery, gonorrhea, leprosy, meningitis, plague, bacterial pneumonia, scarlet fever, septic sore throat, tetanus, tuberculosis, tularemia, typhoid fever, undulant fever, and whooping cough (Wilson and Loomis 1962:377). Viruses (the very name of the group can evoke a shudder of dread to those of us familiar only with the "villains") include such nasties as chicken pox, common cold, encephalitis, influenza, infectious hepatitis, measles, mumps, viral pneumonia, polio, smallpox, rabies, and yellow fever. Fungi have hit us with ringworm and athlete's foot, as well as a diverse arsenal of poisons in a variety of mushrooms. Our fellow vertebrates on this planet, including all those dwelling in the Sutter Buttes, are exposed to an equally impressive variety of deleterious micro-organisms. A city pigeon, the urban counterpart of the Rock Dove that frequents ranches around the Buttes, is known to host up to four viruses, nine bacteria, and two fungi that can cause infectious diseases (Terres 1981:255). In our snapshot observations, we rarely notice either the continuous nor episodic effects of these diseases, yet an omniscient onlooker might find the dramas of infection and reaction to be major indeed.

Green plants suffer from the activities of non-photosynthetic fungi, which exploit the solar converters to meet their own energy needs. "Fungi are more dangerous to plants than bacteria are to us" (Wilson and Loomis 1962:391). Since **we** depend on so many plants, the fungi and other organisms of plant diseases are often in direct competition with us. We spend millions on fungicides, research, quarantines, and various chemical and agricultural treatments as we battle such plant afflictions as rusts, smuts, cankers, wilts, rots, blights, scabs, molds, curls, and mildews. More than a tenth of the annual cultivated crop yields around the world is destroyed or ruined by fungi (Huxley 1978). Losses to forestry are equally staggering in economic terms.

Well then, some of these "simple and lowly" organisms do indeed affect our lives profoundly. As agents of misery and economic loss, they make quite an impact. Yet the emphasis on the negative aspects of our relationships with them may be an oversimplification, or at least a bias that ought rightly to be countered by the "other side". What "good" are the microorganisms to us?

First, good and evil as we tend to apply them to other organisms are defined strictly in relation to impacts on humans either directly or indirectly by effects on resources for which we have plans. We protect a wheat field against wheat rust not because we sympathize with the parasitized wheat but because **we** want to be the consumers of that wheat. In general, we are far more efficient destroyers of cereal crops or forest stands or herds of cattle than are any of the little organisms against which we battle.

Second, perhaps it is presumptuous to think we are entitled to 100% of the production produced by green plants or as converted into animal products by herbivores that we control. The non-green organisms have used green plants for basic sustenance for millions of years before we came along; where we see deterioration or death, they see only survival.

Third, despite the human biases of our definitions, we may find that usefulness of some members of these groups may far outweigh the negative aspects. Many of these organisms can be used to combat the diseases we dislike, as well as insects and other creatures we call pests. Antibiotics such as penicillin and streptomycin are invaluable. Commercial applications also include making organic acids (especially citric acid used in many foods and pharmaceuticals), alcohol, pigments, vitamins, and enzymes (Moore-Landecker 1972). Without the benefits of microbiology, we would lack such "necessities" as bread, beer, wine, whiskey, yogurt, buttermilk, cheese, and soya sauce.

That's not all. The saprophytic fungi and bacteria, with some help from animals, of course, accelerate the decomposition of the enormous quantity of organic debris that otherwise would quickly smother the earth and tie up the nutrients other living things need. They are the great recycling agents, redistributing the world's wealth. We could not live without them. About 80%

of the carbon dioxide required by land plants for photosynthesis comes from the respiration of microorganisms (Moore-Landecker 1972).

Our landscapes would be depauperate in green plants, indeed we would not exist either, without the activities of nitrogen-fixing bacteria (Coulter and Dittmer 1964). These minute bacteria live in nodules on the roots of certain plants, such as many legumes, and somehow manage to extract nitrogen from the air and convert it into a form usable by other plants and animals. Certainly no altruistic intent is involved, so it's not necessary to prostrate oneself before a lupine or clover in praise of the process occurring at molecular level among the soil particles and roots below. Yet it's sobering to realize that nitrogen-fixation **alone** far more than compensates the human race for the occasional inconveniences of poisoning or disease or food spoilage caused by other members of the group we call microbes. Natural nitrogen-fixation greatly reduces our need to add chemical fertilizers to the soil and thus relieves us of the economic and environmental costs of those applications.

Plenty of bacteria, fungi, and algae have developed intimate relationships with other organisms as symbionts — neutral or beneficial partnerships. Algae and fungi coexist in lichens, fungi live in or on the roots of higher plants as mycorrhizal associations, and of course the nitrogen-fixing bacteria occupy nodules on roots of vascular plants. These cooperative arrangements please our sense of fair play as surely as predation and parasitism offend us at times (but only when we don't recognize ourselves as predator or parasite).

In recent years, a scientifically introspective look at ourselves has revealed that some of the organelles, like mitochondria, in our cells seem strangely enough to be more like bacteria than they are like the rest of us. Similarly, the chloroplasts of plants, those invaluable photosynthetic factories, bear striking resemblance to certain independent blue-green algae. The inescapable implication of these and other findings may be that these organelles are the descendants of bacteria and algae which developed in close symbiotic linkage with the primitive organisms — basic cells — that ultimately led to orchid and octopus and orangutan.

Lewis Thomas (1974:84) ponders these imponderables:

> *It is a good thing for the entire enterprise that mitochondria and chloroplasts have remained small, conservative, and stable, the most important living things on earth. Between them they produce the oxygen and arrange for its use. In effect, they run the place.*
>
> *My mitochondria comprise a very large portion of me. ...I could be taken for a very large, motile colony of respiring bacteria, operating a complex system of nuclei, microtubules, and neurons for the pleasure and sustenance of their families, and running, at the moment, a typewriter.*

Well, enough has been said here about the essentially invisible, even though ecologically profound, members of the three "lower" kingdoms. Let's take a closer look at the macro members of the bunch — the larger fungi and the lichens.

A Feast for the Eyes: Mushrooms

Smuts, rusts, molds, and the like are mighty influential fungi, despite their minuteness. Yet the larger fungi capture our attention more readily, drawing or repulsing us ambivalently in a blend of fact and fancy.

It's small wonder that we associate mushrooms and kin with fairies, elves, trolls, and other beings at the edge of our peripheral vision. They often appear overnight, spontaneous eruptions from the underworld. No color or shape is too bizarre, no texture too uncivilized to display impudently. Classic umbrellas and spherical puffballs may satisfy our sense of mushroom-rightness, yet these shapes may be twisted, stretched, and mangled outrageously in less-familiar forms. Then there are fungi which look like globs of butter or jelly, cauliflower heads, coral masses, whale baleen, convoluted brains, wrinkled fingers, powder puffs, leathery ears, crepe-paper petticoats, splay-legged octopuses, birds' nests, pitted potatoes, volleyballs, marshmallows, throat lozenges, fritters, sponges, and plastic orange peels.

Lactarius

Of course, there are perfectly good biological explanations for the diversity of structure and color, yet they can't dampen my awe and wonder. The mushroom we see is but a fruiting body, a temporary and ephemeral phase in the fungal life cycle. Hidden in soil or wood are thousands of fine threads (hyphae) packed together in strands or masses called mycelia (to the scientist) or spawn (to the commercial grower). Unlike green terrestrial plants, the fungal body is protected from dessication by its hidden location. When moisture is plentiful and nutrients abundant, the mycelium sends up the reproductive structures in a quick burst of growth. As saprophytes or parasites, the fungi are unconstrained by photosynthetic design considerations. They can be any color or shape as long as they have a reasonably efficient method of spore dispersal.

The fungi play the numbers game in a big way. A common edible mushroom may release a hundred million spores an hour, some sixteen billion before it's through. The infinitesimal spores need little air movement to defy gravity; they may travel hundreds of thousands of kilometers before descending among raindrops. Needless to say, mortality is astronomically high. Otherwise, the products of a generation or two of mushroom spores could bury us to unimaginable depths in fleshy fungi.

The umbrella form, typical or modified, aids spore dispersal in two ways. It acts as an umbrella ought to, protecting the spores under its cap from rainfall, and also lifts them high enough so that when released, they can ride the winds (in some cases, no more powerful than the breath of a mouse). Few, if any, spores end up beneath the fruiting body.

That umbrella form is geotropic, moving as needed to keep the spore-bearing surface facing the earth (Sterling 1955). The tiny explosive force that releases the spores sends them the 1/10mm or so just so that they fall free from the narrow gap between gills.

It takes a lot of water to support a mushroom mycelium and even more to permit it to thrust up fruiting bodies. Arid places such as the Sutter Buttes support fewer species than the humus-and vegetation-rich forests of coastal regions or the deciduous woodlands of the eastern U.S. Yet certain ones are encountered often enough to justify our special attention.

Keep in mind that mushroom identification is not as simple as, say, bird or mammal naming, despite the fact that mushrooms stay put. Fungi are phenotypically plastic, which means their looks can vary dramatically depending on stage of development, substrate, and conditions of growth. Field guides can't possibly show the range of variability, and even experts disagree as to what constitutes certain species. Common names have not been standardized, and scientific names themselves change as scientists learn new things and discover relationships. Here I use the terms suggested by Lincoff (1981), along with some alternate names. I have made identifications by comparing my photographic records of Sutter Buttes fungi with descriptions and plates in a dozen or more books. Since differences among species can be so subtle as to be detected only by microscopic examination of spores, my names should be taken as close approximations only, subject to expert verification and refinement (checklist in Appendix C).

More than a hundred species of *Helvella* have been described. Though in the same family as the delicious morels, these saddle fungi or false morels, are better contemplated visually than gastronomically. They contain helvellic acid, a potent poison. The Fluted White Helvella may appear in oak leaf litter in the Buttes around February if rains and temperatures cooperate; the rest of the year it is one of the subterranean secrets of the landscape.

There is nothing subtle about the fruiting body of *Tremella*, Witches' Butter. Bright yellow-orange convoluted masses of jelly stand out prominently on de-caying wood in cool damp weather. After a few dry days, each glob contracts into a hard, orange-red mass, but another rain may spark a miraculous revival. If you can get past the name, you may find it edible; some folks use it in soups (Lincoff 1981).

Tan woody-looking fingers projecting from the ground belong to the Pestle-shaped Coral. In the same family is *Sparassis,* an unappetizing-looking fungal mass resembling a convoluted head of cauliflower; despite its looks, it is both edible and choice. I continually marvel at what appears to be such imaginative and playful inventiveness that we find in nature. Oh sure, I can say that these "pestles" and "cauli-flower heads" are products of the interacting forces of their physical and competitive environments, but it astounds me nonetheless that the bio-logical "solutions" can be so extreme, so beyond my imagination. I suspect that's a weakness more of my mind than of the system, so without any need to prove them "logical", I can let myself enjoy their incongruity to the fullest.

Pestle-shaped Coral

The many pored polypores are repre-sented in the Buttes by two conspicuous species and a few unnamed wood decomposers whose names I have not yet tracked down. Living oaks may be afflicted by the Chicken Mushroom (because of its reputed taste as a choice edible) or Sulphur Shelf Fungus (because of its appearance). Puffy overlapping pancakes in shades of yellow, the fruiting bodies are mere symptoms of the destruction of living wood going on inside. Breaking them off is like picking an apple — the main plant is scarcely affected. The hyphal threads of the fungus produce enzymes which digest the woody material outside the body of the thread (Dickenson and Lucas 1979). The solution of digested matter is then absorbed by the threads for maintenance and ultimately reproduction of the fungus. The mycelium advances by digestion into the heartwood, changing solid wood into a soft and powdery (punky) mass. When the tree dies, the shelf fungus lives on as a saprophyte.

Rainbow Shelf Fungus

Another major polypore is the Rainbow Shelf Fungus which occurs in crowded stacks of overlapping crinkled shelves on dead oak wood. Each shelf is marked with concentric semicircular bands of rich colors, suggesting the alternate name, Turkey-tail. Initially mycologists included most polypores in the genus *Polyporus*, but microscopic examination has led to finer taxonomic tuning. This fungus has passed generically from *Polyporus* to *Coriolus* to *Trametes*, presumably without any change genetically. *Trametes* is good enough today; stay tuned for the official word tomorrow.

Amanitas account for about 90% of the fatal mushroom poisonings (Lincoff 1981), so approach this group with caution. The Grisette forms a tall umbrella, its cap gray with white patches. A white species, perhaps *A. virosa* or *A. verna*, also grows in the Buttes; these are called Destroying Angels. For some reason I hesitate to pick them to do the necessary keying. For similar reasons, I suppose, I don't handle Poison Oak or Western Rattlesnakes or Black Widows. Am I a fair-weather naturalist?

The fungal counterpart to the inconspicuous "dickey bird" is the LBM (little brown mushroom). The Yellow Bolbitius is one of the easier LBM's to recognize, if one goes to the trouble to peer down among the overtowering grasses in spring to find it. Young specimens have bright yellow, moist and reflective, egg-like oval caps; older ones become flattened umbrellas tending toward straw color. This species "follows the cow", thriving best in manure or rich compost. The caps are edible but too small and delicate to justify collecting them for the frying pan.

The Suillus, a typical bolete, has a spongelike tube layer instead of gills. Ours may be *S. tomentosus*, but I wouldn't stake my life on it. It has a brownish cap, golden-yellow to ochre tubes, a yellow stalk turning red toward the base. Bruised parts turn dark blue almost immediately.

Yellow Bolbitius

Another **LBM** is *Inocybe,* having brownish caps with elevated centers that any Freudian would describe as areolas with raised nipples, floating breastless on slender stalks. Coincidence or is there a playful side to natural selection?

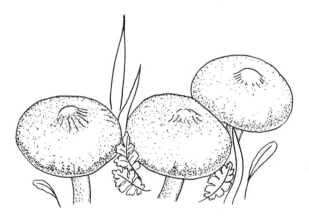

Inocybe

Lactarius and *Russula* are "two of the most abundant, varied, and widespread genera of gilled mushrooms" (Lincoff 1981). The Delicious Milky Cap is a popular edible form in Germany, France, and China but less so in North America. Ours is a "close approximation"; don't consume it without expert assurances. Our Russula has a red cap, yellow gills, and white stem, similar in appearance to the poisonous *R. emetica* typically found in spagnum bogs.

These, like many mushrooms, often form mycorrhizal associations with the roots of certain trees, an arrangement certainly beneficial to the fungus and believed neutral or beneficial to the tree.

Mycenas are gregarious, clustering LBM's on dead wood. Even experts consider the genus "confusing"; one monograph lists 230 species.

Puffballs and earthstars belong to closely related families. *Geastrum*, the earthstar, has an outer skin which detaches from the inner, peeling back in broad rays that raise the inner spore bag as the arms reflex against the ground. The lift thus provided gives a slight altitudinal edge to the spores, aiding their dispersal.

The Papery or Tumbling Puffball, *Bovista pila*, has spherical white buttons attached to the ground by a simple rootlike rhizomorph. Epicure mycophagists (mushroom eaters) consider the species "a bit mealy, but easily collected and identified, hence good for a beginner" (Haard and Haard 1974). Older puffballs become brown, their white flesh turning into inedible powdery spores. The outer skin cracks, and any contact — the hoof print of a deer or the beating of raindrops — forces smoky clouds of spores into the air.

Less common in the Buttes are two other puffballs, both rated "choice" in edibility if selected when young with a firm white interior. The Gem-studded Puffball is top-heavy, turban-shaped, and covered with tiny white spines. The Sculptured Puffball is large, somewhat lumpy, and plated with polygonal scales.

By their very nature mushrooms are easy to overlook, so serious searching in the Buttes is likely to turn up more than the twenty species I've noticed. Field guides (e.g., Miller 1972, Haard and Haard 1974, Smith 1975, Orr and Orr 1979, Lincoff 1981) may help the amateur pin down an identification, but **no** guide covers all species, and people often react differently to ingested pieces of the same mushroom. Fungi-foraging can be fun and rewarding, but unlike bird-watching or plant-keying, a mistake could be fatal. So unless you are **positive** (reasonably confident is not good enough), let most mushrooms be a feast for the eyes alone!

Papery Puffball

Pioneering Partners: Lichens

A typical Sutter Buttes boulder is a colorful patchwork of lichens concealing most of the crystalline face of the rock itself. "New" rock, such as that exposed by a landslide (or originally following the eruptions) provides a wide open landscape for colonizing pioneer lichens, arriving as fungal spores (which must fortuitously meet the appropriate algal partner) or as "vegetative biospores", linked lichenized fragments capable of survival apart from the parental body or thallus (Hale 1974). Wind, water, mammals, birds, reptiles, and perhaps insects transfer the tiny tidbits of potential lichen. The initial pattern reflects arrival rates and abilities to become established on bare rock, often under extreme exposure to harsh elements. As the lichens grow, competition alters the patterns gradually, as those with long-term advantages replace the quick pioneers that may lack staying power. Since lichens grow extremely slowly, the dynamic nature of the community may be evident only to an observer with decades or even centuries of patient watchfulness.

Lichens

Yet even those of us who can't wait a century to measure the centimeter-by centimeter encroachment of one lichen over another can witness fairly dramatic seasonal changes. One day after months of drought we can rub our fingers across the dessicated surface of a lichen and watch it crumble like dust; another day after the first rain, we can see the same lichen swollen with moisture, brilliant with color, literally exuding life and vitality. Both states strike me as equally miraculous: an incredible tolerance for deprivation and environmental extremes, sacrificing almost any semblance of life while somehow maintaining genetic integrity and a quick-response capability for when conditions change, versus a nearly spontaneous resurrection into productivity, growth, reproduction, and even competition with neighbors.

Most plants seem soft, fragile, ephemeral compared to lichens. The toughness of lichens arises from the unique partnership, for neither fungus nor alga alone has the persistence of the symbiotic duo. The alga is the producer, the solar distillery manufacturing food used by itself and its fungal companion. The fungus provides both components with water and minerals and effectively shelters the alga to permit survival in places of high light intensity and occasional extremes of temperature and dryness.

Most lichens seem to exhibit mutualism, a relationship beneficial to both alga and fungus, but some cases may represent mild parasitism, in which the imprisoned alga is exploited by the fungus but manages to reproduce faster than it is destroyed. Lichens appear to have evolved in several lines independently, probably initially with fungus parasitizing alga, developing in many cases to a balanced mutualism (Baker and Allen 1971).

It wasn't until 1867 that botanists recognized that a lichen was a composite organism — neither full fungus nor able alga but something beyond the sum of its parts. Most had been named as if they were simple plants. Should they have a distinct lichen name, as well as names for the component fungus and alga? Since the fungus generally dictates the external appearance, the easy way out was to apply the fungus name to the association as well. The green or blue-green alga, often capable of independent existence anyway, retains its appropriate algal name. Some algae are present in several or many lichen associations.

The lichen-namers have been busy indeed; they've attached handles to at least 16,000 kinds. Yet don't expect to find a handy field guide with common names and arrows pointing to easy field marks. Most are known only by Latin scientific names, and many can be distinguished only by chemical tests or microscopic study of minute spores. Still, some of the common and colorful ones can be recognized to genus and sometimes species, even by us generalists.

Even without knowing specific names, we can recognize three major growth forms: crustlike (crustose), leaflike (foliose), and shrublike (fruticose). Also, we can think ecologically in terms of lichen communities (Smith 1975). We can group them by substrate preference: on leaves, bark, or wood (arboreal); on the ground (terricolous); on rocks (saxicolous); or on almost any substrate, even bones, iron, leather, etc. (omnicolous).

Seeds cast on stony ground, as the Bible points out, are doomed to wither and die; almost all plants require at least a bit of soil to become established. Yet lichens alone can live on bare rock, clinging tenaciously and gradually contributing to rock break-down by mechanical tugging and by production of acids.

A single andesite boulder may support a dozen or more kinds of lichen. After a refreshing shower, some rocks appear gaudy, as if splashed by vivid paints from a mad artist's palette. Simple, weakly differentiated gelatinous lichens such as *Leptogium* may look tacky like fresh paint. A *Lecidia* common in the Buttes is a thin gray encrustation freckled with odd black squiggles; it reminds me of a chromosome map. Another gray encrustation that colonizes tombstones as readily as boulders is *Leconora*. The grayish-white foliose lichens *Physcia*

Cladonia

phaea and *Xanthoparmelia* reach outward with leaflike lobes from centers sometimes packed with fruiting bodies — irregular chalices with deep-brown linings. The leathery brown Rock Tripe or Flake Lichen, *Umbilicaria phaea,* is a thin sheet attached only at its center, like an umbilicus. Each sheet is basically circular but is distorted by folds, cuts, and lobes. Just add water and watch as the flake writhes before your very eyes.

Then there are the real eye-catchers, intensely brilliant crusts of yellow (*Acarospora*) and orange red *(Caloplaca elegans)*. Appropriately called Jewel Lichen, *Caloplaca* may be splashed across the vertical face of a boulder or may grace its apex, where it particularly favors the nitrogenous deposits left by perching birds. The gray-blue-green thallus and "golf tee" fruiting stalks of *Cladonia fimbriata* resemble those of the related lichen, Pixie Goblets. Other well-known *Cladonias,* not found in the Buttes, include the so-called Reindeer Moss and British Soldiers.

Trees likewise provide substrate for lichens, even if not as permanent as boulders tend to be. Stemflow following a rain may deliver extra nutrients,

Ramalina

especially potassium and calcium leached from the bark (Hale 1974). The flaky deciduous bark of manzanitas prevents lichen establishment except on patches of dead wood. On the other hand, the rough, highly textured bark of oaks seems an open invitation to many types of lichens. Grayish, foliose forms such as *Ochrolechia pallescens* are common on oak bark, as is the yellowish *Candelariella.* The arid environment of the Buttes doesn't encourage the dangly tangles of "beards" that festoon trees closer to the California coast. The loose, crinkly straps, coils, and threads of *Ramalina menziesii* drape a few oak branches in the fairly lush lower reaches of Moore Canyon.

References

Baker, J.J.W. and Allen, G.E. 1971. *The Study of Biology.* Addison-Wesley Publ. Co., Reading, Mass.

Coulter, M.G. and Dittmer, H.J. 1964. *The Story of the Plant Kingdom.* University of Chicago Press, Chicago.

Dickenson, C. and Lucas, J., eds. 1979. *The Encyclopedia of Mushrooms.* G.P. Putnam's Sons, New York.

Gould, S.J. 1977. *Ever Since Darwin.* W.W. Norton and Co., New York.

Haard, K. and Haard, R. 1974. *Foraging for Edible Wild Mushrooms.* Cloudburst Press Ltd., Brackendale, British Columbia.

Hale, M.E., Jr. 1974. *The Biology of Lichens.* Edward Arnold, Ltd., London.

Huxley, A. 1978. *Plant and Planet.* Penguin Books, New York.

Lincoff, G.H. 1981. *The Audubon Society Field Guide to North American Mushrooms.* Alfred A. Knopf, New York.

Miller, O.K., Jr. 1972. *Mushrooms of North America.* E.P. Dutton and Co., Inc., New York.

Moore-Landecker, E. 1972. *Fundamentals of the Fungi.* Prentice-Hall, Inc., Englewood Cliffs, N.J.

Orr, R.T. and Orr, D.B. 1979. *Mushrooms of Western North America.* University of California Press, Berkeley.

Smith, A.H. 1975. *A Field Guide to Western Mushrooms.* University of Michigan Press, Ann Arbor.

Smith, A.L. 1975. Lichens. The Richmond Publ. Co. Ltd., Richmond, England.

Stern, K.R. 1982. *Introductory Plant Biology.* William C. Brown, Dubuque, Iowa.

Sterling, D. 1955. *The Story of Mosses, Ferns, and Mushrooms.* Doubleday and Co., Inc., Garden City, N.J.

Terres, J.K. 1981. Diseases of birds — how and why some birds die. *American Birds* 35:255-260.

Thomas, L. 1974. *The Lives of a Cell — Notes of a Biology Watcher.* Bantam Books, Inc., New York.

Whittaker, R.H. 1969. New concepts of kingdoms of organisms. *Science* 163:150-160.

Wilson, C.L. and Loomis, W.E. 1962. *Botany.* Holt, Rinehart, and Winston, Inc., New York.

6

A Place for Plants

The evolution of life is a fascinating subject, perhaps particularly because we must be detectives to reconstruct the story. Most of our clues are in the present — the diversity of living organisms which we can directly compare and contrast and from which we can speculate and draw inferences. Then the fossil record gives us more — snapshots of prehistory. What could be more exciting than the hope of discovering a missing link?

The fossil record fails to give us a nice, neat sequence of organisms from primitive to specialized. Instead of graded series, we more often find long periods with little change, then sudden appearances of completely new types. Rather than a pattern of gradualism, we see alternating periods of quietude, then bursts of evolutionary flowering. Theorists such as Gould and Eldredge call this "punctuated equilibrium", though their conservative "gradualist" colleagues have not all been won over to the idea (Lewin 1980).

Gould (1977) suggests that formation of new species usually occurs in very small populations isolated from the parental group at the edges of the ancestral range. If mutation or genetic recombination creates a favorable variation, it may spread quickly in the small population without being swamped in the large parental group. Of course, mere isolation does not guarantee speciation; only the right circumstances of variability and selective pressures will create a new species.

The Sutter Buttes is a natural place to look for evidence of this process. Presently it is an inland island of upland isolated from similar habitats in the Coast Range and Sierra. Has it been isolated well enough and long enough for speciation events to be evident?

It seems reasonable to look for evolutionary changes among the plants. Within any population there tends to be considerable genetic variability upon which selection can work. A couple million years ought to be long enough for changes to be visible. And even a cursory inspection of the Buttes turns up populations that appear to be far isolated from known populations of their kinds; these are prime suspects.

Yet there are difficulties. Most of us exploring the Buttes are amateurs. If a plant keys out in Munz (1959) reasonably well or nearly matches a field guide picture (e.g., Niehaus 1976, Spellenberg 1979), we let it go at that. It may take a specialist to pry into the private posy places to determine if species designation is appropriate. Even then, there may be debate between the lumpers and splitters — one man's species is another's race.

In addition, today's relative isolation may be far too recent for new changes to have occurred. Before extensive cultivation in the Sacramento Valley, upland plants frequently followed watersheds and stream terraces far out into the valley. Perhaps for many species, genetic exchange was ample to prevent local divergence. Since pollens are so mobile as drifters, maybe even now many plants are less isolated than we might expect. Just 10,000 years ago, cooler climates prevailed and the Buttes were united with foothill habitats in a very real way. That's but a moment ago geologically. Even if some divergence had occurred during prior periods of isolation, the unification may have allowed interchange in each direction, which might obscure any patterns we see today.

While no species of plants are strictly endemic to the Buttes, found there and nowhere else, some species stand out as geographic exceptions. The Rock Gooseberry (*Ribes quercetorum*) typically occurs from Alameda and Tuolumne Counties southward. The healthy stands in the Buttes may be a relict population left from a once-broader distribution, or they may represent a rare successful colonization far from normal range. Arizona Three-awn (*Aristida hamulosa*) typically ranges from southern California through Arizona to western Texas and south to Guatemala. Its discovery in the Buttes was a significant range extension northward, a record lasting until January 17, 1983, when a stand was detected on Table Mt. in Butte County (ah, the joys of discovery can still be attained by the sharp-eyed field botanist!).

Some plants in the Buttes belong to species found today in the Coast Ranges west of the Sacramento Valley but not in the Sierran foothills to the east. A prominent example is Narrowleaf Goldenbush *(Ericameria* or *Haplopappus),* an attractive shrub found in the Coast Ranges from Lake and Glenn Counties south. Other species such as *Silene verecunda, Rafinesquia californica, Gilia achilleafolia, Navarretia cotulifolia,* and *Festuca elmeri* show affinities to the Coast Ranges, not the Sierra Nevada. One wonders whether the Sutter Buttes has ever been or will become the critical link in a cross-valley leapfrog-type of colonization in either direction.

In general, the Buttes contain the same basic habitat types and presumably a floristic potential quite similar to nearby Butte County. Indeed, most Sutter Buttes species do occur on Butte County lists. The exceptions, in addition to those mentioned in the last two paragraphs, are worth noting: *Amorpha californica, Amsinckia retrorsa, Chenopodium californicum, Festuca arundinacea, Gnaphalium californicum, Juncus xiphioides, Koeleria macrantha, Lagophylla ramosissima, Linaria canadensis, Lotus strigosus, Malacothamnus fremontii, Pectocarya penicillata, Potamogeton diversifolius, Pogogyne serpylloides, Rubus ulmifolius.* The *Festuca* and *Rubus* are introduced species, hence subject to the whims of human dispersal. The *Lotus, Pogogyne,* and *Malacothamnus* do not come as far north as Butte County; the Sutter Buttes mark a northern limit. The others vary a great deal ecologically; some may yet be discovered in Butte County but others probably are geographic curiosities worthy of a closer look by enterprising biogeographers.

Perhaps as important in defining the flora of the Buttes are the conspicuous omissions, the plants that *ought* to be there, those that thrive in similar sites in foothill lands west or east beyond the valley floor. Apart from a few recent human introductions, the Sutter Buttes island has no Digger Pine *(Pinus sabiniana),* no California Buckeye *(Aesculus),* no Chamise *(Adenostoma),* no Spicebush *(Calycanthus).* The Black Oak *(Quercus kelloggii),* Canyon Live Oak *(Q. chrysolepis),* and Tan Oak *(Lithocarpus densiflora)* have not been found in its shaded canyons or steep slopes. No *Dudleyas* form rock gardens among its pinnacles. No Meadowfoams *(Limnanthes)* line its vernal pools and creekbeds. These plants, as much as the isolated curiosities, prove that the Buttes are an ecological island. If colonists of these species ever reached the Buttes, they have not managed to survive to the present.

Certainly the **combinations** of plants we find in the Buttes are unique, a product of their location and isolation. The challenge for determining the uniqueness of particular populations lies ahead of us. Here is a way in which the observant amateur can be of great help. Use the preliminary lists in this book as a guideline. Plants suspected of being new species should be brought to the attention of professional botanists for verification.

In recent years major collecting efforts by Lowell Ahart, as well as contributions by John Thomas Howell, John Hunter Thomas, Margit Epperson Sands, Pete Sands, myself, and others, have provided specimens which form a good base upon which vegetational analyses must be based. In turn, these lists and our growing understanding of the ecological relationships they represent, are vital tools for monitoring changes and defending against destruction of a botanically fascinating area.

But if taxonomy is not your bag, if a name means less to you than the graceful curve of an oak's trunk or the spicy pungeance of a bay leaf or the delicacy and brilliance of a penstemon's floral tube, then you have a great deal in common with most naturalists. Names can get us started, even provide us with instant associations appropriate to our individual memories, but there is no substitute for pure, plain physical experiencing. Direct appreciation usually leads to curiosity, and here we can benefit from others' experiences too, can draw on cumulative knowledge of many. And here is where this book may be of service, not only in cueing you in on the variety of plants to be found, but also by sharing tidbits of natural history, the flavor behind the names. Happy sampling!

Frogs of the Plant World: Mosses and Liverworts

Competing with the lichens for space, moisture, and nutrients on boulders and trees are the mosses and liverworts, the bryophytes. Their ancestors were likely the first land plants. From water-dwelling green algae, they managed the transition from sea to land through the blind winnowing of the scythe of natural selection. Their reproductive systems and body forms enabled terrestrial survival in ways impossible to the older algae, yet they have kept a strong dependence on water. They are the "frogs" of the plant world.

Scientists consider them an evolutionary dead end, a group that failed to capitalize on the abundant opportunities offered by transition to the land. They have remained small and insignificant, while a separate line, the vascular plants, diverged and proliferated to exploit the earth more efficiently and, one could **almost** say, imaginatively.

Yet who can say that climbing a ladder that goes nowhere in particular is any less acceptable than its alternative? What's **wrong** with a moss as an end-product in itself? It's all too human of us to think of evolution as progressive and purposeful, plants and animals "improving" with time, growing in complexity and efficiency. Yet nature gives us many examples of "steps backward" (e.g., becoming simplified as parasites or cave dwellers, etc.) to show that differential survival of alternatives is all that matters.

With all due respect to the vascular plants, which I hold in great esteem, I admit to a sympathetic appreciation of these "dead end kids". I share the empathy expressed by Northen and Northen (1970:61): "Like muted strings in an orchestra, the mosses and ferns play their subtle role in nature. Softly they cover moist ground; unobtrusively they seek a foothold in rock crevices, mellowing the contours of cliffs and walls even as they delight the eye with their intricate patterns of velvet and lace."

In very simple terms, these plants breed by alternating generations. Offspring resemble grandparents rather than parents, or if you prefer, a gametophyte generation alternates with a sporophyte generation. In flowering plants, the sporophyte is a dominant; in bryophytes, the sporophyte is a dependent stage, always attached to the plant body of the gametophyte.

The gametophytes produce multicellular sex organs, male and female. Getting their gametes together is the trick. Despite an ability to survive long periods of drought, these simple plants must have a water film present for fertilization to occur; the sperm are swimmers and can reach the eggs no other way. Rain not only revives the dormant plant body, inactive and non-productive throughout the dry season, it also allows the gametophytes to bring off their breeding act, giving rise to the sporophyte stage. The sporophyte extracts nutrients from the gametophyte, essentially parasitizing its parent, while producing millions (yes, millions) of microscopic spores that will be cast to the vagaries of the wind. Those few spores finding a suitable substrate and adequate conditions will germinate to form the plant body of the gametophyte stage. The cycle can be repeated.

Liverworts seem masters of understatement. Some plants practically **demand** to be noticed. The oak bulges with implied muscles and lifts its writhing arms into the sky, the blackberry reaches out and snags your cuffs as if reluctant to let you pass without acknowledgment, and turpentine weed assails your nostrils with its unforgettable perfume. The liverwort, by contrast, tucks itself away beneath rocky overhang or peers out from mossy cover, far more secretive than the proverbial shrinking violet. Only when the rains are frequent and suitable, only when opportunities for reproduction override its typical cryptic tendencies, is it likely to be noticed. Even then, you must look closely and in the right places in the Buttes for these tongue-twisting genera: *Sphaerocarpus, Targionia, Riccia,* and *Asterella.*

Asterella

The leaflike green thallus of a liverwort, low-growing and lobed, suggested a liver in form to the ancients who used the plant to treat hepatic disorders. If I look carefully, in winter and spring I can find clusters of elfin umbrellas, little green domes on slender stalks. These are the gametophytes of *Asterella californica* and *Preissia quadrata*. Under each dome hang the whitish sporophytes, the dependent generation. It's one of the ironies of nature that the elevated umbrellas improve chances for spore dispersal while making it harder to achieve union of egg and sperm, a process requiring rain splash.

Some of the liverworts have three ways to reproduce. The alternation of generations is complicated and dependent upon favorable conditions, but it allows the mixing of genes through sex that can mean a survival edge in a changing or uncertain environment. The growing points of the flattened thallus or body may branch, with each branch becoming a separate plant as death of older material creeps up from behind. A slightly more sophisticated form of vegetative multiplication involves developing little cups bearing "gemmae", tiny bodies capable of dispersal by small animals and growth if allowed to contact moist soil. These methods are the "strategic triad" of a supposedly simple plant. We elaborate higher animals, by contrast, are stuck with a single method, sex, but who am I to complain?

An unlikely place to expect a plant dependent on water for reproduction would be a boulder face, yet that's exactly where we find many of the mosses in the Sutter Buttes. Often lichens may precede them, especially in the more exposed sites and before organic matter has begun to accumulate in cracks and pits in the rock's surface, but moss and lichen may grow side by side. The mosses, photosynthesizers all, provide varying shades of green in contrast to the grays, yellows, oranges, and browns of the common lichens.

Identifying the bryophytes without the aid of magnification is tricky at best. I sent my best slides, mostly well-illuminated close-ups shot with a macro lens, to an acknowledged expert, Alan Whittemore. He sent tentative identifications, prefaced with this caveat: "Your pictures are roughly comparable with photographs of woody plants from a quarter or half mile away — that is, a few species may be recognized with some confidence, many are more difficult to name, while quite a few are totally nondescript."

Since my slides tended to sample lush, colorful growths, they can't be considered unbiased, and the names proferred here are first approximations. I hope that this inadequacy spurs me and others to collect carefully in coming months so that the classification of Sutter Buttes bryophytes can approach the state now existing for the flowering plants.

Alan recognized a bright yellow-green branching moss as a species of *Homalothecium*. Other mosses appeared to be members of the families Pottiaceae (perhaps a *Didymodon*) and Hedwigiaceae (*Hedwigia ciliata*

or *Pseudobraunia californica,* told apart only if sporophytes can be found). A common cushion-forming moss
in the Buttes is *Grimmia,* lovely velvet-green mounds
with rounded contours. *Timmiella* (probably *T.
crassinervis*) forms rich-looking carpets when moisture
is adequate. And what could be more beautiful than a
soft patch of *Tortula* thrusting hundreds of yellow lances,
its sporophytes, above its deep-green carpets?

Tortula

Thanks to tips from a professional, I now can tack labels on a few of the
mosses and liverworts I see in the Buttes. Yet the label is just a start. It helps
me to discriminate differences, helps me to look more closely and curiously
at plants which before I might have glanced over casually as "mosses". The
closer look invites questions, stimulates ecological thinking. Where and under
what conditions do the various types appear? How do moss structures, simple
as they are, function for survival and reproduction? How do mosses relate
ecologically to other organisms — lichens, for example, or mosquitoes or
millipedes or mice? Or me?

Discovering answers to such questions, even debating possible alternatives
when no answers can be proven anyway, takes nothing away from the magic
of pressing one's hands into spongy moss or watching a dry, seemingly lifeless
scrap suddenly spring to life as water is poured upon it. Some botanists may
feel that failure to develop an independent sporophyte or failure to develop
specialized conducting tubes in some way "doomed" the bryophytes to be
lowly, insignificant, minor characters in the great evolutionary play. I remind
them that the play is not yet over, that these bit-part actors appeared in many
scenes before we made our first entrance on the stage, and only later scenes will
reveal whether or not our assessment of the plot has any validity.

In Defiance of Gravity: Vascular Plants

The "three little kingdoms" and the bryophytes are size-limited: most are
microscopic, many (such as lichens and mosses) form crusts or low cushions,
and even the largest fungi are insignificant in size, if not in effect, compared
to a tree. The ferns, then the gymnosperms, and finally the angiosperms, our
typical flowering plants, overcame many of the limitations of gravity and water
transport by developing vessels or vascular bundles, xylem and phloem. Root,
stem, and leaves could function together in "a system which combines liquid

conduction with rigidity, like an architect's dream of a plumbing circuit which supports a whole house" (Huxley 1978:57).

Given a physical solution to the size/transport dilemma, the vascular plants seem to have gone "wild" with evolutionary experimentation, giving us everything from horsetails and tree ferns to oaks and redwoods. Insects and flowering plants proliferated together during the Cretaceous (some 65-135 million years ago) each creating selective pressures and niches enabling ever greater diversification of the other. We may think that flowers are so bright and showy for the benefit of our esthetic appreciation, but we are late-comers on the scene. Plants and insects, food sources and pollinators, reflect the influence of each other. Only later did the birds and mammals exploit **both** these sources of food. Insects helped make the flowers; we mammals may have made the spines!

The plants we observe today are the vector sums of multitudes of forces acting upon them: altitude, weather, soils and chemicals, competitors, predators (acknowledging that devouring a plant is fatal to that plant), parasites, pollinators, etc. Life history characters such as annual versus perennial or woody versus herbaceous reflect successful solutions to environmental testing. Even the amount of energy an individual plant allocates to reproductive organs, physical structures (stem, leaf) and defense mechanisms (chemicals, hairs, spines, etc.), and **when** it does its growing, flowering, resting, etc. depend significantly on both its historical background and its present situation.

It is no exaggeration to say that the vegetation of the Sutter Buttes is unique. Long isolated from other upland areas, the flora represents both relict populations of ancient connections and surviving elements of colonization/extinction as an ecological island (checklist in Appendix D).

Throughout the year the seasonal plot unfolds with flowering and leafing corresponding to ancestral clocks and climatic regularity. The blue and purple "brodiaeas" illustrate the predictability of flowering: Blue Dicks, Ithuriel's Spear, the ookows, and finally the Elegant or Harvest Brodiaea, each appearing in turn. Yet the basic plot still allows natural improvising — the early blooming of a plant on a south-facing slope, the arrested growth or prolonged dormancy of a plant experiencing drought.

Here, then, are the vascular plants, a tremendous radiation without which these words could not have been written, as we would not have been here. See them as they fit in the Sutter Buttes picture; take from them the lessons they can teach us about life beyond the boundaries of the range.

The Quillwort Family: Isoetaceae

The epitaph of a dead quillwort could read: "Beloved by muskrat and wading bird, ignored by modern man''. If one notices these inconspicuous plants at all, one is likely to mistake them for grasses or sedges or perhaps onions. Yet these linear-leaved plants produce no seeds; they are close cousins of the club mosses.

For some 130 million years, the quillworts have been doing things pretty much the same way. No planned obsolescence has led them to radiate into anything fancier, yet like a VW beetle among American sedans, they persist along with the flashy models of flowering plants so recently designed.

The quill-like leaves become rather spoon-shaped at the base, where they form a tight spiral on the crocuslike corm (Stern 1982). Within the shallow curve of these "spoons" develop the sporangia, which produce spores that develop into gametophytes of both sexes. The male side of the line may produce a million microspores at a time; the female gametophyte is the provisioner for the future zygote, so goes for quality rather than quantity.

Look for these small plants at the water's edge, in wet or at least moist soil, along creeks or in vernal pools. If you beat the muskrats to them, you will find them perfectly edible.

The Club Moss and Horsetail Families: Selaginellaceae and Equisetaceae

Club mosses and horsetails are living monuments to antiquity, surviving samples of primitive plants that once dominated the earth. The spores of these representatives are time capsules which have brought them through inconceivable numbers of generations to exist and remultiply little changed from their ancient ancestors. Four hundred million years ago when aberrant vertebrates, the first amphibians, crawled onto the land, the progenitors of these simple plants began to form lush forests. They spread and diversified, equipped with all the latest advances in strengthening structures, conducting systems, reproductive gadgetry. An extraterrestrial looking in might have concluded that they were the logical, successful culmination of plant growth on earth.

Millions of years passed, **millions** of them, and things changed. Reptiles appeared. Beetles came on the scene. Conifers developed as the first true seed plants. None of this happened overnight, even though we list appearances and disappearances in the fossil record as if they were sudden events; yet the changes may have been **relatively** sudden, like punctuation marks between long fairly stable phases. The horsetails and club mosses were part of the changes. Along with other early plants of the times, their unconscious repetition of their life cycles gradually built up tremendous carbon deposits, the future's coal, and filled the atmosphere with the gaseous products of their metabolism. Their very existence created conditions suitable for life forms they themselves had no way to anticipate.

The changes have perhaps been most profound during the last hundred million years, when birds, mammals, and modern seed plants appeared and proliferated. The primitive plants were often outcompeted by new evolutionary approaches — the seed, for example. Those ancient species which have survived, however, dominate their respective niches and provide us with immediate links to the otherwise-inaccessible past.

The spike or club mosses are actually more closely related to ferns than to true mosses. Hansen's Club Moss is a survivor on a day-to-day basis, as well as through geological time. It grows exposed on shallow soils or bouldery faces, dry and brittle and seemingly lifeless as the sun bakes down on it through the dry seasons. Yet add water, and presto! — the "resurrection plant" rises from the dead.

Horsetails prefer moister sites, sending up vertical pencil-thin stalks jointed at nodes every few inches. Silica reinforces the ridged and hollow columns, a fact outdoor pot-scrubbers have exploited often, using the stalks as "scouring rushes".

The horsetails today seem to be a weak echo of their ancient prominence. Only 25 species have persisted, as compared to roughly 250,000 species of flowering plants now extant. Yet the impacts of human populations on plant survival are only now beginning to be seen. Land alteration, especially in the tropics, is accelerating. The President's Council on Environmental Quality has predicted that by 2000 A.D., two-thirds of all tropical forests will be lost, a loss of 10-20 percent of the earth's biota in half a human lifespan (Soulé and Wilcox 1980). If we were to return in a few million years, perhaps fewer, we might discover horsetails continuing their unbroken chain of continuity while many newcomer flowering plants may have disappeared like a flash in the pan. On the other hand, we might find new organisms far beyond our feeble abilities to extrapolate. **We** might be the flash in the pan!

The Pepperwort, Fern, and Water Fern Families: Marsiliaceae, Polypodiaceae, and Salviniaceae

Humid tropical forests are the great strongholds for most of the 10,000 species of ferns in the world. In California, ferns are well represented in dank coastal groves, but a few penetrate into drier countryside (Grillos 1960). There they survive by lurking in relatively cool, moist niches or by facing the drier conditions armed with special adaptations.

Ferns offer few direct economic values to our peculiar species which worries about such things, but many are planted as ornamentals. Indirectly, ferns are economic heavyweights. They and their kin in the rampant lushness of the

Carboniferous Period (a mere third of a billion years ago) were transmuted by chemistry, pressure, and time into the coal deposits which are now being acclaimed as America's key to energy independence.

The **time** involved staggers me. My mind vaguely remembers scattered items from 30 years ago, accepts as reasonable much of what I read of 300 years ago, begins to boggle at the thought of 3000 years, and loses all sense of connection as additional zeroes are added. Who can look at a chunk of coal and make the mental leap to a steamy green jungle some 300,000,000 years ago? It's beyond comprehension, so we don't even try. We cheerfully burn the coal, enjoying a short moment of heat-releasing combustion that reverses great geologic ages of formative processes. Carbon molecules locked in stone for millions of years are released in ephemeral gases to cycle through new systems that also lie beyond our comprehension.

Giant Chain Fern

Limited seams of "inferior coal" occur in the Buttes, all in rock predating volcanic uplift. How judgmental we are in our classifications! It seems to me to be miraculous that coal of **any** kind should exist. We ought to treat it with a great deal more respect. Wasting it is a permanent loss. We can't count on today's ferns to replenish earthly stocks of that incredible, energy-liberating rock. They are but relics of a once-glorious past, subordinates to the upstart seed plants which now dominate the vegetative world.

Unlike the seed plants, ferns propagate by the primitive alternation of generations. The mature fern we recognize is the sporophyte generation, producing spores on the undersides of the fronds where we see them organized in small clusters called sori. Released into the air, spores travel near or far, millions of them doomed to die with their genetic messages unfulfilled. A tiny fraction will land in suitable sites and will develop into the gametophyte form, an inconspicuous prothallus. Distinct sexual organs will develop, and water will mediate the transfer of sperm and egg to productive union to begin a new sporophyte. The resultant "offspring" receives nourishment from the gametophyte until adequate leaf tissue forms to give it independence.

Marsilea

The Sacramento Valley proper is not good fern habitat, yet the Buttes have been successfully colonized by at least a dozen species. A condensation of the successes and failures of early colonization events and the gradual spread through the range would make fascinating reading.

Giant Chain Ferns thrust up their seven-foot fronds from soggy soils near a few springs, far from redwood and Douglas Fir companions with which I would usually associate them. I have hidden among the graceful fronds as an unsuspecting deer trotted down from parched hills to refresh itself in the trickling waters there.

On an intermittent creek where cattle wade and tree frogs chorus, a delicate aquatic fern, *Marsilea*, grows. "Marsilea" has a lyrical quality which I find far more appropriate to its shamrock-like looks than its common name, Hairy Pepperwort. Summer sloughs and ditches at the base of the Buttes contain the floating Duckweed Fern, *Azolla*.

Steep shaded banks near waterfalls or where sunlight rarely penetrates support lush growths of polypody and maidenhair ferns. Their exposed fronds die back during dry periods, while their tough underground rhizomes hold life-sustaining moisture.

California Polypody

Maidenhair Fern

Lace Fern

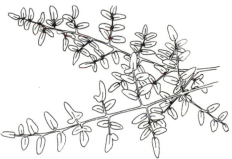

Coffee Fern

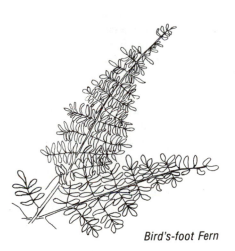

Bird's-foot Fern

Tucked under the sheltering north sides of rocks, Goldenback Ferns are emancipated from creeksides and springs. The rather triangular blades are leathery, deep green above, often densely coated with yellow spores below. The fine yellow powder can leave a perfect imprint of the frond when pressed carefully against a dark cloth (as junior naturalists love to discover).

Finding the California Lace Fern, the Bead Fern, or the Bird's-foot Cliffbrake requires patience and poking into rocky jumbles where one might encounter poison oak or some reptilian tenant, but their delicate beauty is worth the effort. Even more secretive are the Brittle Fern and Wood Fern, tucked away in moist places beneath heavy brush. Coffee Fern is fairly widespread in loose leaf litter beneath oaks. Tolerant of the tannins which leach from oak products, this fern will thrive in captivity if watered with tea!

The Pine and Juniper Families: Pinaceae and Cupressaceae

At comparable altitudes in the Sierra and Coast Ranges, Digger Pines spread their spindly needles above the rounded Blue Oaks. These pines are strikingly absent in the Sutter Buttes. Many people assume that the "timber" of the Buttes, namely pines, was cut or burned off by the white men, but we've found no positive evidence that this was so. Certainly **some** trees in the Buttes were cut by ranchers and by valley settlers needing fuel or timber, but better trees (e.g., mighty Valley Oaks) were available in the lowlands. Even a casual reference, if such exists, to "pine" by a settler could easily refer to the junipers that do survive there. The seeds of pine are carried in heavy cones that stay within the downslope gravitational zone of the tree, so pine propagules rarely cross broad hostile valleys.

Absence of pines supports the idea of the Buttes as a biogeographic island. It's certainly possible that pines colonized the Buttes one or more times in the last million or more years, but the island effect makes local extinction more probable than would be the case in the extensive valley-edge foothills.

California Junipers do indeed occur, scattered on the south side of South Butte. Why shouldn't junipers be more widely distributed in the range? That's a question appropriately pondered with a glass of juniper-cone-flavored gin and tonic in hand!

The Dicots

The greatest diversification of "higher" flowering plants occurred among the dicots. These typically have net-veined leaves; stems with concentric layers of pith, xylem, phloem, and cortex; flower parts mostly in fours or fives; an embryo with two cotyledons. From this basic plan they have evolved an incredible array of variations and specializations — compare a cottonwood to the mistletoe infesting it, for example. There follow examples from most of the dicot families represented in the Buttes. Slight seasonings of humor should heighten the taste of an already flavorful subject.

The Sumac Family: Anacardiaceae

I have never understood **why** the Poison Oak **produces** the toxic juice that makes life so miserable for so many who contact it. Brambles or thorns, stinging or sticky hairs, obnoxious smells or repulsive tastes — all these make evolutionary sense as mechanisms to protect plants from hungry herbivores. The compound apparently doesn't discourage cattle, for they do eat Poison Oak. It could scarcely have been directed at Native Americans, for few of them were affected by it. In fact, Sutter Buttes Indians were noted for using Poison Oak leaves in their acorn meal for baking bread. Many Indians used the plant in basketry, making dyes, curing warts, and healing snakebite.

Perhaps the chemicals deter foliage-eating insects. I have seen spiders and insects on Poison Oak leaves, but I don't recall extensive leaf damage as I have seen on other species. If so, the delayed-action rash and blisters that affect us are perhaps accidental, for the juice would not have the same effect on arthropods.

At any rate, I admit to ambivalent feelings about this family. On the one hand there are the "villains" — Poison Oak, Poison Ivy, Poison Sumac, Florida Poisontree. On the other are the "heroes" — Mango, Peppertree, Cashew, Pistachio. Then there are others in the group with ornamental beauty or which produce useful tannins, waxes, lacquers, or medicines.

Sometimes snaking as a vine high up into trees in shady areas, sometimes squatting as low shrubs in open sites or standing tall in pure, dense thickets, Poison Oak is highly variable in growth form. Its distinctive leaflets in trios are usually shiny, often deep red during early growth, bright green during the summer, and yellow or red in the fall. Flowers are small greenish inconspicuous clusters, and berries are dry white spheres. Leafless winter stalks can still transmit the rash, so avoid them. They tend to be short and thick, blunt at the tips, branching alternately.

Squawbush is an innocent shrub which closely resembles its poisonous cousin. Indians used the stems in basket-making and the fruits to make a beverage resembling pink lemonade. It too has three leaflets, but the central one lacks a distinct petiole and is under two inches long, the minimum size for the terminal leaflet in Poison Oak.

The Carrot Family: Apiaceae (Umbelliferae)

Consider the humble umbel. Its epigynous flowers may be perfect or sometimes imperfect (aren't we all?). It must live with an inferior ovary, pendulous ovules, and sometimes obsolete sepals (seems a crime). Fortunately, its anthers are versatile, and it is blessed with dual mericarps. Moreover, its pericarp has oil-tubes between the ribs and on the commissure. All these and a few other dandy facts from *A California Flora* by Munz help me to recognize a carrot when I see one.

With 3000 species worldwide, this family has other notables: parsnips, celery, lovage, dill, fennel, anise, caraway, parsley, and coriander, to name a few. Some members of the family are poisonous; extracts from Poison Hemlock apparently killed Socrates. That Old World native (Poison Hemlock, that is) has been introduced to America and occurs sparingly in disturbed places in the Buttes. It's a tall weed, with greenish stalks spotted with purple. Children have died from using its hollow stems as whistles.

Poison Sanicle is more often noticed in the spring by its scent than by its inconspicuous balls of tiny yellow flowers. Its foot-crushed leaves emit an odor that some people liken to cilantro (coriander); I think it smells like the inside of a leather baseball mitt after a heavy game.

The broad domes of lomatium umbels are ideal for what one author calls "insect idlers". Unspecialized flies walk about the cushions of tiny flowers, sampling the minute sips of nectar offered and moving the pollen about a bit, effecting a fair amount of pollination. So many insects gather at these spreads, in fact, that crab spiders and other predators hang out there to catch the unwary. A good patch of Giant-seeded Lomatium in bloom is well worth a couple hours of close-up viewing of melodramas in minute scale.

The Birthwort Family: Aristolochiaceae

In February one senses a stirring of life in the plants, an appearance of buds and a haze of green on moist soil that presages the flush of growth that fairly shouts with exuberance in March and April. Still one is hardly prepared at that time to find the precocious enthusiasm of such a tropical-looking plant, the Dutchman's Pipe.

Even by New Year's day, the welter of vines threading up through bushes or over a lichened boulder has hundreds of small dangling pipes emerging from axils of yet tiny leaves. In a month the pipes are swollen fully, crowded together in dense masses. One half expects to hear tiny voices from the protruding lips of haughty characters who would be at home in Alice's Wonderland.

What a marvel these pipes are! From a joint in the stiff, naked stem, the site where the arrowhead-shaped leaves will develop, a short twice-bent stalk descends. The flower begins as a rounded cylindrical dome, broadening as it descends and jutting forward like a bulging jaw. The tube then curves sharply upward, opening outward like a porch with an overhanging canopy. The semi-transparent pipe is greenish with strong reddish veins curving

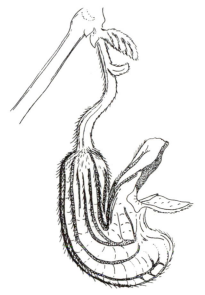

Dutchman's Pipe Flower

around and up to the red, brown or lurid purple lips. Fine hairs, best seen with back-lighting, form a light fuzz over stalk and blossom.

The Dutchman's Pipe is an elaborate fly-trap. A scent of rot or decay wafts from the tube, drawing in innocent flies with irresistible promises. Once inside, the fly can't back up, since downward-pointing hairs jab it in the posterior. Looking for light which should signify an exit, the fly is drawn into a chamber where thin walls let in more light than actually shows at the real, darkened entry. Falsely lured into contact with the flower's female parts, the fly may leave behind pollen picked up at a previous visit to a pipe (most flies never learn!).

The flower avoids self-pollination by having its pistil receptive before its stamens produce pollen. The hapless fly stumbles about in its jail until the plant releases its pollen and in effect opens the exit by letting the guard hairs wither. The flower itself may wither and bend so that the exit is finally made obvious. Some flies never do make it out in time, but those which do may carry pollen to the waiting stigmas of another flower that the naive fly just can't seem to resist!

All this makes the Dutchman's Pipe seem pretty clever, but of course no consciousness is involved. The intricate mechanisms arose from genetic changes that conferred survival advantage to their bearers. That doesn't make the plant any less remarkable.

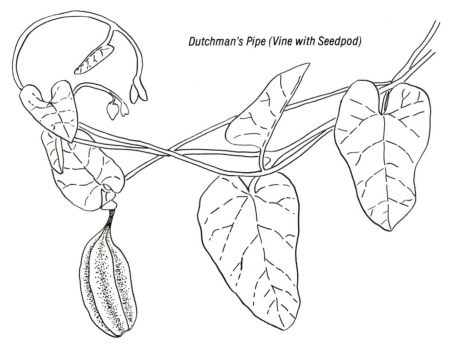

Dutchman's Pipe (Vine with Seedpod)

   The withering flower is replaced by an elongated greenish capsule with raised rusty ridges. The mature pods darken as they ripen and split open to drop the compressed seeds to the ground. The blackened, weathered pod may hang on the plant through the next flowering season.
   The growing tip of the vine is sensitive to contact with other objects, hence twisting and turning around convenient branches to gain the support such a wanderer needs. Once the flowers have passed their peak, the arrowhead leaves take over, solar factories producing the food that the plant uses for growth and future flower production.
   Aristolochia derives from Greek words meaning "best birth", a reference to medicinal properties associated with childbirth. Birthwort is an alternate common name.

The Milkweed Family: Asclepiadaceae

The milky white latex of milkweeds is a splendid chemical defense against most of the creatures that would eat them, but the Monarch butterfly gobbles the leaves with impunity and uses the toxins as a defense of its own.

Pollen transfer is a complicated process in milkweeds. Insects attracted to large nectar glands incidentally pick up sticky pollen on their legs. On the next flower the insect may step into a tight slit that conceals a receptive stigma. In extracting its leg, it leaves the pollen behind. Small or weak insects may find the slit an unyielding trap, dooming them to flutter and expire in the clutches of the heartless flower.

Successfully pollinated flowers develop strong pods filled with silk-tufted seeds. The mature pod eventually cracks open and releases the buoyant seeds to the wind.

The Composite or Sunflower Family: Asteraceae (Compositae)

Stand back for the **big one!** This family has about 19,000 species worldwide, 850 in California, and at least 70 in the Sutter Buttes.

What we call the flower of a sunflower is really an inflorescence, a head composed of many tiny, radially symmetrical central flowers (the disk) and strap-shaped peripheral flowers (the rays). A given head may have disk flowers, ray flowers, or both, but it is invariably a **composite** flower made up of smaller blossoms. There is no hope for discussing this massive group unless I subdivide it into tribes, units of convenience with certain traits in common.

The sunflower tribe includes the mule ears (*Wyethia*), balsamroots (*Balsamorhiza*), and sunflowers (*Helianthus*), all large and showy and easy to recognize. Our domestic sunflower is a race of the wild one, yielding cooking oil and seeds edible to man, livestock, and birds.

In the same tribe but in a separate subtribe, the Cocklebur (*Xanthium*) is a pesky cosmopolitan weed. Its cylindrical burs have wicked hooks that aggravate both man and beast unlucky enough to have picked up the hitch-hikers.

In yet another subtribe we find Blow Wives (*Achyrachaena*) and tarweeds. Blow Wives are far more known for their chaffy, whitish seedheads than for the tight clusters of inconspicuous tubular golden flowers that appear first. *Madias, Calycadenias, Hemizonias,* and *Lagophyllas* are tarweeds, glandular and aromatic late-bloomers, sufficiently repulsive to would-be herbivores to survive as green plants in the yellow-brown landscape of summer and fall. Spikeweeds (*Hemizonias*) are further armed with nasty spines. A walk through a summer field of tarweeds leaves pungent and greasy resin smeared around the pant cuffs and sometimes prick points in the legs.

Blow Wives (Flower)   *Blow Wives (Seedhead)*

The sneezeweed tribe includes Goldfields and Fremont's Lasthenia (both *Lasthenia*), Woolly Sunflower (*Eriophyllum*), and Yellowfields (*Blennosperma*). Many a forty-niner probably failed to strike it rich in the creeks of the Sierra, but the low hills near the valley turned gold each spring in a floral display that may have restored hope for some. Goldfields spreads across the low rocky slopes of the Sutter Buttes rampart, whereas Fremont's Lasthenia and Yellowfields choose the wetter flats. Woolly Sunflower is not as sociable, occurring as showy, many-headed plants on south-facing, often rocky slopes near peaks. Stems and leaves are covered with gray woolly hairs which help retard water loss.

The base of the flower head of a typical member of the aster tribe has greenish bracts which overlap like shingles. These bracts on the gumplant (*Grindelia*) are rolled back and strongly gummy, fitting the general pattern that late-blooming Buttes flowers tend to be resinous, sticky, hairy, smelly, spiny, or in some other way armed against casual consumption.

Narrowleaf Goldenbush (*Ericameria*, formerly *Haplopappus*) is a likely nominee for "showiest flowering shrub" for the month of March in the Buttes. Large yellow heads swarm over bright green foliage on rounded bushes. Later the tufts of silky seeds make an equally attractive sight. This species occurs in the Coast Ranges but not in the Sierra, perhaps giving some kind of clue to the biogeographic origin of the population in the Buttes.

Erigeron translates from the Greek to something like "early old man", a reference to its short grayish hairs and a tendency within the group for early flowering. On Pigeon Peak in the Buttes is a vertical cliff where clumps of Spreading Fleabane sprout from the rocky jumble of ancient mudflows. With a perfect southern exposure and enough altitude to allow basking in the sun when lower areas are smothered in winter fog, the plants here are the first to bloom in numbers in spring. In fact, some were crowned with new blossoms on the date of December 29, 1979! This species occurs on most of the peaks, some plants blooming up until May.

The genus *Baccharis* commemorates Bacchus, originally the Greek god of vegetation, later promoted to god of wine and revelry. Both Coyote Brush and Mule Fat are woody shrubs; the former is uncommon in chaparral and the latter fairly common along creekbeds.

The feathery, finely divided leaves of a young Common Yarrow *(Achillea)* give an immediate impression of a fern. Later it has a stout stem with occasional leaves, branching at the top into flattened clusters of small heads of whitish flowers. As in lomatiums with similar broad "tables" of tiny flowers, yarrows are visited by many insects, especially flies.

The European species of yarrow was a cure-all for innumerable ailments—rheumatism, ulcers, gout, nosebleed, gastritis, constipation, fevers, hemorrhoids, burns, kidney disorders, and so on. Our species makes a pleasant tea and was used by Indians internally much as the Europeans used its cousin. *Achillea* derives from Achilles, the Greek hero, who in the Trojan War reputedly used this plant to cure the wounds of fellow fighters.

Along with yarrow, the mayweed tribe includes Dog Fennel *(Anthemis)*, Pineapple Weed *(Matricaria)*, and Mugwort *(Artemisia)*. Dog Fennel and Pineapple Weed are introduced weeds related to the useful herb Chamomile. Crush the pineapple-shaped flower cones to catch the faint aroma diagnostic of Pineapple Weed, but take my word for it that the Dog Fennel is singularly ill-smelling. Mugwort is a cousin of sagebrush. Its pleasant-scented leaves can be crushed and applied with water as an antidote to accidental touching of Poison Oak.

The groundsel tribe includes the genus *Senecio,* one of the largest genera in the world, with over 1000 species. High on the slopes of Mt. Kenya in Africa we have seen the spectacular Giant Groundsels, some towering to 30 feet high in the Afro-alpine moorlands. Our representative in the Buttes is the inauspicious Common Butterweed, *Senecio vulgaris.* Somehow this scraggly little weed fails to inspire me.

Arnicas also have been assigned to the groundsel tribe. Most are mountain plants choosing moist places in forests on up to alpine meadows. We have found scattered plants of Rayless Arnica on the north slope of Old Man, and it may occur on similar sites elsewhere in the Buttes.

Most members of the everlasting tribe have woolly herbage. Oregon Woolly Marbles *(Psilocarphus)* is a low-growing plant of drying vernal pools. Cottonweed *(Micropus)* is common in grassy woodlands in April and May;

for a long time we thought we had missed the flowering stage until it dawned on us that the woolly "seed-heads" were actually the flowers. The dried stalks with pearly-white heads of the *Gnaphalium* everlastings are popular in floral displays. Their delicious scents, hinting of citrus and butterscotch and more provide a most delightful olfactory alternative to the odors of tarweeds and sanicles and turpentine weeds.

Along gravelly creekbeds in the Buttes occurs a straggly rounded bush that few people notice, even as they step around or over it. California Brickell-bush *(Brickellia)* is a master of understatement. It's a "wallflower" visually if not botanically (the showy yellow wallflower in the mustard family would be popular at **any** dance!). We look right **through** the brickellbush at the background — a bubbling creek, a monkeyflower, even a cow pie covered with flies. Like other members of the eupatory tribe, it has just disk flowers. I think we're predisposed to see ray flowers, enjoying disk flowers when they complement the rays but ignoring them by themselves. Poor old Dr. Brickell of Georgia has been "remembered" by a plant no one sees and a name no one remembers! Let's make a special effort to get to know this long-neglected shrub, shall we?

Most of us have had memorable experiences with the thistle tribe. Lest we forget, they have thousands of barbed reminders. Italian *(Carduus)*, Bull *(Cirsium vulgare)*, Milk *(Silybum)*, and star thistles *(Centaurea)* are exotics; Red *(Cirsium proteanum)* and Cobweb *(Cirsium occidentale)* are natives. Showy heads attract multitudes of insects; star thistle honey is a local favorite. Both ancient and modern foragers counterattacked these spiny plants, eating leaves, stalks, roots, and heads in a variety of tasty dishes. The artichoke, after all, is a thistle. Seed-eating birds relish the seeds; those escaping the birds are blown on the wind, as light as thistle-down.

All members of the chicory tribe have milky sap, exclusively ray flowers, and five teeth at the tip of each strap-like petal. Chicory itself *(Cichorium)*, that beautiful and edible blue-flowered weed, grows along Pass Road and perhaps elsewhere in disturbed areas. Yellow flowers and finely-haired seeds ("hang-gliders") characterize the Common Dandelion *(Taraxacum)* and such relatives as Cat's Ear *(Hypochoeris)*, Woodland Dandelion *(Agoseris)*, Common Sow Thistle *(Sonchus)*, and Woolly Malacothrix *(Malacothrix)*. Twiggy Wreath Plant *(Stephanomeria)* has similar basal leaves and flowers (though pinkish), but its stem is tall, spindly, and highly branched ("twiggy"). It is another late blooming annual, often blossoming in September.

The Barberry Family: Berberidaceae

On April 20, 1891, Willis Jepson reached Sutter County by river steamer and ascended South Butte on foot, the first botanist to collect in "this peculiarly isolated compact group of hills" (Jepson 1891). In a mere four hours, he had identified 110 species of plants, three of them unknown to science. Two of the latter have since been reduced to the status of races of other species, but the Sutter Buttes remains as the type locality for *Mahonia dictyota*, the California Barberry or Jepson's Mahonia.

Since then this holly-like shrub with undulating spine-tipped leaves has been found in the Sierra Nevada foothills, the inner Coast Ranges, and lower mountain slopes in southern California, but it is uncommon and seldom noticed throughout its range. Even in the Buttes it is unusual; Jepson found but a single plant near the summit of South Butte. We have found small patches here and there, but only on the northern slope of Goat Rocks near West Butte have we found an extensive, several-acre patch of the shrubs up to a meter high.

By April, terminal clusters of small yellow blossoms are displayed. The resulting berries dry quickly, unlike its Oregon Grape cousin which provides a moist and edible, if sour, berry for birds and beasts. The prickly leaves are an effective deterrent to the rampaging rooting of feral pigs; perhaps some plant species will escape local extinction only through association with the barberry.

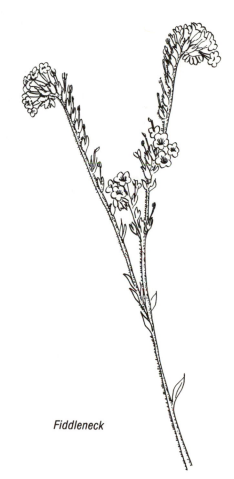

Fiddleneck

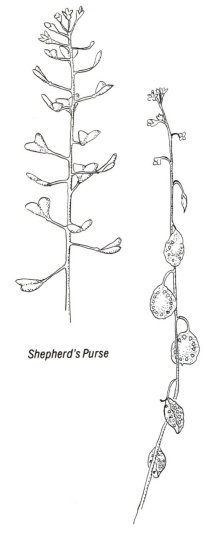

Shepherd's Purse

Lace Pod

The Borage Family: Boraginaceae

Trumpet-like flowers in a one-sided coil, a scorpioid spike, are typical of borages. Open slopes may be blanketed in spring with popcorn flowers or cryptanthas. Lower fields may be dominated by the orange curls of fiddlenecks, to the chagrin of cattle ranchers, who prefer grass. Grand Hound's-tongue, a lovely flower that shows off its close affinities to Forget-me-nots, is more of a loner in the Buttes, apparently finicky in its choice of dry but shaded sites. Salt Heliotrope prefers saline soils and is uncommon in the Buttes. I've found it in sheep corrals; perhaps the concentrated urine of hundreds of sheep has created the salinity it requires.

The Mustard Family:
Brassicaceae (Cruciferae)

This is the fifth largest plant family in the state, with approximately 235 species, but only a dozen or so are commonly found in the Buttes. They share such traits as a pungent watery juice, four crosslike petals, six stamens (two lower and shorter), and seed-bearing capsules. Long, narrow capsules are called siliques; broad flattened ones are silicles.

The pods or capsules deserve a closer look in the field. A hand lens can open up a new world to appreciate. Shepherd's Purse gains its name from its flattened, heart-shaped silicles, though in this era one is far more likely to know the plant than the herder's bag for which it is named. The reflective smooth oval pods of Shining Peppergrass and the delicate papery doilies of Lace and Spoke Pods are well worth the humbling exercise of prostrating the body on the ground. Don't take my word for it; look at them eyeball to silicle!

Many crucifers are edible; after all, cauliflower, cabbage, turnip, rutabaga, radish, broccoli, Brussels sprouts, and mustard itself are in the family. A little watercress from a creek or spring has flavored many a sandwich on Buttes hikes.

The Bellflower Family: Campanulaceae

The two-inch slender stems of Common Blue Cup are easy to overlook amid taller grasses and earlier flowers. Indeed, we didn't find them until 1980, even though we knew Jepson had found some in 1891.

The downingias prefer vernal pools, often forming bluish "bathtub rings" on the drying ground surrounding the retreating moisture of an evaporation flat. In March we may see Killdeer and Greater Yellowlegs and Mallards wading across a soggy flat; in April and May, we may find lizards scampering among the Two-horned and Valley Downingias and other "vernal pool flowers" sprouting from dry and cracking earth in the same place.

The Honeysuckle Family: Caprifoliaceae

Common Snowberry is **not** common in the Buttes, doing best in shady sites not far from water. Mexican Blue Elder, on the other hand, thrives along wooded creekbeds and around seeps and springs. In August and September when much of the landscape is sere, the lush elders look almost tropical and magnetically draw insects and birds to their foliage, flowers, fruits, and stems, plus mammals and reptiles to their shade.

One of the richest natural sources of Vitamin C, elderberry products are used for medicines, teas, wines, jellies, syrups, sauces, and fritters. The pithy stems provide residences for some of our solitary native bees, and hollowed out, they can become whistles, arrow shafts, and flutes. The genus *Sambucus,* in fact, is a Greek word for an instrument of elderberry wood.

We know the Chaparral Honeysuckle from but a few individuals widely separated in the Buttes, though it may occur there elsewhere. How long ago did this species colonize the Buttes, and from whence did it come? How was it transported? Was it more common in earlier years? Will it spread or disappear? A rare colonist raises all manner of interesting questions, but the clues may be gone; the mystery may remain so forever.

The Pink Family: Caryophyllaceae

Our most obvious representatives of this family are aliens introduced from Europe: Common Catchfly, Common Chickweed, Wild Carnation, Ruby Sand Spurry, and Evening Lychnis. Indeed **most** of the exotics sucessful in our area are from Eurasia, since temperate zone species are far more likely to thrive here than are tropical ones. We regard them officially as weeds because they are out of place and often prefer waste areas. Yet the unpleasant connotations of the word "weed" are instantly forgotten when one beholds a pink patch of boutonniere-sized Wild Carnations.

Chickweed, usually frowned upon or ignored, actually has a long history of usefulness to humans for food and medicine. Even the mass-produced chickens of today may receive chickweed seed in their poultry feed as an appetite stimulant.

Catchflys are sticky-haired; woe to any dallying Dipteran that chooses one for a perch! Both Common Catchfly and Evening Lychnis open in the long shadows of late afternoon or evening and wither the following morning.

Wild Carnations

The Goosefoot Family: Chenopodiaceae

The strategic Arms Limitation Treaties are too late to stop the proliferation of a most unpleasant invader, the Russian Thistle. Ironically, its genus *Salsola* derives from a Latin word for "SALT". It forms a huge tumbleweed shape, armed with thousands of diabolical spines. The dried plant is easily uprooted and goes bounding across the landscape on autumn winds, freely scattering its bullet-like black seeds until stacking up with others in fence rows.

The Morning Glory Family: Convolvulaceae

Convolvulus is Latin for "to entwine". Bindweed is a persistent, deep-rooted weed common along roadsides, and Western Morning Glory is a larger, showier vine that ascends and spreads over shrubby vegetation. Both produce handsome five-lobed white or pinkish trumpets. Their seeds contain nasty nitrogenous compounds, effective defense against seed-eating birds.

The Stonecrop Family: Crassulaceae

Our stonecrops are about as small as they come, as Dwarf and Pygmy imply. A hand lens will reveal them for the tiny succulents they are. A thousand or so Pygmy Stonecrops in a square meter looks to a standing person like a reddish moss, yet tiny stems sprout tiny leaves at the axils of tiny flower stalks with minutely perfect flowers. The infinitesimal seeds contain the complex coding **and** the start-up energy to build new stonecrops with the same self-replicating features. Can man with his silicon chips and microprocessors rival this marvel of miniaturization?

Dwarf Cliff Sedum

The Gourd Family: Cucurbitaceae

On one of our early explorations in the Buttes in 1976, we discovered a dried vine with colorful gourds. Leaves had withered, so we were unsure whether it was Stinking Gourd (*Cucurbita foetidissima*) or Coyote Melon (*C. palmata*). For either species, the finding would have meant a range extension, since both occur from the San Joaquin Valley south. Alas, we haven't returned to the site and have found no others.

California Manroot aggressively sends its vines with coiling tendrils up bushes and over fences in the spring. Its delicate white flowers are followed by mace-like spiky green melons which eventually burst to release the brownish seeds. As summer heat begins to rise, the once-lush vine withers and dies back above ground. Moisture and precious nutrients built up during the spring are retained in the massive subterranean tuber, sometimes "as big as a man". Manroot achieves the best of both worlds by having an annual leafy stem with a perennial tuber.

The Dodder Family: Cuscutaceae

"Parasite" — a perfectly neutral word coming from "para" meaning "beside" and "sitos" meaning "food". Yet of all the terms we use to describe interactions among organisms — competitor, herbivore, carnivore, etc. — "parasite" is most likely to arouse a strong negative feeling. Why should we calmly accept a cow devouring an entire clover plant, yet deplore a twining mass of orange dodder threads merely tapping a portion of the nutrients of the "host" plant? A good parasite doesn't kill its host; indeed, if one does, it ought to be redefined as a predator. How neutral is a bulldozer that flattens a stand of chaparral? We too easily overlook the long evolutionary history of interacting organisms, the give and take, changes and compromises, thrusts and deflections that result in coevolved arrangements at which we should rightfully marvel.

The twisting threads of dodder have leaves reduced to mere scales. Wherever twining stems touch the host, a haustorium or point of connection develops — probe, clamp, wedge, penetrate. The plumbing of the parasite links into the xylem, the upward-flowing column of nutrients of the host. Threads proliferate all over the victim, and the acquired nutrients ultimately are converted into flowers and seeds, the dodder's ultimate effort.

Then comes the period of uncertainty. Dodder seeds are scattered blindly, and the sprouting plant from the germinating seed must somehow find a host. Unlike the miniscule seeds of the parasitic broomrape (*Orobanche*), which must germinate in contact with a host's tissues, the larger seeds of dodder are given a dowry of endosperm which will keep them alive for six to eight weeks. Dodder has "unemployment insurance".

The initial thread or threads begin to spiral, first in a wide, sweeping arc in "search" of contact with a host. It's not merely a random wave; the parasite can sense chemicals of the potential host and grow toward them. Both the wide spiral and a tighter vertical coiling continue once contact has been made. As soon as attachment is effected, the dodder abandons its "baby roots" and becomes a true parasite.

So much for the facts! In reality, we relate best to plants when we can draw inferences from them that illuminate or interpret some aspects of ourselves. I find quite charming the verse by Erasmus Darwin in *The Botanic Garden* (quoted in Huxley 1974:289);

> *Two Harlot-Nymphs, the fair Cuscutas, please*
> *With labour'd negligence, and studied ease;*
> *In the meek garb of modest worth disguised,*
> *The eye averted, and the smile chastised,*
> *With sly approach they spread their dangerous charms,*
> *And round their victim wind their wiry arms.*

The Heath Family: Ericaceae

Manzanita, the "little apple" (for its deep red fruits) is a strikingly beautiful small tree or shrub with smooth reddish trunk, twisting branches, and ever-green leaves. The urn-shaped drooping blossoms of white or pink attract a variety of bees and flies, the usual pollinators, but inadvertently supply nectar to hummingbirds if other flowers are scarce. Undoubtedly some pollination is effected by bill-tip contact, but clearly manzanitas and hummingbirds have not coevolved in an intimate system such as occurs between the birds and many tubular red flowers in the American West.

The Spurge Family: Euphorbiaceae

Turkey Mullein or Dove Weed forms low, rounded cushions of hairy gray-green leaves. It produces tiny, easily overlooked blossoms after most spring flowers have passed away, but its seeds are not overlooked by hungry quail and doves. Its milky latex, typical of spurges, is poisonous, and was used by certain Indians as a fish poison.

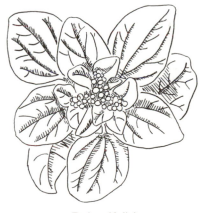

Turkey Mullein

The Pea Family: Fabaceae (Leguminosae)

The pea family is richly represented in California by some 380 species, making it the third most diverse family in the state. That is a blessing to the landscape and to mankind in general, for the family includes such useful or beautiful species as alfalfa, clover, peas, beans, soybeans, peanuts, lentils, redbud, mimosas, acacias, mesquites, and the like. It can be a source of frustration to the neophyte botanist who feels lucky if he can distinguish a lupine from a lotus from a clover, let alone tell **which** of California's 82 lupines, 36 lotuses, and 52 clovers a specimen might be!

Most clovers play by the rules, with rounded heads of pea-like flowers and leaflets in threes (as *Trifolium* implies). Their common names can be plainly descriptive (Rose, White, White-topped, Bur) or more imaginative (Tomcat, Cowbags, Cow, Bull, Maiden, Indian, Pinpoint).

Lupines were vilified long ago for allegedly robbing the soil of minerals and nutrients (*Lupinus* means "wolf"). Both lupines and wolves have been vindicated of most of the accusations directed against them. Lupines don't cause poor soils, but they can survive in them because nitrogen-fixing bacteria in nodules on their roots actually add nutrients to the soil. Farmers may rotate a crop of alfalfa, clover, or beans on their fields to exploit that soil-enriching ability.

Several of our lupines are small annuals. Miniature Lupine commonly adds its blues to the brilliant reds and oranges of owlclovers and poppies. White-whorl Lupine raises creamy white spikes in a salute to April. Our largest lupine, the Silver, is a woody bush with silvery-gray leaves giving it a resemblance to sagebrush (if seen through squinted eyes). That illusion is dispelled in spring when it sends up dramatic purple-blue and white spikes of flowers.

Deerweed is our most noticeable lotus, a rounded shrub that thrives on open slopes following chaparral fires. Cattle relish its taste at least as much as do deer, and a fenceline across a hill may show masses of deerweed on one side, none on the other.

Sulphur Pea or Snub Pea is a sprawling vine with pinnately compound leaves with twining tendrils. Most of the flowers are yellow with rust or orange tints, but the upper blossoms may be white with purple tints.

A final noteworthy example of this family is the Western Redbud. Useful to the Indians medicinally and in basket-making, the redbud is now recognized for its beauty. Brilliant pink blossoms emerge in March prior to the leaves; the flowering trees stand out as bursts of pink in a predominantly green landscape. Then the leaves emerge, broadly heart-shaped, green in summer and reddish in fall. The seed pods are handsomely rusty too, giving color to the leafless branches even through the winter.

The Oak Family: Fagaceae

Our oaks are not only natives, they are endemic to the state, true Californians. Though flowering plants, they lack petals; insect attraction is not crucial to pollination. Dangling clusters of staminate flowers produce pollen prolifically. At times a shaken branch will release a yellowish cloud to be swept away on the wind. Abundant pollen may coat the surface of a pond. Woe to hay-fever sufferers at this time! The pistillate flowers which receive pollen develop acorns, pointed nuts set in cuplike rings. The meat of the acorn provides food for the rapidly growing radicle, which seeks the ground where the first root system develops.

Oaks transform a simple, two-dimensional grassland into a complex,-three-dimensional savannah. The implications are profound. Roots, bark, branches, leaves, flowers, and acorns are oak survival mechanisms, an oak's way of providing for the perpetuation of its genes. Yet ultimately thousands of other organisms may benefit from the existence of a single big oak. It's literally an "acornucopia", a woody horn of plenty.

Consider the birds. Acorn Woodpeckers specialize on oaks, harvesting and storing the acorns as true farmers would. Scrub Jays gather acorns too, storing many and forgetting some, thus inadvertently helping oak seedlings get a start. Nuthatches inch down the rough boles inserting their beaks like tweezers to extract insects from the bark. Phainopeplas flutter between clumps of mistletoe in oak branches, gorging on the pale berries and defecating the seeds, some of which will spread the parasite. Kingbirds nest in the boughs, sallying forth to snap insects from the air. Great Horned Owls grip the furrowed branches with powerful talons.

Valley Oak

hiding in dense foliage in daylight to avoid harassment from intolerant neighbors and plunging into the grasses below at night for food. Titmice, Starlings, and Ash-throated Flycatchers nest in security within cavities, some created by mechanical or insect damage, some by woodpeckers. Even Golden Eagles may build their massive stick nests on mighty oak branches. Thousands of migrant birds visit oaks for food or cover during passage.

Mammals, too, depend on the oaks. Deer rest in their shade and join the rodents and other creatures which feast on the mast, the fallen crop of acorns. Few oak seedlings, in fact, evade the hungry browsers to become real trees. Raccoons, Ringtails, Gray Foxes, and bats find shelter in the cavities within standing or fallen trunks and branches.

Insects use the trees in mind-boggling numbers. Even though basically wind-pollinated, the flowering oaks attract multitudes of flying insects. You can hear a hum from a blooming Interior Live Oak yards away. Caterpillars may proliferate on the leaves, in turn attracting insect and avian predators. Tiny wasps lay their eggs in stems and foliage, stimulating gall production by the oaks. The young wasp larvae inside may in turn be parasitized by other insects.

It is one of the ironies of California land use that thousands of acres of Blue Oak woodland have been sprayed, chopped, burned, and in other ways violated because of the mistaken idea that fewer oaks mean more grass and hence fatter cattle. Oaks and grasses extract their moisture from different parts of the soil horizon. The trees provide shade and interference with wind flow to drastically reduce moisture loss to grasses through evapotranspiration. Stand on a ridge in late spring and look at the pattern of scattered oaks on adjacent ridges. Open areas dry most quickly, leaving circles of green surrounding each oak. Studies have documented that not only is grass lusher beneath oaks, it often contains more nutrients and is more palatable to cattle (Holland 1974). It's equally obvious that cattle seek the shade on warm days. The foothill oak woodland epitomizes the natural beauty and wealth of the Golden State. It is a tragedy to see a wasteland of oak carcasses, like a war-torn battlefield, in its place. Fortunately, most of the Sutter Buttes groves are relatively intact.

The Blue Oak is well adapted to hot, dry foothills. Its pale, blue-green leaves are lightly scalloped and deciduous. The trees do not attain the great girth or spread of ancient Valley Oaks, but old-timers with boldly twisting branches and dark oval cavities develop what I must refer to as "character". Many groves are beautifully parklike: umbrella-shaped trees over smooth, flowing grasses without a clutter of brush.

Valley Oaks are true to their name, typical of the Sacramento Valley lowlands but scattered through the Buttes along streams and where deeper soils have accumulated. Their leaves are greener, larger, more deeply lobed than those typical of Blue Oaks. Like them, they are bare in winter.

Scrub Oaks are "evergreen or tardily deciduous" (McMinn 1939), shrubby elements of the chaparral. The small leaves are highly variable, but the undersides are dry and pale, which helps distinguish them from those of Hollyleaf Redberry. Acorns, of course, give them away.

Interior Live Oaks occasionally mingle with Blue Oaks in open areas but more often flank creeks or form dense groves on valley floors or on shaded northern exposures. The dark green, leathery leaves may have entire or scalloped edges, with prickly tips. The leaves are retained for approximately two years and are replaced so that the

Interior Live Oak

branches are never bare. This oak may grow as a typical tree or remain shrubby in a chaparral formation. It sprouts readily from the stump after fires.

Finally, the Oracle Oak occurs sparsely in the Buttes. Its highly variable leaves are basically evergreen, but during drought winters I found specimens which dropped most of their foliage, leaving a branch or two leafed-out in a most unusual way. Botanists believe this oak is a hybrid between the deciduous Black Oak and the evergreen Interior Live Oak. Since we've never found a Black Oak in the Buttes, we have the interesting biogeographic question of how these Oracles got started. Were Black Oaks once here or are the pollinating mechanisms (e.g., pollen drifting on the wind) such that long-distance colonization could occur? The nonspecific scatter of pollen occasionally results in other combinations of oak hybrids in the Buttes.

The Silktassel Family: Garryaceae

John C. Fremont made history when he camped in the Sutter Buttes from May 30 - June 8, 1846, preparing for the Bear Flag Revolt which ultimately brought California to the United States from Mexico. Fremont appreciated the climate and the abundance of game in the Buttes. He wrote enthusiastically about the flowers he found in California and sent specimens to his friend Dr. John Torrey, a New York botanist, for identification.

In the 1850's he discovered a new shrub along a small tributary of Cow Creek in Shasta County and sent pressed material to Torrey. Having already assigned the genus *Fremontia* to the flannel bush, which Fremont had discovered earlier at the head of the Sacramento Valley, Torrey immortalized his friend in the species name instead: *Garrya fremontii.* If Fremont had searched the Sutter Buttes more thoroughly in 1846, he might have found the species then, for it occurs there uncommonly.

As a soldier, Fremont is remembered in the Buttes by a stone monument. As a flower-lover, his name is affixed to a silktassel, a cottonwood, a globe-mallow, a camas, and a lasthenia, plus a few other species not found in the Buttes.

It is a surprise to discover a silktassel shrub blooming in January or February, but that's its style. We can't stigmatize a plant just because it's different. The yellowish-green catkins and glossy evergreen leaves make it an attractive shrub suitable for home landscaping.

Normally occurring in the 2000-7500 foot elevational zone, the silktassels in the Buttes at such low altitudes are exceptional. I have found a single eight-foot tree in a wooded draw west of Twin Peaks and a half-acre stand of four-to-six-foot shrubs in chaparral in Moore Canyon.

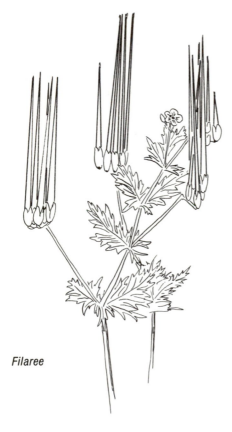

Filaree

The Geranium Family: Geraniaceae

This family is represented in the Buttes by four storksbills and three small geraniums (the cultivated geranium is really a *Pelargonium*). Most of them are native to Europe or North Africa, but the storksbill colonizers of the Buttes are welcomed with pleasure by most sheepmen, since the plants provide early green feed and protect the soil.

Storksbills get their name from the long beak-like projection formed by the clustered styles of five seeds from the original tiny pink flower. As the seeds mature, they detach at the base, and gradually move upward to the apex of the beak as the drying styles slowly turn. The light spirally-twisted tails assist dispersal by wind and respond readily to humidity changes, twisting like drills in a motion which often succeeds in planting the sharp seeds. The seeds are barbed with stiff back-projecting white hairs which keep the planted seed imbedded in the ground. Twisting will drill the seed in deeper, untwisting with reverse humidity will not pull it out.

Storksbills are often called Filaree, derived from a Spanish word meaning "pin". The sharp "stick-pin" seeds are readily imbedded in the pants-seat of an unwary hiker sitting down in a patch where the seeds are just unfurling! Dogs sometimes suffer when the seeds penetrate toe pads or ears; the back-pointing hairs make extraction from the convoluted ear channels a trick even for a veterinarian.

Children have yet other names for these plants. "Scissors" comes from kids using two beaks in snipping fashion, and "Clocks" comes from the turning action of a freshly picked seed whose drying style sweeps in a clockwise fashion.

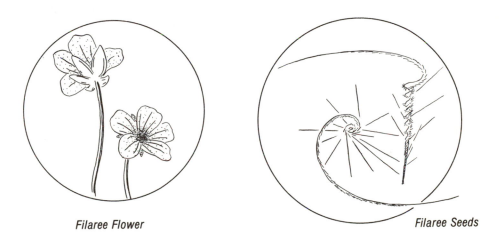

Filaree Flower   *Filaree Seeds*

The Buckeye Family: Hippocastanaceae

Considering altitude and general habitat types, the Buttes **ought** to have buckeyes. They are common in comparable sites in both the Coast Range and Sierra Nevada flanking the valley.

We have found a single California Buckeye blooming in May in an abandoned olive orchard near South Butte Road, a most unnatural site for a buckeye. It obviously was planted.

Looking closely at the species, however, reveals that it would be an unlikely candidate for colonization across unsuitable habitat. Each flower produces a single large pear-shaped capsule, usually with a single large seed. Not wind nor gravity nor any sensible animal would transport such a seed miles to a distant volcanic island.

The Waterleaf Family: Hydrophyllaceae

One Easter a dozen of us nature enthusiasts lay on our backs on a south-facing hillside among scattered Blue Oaks. During the winter this slope had been a quiet place of dead grasses and leafless trees. Now in the peak of spring the same area pulsed with life. All around us the coiled heads of Tansy Phacelia nodded in the breeze, like a rippling purple sea. Above the soft rustle of the wind came the vibrant hum of thousands of bees industriously visiting the brilliant flowers. Other insects moved among the stems of the phacelias, some nibbling on plant parts and others hunting the mild herbivores. Nothing could be more representative of the Easter resurrection than the miraculous renewal of life that spring provides.

A field of Baby Blue Eyes always seems a perfect excuse to abandon our high-headed view of the world to sprawl prone on the ground where the action is. What a classic flower — five broad symmetric blue petals united at the base, a perfect white circle in the center punctuated by the dark central anthers.

Baby Blue Eyes

Yerba Santa, literally "holy weed", bears little superficial resemblance to the annual flowers in the same family, but again the structure of the pale pink, funnel-shaped flower proves to be the unifying link. It is a tall shrub, with sticky, aromatic leaves dark green above and hairy-whitish below. Also called "mountain balm", the plant has many medicinal values. A bitter tea brewed from the leaves is taken for colds, coughs, and sore throats, and a mouthful of fresh leaves may help quench one's thirst.

The Walnut Family: Juglandaceae

The native California walnut occurs sparingly along some creekbeds in the Buttes. Its actual native distribution is somewhat speculative, since Indians transported the edible nuts about with them and white man may similarly have introduced it here and there.

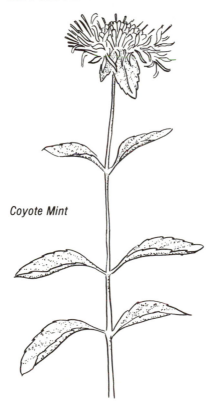

Coyote Mint

The Mint Family: Lamiaceae (Labiatae)

Square stems, opposite leaves, irregular two-lipped flowers, aromatic scent — these cues readily identify a mint (except the exceptions). Thank this productive family for sage, rosemary, and thyme (but not parsley), as well as catnip, spearmint, basil, germander, oregano, and lavender.

Our native Chia was used extensively by California Indians, chiefly (and bravely) as a meal ground from seeds. Its seeds had an open market value of $6-$8 per pound in San Francisco in 1894 (Balls 1962).

The Old World Horehound, which Munz describes aptly as a "common pestiferous weed in waste places and old fields", was already "rank" at the Feather River near the Buttes as early as 1891 (Jepson 1891). It is a coarse perennial herb with small flowers in dense whorls; these later become clinging seeds which torment dogs and sheep and sweater-clad hikers.

Ancient European herbalists, now few and far-between, prized the medicinal qualities of horehound. Its rather bitter taste inhibits coughing and helps cure colds. Horehound is reasonably well-known as a candy, though it doesn't rival jelly beans or chocolate bars.

When the grasses and normal wildflowers of the dry hills and flats in the Buttes have dried and withered in the oppressive summer heat, Blue Curls takes over. Green and flowering when nearly all else is dessicated, the Blue Curls would seem to be a natural target for greens-greedy herbivores, from insects to mammals. Yet its extreme pungence (other names are Vinegar Weed and Turpentine Weed) announces its chemical defense system which seems to work. Moreover, it has little competition for pollinating insects at that season. If I could overcome my olfactory repugnance for the plant, I'd like to study it closely to see if any enterprising arthropods have adjusted to such a highly marinated salad.

Blue Curls

The Laurel Family: Lauraceae

In a family noted for producing such useful products as avocado, cinnamon, sassafras, and camphor, our California Bay (or Laurel) should provide something of interest. Indeed it does. Its pungent leaves are a fine substitute for the unrelated true bay leaves of the Mediterranean used in flavoring roasts and soups. One would expect the strong pungence to deter browsers, but deer in the Buttes prune it back with apparent enthusiasm. A poacher might well find his illegal venison pre-seasoned!

When it can grow beyond the reach of browsing beasts, the bay develops into a substantial tree. In winter months its dark leathery foliage stands out on rocky ridges among the naked branches of adjacent Blue Oaks, for it is evergreen. Basically left alone in the Buttes, its wood is sought elsewhere for

California Bay

furniture, boat building, and stave timber. Oregonians call it "Oregon Myrtle" and sell beautiful lathe-turned bowls and candlesticks. In their zealous promotion of its products, some claim that their "myrtle" grows only in southwestern Oregon and the Holy Land. In fact, the Holy Land has true myrtles, and the Oregon Myrtle or California Bay (*Umbellularia californica*) occurs all the way from San Diego County to Coos Bay, Oregon.

Umbellularia is widely distributed but not abundant in the Buttes. It seems to prefer rocky ridge-tops and thickets of chaparral on northern slopes. A crushed leaf carried in the pocket allows its pleasant fragrance to accompany one throughout a day's hike.

The Loasa Family: Loasaceae

Jepson in 1891 found a *Mentzelia* "quite plentiful" on the southern slopes of South Butte at about 1600 feet. Lowell Ahart has collected it on the same peak, but I've never seen the rather showy plant elsewhere in the Buttes. It has alternate leaves with "sticky" barbed hairs, stout greenish-white stems, five sepals and five larger petals which Dr. Jepson's friend, Dr. Kellogg, described as having "a shining golden color, with lustrous metallic hue, shading from a deep vivid orange to a burnt carmine center."

The Mallow Family: Malvaceae

The mallow family contains such well-known members as the hibiscus, hollyhock, cotton, and, yes, marsh mallow, a European plant from which the original sweet puffy confection was made. Our largest type is the Fremont or White-coat Globemallow, a felt-leaved shrub with broad pink blossoms with darker centers. Its generic name, *Malacothamnus,* appropriately means "soft shrub".

Our two sidalceas are delicate erect pinkish flowers. Superficially they resemble some of the pink clarkias but are easily told by five petals instead of four and palmate (handlike) leaves instead of single, nearly linear ones.

Cheeseweed is an alien which crops up in disturbed areas. English children nibble the cheese-like fruits; Americans just trample them.

Though not found in the Buttes, the gorgeous California Hibiscus occurs along wooded sloughs in the nearby Butte Sink. It is endemic to the Great Valley lowlands and so restricted in distribution that it's classified an endangered species. Other botanists reduce it to a mere race of the widespread *H. lasiocarpus* found from Illinois to Florida. Whether race or full species, it is so impressive and localized in this state that it has become the official flower of the Sacramento chapter of the California Native Plant Society.

The Martynia Family: Martyniaceae

Greatest of the "hookers" in the plant kingdom is the six-inch, two-pronged capsule of the Unicorn Plant or Devil's Claw. Choose your name according to the stage of capsule development: as the pod matures, it splits from a single "horn" into two strongly curved "claws" (Spellenberg 1979). Pity the poor sheep packing around such wickedly-clinging passengers, unwittingly scattering seeds that may lead to its later, greater aggravation!

The striking flower and chubby, heart-shaped leaves would seem at first glance to be redeeming features, but examine them more closely. It is a **most**-unpickable plant, covered with obnoxiously sticky hairs and emitting a foul scent. I found tiny black insects littering its hispid, viscid (sounds worse than "hairy, sticky") leaves and stem; whether they were victims or exploiters, I could not tell. I peered into the broad funnel of its freckled corolla and interpreted the striped "pollinator path" as a most-insulting tongue.

Sure, I've let my emotions run away with me; the plant's design is its survival machine, innocent of malicious intent. **Any** judgment we assign to a plant, good or bad, is an artifact of our own biases. Forgive me my anthromorphic teasing; I trust we both know better but can enjoy the verbal pun-ishment.

The Mulberry Family: Moraceae

I well recall my first encounter with a wild fig. Wrinkled, saggy pear-shaped fruits dangled among the broad mitt-like leaves of a spreading tree ten feet high and twice as broad. I smashed through an enveloping thicket of nettles and pulled myself up among springy white branches. I picked one of the fruits but hesitated at the thought of eating such an alien object. Curious and rather hungry, I bit into the yielding flesh and discovered, to my surprise, a delightful warm mush of seeds and fibers. Describing one is no substitute for eating one! As I descended, I learned that fig trees are capable of giving bare skin an itchy rash, but already I was hooked on a most edible fruit. The rash did suggest that using the proverbial fig leaf in the traditional way might be inadvisable!

Not native to California, figs now grow most often where water is readily available, such as springs and seeps. Summer plants could scarcely be more lush or winter plants more bare. Pollination is achieved through a unique symbiotic relationship with a miniature wasp.

Sharing this family with the edible fig are such well-known plants as the mulberry, rubber plant, hops, and marijuana. The latter is grown illegally in humid parts of northern California, but the aridity and openness of the Buttes would seem to preclude that possibility here.

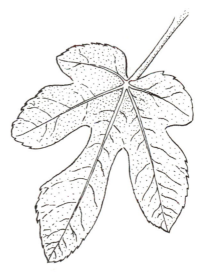

Wild Fig

Lovely Clarkia

Elegant Clarkia

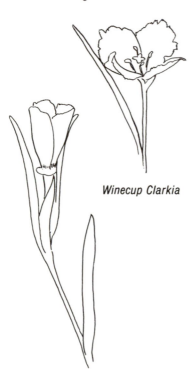

Winecup Clarkia

Slender Clarkia

The Olive Family: Oleaceae

Common in the riparian forests of the Butte Sink and Sacramento River, Oregon Ash ventures into the Buttes only where dependable water supplies occur. Its seeds are winged samaras, tiny helicopters propelled by capricious winds.

The Evening Primrose Family: Onagraceae

To a certain degree, I've always resented naming plants or animals after humans. It seems an act of arrogance to associate a single human being of such ephemeral existence with a species long predating the origin of humans themselves. Descriptive terms, still subjective and often compromised by human bias, nevertheless seem more appropriate.

Parched Fireweed, for example, is an adequately descriptive name. Fireweeds often appear in disturbed ground after fires, and Parched Fireweed is a species blooming in arid areas at the hottest, driest time of year.

Five species of Clarkia bloom in the Buttes. *Lewisia* (Bitterroot) and *Clarkia* commemorate the famous Lewis and Clark Expedition. I suspect that their contributions deserve recognition more than do the friends and political contacts for whom botanists sometimes name plants. *Lewisia* and *Clarkia* have a nice sound to them, musical enough to fit the delicate, lovely blossoms to which they've been assigned. Bilobed Clarkia has a straightforward adjectival name, but our others may have been named in the passion of appreciation that these blossoms inspire: Lovely, Elegant, Slender and Winecup. A toast to our friend Clark and the fine flowers that bear his name.

The Broomrape Family: Orobanchaceae

I'll resist the temptation to play games with the name of the Naked Broomrape, a remarkable enough parasite on the roots of saxifrages and perhaps other plants in the Buttes. The plant is leafless, save for a few scales at the base of the stem, and lacks chlorophyll, depending completely on its host plant for nourishment.

In April we find the broomrape's single snapdragon-like flower on its one- to four-inch stem. The fine seeds it produces **must** germinate in contact with the roots of an acceptable host to establish the vital linkage. The main stem occurs underground, and a dense network of fine hairlike roots transfers nutrients and water from the host. In fact, the broomrape can alter the chemical composition of the sugars it steals, creating an osmotic gradient that literally pulls water from its host.

The Poppy Family: Papaveraceae

When spring hills blaze with the golden-orange of the California Poppy, it's obvious why the plant was chosen the official flower of the Golden State. Three species of poppies grow in the Buttes, but only the California has a broad flattened rim at the base of the ovary.

Californians are caricatured by Easterners as sun-worshippers, and our brightest poppy is a good Californian. It spreads its petals wide on sunny days but closes them at night and in cloudy weather. Petals tend to be large and bright orange early in the season, smaller and pale yellow later. The flowering season is remarkably long, some individuals blooming at any time from February through September. One clump was in full bloom at West Butte on January 1, 1979.

Its open arms posture welcomes all manner of six-legged visitors, but beetles are particularly attracted to its spicy fragrance and serve as chief pollinators. Tiny black seeds develop in its elongated capsules and are popped out forcibly when ripe.

The Plantain Family: Plantaginaceae

The Dwarf Plantain can only be appreciated by changing scale, by lying down for a mouse-eye view of the thin fuzzy leaves and stem ascending from a base and the tiny compact spikes of pale scalelike petals. They can be surprisingly abundant on dry rocky soils which could never support the water demands of larger plants.

Another plantain found along dry roadsides in the Buttes drove us crazy as we tried to key it out. Its characters seemed straight-forward, but each trip through the key led us to *Plantago coronopus*, which, according to the range listed for it, was an alien naturalized in "sea cliffs, about salt marshes, etc." along the California coast. Specimens brought to the herbarium at UC Davis led the curator to the same identification, and comparison with pressed plants clinched it. One collection, not yet listed in Munz, found the species in the Sierran foothills, so this alien does seem to be spreading.

The Sycamore Family: Platanaceae

No local tree could be confused with the sycamore. The gray and white patches of thin, peeling bark form elegant abstract designs on the trunk, and thick branches angle erratically up to form a fairly open crown. Its leaves form broad green mittens, and its seeds are born in bristly balls.

Within sight of the Buttes near Meridian is the community of Sycamore, named for the stately trees that lined the quiet slough where once the Sacramento River sent a meandering arm. There and elsewhere in the valley, this beautiful tree is disappearing. It prefers the high terrace lowlands near water, usually on rich soils. More and more, the trees have been cleared and the ground tilled for farming or orchards.

A few sycamores stand along Pass Road near the Fremont Monument and in yards of Buttes settlers. All these may have been planted, but some of the creekbeds probably supported this increasingly-uncommon native tree.

The Buckwheat Family: Polygonaceae

Naked Buckwheat splays its shamelessly leafless stems above the grasses and forbs that share its open hillsides. Basal leaves like limp spoons sprawl around at ground level. Its stiffened stems rise straight for a foot or more, fork abruptly, then fork again to be crowned with tight clusters of pale flowers. When other plants have bloomed and withered, the buckwheats stand high and have most of the pollinators to themselves.

Smartweed and Lady's Thumb are amphibious. They sprawl or float as long as the mud is covered, yet root at the nodes and send up vertical stems with different-shaped leaves as water recedes. Ducks relish their tasty seeds.

Tawny summer fields often are visually peppered with rusty stalks of Curly Dock. A widespread weed originally from the Old World, dock was important at one time as a medicinal drug, a laxative and tonic.

The Phlox Family:
Polemoniaceae

The phlox family has 136 species in California, of which fifteen, about ten percent, occur in the Buttes. Our species have pretty, upright trumpets. Some, such as the gilias, Evening Snow, and Small Linanthus, have smooth stems and leaves; the others have hairs that range from mildly sticky to downright prickly in the navarretias.

Bird's-eye Gilia produces bright blue pollen. During the peak of flowering, visiting honeybees depart the blossoms with pollen sacs bulging with blue. The darker pollen is segregated in hexagonal storage chambers that both bees and beekeepers can readily discriminate.

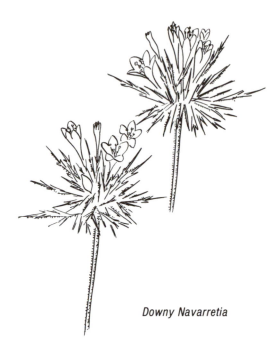

Downy Navarretia

The Purslane Family: Portulacaceae

Captain Meriwether Lewis is honored by the generic name of the Bitterroot, the state flower of Montana. In California it typically occurs in gravelly soils at elevations of 2500-9000 feet, yet we have found a small colony in the Sutter Buttes at approximately 1030 feet. Its bold pink blossoms overwhelm its linear, fleshy, basal leaves.

Red Maids open only in full sun, sometimes covering an orchard floor like a terrestrial red tide. The Miner's Lettuce prefers the shade of oak woodlands. Its basal leaves are like spatulas, its flower-bearing stems poke through round leaves like umbrellas. Otherwise-sane people stuff the succulent greens into their mouths at the peak of its lushness in early spring.

The Primrose Family: Primulaceae

If for no other reason (and I can think of other reasons), this family should be noteworthy for some literary allusions. Who hasn't heard of Scarlet Pimpernel, but who again would recognize it as a low-growing weed? Its genus, *Anagallis,* comes from the Greek "to delight in again", since the petals close in bad weather but open up boldly when the sun reappears. Our other primroses, the shooting stars, are spectacularly streamlined as blossoms that appear to have been turned inside-out by a meteoric plunge toward the earth. Their genus, *Dodecatheon,* means "twelve gods" in Greek; Pliny felt the primrose was under the care of the leading dozen dieties.

Our shooting stars are the purplish Hansen's and the whitish Padre's. Certain hillsides near Old Man Peak have populations, presumably of Hansen's, with strongly curled petals, twisted and rolled inward like Christmas ribbon zipped by the edge of a scissors. Dr. H.J. Thompson of UCLA, **the** expert on shooting stars, has never seen this trait in *Dodecatheons* but has seen similar curling in flowers of some cultivated *Cyclamens,* a close relative. We may be seeing the spread of a new mutation, which could lead to a distinct race unique to the Sutter Buttes.

Hansen's Shooting Star   *Unusual Form*

The Buttercup Family: Ranunculaceae

A field of blue or purple larkspurs in the spring draws us magnetically, as if nature had laid out her finest embroidery for us to inspect. Yet we delude ourselves if we think **we** are the reason the delphiniums show off. Those delicate blossoms are in fact the plants' sex organs unblushingly displayed to attract the pollinators that effect fertilization. Each plant thrusts its flower stalk above the foliage with its flowers arranged in non-overlapping spirals; both traits help give pollinators easy access. The showy blossoms offer rewards of nectar in their spurs for the insects and birds that visit them. These mutually-beneficial associations can lead to extreme specialization and interdependence.

In delphiniums pollinated by bumblebees, the spike contains both male and female flowers, but rarely does self-pollination occur. The lower flowers of the spike mature earliest, so that lower flowers are in a female condition while apical flowers are male. Bumblebees work flowers in a wonderfully predictable way. Each bee starts at the bottom and works up, then flies to the bottom of the next flower stalk. Hence pollen picked up from the upper male flowers is carried to the low female flowers of the next plant, and cross-pollination is assured (Grant and Grant 1968). The bee, of course, is unaware that it is helping the plant, serving as its mobile sex organ. It is drawn to the lowest flowers because they have the most nectar and works its way up until diminishing returns make it profitable for it to fly on to the next.

Of the thirty-one species of *Delphinium* in California, only two have diverged from their bee-pollinated cousins and depend upon hummingbirds for pollination. Both are red, a visual signal conspicuous to birds but not detected by bees, and both lack the pleasant floral fragrances that attract both bees and humans. Our Canyon Delphinium is a gorgeous spike of scarlet flowers blooming in March in partly shaded sites. Anna's Hummingbirds hover at the blossoms, inserting their long beaks and slightly frayed tongues into the deep spurs containing nectar. Pollen sticks to the chins of visiting hummingbirds

Larkspur

who transport it unknowingly to the blossoms of another plant. Hummingbirds do not feed as systematically as do bumblebees, so the plant assures cross-pollination by having all flowers in a single reproductive state, male or female, at a given time. A hummer can stick her pollen-packed chin feathers against a dozen flowers of the same spike, but since they are in the same stage of development, no incestuous selfing can occur.

Thus even in the single genus *Delphinium*, different species display different

Clematis Buds   Clematis Flowers

flowering strategies depending upon their usual pollinator. Ah, this birds and bees business is heady stuff!

This family also boasts the buttercups, the genus *Ranunculus*. With *Rana* meaning "frog", the genus implies "little frog" and alludes to a preference for damp places. Find some *R. occidentalis* (Western Buttercup) and *R. hebecarpus* (Bluntseed Buttercup) in spring and you will be walking in moist, yielding earth. Inspect a blooming patch of *R. muricatus* (Prickleseed Buttercup) and you will find your feet mired in clinging mud. Look eye to corolla at *R. aquatilis* (Water Buttercup) and you'll be as wet as a frog yourself!

Buttercup

Most of the buttercups have five petals and stamens galore. Sniff a yellow buttercup and discover a butter-yellow powder of pollen on your upper lip and nose. The Water Buttercup defies our ideas of what a buttercup should be, for its blossoms are white and its submerged leaves are filamentous on lax stems. Yet a close look at flower structure gives it away. Botanists name plants not

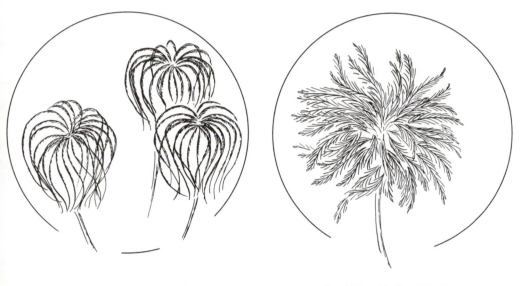

Clematis Seed Head   Aged Clematis Seed Head

on their widely divergent and convergent growth forms but on the floral charac-
teristics which tend to be evolutionarily conservative.

Sharing with the buttercups the trait of many stamens but differing greatly in
growth form are the species of clematis or virgin's bower. Their strong woody
vines twine up and over oaks and coffeeberry and other sturdy plants. Hundreds
of white or cream flowers burst forth in spring on the arbors created by the
climbing vines. Separate plants carry either male flowers with a pincushion-
profusion of stamens or female flowers with many ovaries. After pollination,
the styles of the ovaries form silvery plumes above the seeds, and the many
plumes per cluster form a feathery ball. The feathery plumes aid seed dispersal
by wind.

Our two species aren't illustrated in most plant guides, so here's a free tip.
The Virgin's Bower or Pipestem Clematis has one to three flowers per peduncle
(flower stalk) and three leaflets; the Western Clematis has many flowers per
cluster and five to seven leaflets.

Indians elsewhere (and by inference, perhaps those in the Buttes) used
clematis to treat colds and sore throats, and settlers apparently placed crushed
roots in the nostrils of tired horses to revive them (Spellenberg 1979).

The Buckthorn Family: Rhamnaceae

Coffeeberry and Hollyleaf Redberry are common undergrowth species, sometimes important chaparral elements. Buckbrush is surprisingly uncommon in the Buttes, primarily near the summit of Twin Peaks and in Moore and Huff Canyons.

Our redberry, *Rhamnus ilicifolia*, sounds as if it might have "ilicit foliage", but since *Ilex* is the genus of holly, *ilicifolia* simply means "hollyleaf". The large shrub or small tree has shiny, bright leaves with prickled edges, greenish clusters of blossoms that attract honeybees, and brilliant red berries in late summer.

The Rose Family: Rosaceae

The natural edibility and beauty of this family have been coaxed by man for centuries to become among our most useful plants. Roses, hawthorn, spirea, and mountain ash are popular ornamentals, and the apple, peach, apricot, pear, quince, cherry, plum, strawberry, raspberry, and blackberry are major fruits.

Thickets of prickly wild rose and sprawling blackberry provide excellent wildlife cover in the Buttes. When ripe, the blackberries exude an irresistible fragrance; birds and small mammals must compete with hikers for the attractive berries. The fleshy drupelets of the aggregate fruits are the plant's solution to seed dispersal. After passing through the digestive tract of some animal, the seeds are deposited some distance away, complete with fertilizer. Rose hips, while not as tasty as a good blackberry, are edible and nutritious, supposedly containing more vitamin C, calcium, phosphorus, and iron than oranges (Clark 1977).

Toyon's evergreen leaves and bright red berries (really small pomes, like apples) stand out vividly in December when most small trees and shrubs are bare and dormant. Alternate names of Christmas Berry or California Holly seem highly appropriate. Once abundant near an expanding Los Angeles, the plants provided a good descriptive name for Hollywood.

Ocean Spray or Cream Bush seems a stray from higher, moister forests (Munz says 4000-9600 feet). Indeed we have found it only on shaded, north slopes or well-watered sites in the Buttes, where we also may encounter the Western Choke Cherry. Sweet Cherry, an escapee from cultivation, grows in a draw on the Dean Place near North Butte. Mountain Mahogany is rare in the range; I have found but a single twelve-foot tree on the north slope of Old Man, though it could occur sparsely on other peaks.

The Madder Family: Rubiaceae

The tiny herbaceous bedstraws and the woody Button Willows seem unlikely relatives, but both have rounded clusters of small flowers of similar structure. This diverse family also contains plants which produce coffee, quinine, madder (a dye), woodruff (an herb), and the gardenia.

Buttonbush frequents creeksides and does indeed resemble a willow except for the flowers. Bedstraws grow in shaded areas, sometimes sprawling over other plants. Leaves occur in distinct whorls around four-angled stems. The tiny spherical fruits have grasping hooks that aid their transport by passing animals.

The Rue Family: Rutaceae

Our only member of the family which includes the orange, lemon, and other citrus fruits is the Western Hoptree. It's an attractive shrub with three-part leaves, greenish-white flowers, and flattened, round samaras like tiny flying saucers. Its odor is strong and resembles that of hops; indeed its seeds have been used as a hops substitute in brewing beer.

The Willow Family: Salicaceae

Springs and water courses provide the only usable habitat for these species in the Buttes. Pendulous catkins appear on the trees prior to spring leaf emergence. The pale green cottonwood flowers later become masses of whitish down which can fill the air with blizzards of "cotton". Where the seeds reach moist ground, hundreds of shoots per square foot may sprout, but water must be persistently available if the saplings are to long survive. Orioles may combine the cotton with stiffer fibers in building their pendulous nests at the tips of a cottonwood branch.

Cottonwoods and willows sprout readily from their roots and send masses of root hairs into moist places. With roots in contact with water, they can photosynthesize and transpire freely during hot months, growing significantly when upland trees such as Blue Oaks are nearly dormant as drought protection.

The Saxifrage Family: Saxifragaceae

Saxifraga means the "rock breaker", for numerous species root in rock crevices. Our California Saxifrage opens its delicate white petals in March. The

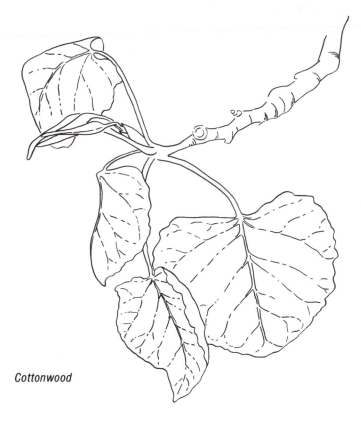

Cottonwood

flowers are spent by April when its occasional parasite, the Naked Broomrape, sends its solitary flower stalks skyward.

Floral constellations of whitish Woodland Stars and pinkish Prairie Stars begin appearing in Sutter Buttes groves in late March.

A healthy stand of gooseberry with yellow blossoms occurs near the summit of Old Man at an elevation of about 1550 feet and on Pigeon Peak even lower. It appears to be *Ribes quercetorum,* the Rock Gooseberry. That comes as a surprise, as its range is traditionally defined by the Southern Sierra (only north to Tuolumne County), the South Coast Ranges, and other southern California mountains. The Sutter Buttes stands apparently represent an isolated population far from normal range, surely a tempting prospect for study by an enterprising biogeographer.

The Figwort Family: Scrophulariaceae

With about 315 species in California, this family is fourth largest in the state. Knowing that "scrofulous" can mean "morally corrupt or degenerate", I sought to track down the origin of the name for this group, expecting to unearth some secret shame. Instead, I found a more positive meaning. Many of the herbs in this family have medicinal uses, and figworts were believed to cure the disease scrofula, a tuberculosis of the lymph glands. That's a much more satisfying origin for a family containing some of my favorite plants.

In damp sites throughout the Buttes is the Common Monkeyflower, blossoms butter-yellow with red spots on the lower lip marking the way to its private parts. In rich, soggy soils it may tower to three feet high; on moist rocks with minimal soil it may struggle to raise its miniature blooms an inch into the air. No other plant in the Buttes shows such variability in growth form (except perhaps that nefarious Poison Oak!). *Mimulus* alludes to a mimic, or comic actor, because of the grinning corolla.

Many in the snapdragon family have red flower tubes or prominent red bracts. As might be expected, most of these are hummingbird-pollinated, an exceptional fifteen percent of the family in California (Grant and Grant 1968). In penstemons, bee-pollination is the basic condition (e.g., the bluish Foothill Penstemon) and hummingbird-pollination appears to have evolved late in the game (e.g., the Scarlet Beard-tongue). Paintbrushes, on the other hand, are basically bird-pollinated; the few purple or yellow bracted species in the West, probably insect-dependent, seem to be derived from reddish ancestors (Grant and Grant 1968).

Foothill Penstemon

Paintbrush flowers are nearly hidden among showy red and yellow bracts. Migrant Rufous Hummingbirds take full advantage of their nectar stores as they pass through in the spring. But the apparent bright-eyed innocence of the paintbrush conceals the fact that the plant tends to parasitize the roots of nearby shrubs, even though capable of manufacturing its own food.

Owlclovers are unrelated to the pea-family clovers, but some have dense pinkish heads suggestive of clovers, and some have hooked beaks, perhaps owl-like, on their flowers. Prolific annuals, the Red Owlclover can create masses of purple amidst the golds of poppies to provide the outstanding floral displays of the spring.

The fancy faces of purple Chinese Houses peer outward in whorls around erect stems. They form showy patches in shady places, far more conspicuous than their frail cousins, the tiny Blue-lips or Spinster's Blue-eyed Mary.

Our two mulleins are biennials, putting out a rosette of of large leaves their first year and sending up stout flower stalks to bear their yellow blossoms the second. Woolly Mullein leaves feel like the softest flannel, and Moth Mullein stalks appear to sport sulphur butterflies. Both are weeds from Europe, though some Europeans have tried to disown them by calling the Woolly Mullein the "American Velvet Plant" (Spellenberg 1979).

The dried stalks in the winter have sometimes impressed me with the elegance of a rustic candelabra. Occasionally injury or disease deforms the usually straight stalks into bizarre writhing, hydra-headed shapes. Seed-eating birds often perch on the winter stalks.

Ancient Greeks and Romans dipped the stalks in tallow to be used as funeral torches. Later Europeans cultivated them for medicinal uses, and found the felt-like leaves to be comfortable insoles for thin boots in winter. Among the many uses of this "weed", perhaps most inspiring is its presence in modern gardens for the blind, "not for visual beauty or for fragrance, but for the pleasure the velvet leaves convey to the sense of touch" (Haughten 1978).

Moth Mullein

The Quassia Family: Simarubaceae

The Chinese reportedly played a major role in the building of rock walls in the Buttes, and perhaps they are responsible for the occasional grove of Tree of

Heaven that now survives there. Male flowers are unpleasantly smelly and on separate trees from female flowers. A tree without a mate can create offspring only vegetatively, sending out roots which sprout into young trees genetically identical to the parent. In this way a lone, old tree can have rank after rank of progressively smaller trees encircling it.

Ailanthus leaves are large and pinnately compound. The tiny black seeds, seventeen thousand to a pound, are borne single in the centers of oblong, twisted samaras in dense clusters that may hang on the leafless trees through the winter. The thin gray bark is diamond-studded with twig scars — a most attractive sight.

The Nightshade Family:
    Solanaceae

No other family tree of plants would branch out so clearly into notorious bad guys and white-hatted good guys. Blanch at the thought of Blue Witch, Bittersweet, Horse Nettle, and Deadly Nightshade. Glow in appreciation of the potato, tomato, chili peppers, and petunia. Choose your side in judging the controversial, but economically profitable, tobacco. Perhaps the symbolism of the Matrimony Vine would be equally controversial in this day and age.

No one could deny the beauty of the violet stars with yellow centers that blossom on the Parish's Nightshade or of the huge white bugles of the Jimsonweed. Beware of ingesting any part of either. Most, if not all, nightshades are poisonous,

Parish's Nightshade

and Jimsonweed contains the drug atropine with dangerous to fatal narcotic properties. That hazardous plant was used by certain Indians to induce dreams, to create hallucinations which they interpreted for decision-making. In those days, consumers were not protected by kid-proof caps and warning labels either.

Jimsonweed

The Nettle Family: Urticaceae

Stinging hairs with formic acid inhibit casual romping through a nettle patch, yet the plant has an astonishing variety of beneficial uses (Clark 1977). From bowstrings to basket-making, medicines to dyes, the nettle has demonstrated values far outweighing the short-term rashes they cause. Rich in vitamins A and C plus protein, nettles make an excellent substitute for spinach. Most children would rather substitute ice cream.

In the Buttes, nettles grow in disturbed areas where water is near or at the surface.

The Valerian Family: Valerianaceae

Our *Plectritis* species are lovely little flowers but not large or bright enough to draw attention among the masses of flowers at the peak of spring. Slender stems with opposite leaves rise up to dense clusters of tubular flowers.

There are eleven species of *Plectritis* in the world, found in western North America and again in Chile. Some of our other Buttes plants, for example Cowbags or Balloon Clover and Chile Lotus, are restricted to our West and to Chile. Spellenberg (1971), writing of the lotus, says; "It is one of nearly 100 western plants also found in Chile and Argentina, but not in the intervening thousands of miles, a natural distribution still not satisfactorily explained."

The Vervain Family: Verbenaceae

Lippia, a South American import, forms dense low mats in disturbed areas, sometimes almost like artificial turf. Its long blossoming period and easy-to-reach flowers attract scores of bees, flies, skippers, and smaller butterflies (e.g., Buckeye, Acmon Blue, Common Hairstreak, Mylitta Crescent).

The Western Vervain is common along drainage ditches in the valley, and the Robust Vervain is occasional along upland creeks.

Lippia

The Violet Family: Violaceae

The "roses are red, violets are blue" aphorism falls on its color-blind face in California, where most violets are yellow, some are white, and a few more are blue to purple. Our Douglas's Violet has a yellow face with rusty streaks radiating mostly downward from its center to mark the landing strip for prospective pollinators. The upper two of its five petals have brown backs. Sometimes called Johnny Jump Up or Wild Pansy, this violet shoots up above the sprouting grass in March and gives one of our most enchanting floral displays.

The Mistletoe Family: Viscaceae (Loranthaceae)

How strange that a parasite should become symbolic of romantic impulses. Apparently the rule applies only to sprigs hung in doorways, for standing under a clump of mistletoe in the Buttes never has the desired effect, at least for me, even at Christmas.

Mistletoe lacks true roots, but its modified stem directly penetrates to the xylem of the host tree, the primary plumbing that delivers minerals, water, sugars, carbohydrates, and other goodies. With green leaves of its own, it can produce some of its food, but if the host tree dies, the mistletoe too perishes in place.

The whitish, sticky berries attract mockingbirds, thrushes, waxwings, and particularly Phainopeplas, which prefer the mistletoe to all other foods. The berries (or at least the seeds) pass through bird digestive tracts remarkably fast, deposited in droppings within ten to thirty minutes after being ingested. The sticky mass adheres to the branch and the seed germinates, fortified with ample nutrition to support it during the time necessary to penetrate the host's tissues. Occasionally seed transport is achieved when a bird wipes its sticky beak against a branch, dislodging the hitchhiking seeds.

Ironically, the stickiness of mistletoe seeds was turned against the birds by clever Europeans, who made birdlime from them. Many a blackbird pie was enjoyed before such practices were ruled illegal.

Greenleaf Mistletoe typically parasitizes cottonwoods in the Buttes; Hairy Mistletoe predominantly infests Blue and Valley Oaks.

The Grape Family: Vitaceae

Along wooded stream beds, shaggy-barked vines twist up into the trees, occasionally dangling in broad loops that invite a Tarzan-like swing. Where adequately exposed to sunlight, the vines are covered with rounded valentines that function as leaves. Rich reds, golds, and yellows in fall give the best color show in this part of California.

The fruits are unmistakably grapes, delicate in flavor even though small and large-seeded. Wild Grape jelly throughout the year helps propel us mentally back to those fine autumn days when we harvested. Indians used the grape for baskets, food, wines, and medicines. Clarke (1977) reports that "Juice from the leaves was used to treat diarrhea and lust in women." Apparently there is no such cure for lust in men.

The Caltrop Family: Zygophyllaceae

A diabolical weapon employed some centuries ago in Europe was the caltrop, an ingeniously simple device of iron with four points situated such that no matter how it lands, one point faces upward to impale the hooves of cavalry horses. Perhaps the first caltrop designed was modeled on the dispersal mechanism of the Puncture Vine. In the Buttes, we find this unpleasant alien along roadways and in disturbed areas, where it may be cursed by the sheepman for occasional damage to the hooves of his charges.

The Monocots

Monocots appear to have diverged early from a dicot ancestor, undergoing a basic physical streamlining usually detectable by casual handling (compare the feel of a lily or onion or grass to that of a sunflower or violet or pea). Monocots tend to have parallel-veined leaves; closed vascular bundles located irregularly through the pith; flower parts in threes or sixes; an embryo with a single cotyledon. Flowering plant species occur roughly in the ratio of three dicots to one monocot.

The Water Plantain Family: Alismataceae

Search carefully among the crowded guests in spring's floral grand ball in the grassy hills and you'll never find an arrowhead or water plantain. Clarkias, poppies, gilias, and penstemons simply don't rub stems with members of this family. It just wouldn't be right!

You must seek them in their own neighborhood, down out of the hills, sometimes across the tracks, into the low-lying districts which we sometimes describe as dank, mucky, buggy. Chances are high that we'll never get there, even though our automobile tires will swish by within a few feet of these plants. We are blinded by our prejudices — our fixation on spring flowers on rolling slopes, our distaste for water-saturated soil which we so quickly dismiss as "mud".

Believe me, even well-intentioned naturalists like myself are guilty of Alisma-neglect. How many times over five years had I lifted my eyes to the hills even as my feet crushed these beautiful plants? This book was nearly written before some quirk of fate brought me face-to-scape with several of these species.

I stopped the car along a weedy ditch and left the engine running; after all, why should I spend much time there? I leaned in closely for a look, found my hands reaching out to touch, and suddenly realized I was hooked, not by barbs but by beauty. I walked back and shut off the engine, then returned to inspect an exotic community no less special than the spring hillsides I already knew.

Everything changed as I abandoned my upright posture for a bittern-level view. Rich scents, surprisingly pleasant ones, surrounded me. The brilliant green blades of *Alisma* and *Sagittaria,* harmless daggers and arrowheads, diverged on long pedicels rising from the buried central stems. Three-petaled flowers stood above the rounded seed clusters on tall flower stalks. To a frog, if there were one with the esthetic sensibilities of a romantic painter, what more beautiful landscape could there be?

The Amaryllis Family: Amaryllidaceae

Showy relatives of lilies, the Amaryllid flowers can be distinguished from those of their aristocratic cousins by their umbel origins. That is, their flower stems radiate umbrellalike from a point on the main stem, not in the lily arrangements of spikes, racemes, or panicles.

Most of these are plentiful, conspicuous, attractive — the kinds of plants that

Ithuriel's Spear

laymen recognize and recall. Seven of our species were known as Brodiaeas, a name that rolls from the tongue so delicately and with such elegant floristic connotations that even the most casual of flower watchers painlessly acquired the Latin name, *Brodiaea.* Imagine the consternation, nay, **uproar,** created when botanists decided to subdivide the group a bit finer, creating new genera with somewhat less memorable names — *Dichelostemma* and *Triteleia* — as well as leaving some species as *Brodiaea.* One could argue that the added names are as pleasant to the ear as *Brodiaea,* but that ignores two persisting problems. First is basic conservatism — "If *Brodiaea* was good enough for me, then *Brodiaea* is good enough for my kids." Second is the "old dog/new trick" syndrome — "how can you expect me to remember **three** scientific names at once?" Botanists, motivated purely by the altruistic goal of improving the system (despite rumors of "splitting" for the sake of another publication), must now cope with the wrath of die-hard amateurs who know a *Brodiaea* when they see one. They simply refuse to accept taxonomy without representation.

Also in this family are onions, leeks, garlics, shallots, chives, and kin. Volatile sulphur compounds in all parts of these plants give them characteristic aroma, especially when bruised or bitten. Long used around the world for dyes, foods, flavorings, and insect repellents, onions and associates have contributed significantly as well to the proliferation of antacids and breath mints.

The Sedge Family: Cyperaceae

"Sedges have edges" goes the quick ditty aimed at separating them from grasses. Try listing all the species you know; one hand has more than enough fingers for most of us. Yet there are more than four thousand species in this family, more than two hundred in California alone. I am appropriately humbled.

Perhaps best known of this bunch is the Common Tule or Bulrush, the goliath of the emergent aquatic plants. Bitterns stand motionless among their towering stems, while gallinules slip quietly among them. In winter, hunters skulk within their thickets in wait of incoming waterfowl. Along with cattails, tules typify the Central Valley marshes. They and other sedges have high tolerance for waterlogged, poorly aerated soils. Their seeds are abundant and can withstand prolonged soaking; an air space around the fruit keeps them afloat for efficient dispersal. Then too, they can reproduce vegetatively, sending out creeping rhizomes to infiltrate the muck.

The Rush Family: Juncaceae

If we tend to overlook the grasses, generalizing "grass" in a most nondiscriminating way, then we probably completely ignore the rushes, their wet-footed counterparts. Soggy soils low in available oxygen are not the easiest of sites for growing plants, but rushes thrive by spreading their rootstocks in network mats and holding oxygen in air spaces in roots and stems. Seeds come wrapped in plain brown bags — no fancy floral trappings for these wind-pollinated plants.

The Duckweed Family: Lemnaceae

A layer of duckweed floating on a pond seems almost like a mat of algae, but don't dismiss it as such. It's among the world's tiniest flowering plants, and it's chock full of surprises.

First, it has no leaves and but a single root dangling in the water. The tiny, rounded pad is a flattened stem or frond, capable of producing new fronds by vegetative division. Rarely does it flower, but when it does, it produces three flowers in a special pouch — two male, each with one stamen, and one female, with a single naked pistil. There are no sepals or petals and no need for the flowers to be tramped on by dirty little bugs. Reproduction, one way or the other, would seem to be efficient enough; botanists have counted 84,000 duckweed plants per square meter! Submergent plants of other species can be deprived of adequate light when duckweed proliferates in dense surface masses. It readily invades other ponds or sluggish streams by hitching a ride on the feet of a duck or other aquatic bird.

Most plants are the epitome of stay-at-home, firmly planted as individuals even if mobile as propagules. The lone root of a duckweed serves more as a rudder than as an anchor. It goes scudding about on the pond, buoyed up by air-chambers that make it unsinkable. Nutrients bathe its simple root in a classical example of natural hydroponics. It's equally efficient as a solar collector; its chloroplasts become arranged horizontally along the cell walls for maximum insolation during times of weak light but stand vertically in strong light.

For duckweeds, small is beautiful.

The Lily Family: Liliaceae

California is blessed with 118 species of lilies in 26 genera. With but four species, the Sutter Buttes seem slighted, but quality is high even if quantity is low.

Anyone waiting until the flower spectacles of March or April will miss the subtle beauty of Mission Bells. Also called Checker Lily, these uncommon and lovely plants bloom in February, nodding purple-brown bells with yellow-green checks. By March, stout, heavily ribbed capsules have replaced the flowers. As they dry, the seeds inside may rattle as the plant sways in the wind (*Fritillaria* is Latin for "dice box").

Three broad lemon-yellow petals, often marked internally with small rusty streaks and a red spot each, crown the Gold Nuggets or Yellow Mariposa Tulip. A Yellow Crab Spider lying in wait on a petal is perfectly camouflaged. Subterranean bulbs are the pantries of these perennials. Food built up during the brief emergence in spring is stored through summer drought and winter cold until those recurrent vernal cues trigger another season's growth.

Gold Nuggets

Wavy-leaf Soap Plant may be a mouthful as a name, but it is apt. The long, slim basal leaves are rolled inward in undulating waves. The bulbs may be crushed with water to produce a cleansing lather, simultaneously stupifying any nearby fish (the Indians used it both ways). Lanky leafless flower stems bear delicate whitish flowers which open at dusk or on cloudy days in late spring or summer.

The spring of 1982 yielded the fourth species, the Fremont's Camas or Star Lily in soggy grassland where moat soils have slumped gradually for many centuries. Perhaps its relative rarity in the Buttes is a blessing, as its bulb is poisonous to man and livestock alike.

The Grass Family: Poaceae (Gramineae)

No group of plants more typifies the Sutter Buttes than the grasses. They march from rampart's edge up the bouldery shoulders; sweep across the concave moat; ascend both valleys and ridges beneath cottonwood, oak, and bay; and stand exposed to the sky from pockets of soil atop or between cracks within the summit boulders. They form the green against which the brilliant flowers of spring are displayed; they are the gold which ripples across the hills in summer breezes.

There may be 10,000 species of grasses in the world, perhaps 500 in California, more than 60 in the Buttes. Indians used the grains in food and the fibers in baskets, matting, and other implements. Grass values in pasture and range lands, turfs, and ornamental plantings are incalculable. Consider these cultivated types — rice, wheat, barley, rye, corn, millet, sorghum, oats, and sugar cane — economic heavyweights. Still there are so many more values that we rarely consider — watershed protection (impacts throughout a drainage, perhaps clear to the sea and its hosts of creatures), wildlife habitat, climatic amelioration, nutrient cycling, and so on.

The Sutter Buttes are less visibly altered than other Sacramento Valley habitats, yet look at the grass list — only thirty percent of the species are native. What have we done to our native grasslands in the past couple centuries?

Back when the tule elk and pronghorn roamed the Buttes, they encountered mostly native perennials such as needlegrass *(Stipa)*, three-awn *(Aristida)*, Pine Bluegrass *(Poa scabrella)*, Deer Grass *(Muhlenbergia)*, the melics *(Melica)*, Junegrass *(Koeleria macrantha)*, and the squirreltails *(Sitanion)*. That type of grassland is gone forever; nothing in our power can restore the original grassland species composition. Oh, remnant populations of those species remain, and they could increase with encouragement. But no one knows how to extract or eliminate the exotics, mostly annuals, which now dominate the landscape — the bromes *(Bromus)*, the oats *(Avena)*, Bermuda Grass *(Cynodon)*, Crab Grass

Purple Needlegrass

(*Digitaria*), Barnyard Grass (*Echinochloa*), the barleys (*Hordeum*), the beardgrasses *(Polypogon)*, and the like. Just as you can't take a loaf of bread and break it down into the original yeast, flour, water, shortening, what-have-you; neither can you take the grassland apart again to eliminate a few ingredients that you don't like. The process is irreversible.

Livestock grazing began in southern California in 1769 and spread as the missions spread (Bakker 1971). Many Old World plants, intentionally or accidentally introduced, found no linguistic or social barriers to inhibit their colonization. Off they spread, hitchhiking with man (sometimes as legitimate guests), creeping along by stolon or rhizome, or letting seeds ride the winds or cling to animals. Some species failed; others were phenomenally successful.

The native grasses were caught with their plants down. Cattle and sheep devoured the standing foliage more thoroughly and repeatedly than had the native grazers. Natural spaces around the bunchgrasses easily were invaded by aggressive annuals, often less desired by the grazers and thus able to persist and displace the weakened perennials. Grazing, drought, fire, competition from exotics, changes in associated flora and fauna — all interacted to eliminate or greatly reduce the populations of California's original grasses. Fortunately, whether by accident or more-than-customary grazing prudence, today's grasslands in the Sutter Buttes have excellent representation of native species, both variety and abundance.

Though the exotic wild oats and bromes contribute much to the golden haze of the summer hills, some botanists feel that areas of Purple and Nodding Needlegrasses, the most prominent of the Sutter Buttes' native perennials, may have remained green well into the hot months. The winter annuals *(Avena, Bromus, Hordeum, Lolium, Vulpia)* exploit winter and early spring rains to flush green in spring, then burn out, leaving seed, by summer. Summer annuals, mostly exotics with tropical or subtropical affinities *(Echinochloa* and others) develop in moist or irrigated areas when the combination of high temperatures and available water turns them on. Johnson Grass *(Sorghum),* beardgrasses *(Polypogon),* and Dallisgrass *(Paspalum)* also thrive in sites appropriately moist in summer.

Despite all we gain directly or indirectly from grasses or lose to those species we call weeds (no insignificant amount), we tend to be woefully ignorant when it comes to **specifics.** Without showy petals to attract our attention, the grasses, sedges, and rushes blur into undistinguished anonymity in our minds. We **may** not even notice that they do indeed have flowers, albeit simple and inconspicuous ones.

Foxtail Barley
(Hordeum)

Soft Chess
(Bromus mollis)

Italian Ryegrass
(Lolium)

Red Brome

The annual and perennial systems are "strategies" in the sense of groups of traits that exist by virtue of their survival or reproductive values to the plants that possessed them. We don't attribute any conscious thought or motivation to them. Natural selection develops a product that **looks and acts** as if it knows what it's doing but is totally outside the realm of intent or judgment.

An annual grass is a seed's way of making more seeds. As the name implies, its life cycle is restricted to a single season up to a year in length. All its bets are on one throw of the dice. A seed must successfully germinate; transmute nutrients, water, and solar energy into an above-ground physical structure; and produce new viable seeds with genetic instructions for building the next generation. Successful annuals tend to spread quickly and abundantly and to set large crops of seed in minimal time. We take advantage of these traits in our cultivated grain crops where grain (seed) is our objective.

Perennials develop for the long haul. Though some may die back above ground at the end of a season's growth, they all can resprout and resume growth over a number of years. Annuals have strict deadlines; failing to set seed means a dead line. Perennials can afford the luxury of sterile, as well as fertile, shoots. Energy can be devoted to growth at the short term expense of seeds. Metaphorically, the annual throws up a prefab and quickly writes its will; the perennial builds an edifice and makes periodic investments, hedging its bets over some years.

Both strategies clearly work. Annuals and perennials occur side by side in the same types of soils. Disturbances (fire, grazing, flood, etc), accidents of colonization, competition, and so forth all help determine the patchwork of plants, and this mosaic changes across time. Of course this applies to other plants, indeed all organisms.

Annuals are ephemeral, transitory. Perennials are ultimately finite in existence, though some approach a form of immortality. "Probably the oldest living things in the world are not the redwoods or bristlecone pines but such lowly grasses as these that live indefinitely in their native habitat by continual vegetative reproduction" (Crampton 1974:9).

Vegetative reproduction by rooting at points along stolons (above ground) or rhizomes (below ground) can create a rather dense, spreading mat of grass with strong competitive abilities, able to draw on parental resources until rooted and established. Look at the overwhelming tenacity of spreading Bermuda Grass! This creeping sprawl is a strategy for **local** colonization, a hand-over-hand (or tiller-over-tiller) approach. Seeds offer a flying, long-range alternative for dispersal.

Whereas rhizomes and stolons are extensions of the parent plant, tended for until rooted, seeds are "weaned" rather abruptly. All a parent plant can do is provision its offspring with devices and materials which can aid its dispersal and establishment — shape, size, projections, endosperm or food, and the like.

Grass seeds are relatively well-endowed, with "embryonic roots and leaves and stem already showing the pattern of nodes of the adult plant; these grains are comparable with a mammalian foetus in their state of development" (Huxley 1974). They make nearly ideal propagules — small, light, independent, dormant, shielded from the hostile environment, grubstaked, programmed. Many can persist years before they germinate, perhaps long after the parent is gone. Seeds from a single parent plant may, in fact, germinate at different times, even different years — a hedge against an uncertain environment.

Some of the floral bracts (e.g., lemmas, glumes) may be armed with bristly projections called awns. It would be tempting to infer that awns function as grappling hooks, enabling seeds to snag free rides on fur or feathers or denim trousers. For some species, that explanation will suffice, but nature is remarkable in her diverse solutions to survival problems. For certain grasses, the awns twist with changing humidity, effectively levering the pointed seeds into soil crevices and driving them in deeper. Still another alternative is defense against seed predators. An Arizona study showed two peaks of grass seed production, each subject to potential seed predation by ants (summer) and sparrows (winter). Pulliam and Brand (1975:1158) concluded: "Seeds produced after the winter rains are smooth in outline and difficult for ants

Ripgut Grass

to carry. Seeds produced after the summer rains have conspicuous awns, hairs, or other projections and usually require husking by sparrows." Even for ants and sparrows, **time** is a valuable currency; they avoid eating foods with longer handling times if they can. A sparrow can pop down a rounded seed in nothing flat, but imagine how frustrating it would be to have to mandibulate a barbed seed, possibly an interminable chore (the feeling of glume goes awn and awn!). The plants appear to have evolved both structure (smooth or awned) **and** timing of seeding to minimize the impacts of seed predation. Darwin would be thrilled to see this support for his theory. I'm impressed myself. The next time I find my socks bristling with foxtails, I must control my natural impulses and render proper respect to a real survivor!

The Cattail Family: Typhaceae

Cattlemen have taken bulldozers high into the Buttes grasslands to scrape out and dam up a likely looking draw. Winter rains gradually fill the new stock pond, and in a year or two, the artificial scrape is alive with cattails and singing blackbirds. To make a marsh, create a suitable earthen bowl, add water, and let Nature provide the rest of the ingredients.

Wind-borne cattail seeds are produced by the thousands at the top of tall spikes, which persist long past flowering but finally burst in silky clouds of fuzz. Millions of seeds perish in unsuitable habitats, but every pond receives a start-up supply.

Nearly all parts of cattails are useful to anyone living off the land. The long strappy leaves can be plaited into mats and baskets. The starchy rhizomes (underground stems, not roots) are edible roasted or ground as meal. Young shoots and the heart of the stem provide choice foods, raw or cooked. The green flower spikes can be eaten like corn on the cob. Pollen makes a good flour substitute or additive, and the seed fluff works as insulation, padding, or fire tinder. Anyone willing to get his feet wet will find the cattail a great source of natural products.

Wild Oats

References

Bakker, E.S. 1971. *An Island Called California.* University of California Press, Berkeley.

Balls, E.K. 1962. *Early Uses of California Plants.* University of California Press, Berkeley.

Clarke, C.B. 1977. *Edible and Useful Plants of California.* University of California Press, Berkeley.

Crampton, B. 1974. *Grasses in California.* University of California Press, Berkeley.

Gould, S.J. 1977. *Ever Since Darwin.* W.W. Norton and Co., New York.

Grant, K.A. and Grant, V. 1968. *Hummingbirds and Their Flowers.* Columbia University Press, New York.

Grillos, S.J. 1966. *Ferns and Fern Allies of California.* University of California Press, Berkeley.

Haughton, C.S. 1978. *Green Immigrants.* Harcourt Brace Jovanovich, New York.

Holland, V.E. 1974. In defense of Blue Oaks. *Fremontia* 4(2):3-8.

Huxley, A. 1978. *Plant and Planet.* Penguin Books, New York.

Jepson, W.L. 1891. Botany of the Marysville Buttes. *Bulletin of the Torrey Botanical Club* 18:317-327.

Lewin, R. 1980. Evolutionary theory under fire. *Science* 210:883-887.

Munz, P.A. 1973. *A California Flora and Supplement.* University of California Press, Berkeley.

Niehaus, T.F. 1976. *A Field Guide to Pacific States Wildflowers.* Houghton Mifflin Co., Boston.

Northen, H. and Northen, R. 1970. *Ingenious Kingdom: the Remarkable World of Plants.* Prentice-Hall, Inc., Englewood Cliffs, N.J.

Pulliam, H.R. and Brand, M.R. 1975. The production and utilization of seeds in plains grassland of southeastern Arizona. *Ecology* 56:1158-1166.

Spellenberg, R. 1979. *The Audubon Society Field Guide to North American Wildflowers.* Alfred A. Knopf, New York.

Stern, K.R. 1982. *Introductory Plant Biology.* William C. Brown, Dubuque, Iowa.

Soulé, M.E. and Wilcox, B.A., eds. 1980. *Conservation Biology: An Evolutionary-Ecological Perspective.* Sinauer Assoc., Sunderland, Mass.

7

The Spineless Ones: Invertebrates

We tend to think that the great period of world exploration is behind us. The ambitious collections of flora and fauna of scientists such as Agassiz, Bates, Darwin, and Wallace are classified and filed away in major museums. It seems as if the biological sciences have in just a few centuries passed from an infancy of great ignorance to a maturity of polished theories, computerized data collections, extreme sophistication of analysis. Perhaps all that is left are minor refinements, fine-tuning and nit-picking.

That judgment might seem intuitively logical, but it is far from right. Yes, most mammals and birds, even fishes, have been found and described, but only five percent of the earth's creatures are vertebrates. Names and type-specimens now exist for more than a million species of animals. Yet some scientists predict that perhaps three to four times that many creatures remain to be identified. The naming process has just begun, particularly for insects. As habitats worldwide are destroyed, many species will disappear nameless. Their potentials for human benefit will disappear with them, a needless tragedy.

Invertebrates are united only by what they lack — a backbone. They represent many phyla not closely related to one another; grouping them all as invertebrates merely shows our bias as vertebrates. It might even be more logical to divide animals into arthropods and non-arthropods, since seventy-five percent or so of the kingdom is made up of the former (Barnes 1968).

The tiniest creatures, though abundant numerically, tend to be "out of sight, out of mind". I will mention a few examples, but urge the reader to explore this realm of life more fully on his own.

In shallow water we occasionally encounter the fine threads of horsehair worms, or, as some scientists prefer to call them, gordioid nematomorphs. They seem the animal ultimate in thinness, linear filaments with minimal differentiation of organs. Their larvae develop as parasites within arthropods, enter a resting stage, then develop as typical worms in the guts of another arthropod, bird, or fish. As I hold a writhing horsehair worm in my hand, I can easily see how anyone not knowing the complicated life history of the parasites might believe that the creatures rise spontaneously from the hairs of a horse's tail. The truth is no less remarkable.

I must at least mention the earthworm, *Lumbricus terrestris,* before passing on to creatures with legs. The humble angle worm generally is more significant ecologically than the robin that searches for it. Burrowing and feeding mixes and churns the soils, aerating and improving soil conditions greatly. Even after his classic work on the origin of species, Charles Darwin devoted considerable research to what some might consider a subject beneath his talents. However, his classic book, *The Formation of Vegetable Mould through the Action of Worms,* not only raised public awareness of the value of earthworms, but also showed the strengths of his theory supported by exhaustive natural history details.

No other animals in the Buttes even come **close** to the arthropods in variety. No field guide could possibly cover California adequately, as there may be more than 30,000 species of insects alone! Most of us are content to be able to recognize general groups, and several books offer examples and illustrations (e.g., Borror and White 1970, Milne and Milne 1980, Powell and Hogue 1979, Swan and Papp 1972).

A complete list of arthropods in the Buttes is virtually unattainable. Rather than producing a long, superficial, and ultimately rather boring annotated list, I have chosen to concentrate on a few conspicuous groups (butterflies, gall wasps, arachnids) or microhabitats with characteristic species (streams and ponds as a general habitat, cow pats as a specialized one). After all, the expected reader of this book will be looking for names and explanations for things he or she is likely to see.

The references available to us in popular form certainly reflect our biases. *The National Audubon Society Field Guide to North American Insects and*

Spiders (Milne and Milne 1980) has photographs of larvae or adults of 78 moths and 60 butterflies; a companion volume on butterflies (Pyle 1981) has more than 800 photos of that group, but as yet there is no comparable treatment of moths. Yet moths far outnumber butterflies, more than 3000 species to 240 species respectively in California. This state has 9 families of butterflies, about 50 of moths; many small, inconspicuous moths have yet to be described (Powell and Hogue 1979). But since we are diurnal animals ourselves, attracted to bright colors rather than to hard-to-find cryptic creatures of the nocturnal realm, we may feel justified in concentrating on butterflies.

The world of invertebrates need not remain an alien world to us. Learning about these "worlds within worlds" proceeds naturally if we open ourselves to receive it, as Maggie and David Cavagnaro did in the California grasslands (Cavagnaro 1972). Their learning was an interactive process, never linear nor fully predictable, a matter of "awakening, discovering, understanding."

It takes little effort to find, observe, and learn from such creatures as millipedes, sowbugs, Jerusalem crickets, antlions. We are wrong if we dismiss them as mere simple organisms, if we think of them as names applied to diverse objects which are therefore understood simply because they have been classified.

It is a common human impulse to swat a mosquito that lands on our arm, to break through the spider web that blocks our path, to step on the ants scurrying in front of us. We treat most of the animals of the world as if they didn't even exist, or if we acknowledge them at all, as if they were nuisances to us. By ignoring them so, we are depriving ourselves of an infinity of lessons, of the joy that derives from seeing, learning, applying. Our peculiarly human capacity to extrapolate mentally far beyond the obvious can be used to great advantage here. As Cavagnaro (1972:180) says: "Only man can stare into a spider web and see, through its design, the web of life and the web of knowledge." If we truly hope to **see** the Sutter Buttes, we must be aware of where we are on many levels. We must see the rugged peaks in a long-term geologic perspective, we must see the soil and leaf litter as a dynamic community of minute organisms, and we must see ourselves as a part of the natural world, a **participant** rather than a passive observer.

The Water Dwellers: Aquatic Insects

Sutter Buttes streams are temporary, though they may trickle on until late spring or summer, long after the winter rains that supplied them are all but forgotten in the dusty hills. The land releases the winter recharge gradually, and that assures enough time for many kinds of aquatic insects, as well as other organisms, to complete their life cycles.

In arid country a creek or pond has particular significance. Solvent and solution support life impossible otherwise, and the ripple of an insect in water may ramify ultimately through many organisms. The sound of running water in the Buttes is exciting to me, a sound I missed during the drought years and whose absence was even more significant to many other creatures.

In April 1981 Dave Woodward returned to the Buttes, having visited earlier as part of a class I was teaching. We waded into the creeks, lifting rocks and sunken logs, straining the waters with fine nets and discovering a surprising variety of aquatic insects (Appendix E). Dave's enthusiasm was infectious; he not only appreciates the creatures themselves, he also understands how they relate to one another in the aquatic ecosystem.

There are those of us who dream of landing on a habitable planet, the first to see and examine the exotic flora and fauna of a new world. The opportunity for an equivalent experience is so available in nearby ponds and streams that it amazes me how few of us are aware of it. We are blinded by our size and by our speciesism, a graduated form of racism that gives us favorable predilections toward "higher" organisms and a bias against the "lower".

Dave's awareness of the fascinating life in even ephemeral waters jolted me awake to that new world, a world I had sampled briefly and with an appropriate sense of wonder as a child but which I had forgotten about as an adult. That was an oversight that I am determined not to repeat again.

Insects do not grow as adults, but change in size is accomplished by molting through a series of stages, then metamorphosing to a different life form. A complete metamorphosis involves egg, larva, pupa, and adult, but there are variations distinctive to different insect groups.

Evolutionarily, the discrete stages enabled insects to occupy an incredible variety of niches and to enter diapause, a resting state, at whatever stage proved, through natural selection, to be advantageous. Thus the temporary water habitats in the Buttes can be exploited fully; a creek dry and lifeless in August can pulse with life in February.

Many of the aquatic insects are attracted to bright lights, often a fatal fascination, as they swarm there unable to fulfill their normal life functions or fall prey to predators quick to recognize an easy meal. Electric lights are a novelty for which the instincts of ancient lives are not programmed. The sparkle of moonlight or starlight on pond or stream surface is an appropriately attractive stimulus for night-flying insects, whose larvae are aquatic, but our lights merely act as a supernormal signal they cannot resist.

Permit me now, as a naturalist just barely at the threshold of learning about aquatic ecosystems, to look a little closer at the organisms that Dave and I found in our nets in Sutter Buttes streams and ponds. The list is incomplete but will serve as a sampler of typical local aquatic insects.

The Mayfly Order: Ephemeroptera

An adult mayfly is a creature of extreme delicacy: slender, with transparent wings and filamentous threads sweeping gracefully upward to the rear. It lives as an adult for a couple hours to a couple days, as ephemeral as the name of its order implies.

The adult is a frail and fleeting package of reproductive material with no desire to eat nor to defend itself. Its "hatch" at the water's surface is really its penultimate molt, giving it wings to flutter up to the underside of a leaf, where it will later molt to be a graceful flier to complete its cycle in spectacular mating swarms. After their aerial alliance, the mated pair separates, the spent male dropping to die, the female flying long enough to lay her egg packets back in the water. That, of course, assumes no interference. In fact, the mayfly may fly into airspace patrolled by hungry dragonflies, birds, and bats, and the "hatch" may create what fly fishermen call "the magic moment", the explosive conjunction of trout and mayfly, the insect instantly disappearing to fuel the flesh of fish (Miller 1981). In the Sutter Buttes, that moment cannot occur, for the streams themselves are ephemeral, hosts to fast-cycle insects but not to fishes.

Mayfly

The larval mayfly or nymph is less ephemeral, a sturdy aquatic herbivore of algae that molts its exoskeleton regularly and relies on its camouflaged appearance to avoid the depredations of giant water bugs, water boatmen, and dragonfly nymphs. When it is transformed so drastically at the water's surface to its subadult form ("dun", to the fisherman), it is temporarily vulnerable to rapacious water striders. As if its milky wings and clumsy flight were an embarrassment, the dun undergoes its final molt to its clear-winged, agile-flying adult form ("spinner", to the fisherman). The molt of the winged adult is unique among insects.

At least three genera of mayflies are common in Sutter Buttes temporary streams and ponds. Their abundance should be proof enough that their life styles are successful, and success should be considered only as it applies to the mayflies themselves. It's clear, however, that we humans are prone to judge creatures by other considerations. The trout fisherman may say that the "mayfly and trout . . . are absolutely gorgeous creatures, have more class than any other insect or fish, and are beautifully suited to one another's company" (Miller 1981). I wonder how mayflies **really** feel about the company of trout! In contrast, the entomologist, looking at the entire life cycle of the creature, may say about the adult mayfly "each lives but a few hours or a day or two, an ignoble end for the immature which has taken months to mature" (Powell and Hogue 1979). But what is ignoble about a quick transformation that manages quite well to provide eggs, and hence nymphs, for the next aquatic generation? Moralizing about mayflies can scarcely concern them, but what we do to their habitat **can** have real biological significance.

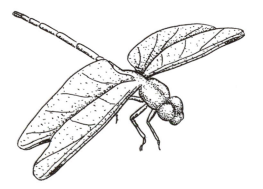

Dragonfly   *Damselfly*

The Dragonfly and Damselfly Order: Odonata

It seems a bit curious to find a colorful dragonfly or damselfly near the summit of a peak in the Buttes, but the odonates are superb fliers, strong, swift, and highly maneuverable. Some which breed in the valley marshlands come to the

Buttes to hunt, where some in turn fall prey to lizards and kestrels. Their four wings can operate independently, so they can zip backward or forward with ease. This not only aids them in capturing flying insects as prey, but also allows them to maintain and defend territories, as a bird might. In some species, a male will closely accompany the female after mating, jealously guarding her lest some other suitor should reach her before she has deposited her eggs. Certainty of paternity, however, does not obligate him to provide any parental care to his offspring, but then, neither does the female.

From those eggs laid in plant stems, mud, or other damp places will hatch the naiads or nymphs, aggressive predators of mosquito wrigglers and other aquatic insects. Their mouthparts fold next to the face like a mask, then snap outward like a mechanical arm to snatch up their prey. From the viewpoint of a mosquito wriggler, a quiet creekside pool might contain many lurking dangers, but natural selection, at which these predators play an important role, has ensured mosquitoes a fighting chance for survival by their sheer fecundity.

Odonate nymphs crawl about using their legs when not alarmed or when stalking prey. Should they feel threatened, they draw water into their rectums and release it in short spurts that provide instant jet propulsion.

Butterflies may claim a disproportionate share of our attention, but dragonflies and damselflies would be strong rivals in any beauty contest. A close look at those bulging, multifaceted eyes reveals a shifting play of light and color. I can't resist wondering what type of consciousness resides behind them. The wings themselves, held horizontally by dragonflies and vertically to the rear by damselflies, are gorgeous. They are functionally light and strong, yet esthetically pleasing — delicate membranes with veins forming patterns like leaded glass, sometimes colored with subtle shadings of yellow, red, blue, or brown or marked distinctly with dark patches symmetrically arranged. Sunlight gleams as it reflects from the tiny panes. The thorax and abdomen display their own brilliant greens, blues, purples, reds — often with scintillating iridescence. Here are insects big enough and colorful enough to make a real impression on us, **if** we bother to look. How ironic it is that we can pay such close attention to a hard, tiny crystal of diamond or ruby, cold and lifeless, yet not seek out the evanescent brilliance of living, dynamic creatures such as the Green Darner, Big Red Skimmer, Common Ruby Spot, and Vivid Dancer!

The Stonefly Order: Plecoptera

Stonefly nymphs or naiads share flowing waters with the nymphs of mayflies, extracting oxygen by means of hairlike or branched gills. One species is very common in the intermittent creeks of the Buttes, proof to an aquatic ecologist that the waters are unpolluted, as stoneflies are sensitive indicators of depleted oxygen.

Adults are poor fliers, often preferring to run, rather than fly when disturbed. Yard lights will attract them; there they flutter weakly around the illumination, easy prey for the nighthawks and bats which sometimes exploit the concentrations of creatures whose instincts have set them up to be victims of a response designed for moonlight glinting off a stream surface.

The True Bug Order: Hemiptera

We call members of this order the **true** bugs, since sloppy usage often labels beetles, ants, even non-insects such as bacteria and viruses as "bugs". But only 40,000 of the world's insects are true bugs, with half-membranous forewings, a characteristic pattern formed by the folded wings on the back, a tubular beak adapted for piercing and sucking, a simple metamorphosis. The word has slipped out into other contexts — to bug a room with a hidden microphone, to annoy or bug a person, to find a defect or bug in a machine or system, to become addicted to a hobby or pursuit, e.g. shutterbug. Perhaps an entomologist specializing in this order could be called a bugbug.

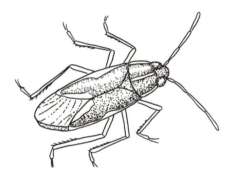

Western Box Elder Bug

Most members of the order are terrestrial. We are well-aware of the stink bugs, plant bugs, shield bugs, milkweed bugs, chinch bugs, assassinbugs, and of course, the bed bugs. Highly noticeable in the Sutter Buttes are the Western Box Elder Bugs (*Leptocoris rubrolineatus*), with their maddening tendency to migrate into buildings in fall to hibernate and to emerge in crawling masses on warm days in early spring.

Other bugs are aquatic or nearly so, and these include some of the most fascinating creatures that a naturalist might encounter by poking his nose down close to or into the creeks and pools. Water boatmen and backswimmers have boatlike builds and rear legs modified as oars. Each carries a silver envelope of air trapped next to its body for continuous respiration. Economies of scale eliminate any need for an external scuba tank, as the air bubble, renewed instantly as the insect surfaces, conforms naturally to the body. Water boatmen, prolific residents of rice field and slow creek alike, are major components in the aquatic food chain, mild-mannered converters of algae to bug, serving incidentally as food for the predatory members of the next trophic level. The upside-down swimming backswimmers prey on other aquatic insects and occasionally small vertebrates. Armed for their

Water Boatman

predatory lifestyle, they can inflict a painful bite to the hand of a curious but incautious human.

The nip of a backswimmer, however, is nothing compared to the snap of a giant water bug, the infamous toe-biter. Now **here** is a predator to admire. Though strong swimmers using their flattened rear legs for power strokes, they usually perch on submerged objects, forelegs poised like great clamps, waiting to ambush passing prey. Without warning (why is it that we persist in saying "without warning", when it would be pure stupidity for a predator to let its prey know that it's lying in ambush?), the powerful legs slash out to seize the victim, which may be another insect, a bug-eyed tadpole, a tiny fish, or even small snake. The killer stabs its prey, inserts its strong beak, and injects a paralyzing toxin. Why is it we cringe at the thought? There ought not be any aversion to the words "killer" and "victim" when we refer to predation, yet somehow we transfer the process to what we consider reprehensible in human beings. By the same logic, we ought to respect the giant water bug because the male is such a devoted father. The female lays her eggs like dozens of billiard balls across her mate's back, and he carries, guards, and aerates them until they hatch. Most cases of toe biting, we must admit, are justifiable in terms of self defense. Most bugs that we step on aren't able to do anything about it — more power to the giant water bug!

Water striders and their shorter-legged relatives, riffle bugs, skate across the water, their toes barely depressing the surface film. The Common Water Strider is found throughout the continent on still waters at almost any elevation. They are gregarious, communicating by ripple patterns sensed through their appendages. The

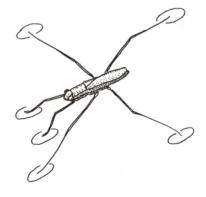

Water Strider

long middle legs are used like oars, as they skate about after prey (aquatic insects or above-water creatures that just happen to drop in) or to avoid becoming prey themselves. Many times I have played the role of predator (albeit with no intention of eating), stalking and grasping in vain after the swift striders. Their shadows, crosses with rounded tips, shoot across the bottom in apparent mockery of my clumsy attempts.

The Dobsonfly Order: Megaloptera

Of all the aquatic insects discovered in the intermittent creeks of the Buttes, the Dobsonfly was perhaps the most unexpected. Its long cylindrical larvae, called hellgrammites, are active predators along stream bottoms and make excellent bait for trout fishing. These larvae normally have a several year life span before metamorphosing to become adults, so what do they do as the creeks dry up in late spring? Apparently they descend and excavate little cells beneath rocks below the creek bed, waiting in estivation until winter rains again swell the creeks (Smith 1970).

The Caddisfly Order: Tricoptera

Adult caddisflies rarely draw our attention. We might take them for nondecript moths, unless we noticed the absence of a coiled proboscis or the presence of minute body and wing hairs, rather than scales. Tricoptera means "hairy wings"; these wings are just barely adequate to get them through the typical adult life of a month.

The caterpillarlike larva, properly called a caddisworm, is the instar attraction. Despite a mental endowment that is no more nor no less than we would expect from a caterpillar, the larva manages to construct an intricate and beautiful case, producing its own silk and adding particles of rock, sand, twig, leaf, or whatever else may be handy. Biologists agree that the primary function of the case is to enhance respiratory efficiency — the tube operates as "a conduit for a channeled flow of water, enabling the larva to create its own current" (Wiggins 1977:16). Clearly natural selection has modified the cases to solve other engineering problems, as well; Wiggins mentions streamlining, ballast, bouyancy, structural rigidity, camouflage, internal water circulation, external water resistance, and protection from predators and intruders.

The four species of caddisworms collected in the Buttes demonstrate a variety of feeding strategies. *Hydropsyche* is a net-spinner, a weaver of elegant silken capture nets to strain food from moving water. The larva itself hides in a retreat it constructs next to its net, emerging now and then to collect the assorted bits of detritus, algae, or tiny aquatic insects swept in by the current.

Ochrotrichia is a micro-caddisfly, unusual in that only the fifth and final larval stage or instar builds a case. It is a purse-case maker, developing a bivalved silken purse upon which sand grains or algal threads may be attached. It lives as a scraper, moving about in its portable purse as it rasps algal and detrital scum off rocks.

Gumaga, very common in the Buttes, builds slender tube cases from fine particles of sand. Its masonry is impeccable, hundreds of particles cemented tightly and efficiently into an elongated cylindrical horn open at both ends.

In the largest North American family of Tricopteras is the genus *Limnephilus,* lowly scrapers of filmy rock surfaces, yet creators of incredible cases of sticks or rocks.

Some entomologists confess to collecting caddis cases as compulsively as philatelists collect rare stamps (von Frisch 1974). I too am attracted by the diversity of their home-spun architecture, yet I admit my interest is casual and superficial, the appreciation of an artist more than that of an entomologist. The latter will distinguish the various caddisflies by examining the "ocelli, maxillary palps, thoracic warts, and tibial spurs" (Borror and White 1970). Somehow I can't help feeling that peering at the palps, warts, and spurs of a living caddisfly is an intrusion too personal for me to justify.

The Beetle Order: Coleoptera

If success is measured in terms of variety and abundance, then beetles must stand at the pinnacle of success. Worldwide there are at least 300,000 species, with 30,000 or so in North America, at least 7000 in California. Chances are high that human alteration of habitat around the globe will eliminate more species even before they are described by scientists. With dazzling colors and incredible body modifications, some are among the most beautiful creatures on our planet. Others are of inestimable importance ecologically. Though terrestrial types predominate, beetles of several families are well-represented in in aquatic habitats.

A slow-moving stream seems at first glance to be a peaceful, tranquil environment. We may be vaguely aware that now and then a garter snake will attack a frog or a raccoon will invade the stream by night in search of a meal, but in general the stream seems a place far removed from violence.

When we change scale, focusing our attention on the creatures from an inch or two long down to the lower limits of our unaided senses, we find a world in which predators of many kinds thrive. Among them are the predaceous diving beetles, which not only subdivide the predatory role by species, but also by age class. Adults are attractively patterned beetles which stroke their flattened, hair-fringed hindlegs simultaneously like oars. They surface periodically for air, capturing a bubble beneath the elytra or wing covers. They are good fliers and can migrate readily between ponds. Their larvae, called water tigers, resemble them little: strong-jawed, multi-segmented elongated creatures more like a centipede in shape than like an adult beetle. They are voracious carnivores, sometimes cannibalistic, even attacking animals larger than themselves. In evolutionary terms, it's hard for a prey species to specialize in escape measures from predators so different in attack features as larvae and adults of these beetles.

Whirligig Beetle

Adult whirligigs exploit the interface of water and air and are functionally four-eyed, able to see above and below the water simultaneously. They are good divers and good fliers, but we are apt to find them spinning in circles at high speed on the surface, always seeming to rebound just before a collision with a wildly spinning neighbor. Apparently each antenna comes equipped with a tiny sensory device, the Johnston's organ, that detects wavelets in the surface film (Hutchins 1966). This radarlike sense prevents the gyrating Gyrinids from what otherwise might become a bumpercar battle of black shiny beetles. Perhaps the designers of VW sedans were inspired by nature's example. As far as I know, no automaker has imitated the long, segmented larvae with lateral feathery gills, though a squinted eye and an active imagination might see similarity to a racing shell bristling with oars.

Somewhat similar to the predaceous diving beetles are the water scavenger beetles, which are slightly less streamlined, have short clubbed antennae held in small grooves near the eyes, and swim by alternating hindleg strokes. Adults feed primarily by scavenging, larvae as intense predators of other small creatures, including hapless others of their own kind on occasion.

The Fly Order: Diptera

Diptera implies two wings; the hind pair has been reduced to knobbed organs, the halteres, presumed to function in balancing. It's hard to be neutral about a family that has members involved in disease transmission, crop destruction, and in many cases, open annoyance. Yet some dipterans are valuable to us as scavengers, pollinators, and controllers, as parasites and predators, of **other** noxious pests.

Long, slender legs and slow flight give a crane fly its name, though a resemblance to an overgrown mosquito suggests another, "mosquito hawk". They are common in the Buttes and easily approachable on a cool, dewy spring morning as the gangly creatures hang suspended on grass blades. They are harmless to man and easily injured when touched; their delicate limbs might seem to be architectural minimalism, the antithesis of the robust bodies of bumblebees or horse flies. Their larvae are dark, thick-skinned maggots, some of them aquatic.

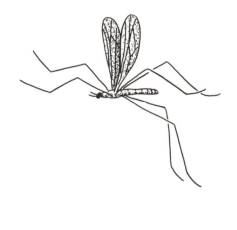

Crane Fly

Midges somewhat resemble mosquitoes, though they're more delicate, have more feathery antennae, and do not bite. During the mating season they may gather in dense swarms, pulsing columns or clouds of insects preoccupied with the most basic of creature compulsions. At such times they can be a nuisance to automobile drivers, house painters, and picnickers. Those which survive the hazards of mating season leave eggs in water in gelatinous strings or masses. The red larvae, called bloodworms because they are unusual among insects by possessing hemoglobin, build silk-lined tubes in the bottom ooze. They breathe by undulating their bodies within the tubes, setting up an aerating circulation, and they feed on minute plants sieved from the water by a silken net placed over the tube mouth. At least two species occur in the streams of the Buttes, but their identification will await the patient examination of a midge specialist.

Another family includes the biting midges, alias no-see-ums, alias punkies, alias sand flies, alias moose flies, alias gnats. These little devils (pardon my lapse into anthropomorphism) produce bites all out of proportion to their size. And they're sneaky, slipping in to attack around a hatband, under one's hair, at the collar, or around the ankles. Mosquito bites tend to produce fairly brief swelling and momentary itch; no-see-um bites are minimal at first, then cause greater swelling and maddening itch that lasts for days. Fortified with her blood meal, the female (the male is blameless as far as biting, but I can't recommend the company he keeps) returns to pond or stream to lay her eggs. Her wormlike larvae scavenge or prey on other aquatic creatures, and they in turn are dietary items for a number of larger beasties, including various fly larvae.

The larger deer and horse flies, family Tabanidae, can inflict a painful bite and can be carriers of certain diseases, but at least we often see them coming or feel them as they land. I figure I've got a fighting chance, though I pity the poor deer, horses, and cattle which must tolerate their attacks and which often lose blood because of an anticoagulant left by the biting females. As is common in this order, the males show no interest in blood and are content to dine on the nectar of flowers. The females relish nectar too, and I suppose I might even find them attractive, in a purely appreciative way, if I were not the occasional victim myself of one of their nasty nips.

No discussion of dipterans with aquatic larvae would be complete without mention of the family Culicidae, the mosquitoes. The Sutter Buttes have several species, including the Western Malaria Mosquito, *Anopheles freeborni*, ubiquitous around rice fields, and the Western Treehole Mosquito, *Aedes siemensis*, which breeds in temporary pools in oak cavities and is implicated as a vector in the transmission of dog heartworm.

As for other biting flies and gnats, the female mosquito requires a blood meal prior to egg-laying and the sugars of plant nectars and juices to sustain flight and to maintain normal longevity (Swan and Papp 1972). I might not even object to sharing a little of my blood with a female or two now and then, were it not for two nasty habits that accompany the feeding. Taking a sample of blood is one thing, but why must the female inject that component of her saliva which causes the infernal itching? In addition, I tend to resent her being a carrier for such diseases as malaria, encephalitis, yellow fever, and the like, though I know I **ought** to blame the viruses or protozoans involved, not the mosquito. Nevertheless, I cheer the dragonflies, swallows, bats, and other creatures who dine on mosquitoes.

Still, the discomforts that mosquitoes cause are among the factors that keep small, nice Sacramento Valley towns like Colusa small and nice. If mosquito abatement work were fully successful, Colusa might yet be invaded by shopping centers, traffic lights, and other symptoms of that pernicious plague, urban sprawl. No doubt some residents of quiet communities such as Colusa would be most willing to tolerate a certain level of blood loss and itching to maintain the status quo, a quality of life becoming ever rarer in California.

Meadows on the Wing: Butterflies

In the spring of the year, as the wildflowers spread bright and varied colors across the meadows and hillsides, the scene in the Sutter Buttes becomes animated with the flashing wings of many butterflies (checklist Appendix F).

They dip and float erratically from flower to flower, appearing as if the petals themselves have suddenly taken wing. As casual observers, we may be tempted to envy their carefree lives of sampling nectar in fields of plenty. This apparent view, however, belies the actual truth of their activities — butterflies are diligently attending to the business of producing more butterflies.

In a single day, a female butterfly may fly many miles in search of a particular plant on which to lay her eggs. Although she herself feeds on nectar from the colorful wildflowers, her young offspring will not have the long hollow, extendable tongue she has for this purpose. In fact, the offspring that hatch from her eggs will not look at all like her — they will be caterpillars! It is hard to remember that those wriggling, often garishly-colored creatures are indeed the larval form of the glorious winged butterflies. Instead of tongues, caterpillars have chewing mouthparts for devouring leaves. Each species needs an appropriate plant or group of plants as hosts for proper nourishment, hence the extensive searching by the female. Once she has found a satisfactory plant, she can lay up to one hundred eggs in one hour.

According to ancient folklore, butterflies were born of drops of dew collected on the leaves of trees. Indeed their eggs are about the size of dewdrops. They vary from species to species in shape, color, and deposition. Most common shapes are spherical, conical, barrel-, spindle-, or pear-shaped, or turban-like. Colors grade from white to black, with greens, yellows, and russets in between. Some species lay their eggs singly on tips of leaves, some in clusters, neat rows, or dangling strings, some even as bracelets around twigs (Swan and Papp 1972).

After two to thirty days of solar incubation (depending on species), the eggs hatch and the larvae begin to eat. Their main function is to eat and grow and store up food for the pupal and adult stages that follow. In the first day of life, each larva may consume more than twice its weight in food and within a month, will increase to nearly ten thousand times its original weight. During this massive growth period, the caterpillar sheds its skin four or five times, becoming larger with each successive stage or instar.

The third stage, or pupal stage, involves the incredible metamorphosis from the caterpillar to the adult winged butterfly or imago (Latin for "image"). During the pupal stage, the insect is stationary and does not eat. The larva attaches itself to a stem or leaf and develops a parchment-like covering called the chrysalis. Inside this protective enclosure, the delicate transformation proceeds. Old tissues are broken down, new ones are formed. In two to three weeks (for some species even years), the butterfly is completely formed, wings, antennae, and legs folded up in many layers inside its chrysalis. As the case splits, the butterfly emerges, wet and weak, but in a few hours the wings are stretched and hardened, ready for flight.

I am constantly amazed at the intricacy and brilliant beauty of the butterflies. The wings, the legs, and body as well are covered with tiny flat scales arranged like shingles on a roof, once counted at ninety-nine thousand per square inch (Riley 1970)! The order Lepidoptera, in fact, comes from the Greek for scaly wings. A light touch to the wings will release a cloud of "butterfly dust", the scales having served as a slippery protection to the wing itself. Too much loss of scales, however, may unbalance the delicate precision of color and weight, thereby reducing the chances of escape the next time.

As well as providing a measure of protection, scales determine the intricate patterns of colors visible on the wings, both by the pigments they contain and their structural arrangement. Many wings show iridescent colors such as the shifting metallic blue-green on the hindwing of the Pipevine Swallowtail. Iridescence is created by the overlapping of the scales which make ridges and planes that break the lateral contact of the light waves into diffracted pieces (Swan and Papp 1972). The amount and hue we see depends upon our angle of vision and can change from pink to purple to blue to green as in soap bubbles. Other colors are produced by refraction of light at the boundary of layered scales which deflect some wavelengths while others pass through.

Why should butterfly wings be so elaborately colored? Undoubtedly, the various colors and distinctive patterns do signal to other butterflies the information of who will be a potential mate and who a competitor for mates and food sources. But what do these bright colors and patterns signal to other animals, especially birds who might use them as food? Although it may seem improbable, bright reds, yellows, and blues do create camouflage and conceal- ment through disruptive coloration. Bold lines and patches of different colors break up regular outlines, distracting a predator from recognizing the true form of the creature as an edible item. Often, especially on the hindwings, the colors form patterns resembling eyespots. A predator's attention is thus drawn away from the vulnerable head to the much less critical area near the tail, or the "eyes" may so startle the predator that the butterfly can escape.

Bright and showy signals may be fine for a distasteful or poisonous butterfly, but an edible one is better off avoiding notice. Many moths particularly have dull brown or gray mottled wings that blend into backgrounds of tree trunks and rocks. As long as the moth has selected a matching background, it can rest for hours perfectly concealed. Other deceptive strategies involve resembling some non-food item such as a bird dropping, a leaf, or a twig.

Table 2.   General Flight Periods for Butterflies of the Sutter Buttes.*

Jan	Feb	Mar	Apr	May	Jun	Jul	Aug	Sep	Oct	Nov	Dec

Pipevine Swallowtail   Orange Sulphur   Painted Lady
Cabbage White   Mylitta Crescent   West Coast Lady

W. Tiger Swallowtail   Common Hairstreak
Monarch   Small Copper
Field Crescent   Eastern Tailed Blue
C. Tortoise-shell   Acmon Blue
Red Admiral   Sootywing
Buckeye   Com. Checkered Skipper
Great Blue Hairstreak

Two-tailed Swallowtail
Anise Swallowtail
Mourning Cloak
Mournful Duskywing

Lorquin's Admiral
Fiery Skipper

Sara Orange-tip
Large Marble
Western Elfin
Bramble Hairstreak
Rural Skipper
P. Duskywing

Satyr Anglewing
Virginia Lady
California Sister
California Hairstreak
Great Copper
Umber Skipper

Eufala Skipper
Woodland Skipper
Field Skipper
Large Checkered Skipper

*Based on personal observations and data from Peoples (1978) and Shapiro (1974).

The Swallowtail Family: Papilionidae

Of the butterflies in the Buttes, swallowtails are perhaps the most conspicuous. They are large and colorful, dazzling the meadows and hilltops with their black and gold or turquoise wings. The swallowtails are so named because of a projecting tip on the hindwings reminiscent of the long outer tail feathers of the Barn Swallow.

Pipevine Swallowtail

One of the first butterflies to appear in the early spring (Table 2) is the Pipevine Swallowtail (*Battus philenor*), closely following the blooming of its host plant, the Dutchman's Pipe (*Aristolochia californica*). The female butterflies visually locate the Pipe vines and deposit linear clusters of rusty eggs. With *Aristolochias* in Texas, which are smaller herbs, a female swallowtail will march up and down a prospective host plant several times inspecting it for earlier-layed eggs, for her larvae will have insufficient food supply if another clutch of larvae gets a head start. Such maternal caution seems less likely in the Buttes where our plants are galloping vines with abundant leaves. Still, a prudent female might leave more offspring if she avoids areas with existing

Western Tiger Swallowtail

egg

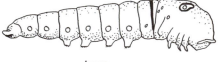

larva

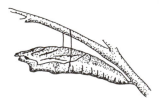

pupa

eggs, since young larvae are voracious enough to devour any eggs they may come across in their munching marches across the plant.

The caterpillars, blue-black larvae with formidable rows of orange spikes, must present a ghastly sight to a hungry bird. If touched, they jab out prongs of hidden horns guaranteed to startle all but the most-hardened larvaphile. They steadfastly devour Dutchman's Pipe leaves, eschewing all alternative plants they may encounter. Eventually they hole up in cryptic chrysalises and undergo miraculous transformations to spectacular butterflies with wings of black velvet brushed with a metallic turquoise sheen. These adults again seek out the Pipe vine to repeat the eternal cycle.

The Western Tiger Swallowtail *(Papilio rutulus)*, the Two-tailed Swallowtail *(P. multicaudatus)*, the Pale and Anise Swallowtails *(P. eurymedon* and *zelicaon)* have the familiar black and yellow tiger stripings although the Pale is more like a zebra with the usual yellow background nearly white. The Two-tailed is the largest of the four, has thinner stripes, and can be distinguished by two tail-like projections on each hind wing. The larvae of these species are deep green with yellow eyespots bordered in black and pupiled in blue. They also have a yellow and black band on the adjoining edges of the first and second segments.

Pale Swallowtail

The Pierid Family: Pieridae

Small to medium in size, the Pierids are abundant especially in agricultural areas. They have nicely rounded wings of creamy white or butter yellow which probably was the original stimulus for the name butterfly (*butterfleoge* in Anglosaxon).

The Cabbage White (*Pieris rapae*) was inadvertently introduced to this country in cargo ships from Europe to Quebec in the mid-nineteenth century and spread rapidly, leaving its larvae to feed on cabbages and other mustards of agricultural fields. Their wings are white with dark edges and one spot on the forewing of the male, two spots on the female. The eggs are yellow and pear-like with strong ribs. Larvae are a black-stippled pale green with a yellow stripe down the back and pale yellow spots on each side. Pupae are stippled pale green, grey, or brown.

The larvae of the Orange Sulphur (*Colias eurytheme*) feed on alfalfa, clover, and other legumes; therefore the species is also commonly known as the Alfalfa Sulphur. Adults emerging in spring are orange, grading to yellow, edged with black. Those from late summer broods have deep orange wings with heavier black margins, under-sides yellow. Tapered white eggs with ribs hatch into dark green larvae with white lines down back and sides, each enclosing a narrow black or red line. Pupae are green with lateral yellow dashes and black markings.

Orange Sulphur

egg   larva   pupa

Aptly described as "a beautiful sprite of springtime," the Sara Orange-tip (*Anthocaris sara*) darts over the meadows in search of shepherd's purse, rock cress, wild radish and other mustards on which to oviposit its yellow-orange spindle-shaped eggs. Pure white wings sport brilliant orange tips framed in black on the forewings. Larvae are green with yellow and black spots and lines; pupae are stippled brown.

Not as common as the previous three Pierids is the Large Marble (*Euchloe ausonides*). Wings are mostly white with faint black forewing tips. The undersides are marbled in green. Larvae are dark green with a stripe down the back and three on each side. Adults patrol along streams.

The Milkweed Butterfly Family:
Danaidae

The rusty stained-glass wings of the Monarch (*Danaus plexippus*) appear in early spring and are in flight in the Buttes through the fall (Table 2). Black and yellow banded bright green larvae hatch from pale green eggs laid on milkweed plants. The milky latex in the milkweed plants contains poisonous toxins which do not harm the Monarch larvae, but predators eating the Monarchs experience violent reactions to

Monarch

egg

pupa

larva

the poison. Monarch pupae are pale green with metallic gold spots and are suspended from their tips.

The Brush-footed Butterfly Family: Nymphalidae

These butterflies have very short, brushy front legs, long antennae, and are usually most active at midday. We have recorded twelve species of this group in

Mylitta Crescent

the Buttes. The eggs are barrel-shaped with net-like ridges. Larvae usually are brown or black, covered symmetrically with hairs or spines.

One of the smallest butterflies in the Buttes is the Mylitta Crescent *(Phycoides mylitta)* with a wingspan of about one inch. Its wings are an orange-brown with fine black markings. Eggs are white, larvae velvety black with yellow underneath and fine yellow lines on back and sides.

They frequent areas with asters and thistles. A close relative, the Field or Meadow Crescent *(P. campestris)* has heavier black markings.

The Satyr Anglewing *(Polygonia satyrus)* flies in spring and summer (Table 2), preferring moist areas. The outline of the wings suggests a rough coastline with a deep bay in the forewing and a peninsular point in the hindwing.

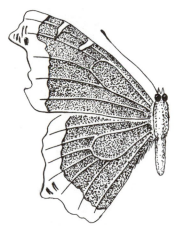

egg

pupa

larva

Mourning Cloak

Coloring is brownish yellow with black spots, underwing mottled brown or grey, often with a silvery comma on the hindwing. Anglewings are not flower visitors, but prefer sap and fruit juices. Pale green eggs are laid in strings on the underside of nettle leaves. The spiny black larvae with one white back stripe form hanging tents called *hibernacula.* Below a leaf axil of a nettle plant, a larva will partially sew up a leaf around itself as a protection. Anglewing pupae are shiny grey-brown with raised golden spots.

Early in the season, the angle-winged Mourning Cloaks *(Nymphalis antiopa)* can be found in the canyons and flying at the tops of trees. Their wings are a velvety purplish-brown with wide yellow trim like fur on a cloak and with inlaid jewels of blue. Eggs are white, larvae spiny black with white and red spots. Pupae are grey and hang from willow and cottonwood branches.

Three Ladies whose names have changed from Cynthia to Vanessa are the Painted Lady *(Vanessa cardui)*, the West Coast Lady *(V. annabella)*, and the Virginia Lady *(V. virginiensis).* This genus is known collectively as "the thistle butterflies" although their plant hosts vary from nettle and thistle to mallow, mule ears, mugwort, lupine and other wildflowers. All three are basically brownish yellow with black markings. The Painted Lady may be distinguished by a rosy tint and four eyespots on the hindwing visible on the underside as well as above. The West Coast Lady has a darker background and more extensive black markings, again with four eyespots repeated underneath. The Virginia Lady has only the outer two of the large eyespots on the under-side of the wing. The larvae of the Painted and Virginia Ladies are lilac colored, spiny,

Virginia Lady

with silvery white spots beneath. The West Coast Lady larvae are black, spiny, with orange blotches.

The Red Admiral is also of the genus Vanessa *(V. atalanta)* but can be separated from the Ladies by the lack of the submarginal eyespots on the hindwing. The forewings are rich black with a bright orange band and white spots near the tip. The hindwings have orange margins with a blue edge at the bottom tip. Males frequently set up territories where they may spend afternoons perching for several weeks. Larvae are black with many white velvety points and seven rows of spines. These larvae sew up hanging leaf tents on nettles similar to those sewn by the Satyr Anglewing but are completely sewn above the leaf axil.

Very intent on defending its territory is the beautiful bark-like Buckeye

Buckeye

(Precis coenia). Its wings are grayish brown with conspicuous eyespots ringed in reddish orange and two black-bordered short orange bars perpendicular to the leading edge of the forewing. Eggs are dark green and flattened, larvae are dark and spiny with longitudinal stripes of pale yellow. They are regularly seen in patches of the low growing plant called Lippia.

Two *Limenitis* species, the Lorquin's Admiral *(L. lorquini)* and the California Sister *(L. bredowii),* are common in late spring through fall. The Lorquin's Admiral has a bold white stripe running across both wings and a golden orange forewing patch. The California Sister is similar but the orange patch is set back farther from the tip and there are blue lines on the underwings. Both species seldom visit flowers but are found along streams flying a series of short twitches of nearly flat wings alternating with leisurely floating and stopping to bask on perches. Lorquin's Admirals lay pale green eggs singly at the tips of willow leaves, California Sisters on oak leaves. Their larvae have two plumelike horns near the front and are camouflaged in coloring. The Admirals' pupae are dull purple and white, the Sisters' are soft brown with metallic spots.

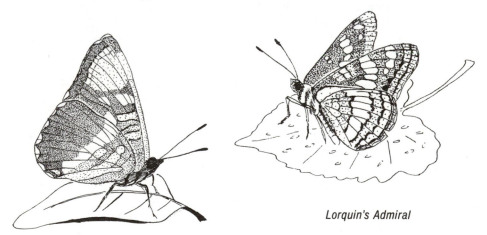

California Sister

Lorquin's Admiral

The Gossamer-winged Butterfly Family: Lycaenidae

This lovely name applies to a family of generally small butterflies often with wings in bright iridescent colors.

Very abundant throughout the Buttes and especially attracted to patches of Lippia is the Common Hairstreak *(Strymon melinus)*. Its wings are slate or blue-gray with two large black spots and smaller reddish orange spots above these, lighter gray underneath with white and black hairstreaks. When perching, they often rub their hindwings together. There is a long projecting tail on each hindwing similar to the Swallowtails. Eggs are pale green, laid singly. Larvae are velvety bright green with fine yellow hairs. Pupae are brown.

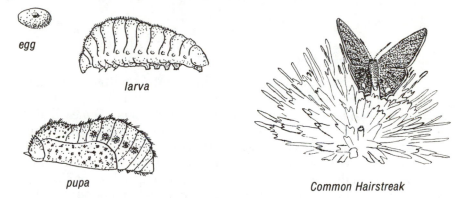

egg

larva

pupa

Common Hairstreak

The Great Blue Hairstreak *(Atlides halesus)* is not abundant in the Buttes but may be seen late in the season around the blooms of Datura. Its wings are iridescent purple with blue-green toward the base and bordered in black; undersides are plain brownish gray with green, blue and red spots. Its larvae feed on the mistletoe on the live oak.

About the size of a penny, the Western Elfin *(Incisalia iroides)* is plain brown above, yellow-brown below.

Two Coppers, the Great *(Lycaena xanthoides)* and Small *(L. helloides)*, have been recorded in the Buttes. Both are brownish orange with gray iridescence and have a band of orange crescents on the hindwings. The Great Copper is creamy white underneath and slightly greater than one and a half inch. The Small Copper is smaller than one and a half inch with pale red to purple underwings.

The Eastern Tailed Blue *(Everes comyntas)* and the Acmon Blue *(Plebejus acmon)* are the azure of a summer sky in miniature. Found along the trails, near creeks, along hillsides, and tops of hills, the Acmon Blue is probably the most common butterfly in the Buttes. The Eastern Tailed Blue is common early in the season.

The Skipper Family: Hesperiidae

Skipper

Named for their habit of swift flight punctuated by rapid starts and stops, the skippers are generally smaller than the butterflies. They are characterized by proportionately larger, stouter bodies and smaller wings. They have broad heads and hooked antennae and tend to be cryptically colored. Their larvae are mostly green and tapered and weave silk and leaf shelters for protection during the day. Pupation is in loose leaf cocoons on the ground.

A Scatological Debate: Dung Flies

A botanist may look at a cow in the Buttes and think of it in terms of its impact on vegetation. Some plants will be injured and will decline in the face of grazing, some will be stimulated to heightened productivity, some will gain as their competitors decline, some will send their seeds as hitchhikers on the animal's hair. A wildlife biologist may see the cow in terms of its indirect effects on wildlife: compaction of soil, impacts on food plants, competition at springs, or introduction of diseases. An entomologist, however, may recognize the cow as a magnet to parasites, biting insects, and the like, as important to a diverse group of arthropods as a full patch of flowers is to pollinators.

Let me propose an unusual way to spend an hour. Pick a cow — any will do — and watch it for a while. Observe it tearing off the grasses, grinding them slowly; you can practically see the continuous conversion of grass to flesh. That conversion has its byproducts, of course, and before long the cow will raise its tail and a postdigestive pat will appear, fresh and steaming, on the ground.

Now ignore the cow and concentrate on its pat. Within a few minutes you will see a small fly arrive from downwind. Look more closely, though avoid rapid movements. It's a male Dung Fly, *Scatophaga stercoraria*, a hairy-legged little creature, golden brown with bright red compound eyes. Native to Europe, its kind followed the cow to the New World; rather, it followed the cow pie.

Perhaps, if you're squeamish, you think you've

Dung Fly

seen enough. More flies are arriving, some the metallic Green Bottle Flies, glistening emeralds with brick red eyes. They seem to delight in touching the gooey mess, and your mind begins to extrapolate to the seething mass of maggots that will eventually be their progeny. Dung watching requires either a hardy disposition or a field entomologist's love for insects that transcends what we normally would call common sense.

Fly and beetle visitors to dung pats are excellent subjects for observation, and enough scientists have had the proper disposition that these insects are among the best known behaviorally. Parker (1978) has compared his extensive data to predictive theories on mate search, mate-guarding, sexual competition, immigration and emigration, and the like. Fascinating stuff!

Cow pats are classic examples of a patchy environment. Male Dung Flies, attracted by the scent of a fresh scat, fly in from downwind to land either on the pat or just upwind of it. Females arrive soon, usually landing just upwind of the pat but occasionally on it. Since males outnumber females in this species by about 4:1, there is intense competition among the males for mating opportunities. This places a premium on males being in the right place at the right time, and Parker did find that males were distributed on cow pats and in the grass just about as theory would predict in terms of pay-off probabilities. This distribution changes gradually with time, as male competition increases and as mated females move in to the pat to lay their eggs.

Getting a mating isn't enough. Females remain receptive even after copulation and males sometimes attack a mating pair for a take-over. The last male to mate with a female prior to egg-laying will fertilize about 80% of her eggs. Even though a male could leave a female right after copulation to go after other females (these guys seem to have little on their minds but sex), there is a high likelihood that another male would get to her before she lays the eggs. If so, the first male's fertilization success will drop to 20% or less. Hence it pays off for a male to escort his mate until egg-laying occurs and to fight off attempted take-overs by other males. It also means that a male may mate with a female encountered on a dung pat right there if few other males are around but should take her off into the grass for more privacy if many other males are present.

Parker's predictions and analyses based on optimization theory are elegant. His models seem to be reasonably well-satisfied by observed data, but Hanski (1980) expresses doubts. Hanski feels that optimization models imply a necessarily high level of sensory sophistication by the insects. They would seem by those models to be assessing population densities, degree of competition, and the like on a continuous basis. In his own work on dung beetles of the genus *Aphodius* (one species, *A. fimetarius*, is another European immigrant widely distributed in California where cattle occur), he found that their movements be-

tween cow pats could be explained better by simple models of random movement
than by complicated models of optimization. He feels the environment itself is
too variable to allow the fine tuning that Parker describes, so he suspects that
Dung Fly behavior too could be described more simply. He refuses to say that
Parker is wrong but feels his hypotheses are simpler and hence perhaps
more likely.

The debate may continue, as Parker and Hanski and others spend more time
watching and quantifying the antics of insects on cow pies. I am impressed by
the gentlemanly nature of this debate: no scat-flinging at all. Perhaps the
nature of the work breeds respect for other practitioners of the art of scat-
scanning, undoubtedly a rather limited fraternity.

A Gallery of Galls: Cynipid Wasps

A great, spreading Valley Oak seems like a monumental effort to go through
to produce acorns, hence future Valley Oaks. The massive tree, of course, is a
product of the winnowing effects of countless forces, such as weather,
competitors, predators, parasites, and so on. The existence of an oak, even
though basically designed to produce more oaks, opens up opportunities for
many new organisms, creates niches and potential for exploitation as side
effects of its own evolution. Maidu Indians and Acorn Woodpeckers are obvious
examples of vertebrates that exploit the oak.

It is not surprising that many tiny organisms, with rapid population
turnover, have coevolved with the oaks and with other plants. Close inspection

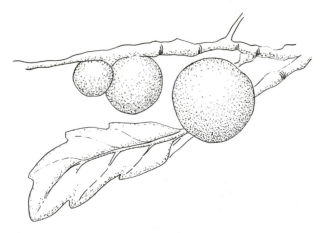

Oak Apple

of an aged Valley Oak is likely to reveal structures ("oak apples", swellings and buttons of many types) that have nothing to do with the oak's reproduction but provide shelter and food for gall-forming parasites. More than 2000 types of gall-making organisms have been described in this country, and more remain to be identified.

Galls are growths or swellings, tumorlike, beginning in response to mechanical or chemical stimulation by an invading organism. Though a gall does provide both food and shelter to the gall-maker, it is not a willing host; the plant reduces the damage it might otherwise sustain by localizing the toxins and activities of the invader and by forcing the invader to extreme specialization (Mani 1964, Russo 1979).

Galls can result from the activities of bacteria, fungi, higher plants (mistletoe), copepods, rotifers, nematodes, mites, and others. Numerous insect groups contain gall-makers. In the Sutter Buttes one often finds rounded swellings on the petioles of the leaves of Fremont Cottonwood; these galls are the work of the aphid, *Pemphigus populitransversus*. Coyote Brush may harber the galls of a midge, *Rhopalomyia californica* and of a moth *Gnorimoschema baccharisella*. Great Valley Gumplants form rosette galls in response to the actions of a midge; these galls remain green even when the rest of the plant is relatively dry and dormant, evidence of the type of metabolic strain such parasites can inflict on the host.

Most types of gall-inducers seem like dilettantes compared to the gall wasps of the family Cynipidae in the order Hymenoptera. The adult wasps are tiny, inconspicuous, hump-backed insects in plain blacks and browns, not likely to draw our notice, but the galls their larvae occupy are often "fascinating jewels . . . like miniature stars, sea urchins, golf balls, cups, saucers, clubs, and teardrops" (Russo 1979:36).

Wasps are most easily identified by the galls they induce and the hosts they prefer. Some species have an annual alternation of generations: a spring generation of males and females which reproduce sexually and a summer-fall generation of females which reproduce parthenogenetically, that is, without the help of males. The fact that males are haploid (one set of chromosomes), the females diploid (paired chromosomes, as in vertebrates), makes that arrangement easier than one might at first suspect. In some species, only parthenogenetic females are known. Often members of the alternating generations seek different egg-laying sites so that galls may be completely different, a fact that long complicated the process of identifying and classifying them.

A big breakthrough in the understanding of the complex sex lives of the Cynipid wasps came from the thorough research of Alfred Kinsey around 1920. Apparently this pioneering work warmed up Dr. Kinsey on the subject, preparing him for his well-known "reports" on human sexuality in later years.

Certainly the most conspicuous gall in the Sutter Buttes is that of the California Gallfly, a cynipid wasp, *Andricus californicus*. Eggs laid in Valley Oak stems hatch into maggotlike larvae which apparently secrete chemicals that trigger gall formation. The galls enlarge into spherical or kidney-shaped "oak apples", greenish with a tint of red at first. Sliced open, they are moist and succulent, as tempting as a fresh apple. My first bite into the "apple" was certainly my last, as the high concentration of bitter tannins set my teeth on edge instantly!

As summer progresses, the galls turn creamy, then tan. In fall the surviving larvae pupate, and the resulting adults chew their way out, leaving little exit holes. The galls can persist on the tree for several more years, often turning dark with black, sooty mold.

The free-flying adults (all females; males have not been found for this species) lay their eggs again in late fall and the eggs overwinter. Progression from larva to pupa to adult may actually occur a year or more after the development of the gall (Russo 1979).

These large galls are more than board and room for the cynipid parasites; they also attract a great many other creatures which exploit the plant growth on the gallfly larvae or even the other exploiters. Few galls escape multiple exploitation by such things as bacteria, fungi, mites, midges, other wasps. Many of the predators and parasites are themselves attacked by yet other parasites and predators. The complexity of the oak gall community simply astounds me.

Sea Urchin Gall

Blue Oaks support their share of galls too. The fall, unisexual generation of the Urchin Gall Wasp, *Antron echinus*, is both common and conspicuous. The galls appear about the time the leaves drop, an ecological timing that may be adaptive for the emergence of the adult wasp stage in November. The bright red or pink rounded leaf galls bristle with thick spines that bend slightly or fork near their tips. They are slightly sticky to the touch and emit a light, sweet fragrance. Russo (1979) describes the common form as deep red to purple, a rarer form from Sonoma County as pink with white-tipped spines. In the Sutter Buttes I found the "rarer" pink and white form to be more common than the red ones.

Equally fantastic are the galls of the Spined Turban Gall Wasp, *Antron douglasii*. Attached to the leaf by a narrow stem, the gall broadens as it rises, then flares out into a flattened circle with heavy spines encircling its perimeter.

The genus to which the California Gallfly belongs has other representatives in the Buttes. *Andricus wiltyae*

Spined Turban Gall

(Felt 1940) or a look-alike makes a leafy bud gall on Valley Oaks. *Andricus crystallinus*, the Crystalline Gall Wasp, chooses Blue Oak leaves as sites for its fibrous, hairy galls; aborted galls lack the crystalline hairs. The Saucer Gall Wasp, *Andricus gigas*, creates tiny galls on leaves and staminate flowers of Blue and Scrub Oaks, tepees in the spring and saucers in the fall. *Andricus pattersonae* produces flattened discs, mint-green in color.

Interior Live Oaks support several conspicuous types of galls. The Live Oak Gallfly, *Callirhytis pomiformis*, induces tiny gobletlike galls beneath the leaves in its spring bisexual generation and much larger spherical balls with short spines in its summer unisexual generation. The Ruptured Twig Gall Wasp, *Callirhytis perdens*, lays its eggs in stems, which swell and develop cracks before the larvae mature into adults. Since these galls are integral, built right into the stem, rather than detachable, as are many of the leaf galls, they do interfere with the normal plumbing of the stem, and twigs beyond the galls may be stunted or deformed as a result. Another integral gall is created by the Live Oak Petiole Gall Wasp, *Callirhytis flora*. Several larvae develop in the woody swelling which involves the petiole and midrib vein of the oak leaf. This bisexual generation leads to eggs deposited in acorns, which abort and drop to the ground, where the unisexual larvae develop. After about an 18-month period, the parthenogenetic females emerge and deposit the next generation of eggs in oak petioles again. Also in the Buttes we can find the globular potato-like stem galls of the Twig Club Gall Wasp, *Callirhytis quercussuttoni*, the most obvious product of a complicated several-year, two-generation life cycle.

Scrub Oaks are not ignored by the gall-makers either. Most impressive are the products of the Beaked Twig Gall Wasp, *Disholcaspis plumbella*.

Beaked Twig Gall Wasp

The galls are almost spherical but stretched toward the attachment point at one end and the projecting beak at the other. Ground color is yellowish to deep red, with raised blotches of bright yellow. Older galls lose the bright coloration and persist as brownish to blackish lumps amid the crinkled oak leaves.

Though parasites, the various gall-makers rarely exploit a host so heavily as to kill it; any parasite that kills its host is in fact a predator and is faced with the need to find a new host/prey. A "prudent parasite" does not overtax its host, as declining vigor of the supporting plant may lead to the decline of the parasite as well. But a host tree or shrub may be inflicted with galls of **many** parasites, each minor in its own effects but contributing to a **cumulative** effect that may be serious. Occasionally the activities of a gall-maker may tip the scales against a tree weakened by diseases and injuries. On the other hand, the spread of galls on a plant may be self-limited by density-dependent effects; as populations rise, the gall-inducers may be held in check by parasites, predators, or disease.

Galls are rarely distributed uniformly among all potential host plants. Russo (1979:12) notes that "isolated trees and shrubs and those at the top of a hill or at the edge of a woodland or brushland generally support more gall organisms and galls than plants of the same species in other ecological situations." This is related to the dispersal abilities of the light-bodied wasps, so easily deflected by winds. Then too, some potential hosts seem able to defy the development of gall-makers' eggs, perhaps because of personal vigor capable of withstanding incipient parasitism.

In fall in the Sutter Buttes when flowers are few, a search for galls may yield fascinating discoveries. They are often esthetically pleasing in themselves, but galls also offer us insight into the complexities of natural communities. The life histories that have been studied are often as unusual as anything our imaginations could conceive, and the potential for **new** discoveries is as high as any adventurer could wish for.

The Eight-leggers: Arachnids

Most people would laugh derisively if someone called an eagle a fish or a frog a mammal. Yet far fewer would object to equally invalid assignment of the daddy-long-legs with spiders or even spiders with insects. Class distinctions tend to blur when we look at invertebrates; let's accord them the class they deserve!

Look closely at a spider or scorpion, at a mite or tick. Instead of the insect's three body segments and six legs, the arachnids have two body parts and eight legs. They lack antennae and wings, possess a set of jawlike or fang-bearing chelicerae near the mouth and leglike pedipalps before the first walking legs.

Members of this class share with the class Reptilia a bad press, often undeserved. Opinion polls often rank spiders close to snakes as objects of fear and loathing. Our prejudices often blind us to remarkable adaptations and beauty, always there for any who can **see.**

Because its sting has neurotoxic venom, a scorpion is somewhat dangerous to humans, though **far** more dangerous to its insect and spider prey. We encounter one occasionally in the Buttes beneath a rotting log or flat stone, where it is an object of curiosity, nothing to fear. Once we found a female with dozens of pale miniatures riding her back, a type of maternal solicitude seemingly at variance with the reputation she has as a lover (after a prolonged and very cautious courtship, the male may become the female's next meal!).

Daddy-long-legs or harvestmen, superficially like extended spiders, are in an order of their own. They build no webs, but scavenge or catch other invertebrates for food. Paired stink glands deter some predators, and brittle, easily lost legs may distract others, at least briefly.

More than 35,000 species of spiders occur worldwide; North America has fewer than 10% of these. All are predatory, piercing their prey with fangs and digesting them at least partially outside the body by secreting enzymes, later pumping in the broth.

Nearly all North American spiders are harmless to man; it is ironic that the occasional poisoning, rarely fatal, from a Black Widow has been generalized into a wholesale fear of the entire group. Terror of the outhouse seat, *Latrodectus mactans* normally stays in her irregular web, where she bites only in self-defense or to protect her egg sac which she suspends in the web. She is a handsome spider, her large spherical abdomen shiny black with a red hourglass pattern underneath. The male is smaller, proportionately longer-legged, with a slender abdomen marked with red and white. He doesn't bite. Like most spiders, the male must approach the female with caution. Many a successful mating ends with the ultimate sacrifice, the male's devoured proteins reorganized within the "widow" to become the future bearers of their genes.

Garden Spider

Autumn is spider season, when morning dew sparkles on each night's production of webs, when males seek out females for mating and when females construct their egg cases to overwinter. An ambitious web-spinner, the female Black and Yellow Garden Spider, *Argiope aurantia,* is perhaps most conspicuous, an inch long creature with banded legs and black, egg-shaped abdomen with vivid yellow spots. Once I accidentally startled a grasshopper, which struck a garden spider web, with considerable force. The web rebounded but held the struggling grasshopper. With amazing speed, the female *Argiope* dashed out and began wrapping her prey, twice her size. Once subdued, the grasshopper received the spider's kiss of death, soon becoming a major meal for a creature which lives a feast-or-famine existence.

Then there are Long-jawed Orb Weavers, *Tetragnatha,* which hold their

Funnel Web Spider

long legs in the same plane as their elongate bodies, adept at hiding on one side of slender grass stems. Their webs are generally horizontal and, by keeping in touch with radial threads, they can respond quickly to those vibrations indicating that a guest has arrived for dinner.

The Funnel Web Spider of the genus *Agelenopsis* builds sheet webs of nonadhesive silk, barrier webs above, and funnels in which the predator itself lurks. Alert and quick-footed, the spider dashes out to seize insects blundering into its barriers. Like most spiders, its eight eyes suffice for prey detection and capture but probably do not give it a sharp image to study. Hence one can move in slowly to within a few inches, look it in the eyes, and ponder that unbridgeable gulf between us that neither will ever span.

Sometimes while admiring the lacy fronds of Maidenhair Ferns on a shady hillside, I have found mysterious turrets in the soil, vertical cylindrical shafts with elevated lips of plant debris bound together by silk. Though their inhabitants were hidden away below ground, I reasoned that the silk construction implicated spiders. Research then led me to the name *Atypoides riversi*, appropriately the Turret Spider. Turrets come in different sizes, reflecting the size of the maker. They are fascinating constructions, and I vow that some day I will sit nearby to learn what I can first-hand.

The family Salticidae contains the jumping spiders. They are leaping predators, eschewing the use of capture webs but spinning little silken shelters and using a silk dragline like a safety rope. In the Buttes I have found the tiny *Phidippus,* a compact black, hairy-legged spider with dazzling metallic green chelicerae. Its eyes are well-developed, the two largest being intense black beads with strong highlights reflected in them. Unlike most spiders, it hunts visually, actually able to form a sharp image of

Jumping Spider

objects within the distance of a foot or so. It also employs visual signals, bright colors and elaborate dances, in its courtship. As Dave Cavagnaro said (1972:73): "If only this magnificent creature were larger he would be as familiar to us as the hummingbird, peacock, or bird of paradise."

A colorful patch of spring wildflowers is sure to attract a good variety of insects, and it's common to find the arachnid equivalent of a highwayman lying in wait. Crab spiders of the genus *Misumena* in the family Thomisidae are yellow or white, actually able to change between the colors in a week or two. They are broad and crablike in shape and movements, scuttling over quickly to snatch a flower visitor, often larger than themselves. I've seen them with the relatively enormous Pipevine Swallowtail, Bumblebee, Honeybee, and Crane Fly, as well as smaller insects. Fortunately, swallowing such huge prey is unnecessary; digestive juices can do the trick externally, and the spider can extract the nutritive soup while leaving the hollow hulk behind.

Sometimes a yellow crab spider may blend perfectly with its substrate,

Crab Spider

perhaps a Gold Nuggets. Other times it may stand out like a sore thumb, bright yellow against the violet-blue of an ookow or the green or red of a Poison Oak leaf. Whether or not the color is effectively cryptic for prey deception, it obviously is not important much of the time. I have seen flies walking on flower clusters right next to another of their kind in the clutches of a crab spider.

These fascinating spiders are only too willing to cooperate in simple predation experiments. I have experimentally introduced small caterpillars to the flowers upon which a crab spider resided. Zap! Students of all ages are thus given a vivid demonstration of one of the forces of natural selection.

Mites and ticks make up yet another arachnid order, Acarina. Ubiquitous in nearly all environments and abundant in numbers, these miniscule creatures are of enormous economic importance to man. Many are parasites of vertebrates, invertebrates, and plants; we consider them pests if we have other plans for those hosts but useful biological control agents when they attack other species that we define as pests. At present scientists have names for roughly 1000 species of ticks and 30,000 species of mites, but perhaps a **million** more species of mites remain to be identified (Milne and Milne 1980). That impresses me, avid collector of Latin names that I am, for I'm incapable of calling up from memory a **single** genus of mite or tick. Now if they had feathers, I might do better!

A walk through brushy woods in North America is the way to go tick-hunting, though I have been surprised how rarely I find one in the Sutter Buttes. Most of the ticks I have seen have been attached near the ear openings of larger Western Fence Lizards. Deer, foxes, hares undoubtedly have them but usually do not allow me the luxury of close examination that a lizard in the hand affords.

A close look at a patch of cushion mosses or the leaves of shrubbery may reward me with sight of a mite, a tiny red Velvet Mite (*Trombidium*) or a paler Spider Mite (*Tetranychus*). In slow-moving water I often find the surprisingly bright Red Freshwater Mite (*Limnochares*). It seems to me as it scoots about through the water as a totally benign and innocent creature, yet I know that as a larva, it is parasitic; as a nymph or adult it is predatory.

Trombidium, Tetranychus, Limnochares — I forget them as soon as I read them, try as I mite.

References

Barnes, R.D. 1968. *Invertebrate Zoology.* W.B. Saunders Co., Philadelphia.

Borror, D.J. and White, R.E. 1970. *A Field Guide to the Insects.* Houghton Mifflin Co., Boston.

Cavagnaro, D. 1972. *This Living Earth.* American West Publ. Co., Palo Alto, Calif.

Edmunds, G.F., Jr., Jensen, S.L., and Berner, L. 1976. *The Mayflies of North and Central America.* University of Minnesota Press, Minneapolis.

Emmel, T.C. and Emmel, J.F. 1973. *The Butterflies of Southern California.* Natural History Museum, Los Angeles Co. Science Ser. 26.

Felt, E.P. 1940. *Plant Galls and Gall Makers.* Comstock Publ. Co., Ithaca, N.Y.

Hanski, I. 1980. Movement patterns in dung beetles and in the dung fly. *Animal Behaviour* 28:953-964.

Hutchins, R.E. 1966. *Insects.* Prentice-Hall, Englewood Cliffs, N.J.

Mani, M.S. 1964. *Ecology of Plant Galls.* Dr. W. Junk, The Hague.

Menke, A.S., ed. 1978. *The Semiaquatic and Aquatic Hemiptera of California.* Bulletin of the California Insect Survey, Vol. 21. University of California Press, Berkeley.

Merritt, R.W. and Cummins, K.W. 1978. *An Introduction to the Aquatic Insects of North America.* Kendall/Hunt Publ. Co., Dubuque, Iowa.

Miller, J.W. 1981. An insect and a fish. *Audubon* 83(4):60-65.

Milne, L. and Milne, M. 1980. *The Audubon Society Field Guide to North American Insects and Spiders.* Alfred A. Knopf, New York.

Parker, G.A. 1978. Searching for mates. Pp. 214-244, *in* J.R. Krebs and N.B. Davies, *Behavioral Ecology: an Evolutionary Approach.* Sinauer Assoc., Sunderland, Mass.

Peoples, K. 1978. *Butterflies of the Sutter Buttes.* Unpubl. ms.

Powell, J.A. and Hogue, C.L. 1979. *California Insects.* University of California Press, Berkeley.

Pyle, R.M. 1981. *The Audubon Society Field Guide to North American Butterflies.* Alfred A. Knopf, New York.

Riley, N., ed. 1970. *Butterflies and Moths.* Viking Press, New York.

Russo, R.A. 1979. *Plant Galls of the California Region.* Boxwood Press, Pacific Grove, Calif.

Shapiro, A.M. 1974. The butterfly fauna of the Sacramento Valley. *J. Res. Lepidoptera* 13:73-82, 115-122, 137-148.

Smith, E.L. 1970. Biology and structure of the dobsonfly, *Neohermes californicus. The Pan-Pacific Entomologist* 46:142-150.

Swan, L.A. and Papp, C.S. 1972. *The Common Insects of North America.* Harper and Row, New York.

Usinger, R.L., ed. 1956. *Aquatic Insects of California.* University of California Press, Berkeley.

von Frisch, K. 1974. *Animal Architecture.* Harcourt, Brace, Jovanovich, New York.

Wiggins, G.B. 1977. *Larvae of the North American Caddisfly Genera (Trichoptera).* University of Toronto Press, Buffalo, N.Y.

8

Stepping Out: Amphibians

Amphibians get the credit for a great evolutionary breakthrough — the transition from an aquatic to a terrestrial environment for a vertebrate. This was no small step. Air and water are drastically different media. Water provides more support for the body against the tugs of gravity, yet offers much more resistance against movement. Body water and salts are more available in the aquatic medium, oxygen more so in air. Temperature changes are far more pronounced upon land than in water. The transition offered incredible opportunities for exploitation of a new environment, but it required rather drastic changes in body structure, locomotion, respiration, sensory control, and so on. It did not occur in an instant.

That great step is buried deep within our own genetic memories. As embryos, we pass through stages which reflect the evolutionary sequence from water to land. Gill clefts develop well before we develop lungs. Our kidney proceeds from fishlike to froglike to mammalian. Our heart goes from two-chambered, as in a fish, to three-chambered, as in a frog, to four-chambered, as in a bat or rat or any other mammal (Baker and Allen 1971). In a sense, we are genetically indebted to the first amphibians. When's the last time you thanked a frog?

The frogs, toads, and salamanders have moist, glandular skin. They differ from all other vertebrates by lacking specialized "dermal appendages", such as the scales, feathers, and hair that adorn fishes and reptiles, birds, and mammals respectively (Stebbins 1951). Protecting their moist skins constrains their movements, yet even by keeping a low profile, they have succeeded admirably in colonizing many habitats.

Amphibians may be mostly aquatic (many salamanders) to highly terrestrial (many toads). It is their **eggs** that tie them to water. As Baker and Allen (1971:598) so aptly say: "Water supplies oxygen and carries off metabolic wastes. Water serves as a shock absorber to prevent damage to the eggs from sudden jarring. Indeed, the complexity of the amphibian egg is an **internal** complexity; on the outside, the presence of water allows the luxury of simplicity". The reptiles, mammals, and birds are the results of the evolutionary solutions to independence from water for reproduction, and their eggs are complex relative to those of amphibians.

Most amphibians thus have two very different generations — an aquatic larval stage and a terrestrial or semiterrestrial adult life. Parental care is rare, so most parents emphasize quantity instead of quality in offspring. They make large bets of small denominations. For Bullfrogs, where a big female may produce up to 20,000 eggs in a mating period, the chances of an egg becoming a sexually mature frog are about 1 in 10,000 (Howard 1979).

In the Sutter Buttes area, we have but four known species of amphibians: the California Slender Salamander, Western Toad, Bullfrog, and Pacific Treefrog (checklist Appendix G). Compare them with the diverse forms occurring elsewhere in North America by consulting a field guide (Stebbins 1966, Behler and King 1979, Ransom 1981). North of Mexico, this continent hosts approximately 112 species of salamanders and 81 species of frogs and toads (Behler and King 1979).

The Lungless Salamander Family: Plethodontidae

Salamanders may have made the great evolutionary step from water to land, but they certainly are not the type to crow about it. Frogs and toads, at least in the breeding season, proclaim their presence in choruses audible over great distances. Not only do salamanders tend to be mute, they are secretive as well. For six years I have looked in springs, streams, and water tanks; lifted boards and logs; looked in nooks and crannies that no one but an avid naturalist or genuine raccoon would consider. No salamanders.

Perhaps it takes an authentic herpetologist to find one. Tom Rodgers, the real thing, tells me of collecting a California Slender Salamander along the edge of a valley in the north part of the Buttes. So they are there, hiding effectively underground, in leaf litter, beneath logs and debris. A mere three to six inches long, an adult salamander of this type seems scarcely more than a fat worm with two pairs of miniscule legs seemingly tacked on as an afterthought. When unpressed, they actually pull themselves along with those minute appendages, but when alarmed, they lash their bodies with snakelike undulations. It apparently doesn't require great speed to come up with their diet of insects, sowbugs, millipedes, small slugs, and earthworms (Stebbins 1951).

Adults are truly terrestrial creatures, vulnerable to drowning if caught too long in water. They lay their eggs in moist areas in rotten wood or the soil, generally in our winter months, the wet season.

The Sutter Buttes population appears to be a relict one, survivors of a population more widespread during a time of moister climate. The species does occur in the Sierran foothills, and occasionally an individual is found on the floor of the Sacramento Valley near streams where it could have been washed out as a rider on debris. As an isolated population, the Sutter Buttes animals are potentially a source of genetic novelty. Seeing even **one** of these elusive creatures would be a novelty for me!

The Toad Family: Bufonidae

As a freshman in high school, I undertook a year-long biology project raising and observing a variety of frogs and toads, my "amphibifamily". The slick, graceful, colorful frogs were a challenge to capture and a delight to behold. Almost as an afterthought, I added a drab and sluggish Western Toad to the the terrarium.

I had mostly ignored toads up until then. Now I could look at one within a few inches of my nose. By human standards, the creature looked pathetic: squat, stout body like a lumpy, hunch-backed beanbag; bowed legs and stubby, splayed fingers; broad, ear-to-ear mouth permanently down-turned; bulging eyes with bulbous glands behind them; a toothless gape with thick tongue; a weak and sagging, undercut chin; a pale yellow stripe down its back (symbolic of cowardice?); a loose, blotchy skin with

Western Toad

innumerable pits, pocks, and warts. The toad wasn't even a good leaper, moving slowly and awkwardly by alternating its chubby limbs in a foot-dragging shamble.

In time, the toad became my favorite, the amphibian with the most "personality". I grew to admire the functional beauty of the very traits that at first for me, as for many casual observers, epitomized "ugliness". I realize now that my conversion to toad champion from toad detractor was just a change of polarization, in neither case defensible. I had in each case personified the toad, judged it by human standards which likely are totally irrelevant to toad standards.

Ironically, even as a trained and ingrained biologist, I find it impossible to view animals except through my human eyes, and totally impossible to empathize with how a toad would view another toad! Yet if I were able to convince myself and others to adopt a truly impartial view of an animal, could we remain "disinterested" without becoming "uninterested"? Would we lose our ability to care about and relate to other organisms and in that "unbiased" ignorance accelerate the destruction of them and ourselves? Animals **are** interesting, and studying them can be stimulating, provocative, even self-illuminating. It's not hopelessly foolish or irresponsible to **like** animals; they need all the friends they can get! The best we can do is not be blinded by our human viewpoint and be cautious about our judgments.

Now that I've justified my changing attitudes toward toads, I can return to discussing them. What ancient creatures they are! Proto-toads slipped through the aquatic-terrestrial boundary layer repeatedly for a hundred million years or so before the first birds took flight. We newcomer primates had nothing to do with the evolutionary making of a toad, yet our present activities are often their undoing. Habitat changes and introduction of aliens (e.g., Bullfrogs) have knocked them back in many places. And how can they defend themselves? If we were to **bite** one, we'd have the same reaction of nausea, irregular heart beat, and throat inflammation that a dog or other would-be predator suffers upon mandibulating a *Bufo*. Yet biting isn't our style, so we are spared the only effective counter-measure a toad has. Despite the mythology, a toad can't even give us warts.

The insect-eating habits (ants, flies, mosquitoes, beetles, weevils, caterpillars, etc.) of toads make them useful allies to man, though occasionally they take advantage of bees at the entrances to their hives. Slightly elevating the hive eliminates this temptation to toads.

Most of the day, a toad will hide out in cool, moist surroundings beneath vegetation or a log or in a rodent burrow. As evening comes on, they amble forth in search of food. On our evening Buttes walks, we hear them shuffling among the dry leaves or see them by moonlight as they stolidly climb over cobbles and limbs in unwavering determination.

Though individuals are by nature stay-at-homes, living within a half-acre most of their lives, the species has managed to occupy an incredible variety of habitats, from Alaska to Baja and through much of the intermountain west, from sea level to 10,000 feet. Basically land-lubbers as adults, they return to shallow, fairly still waters for breeding. The small male (up to 3½ inches) calls with "a birdlike chirping sound consisting of mellow, tremulous notes" (Stebbins 1951) to attract the burly (4-5 inches) female. He clasps her from behind the forelimbs and fertilizes the two gelatinous strings of eggs (ten thousand or so) as they are laid in the water. The strings tangle in the vegetation, eventually hatching out tiny black tadpoles, which feed by scraping algae from plant and bottom surfaces. In 30-45 days, they metamorphose into black mini-toads and leave the water.

Some of the temporary ponds may be gone soon thereafter; I wonder if young toads can accelerate the change if they sense that the pond will dry up from around them. At times the shoreline swarms with thousands of emerging toadlets; I've seen garter snakes bloated and lethargic during the mass emergence, too sated to eat but a small fraction of the emigrants. That, presumably, is why Nature favored the synchrony of development. Once again, I am impressed by the apparent cleverness of that nonconscious sieve, natural selection. Were I to make a toad, I could not have done better.

The True Frog Family: Ranidae

Of the 21 North American species of *Rana,* only one was native to the Sacramento Valley, and its range has been sharply reduced by habitat changes and competition from introduced Bullfrogs. The Red-legged Frog, *Rana aurora,* was considered common at Gray Lodge in the 1940-1950 era but presumably is gone now (John Cowan, undated checklist).

Many of the valley backwaters and marshes resound on summer evenings with the *basso profundo* choruses of Bullfrogs. Native to the eastern United States, the meaty-legged frogs were introduced to the Sacramento Valley in 1905 or so and spread readily. The marshes gained a voracious predator on insects (mostly aquatic forms), spiders, snails, crayfish, small fish, frogs and tadpoles (including some of their own species), small snakes, mice, a few birds. In turn, Bullfrogs and their larvae fall prey to many mammals (mink, otter, raccoon, etc.), birds (herons, bitterns, egrets, some hawks, cranes, etc.), snakes, large fish, and, of course, people, who prize their legs in an equally predatory way. Tossing the Bullfrog into a tightly woven ecological web must have sent major reverberations in all directions!

The breeding system of Bullfrogs is complex and fascinating (Howard 1979). The throaty "jug-o'rum" bellows emanating from a pond at night reflect a territorial system among the larger males, simultaneously advertising for mates and warning rivals of their proprietary claims. A male intruder is

Bullfrog

warned by more threats, then attacked physically and engaged in wrestling combat of brute strength. Several battles may recur if the males are similar in size, but almost invariably, the larger male wins. Thus size makes might, allowing the biggest males to control areas which may be most attractive to potential mates.

Unlike the braggadocio males, the females seem secretive, staying in sheltered areas near shore away from the noisy males until the mating urge overcomes them. Then they venture out and approach males silently, "shopping around" among several, presumably judging them as suitors and/or their territories as nurseries for their eggs. It pays to be choosy and to go for the biggest males, for they control the best territories, and tadpole survival through faster developmental rates and lower predation is much higher there.

Since fertilization is external, a male can have 100% certainty that he is father to the fertilized eggs; there are no secrets such as those hidden by the internal plumbing of salamanders, reptiles, birds, and mammals. If the paternal Bullfrog were the type to invest in his offspring — food, protection, gifts of any kind — he could do so without fear of wasting his effort on someone else's progeny. Alas, the life styles of tadpole and frog are **so** different, the ultimate generation gap, that his confidence of paternity can hardly be translated into parental solicitude. He and his mate for the evening can do little for their offspring but provide them the best possible nursery site.

Older, bigger females are particularly mate-conscious and go for those macho goliaths dominating the best sites. A big female may lay up to 20,000 eggs during a mating; a small one perhaps as few as 6,000. Hence the biggest males can corner the market on a season's gene production, scoring with multiple matings and with the most fecund females. Often more than half the males in a local area may not mate at all, and those which do mate on inferior territories often have low survival of eggs and larvae.

Obviously, bigger is better in Bullfrogs. But recall that Bullfrogs don't live alone in their ponds. Big males, active and vociferous, often are prime prey prospects for hungry predators and are picked off at a higher rate than the quieter members of the population. Big mouth means bigger risk.

Then too, the popularity of the big boys with the females can be exploited by small males. Physically inferior, a younger male may seek out the territory of a "big daddy", hanging around inconspicuously, quietly, ready to flee if challenged by the territory owner, and, most of all, ready to grab at a female attracted in by the waterlord. If he grabs one, she resists, kicking violently, but eventually she ceases to struggle and lets out the eggs. By this time the small male and "reluctant bride" have moved away from the big male's territory (he won't tolerate them there and can't disengage them), probably to a lower quality site where most of the eggs will fail. Yet this opportunism, really parasitism of the big males, is a small male's only chance of any short-term reproductive success. In the long run, he could eat a lot and try to become **big**, but there are many possible unknowns (accidents, predators, diseases, etc.) between little and large.

Medium-sized males employ a mixed strategy. They call and act as if they had territories whenever they can get away with it, but move off elsewhere and try again when challenged by a bigger male. They keep an eye on their neighbors. If mostly bigger males are around, they may act "small" — satellites orbiting the nuclear male, ready to intercept the trajectory of an approaching female. If neighbors are mostly smaller too, they will likely set up their own territories.

Flexible and opportunistic, the Bullfrog is beautifully adapted to a variable physical and biological environment. How can we so blithely dismiss frogs as dull and simple based on our random observations of sleepy but wary amphibians on their off-hours? To see them for what they are, we need a headlamp, copious applications of insect repellent, boots or boat, and the gumption to venture into the marsh at 3 a.m. Time, patience, careful observation, and an appropriate philosophical mind-set can reveal remarkable things.

The Treefrog Family: Hylidae

There are nights in the Buttes when it is so still that only your own coarse movements can convince you that you haven't become deaf. You strain your ears but fail to pick up any molecular excitation stimulated by moonbeam on oak leaf. You press your face hard against an andesite boulder in hopes of detecting in those crystalline bonds echoes of far-off seismic tremors. Nothing.

Then there are nights when the treefrogs sing. A tiny pond can become the amphitheater for a hard-rock concert of hundreds of amphibian voices, an incredible chorus that can drown out all other nearby nocturnal noises. Walk slowly up to the edge of the pond. Suddenly the din ceases and silence rushes in. Wait. A tentative "kreck-ek" begins, repeats, is joined by another. In a few minutes, the pond is again rocking with high-decibel sound.

The Pacific Treefrog belts out his high tenor tones at an amplitude wholly out of proportion to his sub-two-inch size. His throat expands to a sizeable globular pouch that serves as a reson- ating chamber and amplifier. Many males assemble in stock ponds, springs, ditches, marshes, and the like and to- gether produce a chorus loud enough to attract females from some distance.

Pacific Treefrog

When ready to mate, the female ventures into the pond where many suitors await her. The mating pair spends perhaps four to twenty or more hours in the amphibian embrace, amplexus, in which the male clasps the female over her back and just behind her forelimbs. Egg-laying and fertiliz- ing is an extended process, the eggs issuing in irregular clusters of 9-70 eggs each until the full number of perhaps 600 eggs has been achieved (Stebbins 1951).

Eggs are enclosed in two gelatinous envelopes, the outer one sticky. These clusters become attached to many kinds of objects, effectively anchoring them in favorable developmental sites. The envelopes also inhibit certain types of egg predation.

Hatching in about two weeks, the young tadpoles in temporary ponds must grow quickly enough to metamorphose into tiny frogs before their aquatic environment disappears. They are lovely larvae — dark above and light below with bronze or coppery iridescence; golden iris; full-bodied torsos with vertically flattened tails.

The adult frog is equally beautiful, with large (expressive?) eyes, slim waist, stylish black mask, and attractive patterning of dark spots against the ground color. We usually think of treefrogs as green, but they may be gold, tan, reddish, brown, grey, or black. In fact, an individual frog can change from blackish to pale in a matter of five to ten minutes — dermal camouflage to match the substrate.

Primarily ground-dwellers who scorn trees, the Pacific Treefrog is neverthe- less an able climber with the aid of adhesive pads on its expanded toe tips. When away from water, it retreats to cool, moist areas to protect its skin. This species occurs all the way from British Columbia to Baja, from sea level to 13,000 feet, a most remarkable range of tolerance for a "cold-blooded" animal.

References

Baker, J.J.W. and Allen, G.E. 1971. *The Study of Biology.* Addison-Wesley Publ. Co., Reading, Mass.

Behler, J.L. and King, F.W. 1979. *The Audubon Society Field Guide to North American Reptiles and Amphibians.* Alfred A. Knopf, New York.

Howard, R.D. 1979. Big bullfrogs in a little pond. *Natural History* 88(4):30-36.

Ransom, J.E. 1981. *Harper and Row's Complete Field Guide to North American Wildlife, Western Edition.* Harper and Row, New York.

Stebbins, R.C. 1951. *Amphibians of Western North America.* University of California Press, Berkeley.

Stebbins, R.C. 1966. *A Field Guide to Western Reptiles and Amphibians.* Houghton Mifflin Co., Boston.

9

Scaling Down: Reptiles

Considering our ancient origins, we show a surprising lack of gratitude to reptiles. Our folklore is replete with scandalously inaccurate depictions of the creatures. We harass and destroy many species without mercy. Even the name "reptile", derived from Latin for "a creeping thing", has rather negative connotations that do not characterize these creatures universally or exclusively (Oliver 1955). Let's give them a break, taking a closer look with a stout promise to be fair and impartial.

While the great debate rages over "which came first, the chicken or the egg?", reptiles continue to produce the complex types of shelled eggs that enabled the major evolutionary conquest of land. No longer was it necessary to depend upon the aquatic environment to shelter and buffer a fragile egg. "The birds did not invent the shelled egg, they inherited it" (Carr 1963).

Reptiles went another step beyond the amphibians for terrestrial living by developing a tougher, less permeable skin armored with scales and reduced in glandular function. Gills were out; all reptiles breathe using lungs, though some turtles absorb oxygen through the pharynx, as well.

The Age of Reptiles saw incredible diversity of forms develop to exploit the land, the seas, the air. Some of the large predatory dinosaurs very likely were warm-blooded, endothermic, able to control body temperature internally to some extent. From 100-200 million years ago, reptiles dominated the earth, as yet free from competition from birds and mammals. These latter-day offshoots from reptiles, though probably not the sole causes of declining reptile influence, clearly had a negative impact on a good many species. Perhaps the final reptilian revenge, albeit unwittingly, was the very late evolution of the snakes with their subsequent impacts on the feathered and furred. The serpent in the garden bothers us still.

Turtles, crocodiles, and a few other minor reptiles constitute about 5% of the living reptiles; most of the 6000 or so species belong to a single order, Squamata, containing the typical lizards and snakes. Usually lizards have limbs and snakes do not, but there are minor exceptions. Lizards have ears, movable eyelids, a fixed mouth size; snakes lack ears, have permanently open eyes protected by glassy transparent scales, and expandable jaws. Internally, they differ significantly. Most lizards feed fairly regularly, while snakes employ the feast-and-famine approach, having great ability to fast, then eat prodigiously. Both have internal fertilization by means of a pair of hollow hemipenes, inserting one side only according to angle of approach.

Though hardly model parents along the lines of some birds and mammals, reptiles have eliminated the need for the profligate production of "cheap" eggs employed by most amphibians. Unlike the thousands of eggs spewed out by a frog or toad, a small number of higher quality eggs, or in some cases live-born young, are generated by reptiles. Based on average clutch/brood sizes for Sierran reptiles (Verner and Boss 1980), I calculated that in the Sutter Buttes area, our average turtle produces 7 eggs, lizard 8 eggs, and snake 12 eggs or young. Once they enter the world, however, the young reptiles are basically on their own, and some of their potential predators include bigger members of their own species.

North America north of Mexico has about 115 species each of lizard and snake (Behler and King 1979); we have 5 and 9 respectively in the Buttes (checklist Appendix G). Our lone turtle has 25 other family members in the United States, mostly in the east.

The Freshwater Turtle Family: Emydidae

The toothless fixed "grin" of a Western Pond Turtle gives it an air of smug tolerance for the lately-arrived mammals and birds that share its world. It basks in the sun on log or bank and slips quickly into the water if approached by a large, possibly dangerous vertebrate. For 175 million years, its rigid shell has served its kind as built-in armor. Though amphibious in choice of habitat, it is far from being an amphibian. It is completely reptilian in having internal fertilization and in producing a small number (3-11) of shelled eggs in a nest on land.

Each turtle embryo must go through great contortions to come up with that protective shell. Acrobatics are out for a turtle; its backbone is fused to its shell. Its ribs are flattened and broadened for structural support, and its shoulders and hips occupy what in most vertebrates would be the chest. It can't breathe by expanding its chest, so it must use special muscles to push around its viscera and other organs to achieve air flow through its lungs (Carr 1903).

No one can accuse the turtle of hastiness or hyperactivity. At Gray Lodge or in the Butte Sink, a pond turtle may spend much of the daytime basking in the sun. During drought, it may spend weeks in virtual inactivity buried in sheltering mud. One may go months without eating and years without sex, yet a female may produce viable eggs several years after her last contact with a male. The slow pace often goes with a long life — dull, perhaps compared to that of a shrew or man, but who are we to judge?

The Lizard Family: Iguanidae

The Western Fence Lizard, alias Blue-belly or Western Swift, is the most conspicuous reptile in the Sutter Buttes. They scamper about boulders, along fences, and up the rough bark of oak trees. Males give exaggerated push-up displays, flashing the brilliant blue scales of throat and belly to intimidate rivals. For a cold-blooded animal that prefers open, conspicuous basking sites, a visual signal, economical to produce, is better than a vocal one; the blue patches are the lizards' counterpart to bird song.

Sagebrush Lizard

Western Fence Lizard

A close relative, the Sagebrush Lizard, shares the Sutter Buttes with the Western Fence. They look much alike, but the somewhat smaller Sagebrush has finer (and hence more) back scales, smoother scales on the backs of the thighs (which are grey rather than yellow to orange), and rusty armpits (Stebbins 1966, Ransom 1981).

The Sagebrush Lizard "ought not" to be here, for most populations are found at higher altitudes (it's also called the Mountain Swift). According to Rodgers (1953), the Sutter Buttes population is 40 miles west of its nearest range in the Sierra Nevada and 45 miles east of its nearest habitat in the Coast Range. The Buttes area is both the hottest and lowest environment in its range. Presumably during glacial advances the cooler climate allowed continuous contact between Buttes and Sierran populations, but postglacial warming and drying forced Sierran populations to higher altitudes. Sagebrush Lizards in the Buttes had nowhere up to go! The change must have been gradual enough for some members of the population to adapt, leaving descendants in a rather unlikely location. Rodgers believes the Sutter Buttes Sagebrush Lizards have been isolated from their Sierran kin for at least 10,000 years.

The two species overlap in size and food habits (insect eaters) and might be expected to compete. Both here and in Santa Clara County where the two overlap, competition seems to be avoided by habitat segregation (Rodgers 1953; Rose 1976). The Western Fence Lizard prefers grass-oak woodlands and is somewhat arboreal; the Sagebrush Lizard frequents more open habitats such as rock outcrops, talus slopes, and the gravelly dry creek bed. The Sutter Buttes Sagebrush Lizards may take refuge from the heat in rock crevices, a habit quite unusual for the species (Rodgers, pers. comm.)

Both species defer breeding until their second year. The larger species lays clutches of 8-9 eggs, compared to 3-4 for the smaller, but the Sagebrush Lizard tends to live longer (Oliver 1955).

The activity thermostats of these cold-blooded creatures are dependent on external heat sources, so they move from shade to sun and back, orient their bodies accordingly, and even control the pigment in their skin to change from light to dark for heat absorption. Cold weather will keep them inactive underground for days.

Basking and displaying in the open have clearcut lizard advantages, but they expose the performer to possible predation by snakes (e.g., Racers) or birds (e.g., American Kestrels, Loggerhead Shrikes) or mammals (e.g., curious young naturalists). The direct approach by a zealous human usually ends in an empty-handed grasp of lichens and rock where the lizard was a second before. The indirect approach using a noose formed from a Wild Oats stem is more successful. Nothing in the evolutionary history of a Western Fence Lizard has prepared it to be suspicious of a grass blade weaving strangely near its head.

Many of the larger lizards we handle have ticks attached in or around the ear openings. The closer we look, the more complicated things become. I often wonder whether the tiny ticks have their own minute parasites attached beyond the range of my unaided vision. I sometimes feel that my senses are as limited in detection as are those of an orb-weaving spider to whom a fly is reality but a person is some unimaginable force that may affect it without warning but is beyond normal comprehension.

The Skink Family: Scincidae

Young children, until indoctrinated with the hesitations and preoccupations developed by so many adults, are natural naturalists. They delight in exploring and are not afraid to use their hands, as well as eyes, in examining things. I love to watch them lifting corners of rocks or rotted logs with expectations of momentous discoveries — and they find them! A shout of surprise erupts when a child spies the dazzling turquoise tail of a Western Skink. Eager hands grasp for the jewel and end up with a twitching whip of blue as the lizard makes good its de-tailed escape. Even grasping the fore part of the lizard is no guarantee of capture, for the overlapping scales are smooth and slippery. The small head and thick neck, along with general wariness, make them hard to noose, as well.

Unlike the *Sceloporus* lizards which use their blue throats and bellies for advertising, the skinks prefer an undercover life and rely on their brilliant tail coloration for its surprise and deflection effects when a would-be predator exposes them. The blue is most evident in juveniles, often changing to the general body color at adulthood. A disposable tail is a small price to pay for survival, and a new tail can be regenerated in time.

Skinks have short legs and propel themselves through leaf litter and soft soil mostly by snakelike undulations of their bodies. Relying more on their sense of smell than on vision, they capture beetles, crickets, moths, spiders, and sow bugs. Lack of visibility in their down-to-earth haunts makes maintaining a true territory impractical and unnecessary.

The female lays 5-10 eggs in a below-ground excavation in early summer. Somewhat surprisingly, she attends the eggs — defending them, turning them as they develop, even brooding them with heat she has absorbed by basking. Such maternal solicitude is rate among reptiles, even though common in the bird and mammal lines which arose from reptilian stock that may have had such tendencies.

The Whiptail Family: Teiidae

Whiptails are runners, not climbers, and their slender balancing tails, long-toed hind feet, and stream-lined bodies are perfect for quick dash/ sudden stop tactics to evade capture. At high speed they run on hind feet with front feet drawn up to the chest, the tail raised for balance, like miniature versions of certain bipedal dinosaurs. During the sprint, the animal's tail lashes about like a whip — hence the name. Yet even whiptails can be captured by the speedy serpent, the Coachwhip. In May of 1981 we found a long, red Coachwhip with half a whiptail still protruding from its mouth. The snake quickly disgorged the lizard and sped off. The lizard appeared dead, but after a few seconds made a gasp and began to breathe. We watched the dazed lizard progress from helplessness to bright-eyed alertness. Finally it moved off in the typical jerky, hot-footed gait of a normal whiptail. Soon it would again be hunting the insects, spiders, and scorpions upon which it feeds, perhaps more alert than before to its own vulnerability to the Coachwhip.

The Western Whiptail has a normal enough sex life, resulting in 4-8 eggs laid in loose soil in May and June. Some whiptails, however, dispense with sex — in fact, dispense with males! These populations, entirely females, produce eggs parthenogenetically and have offspring identical to themselves. The genotype, if not the individual, thus attains something close to immortality.

There are some real advantages to doing without sex. Its not necessary to waste energy finding and satisfying a mate. All one's offspring are identical to oneself, not diluted by a non-relative's genes. Sexual discrimination and male chauvinism are unheard of in all-female populations. Then why are unisexual species so rare?

First, a unisexual population will gradually pick up adverse mutations and can't reverse the process (back mutation is unimportant). Sex allows some offspring to end up without the deleterious genes, since only half the complement of genes comes from each parent. So in the long run, the bisexual population should end up more vigorous than the unisexual one.

More importantly, though, the changes resulting from recombination of genes by sexual reproduction allow better adaptation to changing conditions. If offspring compete for some limited resource, a "patch" so to speak, then a parent producing variable offspring may have the best chance of having one appropriately matched to that somewhat unpredict- able patch. Maynard Smith (1978:167) phrases it well: "Each asexual parent is like a man who buys a number of tickets in the raffle and finds that they all have the same number; in contrast, the sexual parent resembles a man who buys fewer tickets, but all with different numbers".

Thus in the great raffle of life, some whiptail species still hold winning tickets by maintaining all-girl clubs, but they are exceptions (perhaps by habitat choice, they have a less variable environment). A few fishes and amphibians have adopted that style, but no birds nor mammals. Like it or not, we're stuck with sex.

The Alligator Lizard Family: Anguidae

One's heart may jump when one looks among rustling leaf litter and finds a stern yellow-eyed visage peering back from a diamond-shaped scaly head. Even the wriggly locomotion of the Southern Alligator Lizard reminds one of a snake, and that resemblance may at times deter a predator. When grabbed, the lizard may squirm, bite, and discharge excrement, further discouragement to an attacker. It may leave the end of its tail behind, regenerating another in a few weeks. Yet the many individuals I have handled have been inoffensive and gentle, pleasurable to hold and observe.

The broadened head and stiffened skin provide a fortuitous resemblance to

Southern Alligator Lizard

the unrelated alligator. An "expansion joint" (Grinnell and Storer 1924) of soft grainy scales along the side of the body allows some flexibility of movement, breathing, and eating. We have occasionally found perfect shed skins of these lizards in the Buttes. Apparently they are the only lizards that, like snakes, shed their skins in a single piece (Oliver 1955).

These blond-eyed lizards prefer the cover of oak groves, chaparral thickets, and streamside vegetation where they hunt for the Black Widows, other spiders, scorpions, centipedes, millipedes, sowbugs, moths, beetles, caterpillars, mosquitoes, termites, and other small creatures they feed upon. They are our only lizards with a prehensile tail, capable of pulling themselves up on a branch without the aid of other limbs.

The alligator lizards demonstrate how breeding patterns relate to environmental constraints. The Southern Alligator Lizard lays eggs in warm soil or debris to incubate; hatching occurs about two months later. The Northern Alligator Lizard *(Gerrhonotus coeruleus)* occupies cooler, moister habitats and is a live-bearer, retaining the eggs in the female's body until development is complete (Stebbins 1951).

The Common Harmless Snake Family: Colubridae

Seven of the eight species of snakes known for the Buttes belong to this large, diverse family. Worldwide, more than three-fourths of the 2700 or so snake species are Colubrids (Behler and King 1979). Most, ours included, are harmless to man, but they take a great deal of flak by association with their venomous kin. Some benefit indirectly by what appears to be defensive mimicry of their well-armed cousins; they may coil, hiss, and shake their rattleless tails in a rather intimidating display that may discourage an attack by a rattler-wary predator.

Our species have large eyes and large head scales, round pupils, a double row of scales beneath the tail; they lack the sensory pits and poison fangs possessed by rattlers. In general, the more terrestrial types lay eggs and the aquatic types give birth to living young (Goin et al. 1978).

I admit to a certain aversion to snakes myself, but the tiny Ringneck appeals to me—small, colorful, inoffensive, and secretive. Its olive to slaty black contrasts strikingly with its bright orange belly and neck ring. Threatened, it will flash its brilliant underside upward and coil its tail in a tight "thimble", presumably startling or distracting a predator from its more vulnerable parts (Stebbins 1954). Of course, that ruse doesn't always work; I once found a Ringneck dangling in a Coffeeberry bush like a gaudy ribbon, victim of a shrike. In turn, the little snake hunts under logs, stones, and leaf litter for lizards (such as the Western Skink), small snakes (such as young garter snakes), worms, frogs, some insects. It's a sociable snake, seeking shelter under rocks with others of its kind, tracking them there using chemical senses, and even preferring areas where other Ringnecks have recently been (Goin et al. 1978). As to **why,** we can speculate endlessly and run innumerable experimental tests, but in the end we will have no more than statistical probabilities about certain hypotheses; we have no way directly to fathom the reptilian mind.

Racers are found in all states south of Canada. Ours are plain brown or olive above and yellowish below as adults; light with dark blotches as young, rather like a Gopher Snake. Adults and young are so different, more so than any other western snake, as to be easily mistaken for different species (Stebbins 1954). In the eastern United States, Racers tend to be large and black, easily mistaken for the Black Rat Snake, *Elaphe obsoleta.* Linnaeus apparently confused the two when assigning the name *Coluber constrictor* to the Racer, for the latter does **not** constrict its prey but holds it down with loops of the body (Ditmars 1931).

Racers are appropriately named — swift snakes that hunt with head raised, dashing in to seize lizards (especially *Sceloporus* in the Buttes), frogs, small mammals, birds, and large insects. They are capable climbers too and occasionally raid bird nests in shrubbery. Ironically, some fall prey to the talons of swift raptorial hawks and falcons. One bird's enemy may be another's meat.

The Coachwhip, alias Red Racer, takes its common name from its slender body and tail and pronounced scale pattern resembling a braided whip (Stebbins 1966). It amazes me how serpentine undulations of a legless body can propel one so effortlessly across the ground or up into a tree. When threatened, this snake may act most aggressively — coiling, vibrating its tail, striking boldly — or may dash away, as did the fine specimen we found in the process of engulfing a Western Whiptail lizard. "Fine specimen" to me is the individual that goes the other way, not the one that stays to fight, and perhaps a startled snake would define me as a "fine specimen" using the same criteria!

The Gopher Snake is another intimidator, putting on a grand bluff of vigorous hissing, striking, head-flattening, and tail-vibrating which can simulate the behavior of a rattler closely enough to discourage much closer inspection. On the other hand, this tactic may backfire when a human mistakes the harmless snake for a rattler and kills it. Even the cream-colored skin with dark dorsal patterns suggests "rattler" at first glance.

Yet the Gopher Snake benefits man considerably by its liking for rodents (rats, mice, ground squirrels, etc.) which are killed by constriction. Unlike most bird and mammal predators on rodents, the snake can follow its prey beneath ground. It can even dig, loosening the soil with its snout and passing

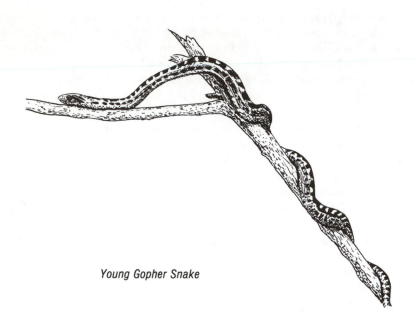

Young Gopher Snake

dislodged dirt back in a loop of the neck. An opportunistic forager, it may occasionally seek birds and their eggs in bushes or small trees, utilizing a special muscular technique to collapse swallowed eggs (Ditmars 1931).

Smooth, reflective scales (*Lampropeltis* means "shiny skin") and alternating patterns of black and white links down the body characterize the Common Kingsnake. These constrictors take both warm-blooded and cold-blooded prey, including other snakes. Rattlers may be victims and react to kingsnakes differently from other creatures. Instead of rattling or striking, they hold their heads low to the ground and use part of the mid-body to make blows; kingsnakes seem to be immune to their venom. Predatory dominance over other snakes accounts for the nomenclatural royalty of the kingsnake. They tame easily, however, and are a delight for appreciative naturalists to hold.

The western race of the Long-nosed Snake has an alternating pattern of black and white bands and could easily be mistaken for the Common Kingsnake. However, its black bands are flecked with white on the sides and its snout protrudes beyond the lower jaw (hence "long-nosed"). Good burrowers, these slim snakes are rarely seen in the daylight. Tom Rodgers collected one at the Dean Place near North Butte in 1946. There surely are others. I often wonder how many nocturnal creatures escape our detection, sometimes so completely that we could alter the landscape and wipe them out without even being aware of their existence. Unfortunately, that too often happens even to conspicuous diurnal creatures; visibility is not always a protection against ignorance.

Our two garter snakes prefer moist areas, swimming readily and relishing aquatic creatures such as frogs and their tadpoles. Our other Colubrids lay eggs; these bear living young, perhaps two dozen at a time. A true placenta is formed through which substances are exchanged between the bloodstreams of mother and embryo (Goin et al. 1978). Maternal protection gives offspring a critical head start in colder environments; the widespread Common Garter Snake extends farther north on this continent than any other reptile (Stebbins 1966).

The Common Garter is a beautiful snake with strong yellow stripe down its back and red patches bordered in black on its sides. The Giant Garter tends to be fairly dark and drab, with stripes obscure or lacking. Both species exude a rather repugnant anal gland secretion when upset and may bite in self-defense when picked up.

The Pit Viper Family: Viperidae

In the West there is a dance that every rancher knows, no matter how limited his social life may be. At the very instant he hears a certain dry, buzzy "s-s-s-s-s-s-s-", he leaps spasmodically into the air, limbs flailing, eyes popping, mouth gasping, often with the utterance of some explosive epithet. No other natural sound can stimulate such an immediate and extreme reaction as the buzz of a rattlesnake. Even a modest imitation, as by a cicada or a Colubrid snake twitching its tail in dry leaves, can provoke the dance. My own pulse quickens, my limbs stiffen, and my throat goes dry just thinking about it.

The Western Rattlesnake tends to be fairly docile, pacific, sluggish, and retiring. Sensing our approaching footsteps by vibrations picked up through its head bones, a snake will usually retreat where it can avoid the risk of being stepped on — or worse. We encounter them far more rarely than we would expect, and then the interaction is usually one of mutual respect and avoidance.

If you look closely (and carefully), you can see how this pit viper differs from the harmless Colubrids. It has vertical, elliptical pupils; pits before the eyes; many small scales on the head; a single row of scales beneath the tail; a blunt tail with dry flattened rattles; a triangular head; and (don't look **too** closely) very big fangs that it can whip out from folded-back sheaths to inject venom hypodermically.

Western Rattlesnake

The rattler is highly evolved for specialized foraging on rather large, warm-blooded prey. The sensory pits on its head enable it to strike effectively at sources of warmth, even when blinded. It is a heat-seeking missile armed with chemical weapons. After the strike, the victim (e.g., a ground squirrel) may flee, but the snake can track the doomed creature by extending its tongue, sampling the ground and air, and performing analytical tests with the sensitive Jacobson's organs within its mouth (Carr 1963). The poison not only incapacitates the prey by action on the blood system but also begins the process of digestion of tissues, even before the snake arrives for its meal.

The typical snake ability to disarticulate its head bones allows it to swallow good-sized prey, even up to rabbit size. Of course people are not intended prey and are occasionally struck only because of defensive gestures by the snake. Striking at a non-edible creature consumes energy and entails considerable risk; a "prudent" snake would gain by avoiding the close encounter entirely. The rattle appears to have no other function than to serve as a warning and reduce chances of injury to its bearer by the large feet or hooves of other animals. The rattle is not used while foraging, when competing physically with another rattler, or when a predatory kingsnake threatens.

The activity of a rattlesnake is limited by temperature. Most retreat to communal dens in rocky areas during winter months though can be encountered on rare, warm winter days. A rancher killed one in the Buttes on January 1, 1981. Another in a boulder patch on South Butte on February 15 rattled its displeasure at our tripping like trolls across its claimed terrain. By mid-March or so, you may be able to find one sunning among rocks, ready to slip away to cover. By May it's possible to encounter one in taller grass away from rocky retreats. By June, hot days inhibit diurnal activity, sending the snakes out to forage at dusk or later. After October, you'd almost have to be a serious herpetologist to locate one.

Mice, rats, and water can attract rattlers, so occasionally they show up at ranch houses at the base of the Buttes, especially late in spring. Newspaper articles have capitalized on public interest/paranoia, sometimes proclaiming, "Rattlesnakes Pour out of the Buttes in Record Numbers". Landowners generally accept, even encourage, such publicity. A good snake story is as good as a fence in keeping trespassers out.

Rattlers do occur in the Sutter Bypass, along the Sacramento River, and elsewhere in the valley, though they are rarely seen. There are but two records for Gray Lodge. The geologist, Howel Williams, who tramped nearly every acre of the Buttes, especially **rocky** ones, never saw one.

Despite a hefty girth and very capable defensive weapons, it may not pay even a big rattler to be brazen about showing itself. Hooves of large grazing animals are dangerous, and so is man (the score of fatalities in man-snake interactions is heavily skewed against the snake). One of my strongest visual memories in the Buttes occurred one summer evening. A full moon rose to the east as the sun set in gory glory to the west. Low overhead flew a mighty Golden Eagle with a 3-4 foot rattlesnake dangling from its talons, a Mexican symbol come to life. So it is in nature, where predator becomes prey, where all creatures provide nutrients for other creatures, where there are no genuine distinctions between the "high" and the "lowly".

References

Behler, J.L. and King, F.W.   1979.   *The Audubon Society Field Guide to North American Reptiles and Amphibians.*   Alfred A. Knopf, New York.

Carr, A.   1963.   *The Reptiles.*   Life Nature Library, Time Inc., New York.

Ditmars, R.L.   1931.   *Snakes of the World.*   Pyramid Publications, New York.

Goin, C.J., Goin, O.B., and Zug, G.R.   1978.   *Introduction to Herpetology.* W.H. Freeman and Co., San Francisco.

Grinnell, J. and Storer, T.I.   1924.   *Animal Life in the Yosemite.*   University of California Press, Berkeley.

Maynard Smith, J.   1978.   The ecology of sex. Chapter 6, in J.R. Krebs and N.B. Davies, eds. *Behavioural Ecology: an Evolutionary Approach.* Sinauer Associates, Inc., Sunderland, Mass.

Oliver, J.A.   1955.   *The Natural History of North American Reptiles and Amphibians.*   D. Van Nostrand Co., Inc., Princeton, N.J.

Ransom, J.E.   1981.   *Harper and Row's Complete Field Guide to North American Wildlife, Western Edition.*   Harper and Row, New York.

Rodgers, T.L.   1953.   Responses of two closely related lizards (genus *Sceloporus*) to different environmental conditions. PhD thesis, University of California, Berkeley.

Rose, B.R.   1976.   Habitat and prey selection of *Sceloporus occidentalis* and *Sceloporus graciosus.*   *Ecology* 57:531-541.

Stebbins, R.C.   1954.   *Amphibians and Reptiles of Western North America.*   McGraw-Hill Book Co., Inc., New York.

Stebbins, R.C.   1966.   *A Field Guide to Western Reptiles and Amphibians.* Houghton Mifflin Co., Boston.

Verner, J. and Boss, A.S., eds.   1980.   *California Wildlife and their Habitats: Western Sierra Nevada.*   U.S. Forest Service Gen. Tech. Rep. PSW-37, U.S. Dept. of Agriculture, Berkeley, Calif.

10

Getting High: Birds

Standing among lofty crags, I can admire the great forces that shaped the rocks and incredible green fabric of plants working to cover them. Yet a special thrill comes when the passiveness of the scene is interrupted by the awesome swoop of a Golden Eagle or the clear, descending series of whistles of a Canyon Wren. A landscape without birds seems alien and incomplete.

Yet systems ecologists who measure biomass, productivity, energy flow, and other factors reducible to numbers and equations often conclude that in many communities birds are fairly insignificant. Invisible microbes and scarcely noticeable insects may be far more abundant and incredibly more vital to the workings of the ecosystem. Remove an eagle here or a half dozen bluebirds there, and there's scarcely a ripple in the biotic pond.

That is not to say, the scientist may quickly add (perhaps sensing the rise of ornithological wrath), that birds might not be important "as governors or controllers rather than direct participants in the functional patterns of ecosystems" (Weins 1973). For example, insect-eating birds might control populations of depredating arthropods that could, unchecked, destroy vegetation for which we might have other consumptive plans (e.g., crops, forests).

Even if birds were to prove to be the frills of an ecosystem, let's freely admit that we like to look at the frills! It's tempting, though foolhardy, to think that

Brewer's Blackbird

birds are showing off for our benefit. A brilliantly-colored Lazuli Bunting perched conspicuously on a high twig, filling the air with liquid melodies, can scarcely be ignored. Yet admitting that the beauty and grace of a bird are functional traits useful to the bird itself, not present for our benefit or delight, in no way detracts from the miracle of that bird.

Darwin was as moved by the sight of a bird as was Thoreau. He found no need to interpret bird structure or behavior in purely human terms, for there were perfectly good biological explanations no less remarkable.

The birds we see in the Sutter Buttes today (checklist Appendix H) reflect some two million years or so of change and interaction at that location, as well as a much longer period of time in which organisms were developing and "being fitted" for their niches. We, or more precisely, our human predecessors, have been part of the selective interaction, at least on populations and behaviors of birds, if not on shapes of bills or hues of feathers. No doubt birds have reciprocated in a way; my reaction to eagle or wren reflects both biological and cultural background.

Please forgive me, then, if my attention to birds seems to outweigh my interest in certain other animals and plants, especially those best viewed through a hand lens or microscope. The very visibility of birds — their usually diurnal habits, songs, flight patterns, bright plumages, and relatively high diversity — renders them especially appropriate for observation and yields abundant data for us to examine.

Compared to staid and stable oak trees, birds are mobile and flighty. Populations turn over fairly rapidly, migration constantly reshuffles the cast of characters, and local distribution may vary greatly even within a single day. Yet on a more general scale, we do find a fairly high degree of predictability.

Walk through a Sutter Buttes oak woodland with me. Any day of the year, we would probably find a Plain Titmouse, Nuttall's Woodpecker, or Scrub Jay.

If we saw a Ruby-crowned Kinglet, Dark-eyed Junco, or Hermit Thrush, it could not be summer. If we encountered a Western Kingbird, Northern Oriole, or Black-headed Grosbeak, it could not be winter. The presence of a Solitary Vireo, Townsend's Warbler, or Lawrence's Goldfinch would strongly imply April or May.

Birds, then, are reasonably predictable by habitat and by season (Table 3). Some habitat generalists may appear almost anywhere, and exceptions do occur; birding would lose a bit of its appeal if rarities out of place and time could not be found. Still, it's rather remarkable that creatures "as free as a bird" should so strikingly seem constrained by habitat and seasonal changes.

The table reveals that year-round residents are common and that winter residents outnumber those coming just for the summer breeding period. Mild winter weather of the low elevation Sacramento Valley permits mingling of "locals" and winter fugitives from higher latitudes or altitudes. Even species breeding here in small numbers may be supplemented by birds of the same species which bred elsewhere (American Robin, Northern Flicker, Rufous-sided Towhee, some waterfowl).

Table 3 indicates general seasonal occurrence and habitat preference but not abundance. Appendix H serves as an overall checklist of Sutter Buttes birds and suggests the likelihood of encountering the species within the appropriate habitat at the proper season. Abundance codes are not hypothetical but closely tied to our extensive data for five years. Certain species associated with valley marshlands and riparian forests were omitted because they are not typical of Buttes habitats, yet "spillovers" can be expected occasionally.

I invite you to use this list to keep a running total of species seen in the Buttes or to duplicate it and keep daily records. Unusual species or out-of-season sightings should be carefully documented and submitted to the regional editors of the journal *American Birds* (check a current issue). Recording numbers seen, even of common species, adds to the usefulness of the data. Make full use of national and regional guides (Peterson 1961, Robbins *et al* 1966, Small 1974, Udvardy 1977), and take advantage of local field trips, lectures, etc. to gain experience and confidence.

Table 3.   Birds of the Sutter Buttes in Habitat Groupings.

Seasonal terms defined:

year-round residents	breed in the Buttes but not necessarily in every habitat in which they forage
winter only	may be expected to stay lengthy periods during non-breeding season
spring/summer only	definite or presumed breeding in the Buttes but absent in non-breeding season
visitors	generally migrating through or wandering from breeding habitats clearly outside the Buttes

Open Grassland and Farmland.

Lower slopes and occasionally high ridges entirely grass and small forbs, plus weedy fencerows, fields, orchard edges. Sometimes rocky.

year-round residents

Turkey Vulture	Mourning Dove	House Sparrow
Red-tailed Hawk	Common Barn-Owl	Western Meadowlark
Golden Eagle	Great Horned Owl	Red-winged Blackbird
Northern Harrier	Horned Lark	Tricolored Blackbird
Prairie Falcon	Yellow-billed Magpie	Brewer's Blackbird
American Kestrel	American Crow	Brown-headed Cowbird
Ring-necked Pheasant	Rock Wren	American Goldfinch
Killdeer	Loggerhead Shrike	Lesser Goldfinch
Rock Dove	European Starling	Lark Sparrow

winter only

Rough-legged Hawk	Mountain Bluebird	Savannah Sparrow
Ferruginous Hawk	Water Pipit	Vesper Sparrow
Burrowing Owl	Northern Shrike	White-crowned Sparrow
Say's Phoebe	Pine Siskin	Golden-crowned Sparrow

spring/summer only

Lesser Nighthawk	Cliff Swallow	Barn Swallow
Western Kingbird		

visitors

Black-shouldered Kite	Poorwill	Northern Rough-winged
Swainson's Hawk	Vaux's Swift	Swallow
California		Lark Bunting
or Ring-billed Gull		

Chaparral and Thickets.

Brushy slopes (California Coffeeberry, Northern Redbud, Toyon, Scrub Oak, California Bay, Poison Oak, etc.) or streamside thickets (willow, Mulefat, cottonwood, Button Willow, grape, elder).

year-round residents

California Quail	Northern Mockingbird	Rufous-sided Towhee
Great Horned Owl	American Robin	Brown Towhee
Scrub Jay	Loggerhead Shrike	Rufous-crowned Sparrow
Bushtit	American Goldfinch	
Bewick's Wren	Lesser Goldfinch	

Chaparral and Thickets (continued)

winter only

Sharp-shinned Hawk	Golden-crowned Kinglet	Golden-crowned Sparrow
Cooper's Hawk	Ruby-crowned Kinglet	Fox Sparrow
Band-tailed Pigeon	Yellow-rumped Warbler	Lincoln's Sparrow
Varied Thrush	Dark-eyed Junco	
Hermit Thrush	White-crowned Sparrow	

spring/summer only

Western Wood-Pewee	Blue Grosbeak	Lazuli Bunting
Northern Oriole	Black-headed Grosbeak	

visitors

Western Flycatcher	Blue-gray Gnatcatcher	Black-throated Gray Warbler
Willow Flycatcher	Warbling Vireo	MacGillivray's Warbler
Olive-sided Flycatcher	Orange-crowned Warbler	Yellow-breasted Chat
House Wren	Nashville Warbler	Wilson's Warbler
Swainson's Thrush	Yellow Warbler	Evening Grosbeak

Oak Woodland.

Extensive at higher elevations and on northern slopes. Primarily Blue Oak with patches of Interior Live Oak and occasional Valley Oaks. Often open and grassy beneath.

year-round residents

Red-tailed Hawk	Nuttall's Woodpecker	Brewer's Blackbird
Golden Eagle	Scrub Jay	Brown-headed Cowbird
American Kestrel	Plain Titmouse	House Finch
Mourning Dove	Bushtit	American Goldfinch
Great Horned Owl	White-breasted Nuthatch	Lesser Goldfinch
Anna's Hummingbird	American Robin	Lark Sparrow
Northern Flicker	Phainopepla	
Acorn Woodpecker	European Starling	

winter only

Sharp-shinned Hawk	Varied Thrush	Yellow-rumped Warbler
Cooper's Hawk	Hermit Thrush	Purple Finch
Band-tailed Pigeon	Western Bluebird	Pine Siskin
Lewis Woodpecker	Ruby-crowned Kinglet	Dark-eyed Junco
Red-breasted Sapsucker	Cedar Waxwing	

spring/summer only

Western Kingbird	Western Wood-Pewee	Black-headed Grosbeak
Ash-throated Flycatcher	Northern Oriole	

visitors

Rufous Hummingbird	Solitary Vireo	Hermit Warbler
Tree Swallow	Warbling Vireo	Western Tanager
Brown Creeper	Black-throated Gray Warbler	Lawrence's Goldfinch
Blue-gray Gnatcatcher		Chipping Sparrow
Hutton's Vireo	Townsend's Warbler	

Table 3. (continued)

Rocky Peaks.
Craggy summits, occasionally with cliffs or boulders, sometimes brushy (Scrub Oak, California Bay, Toyon, California Coffeeberry, Poison Oak, etc.).

year-round residents

Turkey Vulture	Prairie Falcon	Canyon Wren
Red-tailed Hawk	Great Horned Owl	Rock Wren
Golden Eagle	White-throated Swift	Rufous-crowned Sparrow

winter only

Sharp-shinned Hawk	Band-tailed Pigeon

spring/summer only

Violet-green Swallow	Cliff Swallow

visitors

Bald Eagle	Merlin	various warblers
Northern Harrier	Poorwill	and sparrows

Wetlands
Restricted to a few stock ponds and reservoirs, a few deeper ponds (Butte Rock & Gravel), and upland habitat occasionally used by waterbirds.

winter or migration, mostly overhead

American White Pelican	Ross' Goose	occasionally other ducks
Tundra Swan	Mallard	Sandhill Crane
Canada Goose	Northern Pintail	Long-billed Dowitcher
Greater White-fronted	American Wigeon	California or
Goose	Wood Duck	Ring-billed Gull
Snow Goose		

winter, small ponds and marshes in lower part of Buttes

Pied-billed Grebe	Common Goldeneye	Common Moorhen
Mallard	Bufflehead	American Coot
Lesser Scaup	Ruddy Duck	Common Snipe

uncommon but regular breeders (much more common in valley proper)

Mallard	Red-winged Blackbird	Tricolored Blackbird
Killdeer		

visitors, usually lower areas

Cinnamon Teal	Black-crowned Night Heron	various swallows
Great Blue Heron	American Bittern	Marsh Wren
Green-backed Heron	Greater Yellowlegs	Water Pipit
Great Egret	Belted Kingfisher	various blackbirds
Snowy Egret	Black Phoebe	Song Sparrow

Wintering Birds

To year-round residents, winter in the Sacramento Valley implies decreased temperatures, increased precipitation, and the arrival of hordes of other birds to share the mixture of cover and foods established during the growing season. To incoming birds, "winter" need not imply escape from cold or short days but rather an alternative, non-breeding site where survival is somehow enhanced relative to other areas. The sweltering heat of late August may feel little like winter to us, but already the first sizeable flights of Northern Pintails begin to arrive, settling into the rice fields and marshes where they will spend the "winter". In mid-September the Greater White-fronted Geese appear, and in October the clamorous calls of Snow Geese send surges of excitement through the spirits of hunter and non-hunter alike.

Northern Pintails

The annual return of literally millions of birds triggers an equally impressive immigration of sportsmen and birders to the area. Armed with decoys and shotguns or spotting scopes and field guides, hundreds of hardy souls brave the winter chill to witness, experience, and absorb the thrill of seeing the sky alive with birds. Despite the polarization that often occurs between hunters and non-hunters, much of the motivation is the same — the experience differs mainly in final punctuation.

Sometime just before Christmas each year, zealous birders gather in pre-dawn rendezvous and then fan out for an intensive day of recording all birds of all species found within a fifteen-mile diameter circle centered on Peace Valley in the Sutter Buttes.

The Christmas Bird Count (CBC) originated on Christmas Day in 1900 when 27 participants covered 25 areas. It was promoted through *Bird-lore* (now *Audubon* magazine) as a non-destructive alternative to the widely practiced Christmas Day big kill engaged in by some hunters. It caught on quickly, and in the two-week period bracketing Christmas of 1979, some 33,000 people participated in 1320 counts.

The Peace Valley count covers the entire Sutter Buttes, Butte Sink, Gray Lodge Wildlife Area, and town of Sutter. Of the more than 80 CBC's held in

California, it stands out as one of the richest inland counts in the state, with about 135 species recorded each year, 165 total over the last 9 years (Appendix I).

On count day small teams are assigned sectors to cover thoroughly. Many birds don't move far during a day, but efforts are made to avoid duplicating counts of large, mobile species such as swans and eagles. Teams assemble at the end of the day to compile results and share adventures. The day serves its social function, uniting novice and expert alike, but the resulting data are useful in analyzing bird distribution on both short- and long-term bases.

Even though the entire Sutter Buttes range is covered, the CBC effort is weighted somewhat toward the lowlands where access is easier and waterbirds are abundant, hence demanding more counting time. In percentage of coverage time, the various habitats average as follows: riparian or riverland forest and thickets, 19 percent; marsh, 18 percent; oaks, 18 percent; fields and irrigated pastures, 18 percent; dry grassland, 13 percent; open water, 8 percent; orchards, 4 percent, and residential areas and gardens, 2 percent.

Northern Pintail

Note in Appendix I that the Peace Valley area frequently has had highest total counts n the nation for a number of species. Few of .he more than a thousand counts in the country come close to this area for total abundance, especially of waterfowl — the otherwise rare Ross' Goose, the Northern Pintail, the Green-winged Teal, the American Wigeon, the Northern Shoveler, sometimes even the rare Eurasian Wigeon.

Variation in waterfowl numbers from year to year on this count can't be used as a direct measure of population change, since the Sutter, Colusa, Delevan, and Sacramento refuges are **not** in the Peace Valley CBC area but do harbor birds which may move in and out of the count area throughout the winter season. Blackbirds, like waterfowl, tend to move in flocks and have ample habitat outside the CBC area; hence numbers may shift dramatically from year to year on the count without reflecting population changes. The Peace Valley total of 44,560 Tricolored Blackbirds in 1976 set a national record, yet only 73 were tallied in 1978, when the honors went to Thousand Oaks, California with 2000. Ironically, literally thousands of Tricolors were using the Gray Lodge marshlands in 1978 but evaded the censusers by staying out late beyond the boundaries of the count area. Such are the vagaries of bird census work.

Birds preferring the uplands of the Sutter Buttes are sufficiently isolated from similar country that the annual counts may reflect population levels more accurately (Appendix I). Some resident species (e.g., Nuttall's Woodpecker, Scrub Jay, Plain Titmouse, Loggerhead Shrike, Western Meadowlark, Lark Sparrow) fluctuate surprisingly little considering variability in coverage; they may reflect a fairly steady carrying capacity of their habitat. The resident California Quail population, on the other hand, bounces up and down rather erratically. That variation may reflect population changes, for quail exhibit high annual turnover. Alternatively, quail bunch into large winter flocks and chance discovery or missing of one or two large coveys may greatly affect count totals.

Other annually-variable counts suggest a population patchiness superimposed over food supply patchiness. Band-tailed Pigeons are notably erratic, present on only four of the last nine CBC's. Twenty pigeons showed up on the 1977 count, but less than a month later a single flock of 132 flew silently over me. Appendix I shows great yearly fluctuation for such erratics as the Horned Lark, American Robin, Varied Thrush, Mountain Bluebird, Golden-crowned Kinglet, Water

California Quail

Pipit, and Cedar Waxwing. These birds are not loyal to a particular wintering area but flock opportunistically wherever they can find abundant food.

Breeding Birds

At least 58 species of birds nest within the Sutter Buttes proper (Appendix H), and that total would rise if marsh and river nesting species nearby were included. Most of the nesters are year-round residents, flexible enough in diet to switch foods as seasons change.

Only nine of the local breeders — Lesser Nighthawk, Western Kingbird, Ash-throated Flycatcher, Western Wood-Pewee, Violet-green Swallow, Barn Swallow, Cliff Swallow, Northern Oriole, and Black-headed Grosbeak — typically winter far to the south in warmer climes. Most of these feed aerially on insects, a dietary choice seldom available in cooler winter months. A much greater number of winter visitors to the Buttes have moved northward or upward in the mountains to exploit the summer flush of insect and plant life in those environments.

The tolerance among flocking birds in winter gradually yields to rising testiness as hormones surge and birds begin to pair off and claim territories. What we perceive as beautiful symphonies of bird song are veritable shouting matches in which rivals alternate threat with counterthreat.

Not all singing implies nesting, however. Many migrating birds sing as they pass through, perhaps tuning their syrinxes for the true vocal battles ahead. On fair winter days, rich melodies can pour forth from White-crowned and Golden-crowned Sparrows still in flocks and destined to breed elsewhere.

All the same, the advance of spring coincides with increasingly persistent singing and territory defense by local breeders. Indeed, it's possible to map the locations of singing males over a period of time to gain an idea of actual breeding density on a piece of land. An example of such a census, using standardized procedures, is shown in Table 4 (Gaines 1979).

Gaines established a 16 hectare (39.5 acre) square plot along the north drainage of North Butte. Primarily rolling hills varying from 110 to 340 feet in altitude, the census plot had open groves of Blue Oak and strips of Interior Live Oak festooned with vines along two temporary creek channels. Gaines spent 24 total hours censusing the plot on six dates: April 5, 16, 23, 30 and May 7 and 23, 1978. The results (Table 4) list number of territorial birds of each species within the plot, then density conversions to hypothetical standard plots of one square kilometer and one hundred acres.

The census results, including visitors which likely bred in the Buttes but outside the plot, confirm the predictions for oak woodland species listed as year-round residents or spring/summer breeders in Table 3. Those listed in the table but not on Gaines' plot tend to be species with large home ranges (Golden Eagle) or species uncommon as breeders in the Buttes (American Kestrel,

Table 4. Breeding Bird Census of Oak Woodland, Sutter Buttes
(from Gaines 1979).

	Territorial birds per:		
	Plot 16 ha/39.5 A	km²	100 A
Plain Titmouse	8	50	20
House Finch	6	38	15
Bewick's Wren	5	31	13
Ash-throated Flycatcher	3.5	22	9
Mourning Dove	3	19	8
Lesser Goldfinch	3	19	8
Nuttall's Woodpecker	2	12.5	5
Western Kingbird	2	12.5	5
Scrub Jay	2	12.5	5
Northern Mockingbird	2	12.5	5
Brown-headed Cowbird	2	12.5	5
Lawrence's Goldfinch	2	12.5	5
Anna's Hummingbird	1.5	9	3.5
Acorn Woodpecker	1.5	9	3.5
Phainopepla	1.5	9	3.5
Blue-gray Gnatcatcher	1	6	2.5
California Quail	+	+	+
Northern Oriole	+	+	+
Brown Towhee	+	+	+
	46	288	116

Visitors: Turkey Vulture, Red-tailed Hawk, Great Horned Owl, Violet-green Swallow, European Starling, Lark Sparrow

+ indicates less than half a territory on the plot.

Northern Flicker, White-breasted Nuthatch, American Robin, Western Wood-Pewee). Estimates for the late-nesting goldfinches, Gaines admitted, were "educated guesses". My own feeling is that Lawrence's Goldfinches are best considered April-May migrants passing through and that Blue-gray Gnat-catchers are simply visitors, until there are records to substantiate breeding.

Because the Sutter Buttes constitutes the only real upland habitat within the entire Great Valley, it's indeed conceivable that habitat cues or resources extend the likely periods of occurrence of several species. Orange-crowned Warblers are spring and fall migrants, with latest spring date on May 14 and earliest fall record on June 25 (Laymon and Gaines ms). What, then, must we do with our definite Orange-crowned Warbler sightings on May 15, May 17, May 25, and June 23? Are these late spring and early fall records or did some birds spend the summer?

The Lazuli Bunting nests on the valley floor but its breeding status in the Buttes is uncertain. Our Buttes records range from April 22 to May 20, with a single sighting on June 23. Maximum number seen was 45 on May 8, 1979. Clearly **most** of the buntings pass through the Buttes, but a few nesters could easily have escaped detection if the conspicuous males, those dazzling jewels of tropical blue, ceased singing and displaying.

The end of the breeding season is much less noticeable than its inception. Young fledged birds such as orioles are noisy for a few days, then fairly quiet and furtive just prior to migrating south. The picture is further complicated by birds migrating through after nesting elsewhere. In late summer when the young have joined the adults, bird populations overall are at their annual highest, but local distributions can sometimes change markedly from day to day. The fall migration is underway.

Migration of Birds

The first flight of noisy geese in the fall or the first flash of brilliant oriole-orange in the spring are stirring examples of a process familiar to each of us. The fortunes of a "civilized" world may bounce up and down with staggering unpredictability, but we take solace in the arrival of the swallows each March and the bugle-announced return of the cranes in October.

Migration is not universal among birds, for many species adapt to seasonal changes at one location and dwell there continuously as residents (Table 3, Appendix H). Through the course of a year, they are joined temporarily by summering birds from the south, wintering birds from the north or higher altitudes, and transients stopping in for refueling.

Migrating Pintails

Migration enables birds to avoid climatic extremes and to exploit seasonal food abundance. The high mobility of most birds gives them that option, though the more earthbound pheasants and quail are like most mammals and reptiles in their sedentary natures.

Non-migrating resident species forego the suggested advantages of travel for what must be, for them, greater advantages of staying put. Migration, after all, consumes considerable energy, entails higher risks, and brings the wanderer into areas where it cannot be as experienced as the resident in its home neighborhood. These countering selective pressures are evident in species in which some individuals are resident, some migratory.

Most of the waterbirds which occasionally appear in the Buttes are listed as "visitors", but only because they find little suitable habitat in the dry uplands. In general, the tall wading birds (herons, egrets, etc.) are residents in the valley while waterfowl (swans, geese, and ducks) are mainly wintering birds. Shorebirds spend the winter, sometimes increasing in spring and fall movements. Exceptions are avocets and stilts which breed in the valley, but seem to avoid the Buttes. The common woodpeckers (flickers, Acorn and Nuttall's Woodpeckers) are residents but the rare ones visit during winter. Swallows and most flycatchers, which feed on flying insects, spend the warmer months here when such insect prey are active; the water-loving Black Phoebe stays year-round and the Say's Phoebe settles into our grasslands during the winter. Crows and magpies, titmice, wrens, mockingbirds, robins, Loggerhead Shrikes, starlings, House Sparrows, blackbirds, and meadowlarks are always present throughout the year. Vireos and warblers are chiefly spring and fall migrants. In general, except for the finch and sparrow groups, we find that most members of an avian family share the same basic migratory patterns, closely linked to methods of feeding.

If migration serves to take advantage of different environments to meet birds' basic needs, then the timing of migration should coincide with optimal conditions. Our expectation is nicely reinforced by what we see — birds often move through in sharp peaks of migratory activity. Return dates are often within a few days of the average year after year.

Table 5 shows that many birds in the Buttes have been recorded outside the bracket of dates that are known to be typical of Sacramento Valley birds (Laymon and Gaines ms). "Records" of a few days outside the brackets probably mean little since greater coverage often can extend such intervals lightly by picking up those rare "tail" observations of a normal bell-shaped frequency curve. Surely other valley observers have made sightings elsewhere that extend these intervals too.

Dates a week or more outside the brackets (and there are about twenty of them) may have some biological significance. After all, the Sutter Buttes range is an ecological island of upland and may be sought earlier or stayed in later because habitat cues there are different from the rest of the valley. Arriving in a totally foreign environment, a naive American may spot and head to a McDonald's or Burger King because of familiarity, or he may linger there longer because at least he is confident as to what he'll find to eat. A glance through the list in Table 5 suggests that most of the species are those one might expect to find associated with grassland and oaks rather than with lowland valley habitats.

Particularly interesting is the apparent **peak** of migration of Lawrence's Goldfinches later than the interval suggested by Laymon and Gaines. Much more needs to be known: the size of the sample upon which the first interval was based, whether or not some other variables (food, weather, etc.) could have shifted migration time away from what is "normal", whether or not this later migration in the Buttes is a real phenomenon different from valley floor migration but unknown because of inadequate prior coverage of the Buttes.

One thing is clear: the amateur can still contribute in valuable ways to our understanding of birds. I urge the reader to make good use of Appendix H, to pass data on to field ornithologists (particularly the regional editors of *American Birds*), and to remember that data on "everyday" birds may ultimately be more useful than a chance sighting of a vagrant that may never appear again.

Table 5. Early and Late Migration Dates for selected Sutter Buttes Birds. (October 1976 through December 1981, compared with extreme dates for these birds in the Sacramento Valley as reported by Laymon and Gaines, 1976 ms.)

species	early dates	late dates	extreme valley dates
Sharp-shinned Hawk	Sep 20	Apr 10	Sep 28 - Apr 21
Cooper's Hawk	Oct 7	Apr 30	Sep 25 - Apr 21
Common Poorwill	**Mar 5, 31, Apr 5, 6**	Oct 30	Apr 19 - Oct 22
Vaux's Swift	Sep 7	Sep 20, 21	Aug 23 - Sept 19 (fall)
Rufous Hummingbird	Mar 22	Oct 30	Feb 2 - Oct 5
Lewis' Woodpecker	Sep 22	May 3, 6	Sep 17 - Apr 23
Red-breasted Sapsucker	**Sep 22**	Feb 4	Oct 2 - Apr 7
Say's Phoebe	**Sep 18 (2 years)**	Mar 23	Sep 19 - Mar 18
Western Flycatcher	Apr 29	May 31, June 23	Apr 3 - May 29 (spring)
Olive-sided Flycatcher	Apr 26	Jun 12	May 2 - May 24
Varied Thrush	**Oct 1**	May 3	Oct 8 - Apr 22
Hermit Thrush	Sep 23	May 9, 18, 20	Sep 14 - May 5
Cedar Waxwing	Aug 30	May 19	Sep 12 - Jun 8
Solitary Vireo	Apr 17	May 15, 19	Mar 18 - May 13
Orange-crowned Warbler	**Jun 23**	May 15, 17, 25	Jun 25 - May 14
Yellow-rumped Warbler	Oct 7	May 17	Aug 19 - May 14
Black-throated Gray Warbler	**Apr 5-7**	May 9-11, 18	Apr 8 - May 8 (spring)
Wilson's Warbler	Apr 26	May 28	Apr 12 - May 24 (spring)
Lawrence's Goldfinch	Mar 22	Apr 26, 27(15), **May 6, 10(5)**, 16(6), 18, 19, 23(4), 24, 30(8)	Dec 8 - Apr 21
Lark Bunting	**Sep 27**	Apr 4	Nov 10-Feb 10(Buttes) -Apr 3 (Colusa)
Vesper Sparrow	Oct 7	Apr 7	Sep 16 - Apr 6
Dark-eyed Junco	**Aug 18**	May 3	Sep 19 - May 7

Boldface indicates sightings outside the extreme dates of bird observations in the Sacramento Valley through 1976 (Laymon and Gaines ms).

Further Words on Birds

As an environment for birds, the modern Sutter Buttes has come a long way from the smoking, ash-buried landscape of two million years ago. The new, raw land was gradually colonized by plants and insects, and finally by higher creatures which fed upon the pioneer forms. Gradually the complexity of the living community grew; new colonizers often created a resource which would allow further species to survive. The process is an active, continuous one, even today.

Blessed with wings, birds in general are excellent colonizers, particularly when crossing land rather than sea barriers. It would seem reasonable to assume that sooner or later all bird species found in similar habitats in the Coast Range or Sierra Nevada would settle in the Buttes, despite the island-like isolation of the range.

Nevertheless, some species are missing. Wrentits are common in valley-flanking foothills and occur along the Sacramento River north of Colusa but not in the Buttes. California Thrashers and Sage Sparrows breed in foothill chaparral but are absent from Buttes chaparral. Each of these tends to be a local year-round resident in preferred habitat, so perhaps there is built-in inertia against the kinds of long-distance movements which would permit a founding group to get established. The Dipper follows streams to lower altitudes in winter in foothill regions, but of course no permanent streams occur in the Buttes which would support the species.

Absence from the Buttes today by no means indicates that individuals of a species have never occurred there. Colonization is dependent not only on arriving there but also on successfully breeding. That can be foiled by lack of mates, by lack of suitable food or cover, or by predation or accidents. Small populations are easily vulnerable to local extinction, particularly if arrival rate of potential colonists is very slow. The Roadrunner was a Buttes' resident at least until the early 1920's but appears to be extinct there now. We can only speculate as to why or how it went extinct — shotgun, changes to habitat by grazing, the Depression (?). Nevertheless, its ecology made it a likely candidate for extinction from the start — fairly large home range requirements, non-migratory nature (hence infrequent recolonization), etc. The California Condor is believed to have nested in the Sutter Buttes and disappeared much earlier, suspiciously coincident with human settlement. Its life history traits again made it susceptible to local extinction, and now the entire species may be doomed.

Most of the increases — those birds that tolerate us quite well — for some reason tend to be those we view as pests. Our agricultural changes have encouraged some populations to expand so that normally innocuous and welcome birds such as Northern Pintails and Red-winged Blackbirds can become enormous agents of crop destruction through sheer numbers. Roughly **three million** Red-winged Blackbirds were present on the 1978 Peace Valley CBC. A million or more birds means a million or more daily portions of grain to fuel them, and most farmers find feeding blackbirds to be economically unrewarding.

Potential damage to crops, especially rice, is one of the main reasons that local refuges were established. Refuge food crops divert some or all of the hungry birds from private croplands until harvest is over. Once the crops are harvested, of course, the farmer and lease-holding hunters are only too happy to have the pintails return to the same fields in which they would have been cursed and denounced just a few weeks before.

Sometimes our strongest ire is reserved for unwanted immigrants. It's practically un-American to admit any sympathy for Rock Doves (feral domestic pigeons), House (or English) Sparrows, and European Starlings. Each of these aliens has reduced some native populations through competition, disease, or nest usurpation. We think them noisy, destructive, and obnoxious, yet we may be only beginning to feel the impacts of these pests. Starlings have occupied Sutter County only about thirty years. In 1978, the Peace Valley CBC had 3,342 Starlings; that year, Little Rock, Arkansas had 4,758,443! We had 238 House Sparrows that year, while Chicago had 125,000.

On the other hand, one immigrant has been welcomed with open arms. The Ring-necked Pheasant, first established in Oregon around 1880, has accepted

Ring-necked Pheasant

man's environments without obvious negative effects on native birds or
our crops. It has done well in this agricultural region; something like 35
percent of the state take (alias "hunting kill") comes from Butte, Sutter,
Colusa, and Glenn Counties.

Another newcomer to the valley is increasing steadily, first being recorded on
the Peace Valley Christmas Bird Count in December 1979. The Cattle Egret is
believed to have made it from Africa to South America on its own prior to 1930.
It reached Florida in the early 1940's, spread north and west until reaching
California in 1962 (Cogswell 1977). As it continues to populate the valley, we
will have to watch closely to determine its effects on existing communities.

The native egrets and herons, once abundant in the Sacramento Valley,
nearly disappeared in the "Silent Spring" era a couple decades ago. High on
the food pyramid/chain/web (take your pick), these fish-, frog-, and crayfish-
eating birds accumulated deadly pesticide chemicals such as dieldrin and
aldrin. Since the hard pesticides have been banned, the big wading birds have
staged a major comeback. Now their greatest threat is loss of habitat, as riparian
forests where they nest and marshlands where they feed are disappearing
rapidly through agricultural conversion.

Loss of habitat is surely the greatest threat to local birds. Fortunately the
near-natural conditions of the Sutter Buttes continue to support birds in
good numbers.

Some species in the valley have declined despite having adequate habitat
remaining. The decline or disappearance of valley nesting birds of such species
as Bell's Vireo, Warbling Vireo, Willow Flycatcher, Yellow Warbler, and
Common Yellowthroat may be related to the phenomenal increase in Brown-
headed Cowbird numbers since 1900 (Gaines 1977). Cowbirds are brood-
parasites, laying their eggs in the nests of other species and leaving incubation
and rearing of their young to the unsuspecting "hosts". Agriculture has given
cowbirds footholds in areas where local birds had no evolutionary history of
interaction with the parasites; the evolutionarily naive foster parents suffer
genuine drops in breeding success. Since cowbirds parasitize many species, the
decline of a few host species doesn't reduce cowbird numbers accordingly; the
pressure remains high on the few survivors. Bell's Vireos have become extinct
in most of their California range, presumably victims of the cowbirds.

Human-built structures have created new habitats as well as destroying old.
Even though Cliff Swallows still build their funnel-shaped nests on Sutter
Buttes cliffs, we more often find them on bridges or the sides of barns. Black
Phoebes have taken to nesting on small bridges and culverts wherever a stream
passes beneath a road. And where in the **natural** world these days do we look
for the nest of the Barn Swallow?

Yes, though individual birds continue to lead the lifestyles dictated by their genes, populations of essentially all have felt the impact of modern humans. A closer look at certain bird families may help develop a bit of perspective about some that a visitor may see in the Buttes.

The Heron and Bittern Family: Ardeidae

That impressively angular ambusher, the Great Blue Heron, may be called a "crane" by mistake, but its folded neck during flight and typically solitary ways distinguish it from the Sandhill Crane, an elongated relative of the coot. Herons and egrets disdain grain, preferring live prey such as fish, frogs, salamanders, lizards, snakes, large insects, small rodents, and occasionally little birds (Cogswell 1977).

When the day's (or night's) work is done, some of the egrets and night herons discard their aloofness in favor of joining a gregarious roosting party. Nesting tends to be a social event too, as dozens of long-limbed herons and egrets cling incongruously to tree limbs far above the valley floor. No crowds for the bittern! It's camouflaged pattern, feathered fakery of dried tules and reeds, renders it relatively inconspicuous as long as it remains alone. Gray Lodge may qualify as the bittern capital of the country, at least during the winter (Appendix I).

The Sutter Buttes is marginal habitat for these birds. A gangly heron or egret or bittern on a rock wall at the edge of the range is but a few wing strokes away from the marsh where it would seem to belong. Few even fly over the Buttes, preferring to circle the perimeter, low above the ground. Imagine my surprise in April 1980 when I flushed a Green-backed Heron from an intermittent Creek well up in the interior near North Butte.

The Waterfowl Family: Anatidae

Fog rolls over the ridges of the rampart, glides down into the moat, sends tentative chilly fingers up the canyons toward the interior of the range. From the valley comes the inquiring "wow, wow, wow" of approaching swans. There they come, spaced evenly in a line as they emerge from the mists, tilting their heads slightly as if to acknowledge our presence, then disappearing again minutes before we hear the last faint calls.

The jagged battlements of the Buttes thrust above the low-lying mists are natural landmarks that have guided untold numbers of wintering waterfowl. Remnants of stone blinds recall past days of pass-shooting, available only when clouds and winds brought the birds close. At times I have walked in dense fog as pintails passed so close that the whisper of their primaries made me jump.

Canada Goose

On clear days I have looked out from the Buttes to see great expanses of white, like salt flats in the distance — Snow and Ross' Geese by the tens or hundreds of thousands! Nowhere can you find greater wintering concentrations of the diminutive Ross' Goose, "the smallest and rarest of the North American geese" (Robbins *et al* 1966). The rare "Tule Goose", a race of the Greater White-fronted Goose, and the endangered Aleutian race of the Canada Goose return here too. With them come the biologists to keep tabs on the rarities, even though government cutbacks have put some of the biologists on the threatened lists, as well.

As spring flowers begin to decorate the hills, the geese and ducks are leaving, some for destinations as far away as Arctic Canada, Alaska, even Siberia. Small numbers of ducks remain to breed in the valley, and a few pairs of Mallards, Wood Ducks, and perhaps Cinnamon Teal stake claims to small ponds in the Buttes.

The American Vulture Family: Cathartidae

The bare head, awkward stance, and carrion-consuming habits of Turkey Vultures endear them to few of us, though their services are clearly beneficial. A warm day finds them circling on rising columns of hot air deflected upward by cliffs and domes. Dozens, even hundreds of the tilt-winged craft glide effortlessly overhead, using keen eyes and a sense of smell (rare among birds) to locate potential food.

We often marvel that so many birds can survive where we seem to find so little carrion. A single roost among trees in the Butte Sink, just west of the Buttes, yielded more than 500 vultures as they took flight one autumn morning. Despite a six-foot wingspan, a vulture weighs but four or five pounds, needs not feed every day, and conserves energy by its efficient soaring flight. Spreading its wings in the classic thunderbird pose, a sitting vulture becomes a natural solar collector, reducing its own metabolic needs by the capture and retention of the sun's heat.

Turkey Vultures

The Kite, Hawk, Eagle, and Harrier Family: Accipitridae

While the vulture projects an image of effortless, slightly tipsy flight, the Golden Eagle projects pure power. Eight to twelve pounds of compact torpedo are carried by wings spanning seven feet. Intense eyes set beneath a bony shield seem to epitomize fierceness and pride. Massive talons and sharply hooked beak accent the impression of strength. The synonyms we apply to the species — American War Bird, Bird of Jupiter, King of Birds, Royal Eagle — fit our mental image of the great and majestic creature (Terres 1980).

Of course these impressions and projections are simply **that,** associations we make in reference to features or behaviors that relate to human traits. A sheepman with hundreds of wobbly-legged lambs may view the eagle with a different eye. So may a jackrabbit, the eagle's foremost prey!

Golden Eagles typically nest on cliffs in the Buttes, though occasionally use the stout branches of an ancient oak. Even as early as November, a pair of eagles may begin to deliver fresh boughs to decorate one of several nest sites that they will frequent until choosing one in early spring for actual nesting. Since they are sensitive to human disturbance, I avoid the nesting areas during the breeding season.

Eagle Nestling

Immature eagles show a broad white tail band and white marks at the "wrist". These "Ringtails" are easier to distinguish among the vultures circling a peak than are the dark adults.

Redtails are the most common hawks in the Buttes on a year-round basis. The tails of immatures are finely-barred browns, unlike the deep rusts of the adults. A fat, lazy ground squirrel is a short-lived one in Redtail country.

I freely admit a favorable bias toward these birds: the graceful kite hovering above a weedy field, the intense-eyed Sharp-shinned and Cooper's Hawks dashing boldly through the brush to ambush some small wintering bird, the Redtail screaming dramatically as it circles above, the uncommon Ferruginous and Rough-legged Hawks dropping in for a brief winter stay, the white-rumped Northern Harrier gliding low to "come in under the radar", to nab some mouse or other victim, a Bald Eagle soaring over as it wanders from the Butte Sink where it finds an occasional crippled duck, and, of course, the Golden Eagle. Often as I stand near the cliffs of Old Man or the domes of North Butte, I wish I possessed the telescopic eyes and powers of flight of these predatory birds, though thoughts of meals of mouse or snake fail to inspire me equally.

The Falcon Family: Falconidae

Several times we have flushed a Great Horned Owl from its daytime roost in a thicket. As the owl flew off on silent wings, we'd hear far above the sharp, staccato cries of a Prairie Falcon stooping in a power dive toward its perceived enemy. The mutual antagonism between owl and falcon (each has been known to kill the young of the other species) comes as close to apparent hatred as anything I've seen in nature.

Prairie Falcons are present in the Buttes throughout the year. Their defensive behavior near a certain cliff in the summer strongly suggests nesting. This may be the only breeding pair of these falcons within the entire Sacramento Valley.

Occasionally the Buttes is visited by a passing Merlin, perhaps rarely a wandering Peregrine. The only falcon encountered there regularly, however, is the diminutive American Kestrel, once known inappropriately as the Sparrow Hawk. In winter a drive around the base of the Buttes yields sightings of dozens of these birds perched on wires and fence posts. Laymon and Gaines estimate the mid-winter population to be seven times that of the breeding season.

The Quail and Pheasant Family: Phasianidae

That successful import, the pheasant, seems to prefer landscapes altered by its benefactor. Fields and fencerows in the lower valleys and margins of the Buttes support the colorful birds, but open grasslands, oak woodlands, and chaparral do not. Quail are distributed a bit more widely but prefer the dense cover of introduced blackberry tangles where available.

The Turkey Subfamily: Meleagridinae

In early March of 1981 I rested on a rock wall in a saddle near Old Man. Sitting quietly, I watched an eagle displace a score of meadowlarks from the peak and a Prairie Falcon swoosh by. In a clearing in the Live Oaks below, I saw a couple large, dark birds step out from the shadows. Turkey Vultures? No, turkeys! A gobbler fanned his tail and strutted before six hens. I was astonished, as Wild Turkeys aren't native to California and I hadn't heard of any introductions. In this case, a landowner had made a release, and the turkeys subsequently wandered about the range, oblivious to property lines. Whether this flock will make it in the long run remains to be seen, as an introduction by the state some years ago failed to take. In the short run, at least the Wild Turkeys are there, and seeing or hearing them is an unexpected treat.

The Crane Family: Gruidae

What a thrill it is to see a flock of majestic Sandhill Cranes spiralling upward in the thermals above a volcanic peak! Vultures seem to drift aside, yielding to the great gruids. Hornlike calls and rattles descend to us earthbound mortals as the cranes ascend to the limits of our vision.

The Butte Sink vicinity is a major wintering area of this gregarious species, and the tall, alert birds often can be seen in flocks along West Butte Road during that period.

The Rail, Gallinule, and Coot Family: Rallidae

The marshes of Gray Lodge and the Butte Sink support healthy populations of the Virginia Rail, Sora, and Common Moorhen, though the rails are secretive, more often heard than seen. Coots are abundant and certainly not shy. Even though classified as legal gamebirds, coots continue to frequent the Gray Lodge hunting areas when most ducks have left for safer sites. Hunters tend to tolerate or ignore them — "nothing but Mud Hens".

Coots not only rank low in our subjective estimates of beauty, edibility, and sporting quality. Some people feel they compete to the disadvantage of desired waterfowl. Their very lack of wariness, which endears them to little children and dogs in city parks, makes them look weak, stupid, dull to a hunter confronted by hundreds of grunting, head-pumping coots and few, if any, alert and elusive ducks.

Of course, a closer look finds traits that we **ought** to consider commendable: an ability to walk on water, for example, and considerable devotion by both parents to rearing their young. I have cautioned before about making judgments of animals from a purely human perspective. Yet I suspect even other animals make judgments and form biases about other species. For example, a friend of mine conducted a study of Sandhill Cranes in Eastern Oregon, using the vantage of a rocky rimrock from which he could observe cranes and other creatures in the marshlands below. Each morning a coyote would trot out from the rimrock into the marsh, where it promptly caught a coot. It took its catch ashore and placed it on the dike. Then it spent the rest of the morning in the marsh trying to catch a duck. If it failed, it returned to the dike and consumed the coot. The hunter's disdain for the Mud Hen may indeed be justifiable!

The Plover Family: Charadriidae

The Killdeer is the most emancipated of the shorebirds, defining a green pasture or even a gravel road far from water as a suitable "shore". Occasionally I have found a clutch of four cryptically-mottled eggs among low weeds near a stock pond high in the Buttes. Some years the birds had better start early, as the ponds may go dry before the end of the 50 days from egg-laying to flight of young.

If nest or chicks are approached by a human or other threat, real or implied, the parent bird goes into immediate action, fanning its tail, dragging its wing, trilling a cry of apparent desperation. No **typical** predator could resist such a beguiling broken-wing act. Wise to the ways of Killdeer, I am alerted, not diverted, by the behavior, and usually locate the nest quickly. Sometimes it would pay to be a less vociferous *Charadrius*.

The Sandpiper Family: Scolopacidae

Nearly 1500 feet of dense fog buried the Sacramento Valley below me. Occasionally swirls of mist obscured the few rocky pinnacles near me, then withdrew to let the sun gleam on dew-beaded leaves. With most reference points gone from view, I felt as if the isolated crags about me could be in the clouded heights of the Himalayas. Suddenly a squadron of seven birds, a tight formation in synchronized flight, appeared from the mist and shot past, disappearing again as quickly as they had materialized. Dowitchers they were, long-billed probers of muddy shallows. They were birds in passage, shooting past an alien landscape where no self-respecting dowitcher would ever set foot. That incongruity, the juxtaposition of shorebird and eagle cliff, left me tingling, aware of the once-in-a-lifetime intersection of my life with an exception to the ordinary predictability of nature.

While the marshlands and rice fields surrounding the Buttes may at times teem with sandpipers, stilts, avocets, and the like, the upland hills repel them. "No trespassing" signs could not be as effective. Occasionally a flooded flat will have yellowlegs criss-crossing the temporary shallows, where a few months later the vernal pool wildflowers — *Pogogyne, Downingia, Mimulus,*

Dowitchers

Navarretia, Lasthenia, etc. — will carpet the cracked and hardened ground. A lone snipe may hunker among tall pondside grasses as cows suck algae-flavored water from the overlapping craters of their hoofprints. A curlew may give its lonely cry as it passes overhead. Yet by summer even these occasional shorebird visitations are but memories, and the water that attracted them has long since become stem or leaf or fleeing vapor.

The Pigeon and Dove Family: Columbidae

A dove's egg — a pure white, smooth, slightly glossy ellipse of 21 x 28 mm (C. Harrison 1978, H. Harrison 1979) — is a bundle of potential far beyond what the deceptively simple packaging would suggest. Two of these "time capsules" form an average clutch, balanced rather precariously on a flimsy platform of loose twigs. The parents alternate shifts on the nest, the male by day and the female by night. Their warmth permits a miraculous transformation to occur within the shell. At the end of two weeks, the calcitic case ruptures and a sparsely downy, pot-bellied squab emerges. Frequent feedings of "pigeon milk" result in rapid growth of the nestling so that a fortnight after hatching, the young fledgling takes wing.

The Mourning Dove is the most abundant, most widely distributed game bird in North America (though 17 states protect them as **songbirds**). In 31 states, California included, doves must run the gauntlet of hunters in fall, twisting nimbly in the air as bird shot hurtles around (and occasionally through) them. Perhaps 30 million of the 400 million American doves bite the bullet annually (Terres 1980). As the shotgun blasts erupt in their seasonal chorus, some of the lowland doves move up into the Buttes where human access, hence hunting pressure is lower. Numbers in the Buttes seem to decline in winter, then pick up in spring, when mellow *coos* float through the oak woodlands as pairs of doves repeat the nesting cycle.

Band-tailed Pigeons are gregarious, unpredictable winter visitors to the Buttes. I've seen them as early as September, as late as May, but January and February offer most chances for a sighting. Thirty, fifty, even one hundred individuals may race overhead in silence, bringing a hint of pinelands miles away.

Their white-rumped relatives, Rock Doves, frequent barns around the periphery of the range and wander extensively. They are feral (domestic birds gone wild) descendants of Old World birds first tamed by man some 4500 years ago (Terres 1980). Many still wear the multi-colored patterns imposed on them by domestication. Thus branded, they seem out of place in a natural landscape, just as a basset or cocker running in the hills is a poor substitute for a wild-eyed coyote.

The Barn-Owl Family: Tytonidae

Few birds go in for the night life — mostly owls, nightjars, night herons on a regular basis; a fair number more which moonlight on brighter nights; and "red-eye travelers" migrating under nocturnal cover. The Common Barn-Owl avoids the light of day, and supplements its keen night vision with ultrasensitive hearing. Studies have found the species capable of capturing mice in complete darkness. A healthy full-grown owl captured near Davis, California, had no functional eyes — a birth defect apparently compensated for by acute hearing.

The screeches, gasps, and clicks of flying barn-owls can be unsettling to someone unaccustomed to the night, and the eerie, silent passage of a ghostly white shape overhead may seem more apparition than owl. No one has ever developed another rat- or mouse-trap as effective or interesting as a barn-owl.

The Typical Owl Family: Strigidae

Even the normally confident Striped Skunk may fall victim to the Great Horned Owl, whose olfactory sensibilities are not offended by the mammal's musk. Smaller owls must avoid their larger cousin during the nightly forays. In fact, this aggressive species doesn't hesitate to attack prey as diverse as cats, coots, chickens, crows, crickets, and crayfish (Terres 1980).

These resident owls get a head start on most other birds, laying eggs as early as January or February. Often a shallow cave is the home of choice for Sutter Buttes *Bubos,* who litter its floor with bits of bones, feathers, and cast pellets, mementos of past hunts.

The lower rocky slopes of the Buttes may host an occasional Burrowing Owl in winter. Some individuals spend long hours sitting motionless at burrow mouth or on a low rock; there probably is a direct correlation between number of prey to kill and amount of time to kill.

Burrowing Owl

The Goatsucker or Nightjar Family: Caprimulgidae

Master of camouflage, the Common Poorwill sits motionless throughout the day, often tucked beneath an overhanging rock. What a surprise it is to be walking across lichen-crusted rock when an apparent piece of that rock flutters up ahead!

Laymon and Gaines considered the Common Poorwill very rare on the valley floor from April 19 through October 22, though they speculated that the species may breed in the Sutter Buttes. My observations, few as they are, suggest that poorwills are infrequent spring migrants: March 5, March 31, and April 5 in 1977 in Brockman Canyon and on West Butte; April 6 and April 20 in 1981 on North Butte. Yet the secretive birds **could** nest in very low densities in the Buttes and still escape detection. A real surprise was finding one on the very late date of October 30, 1982.

Lesser Nighthawks course over fields and stock ponds in summer months at lower elevations in the Buttes. Gentle trills rather than *peents* or booms, smaller size, and wing bar position distinguish them from Common Nighthawks, though that doesn't mean that the latter is greater than the Lesser. I have found them nesting on open rocky ground, their cryptic plumage concealing the two white eggs layed among the pebbles.

The Swift Family: Apodidae

Scimitar-winged projectiles hurtling past rocky summits, White-throated Swifts seem to be trying to leave their shrill twitters behind. Violet-green Swallows, usually graceful to behold, look absolutely clumsy next to them. The six- to seven-inch swifts can evade the 200+ mile per hour stoop of a Peregrine Falcon (Terres 1980), and the pair may "fly united" in a mid-air mating. We find the impressive birds year-round near the craggy peaks they prefer. Vaux's Swifts, on the other hand, barely deign to tip their wings as they swiftly migrate by.

The Hummingbird Family: Trochilidae

Smallest but never least, hummingbirds are marvels of helicopter-like flight and brilliant iridescent plumage. The Anna's is our only non-migratory hummingbird; we have found up to 26 on the local Christmas Bird Count (Appendix I). In winter they may frequent the early-blooming manzanitas. Spring and summer find them favoring red-flowered plants such as Western Redbud, Canyon Delphinium, Red Owlclover, Coast Paintbrush, and

Brewer's Snapdragon. The common color red is no mere coincidence; plants have coevolved with hummingbirds as pollinators, and the red "flag" is but one adaptation to promote visitation by hummers rather than by beetles, bees, and bugs (Grant and Grant 1968).

The Kingfisher Family: Alcedinidae

The fishless, temporary creeks of the Sutter Buttes offer little to attract the Belted Kingfisher. Yet in September 1977, when creeks had long been dry, a kingfisher appeared above our cabin, circling and rattling repeatedly, finally descending to land in a nearby Live Oak. Did it mistake the sun's glare on the metal roof of the cabin for the reflective surface of a pond? Stockponds in the rainy season occasionally do attract these lowland birds.

The Woodpecker Family: Picidae

The oak, its acorns a vital source of food, was a central part of the Maidu culture. Thus "Panaak", the Acorn Woodpecker, was seen as a bird of power (Simpson 1977). Its head feathers adorned special baskets, its bones became whistles for spiritualistic rites, and acorns from its storage trees yielded cures and poisons, depending on how the Indians prepared them. "Panaak" was both revered and feared.

The Acorn Woodpecker is indeed an unusual bird. Most other birds pair off, defend exclusive territories, perhaps join winter flocks for protection. Acorn Woodpeckers, instead, live year-round in groups and share their property — nest and roost holes, acorn storage sites, sap trees, and food items — communally. Each group defends its communal resources from other woodpecker groups and from squirrels, jays, crows, and other acorn-eaters. Instead of pairing off and going elsewhere to breed, younger group members hang around and share in incubating and feeding duties. At first look, such cooperation

Acorn Woodpecker

appears altruistic, but a closer look and hard scientific data dispel the illusion (MacRoberts and MacRoberts 1976, Stacey 1979, Koenig and Pitelka 1981). Apparently, given a choice, young woodpeckers **would** go off and breed by themselves, but that option is prevented by ecological factors, by the nature of acorns and oaks.

You see, Acorn Woodpeckers are true farmers, harvesting a temporarily abundant resource (acorns), storing the harvest in special sites called granaries,

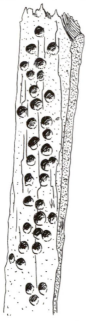

Woodpecker Granary

adjusting the acorns into tighter holes as they shrink while drying, and removing the acorns during the rest of the year for food. The granaries tend to be old oaks or cottonwoods, fence posts, utility poles — dead wood, not live. Storage holes are community efforts too, and over the years a granary may become riddled with thousands of holes which can store thousands of acorns.

It seems that long-term survival of these woodpeckers depends not only on having fairly reliable acorn crops (areas with several oak species are more dependable than those with one), but also on having granaries, which represent tremendous cumulative work effort. Starting a new homestead in marginal oak woodland is a losing proposition for a typical young woodpecker. Instead, helping or apprenticing in the home group may allow eventual succession to a breeding role in a territory with proven oak production and sufficient storage capacity. Helping or cooperating thus benefits **self,** in the long run, and isn't purely altruistic.

When we hear the *waka waka* or *karrit cut* calls or see the white-on-black flashes of a woodpecker in its undulating flight, we can be sure that we are near such a commune. A little stealthy following may show us these farmers at work on the granary, hammering open an acorn at a special anvil, sipping from a designated sap tree with shallow holes in its bark, or launching out into mid-air to capture a flying insect.

The Buttes also host good numbers of flickers and Nuttall's Woodpeckers, occasional sapsuckers, and once in a while a Downy Woodpecker, usually more at home in riparian groves in the valley. The Lewis' Woodpecker, unlike the fairly stable populations of the Acorn Woodpecker, is an exceptional erratic. Christmas Bird Count data (Appendix I) show none from 1973-1975, 2 in 1976, 19 in 1977, an astonishing 148 in 1978 (high in the nation), none in 1979 4 in 1980, none in 1981. Irruptions as in 1978 are believed to be triggered by failure of preferred food crops in normal wintering areas, presumably in the Digger Pine/Blue Oak forests of the Sierra. For us, these are bonus birds, unpredictable on a local scale, mysterious red-faced visitors that drop in unannounced to sample our acorns now and then.

The Tyrant Flycatcher Family: Tyrannidae

Tyrannus, the kingbird, is a true tyrant when an intruder, large or small, chances to violate its boundaries. Even an eagle or hawk, if flying low enough, may receive its heated attacks. Yet its ultimate wrath is reserved for its greatest competitor — some other feisty yellow-breasted (but not yellow-bellied) Western Kingbird. Most of the time this regal bird conceals its brilliant red crown feathers; its reputation for touchy temper is a better deterrent than a badge of rank anyway!

The Western Kingbird seems tough in other ways. Even on the hottest summer day we may see one perched on a fence post in wide-open grassland with sun baking the landscape to a blur of heat waves. From the post, it swoops upward in a quick arc and snaps some hard-cased insect from the air. It won't hesitate to snap up and gobble down a bee, as any beekeeper will attest. When specializing on bees, a single Bee Martin can be a significant threat to young queen bees emerging for their nuptial flights; a large-bodied queen is an irresistible treat compared to a drone or worker. Otherwise, a drone now and then keeps the Bee Bird happy.

Western Kingbird

Like a changing of the guard, when the Western Kingbirds depart the grasslands in September, the Say's Phoebes appear in their place. By comparison, the latter are low-key, inconspicuous, almost timid. In March they are gone, and soon the incessant chatter of the Western Kingbirds, more plentiful and twice as noticeable, replaces the soft, plaintive cries of the Say's Phoebe.

Black Phoebes are hydrophiles, water-lovers, attracted to stock pond, water trough, creek, slough, river, lake, and swimming pool. If you were perishing of thirst, lost in the rugged wilds of the Sutter Buttes interior in the torrid ovens of July, you should look for a Black Phoebe. Learn to recognize that big-headed, black-hooded, white-bellied, tail-wagging little bird, for if you locate one, you should find liquid water nearby. No, those big blackish birds with bare red heads, white-tipped beaks, and hungry-looking eyes don't count — try again.

Flycatchers, as the name implies, catch flies and other insects and hence tend to visit us in the warmer months when insects are active. Somehow the two phoebes make it through our relatively mild winters, but the Western Kingbird, the Western Wood-Pewee, and the Flycatchers (Western, Willow, and Ash-throated) are fair weather fellows.

We call them "tyrant flycatchers" (even though some are far more benign than the kingbirds) to distinguish them from the "Old World flycatchers", an unrelated family whose members **look** much the same as our New World species because of similar ways of life (convergent evolution). That a kingbird, a pewee, and a flycatcher are called "Western" is a convergence of another sort. The appellation is perfect for the wood-pewees, Western and Eastern neatly dividing their breeding ranges down the middle of the country; fits reasonably well for the kingbirds, though the Eastern overlaps broadly across the map where only the Western **ought** to be; and seems inappropriate for the flycatchers, since the Western is but one of a half dozen or so species inhabiting the West.

The Western Flycatcher, incidentally, is ordinarily a spring and fall migrant through the Sacramento Valley (Table 5), yet in 1978 we discovered a nest in the Sutter Buttes, first for the valley area. Actually, it had been a wet spring; even in late May, water continued to trickle over a waterfall often dry much earlier. The wet spring created habitat similar to that usually sought in the Sierra Nevada for nesting, so the breeding attempt doesn't surprise me. Perhaps some thousands of years ago when cooler, moister conditions prevailed, this species and other "mountain birds" regularly bred in the Buttes. Nests rarely, if ever, leave fossilized remains, but this nesting observation is a clue from which we can, if we dare, make predictions, extrapolations, and educated guesses. Of such stuff comes the fun of science.

The Swallow Family: Hirundinidae

Suddenly in mid-March they are back — thousands of Cliff Swallows swooping, wheeling, gliding and flapping, gathering on muddy margins to collect beaksful of mud for nest-building. A few weeks before they were in southern South America. We think they are **our** swallows, yet an Argentinean may feel equally possessive of the "golondrina risquera". They use our bridges, barns, quarries, and other structures as cliff-substitutes, yet we have no way of knowing if they acknowledge our usefulness to them. A colony of 2500 pairs, as typically nests on the old causeway by Mawson Bridge near the Buttes, consumes prodigious quantities of mosquitoes, midges, and other minute insects. Smaller colonies occupy shallow caves and cliff faces in the Buttes, independent of human activity and much safer from the threat of stone-throwing boys who occasionally attack roadside colonies.

Tree Swallows come back even earlier, typically in January and February, though some annually appear on our Christmas Bird Count in December (Appendix I). In the Buttes we see them over reservoirs and in lower areas, whereas the Violet-green Swallow prefers the craggy domes, often in the company of White-throated Swifts. The Violet-green is poetry in motion, clean whitish undersides and flank patches setting off the emerald-green back and violet rump. In Latin it is *Tachycineta thalassina*, translated "swift-moving, sea-green".

The Jay, Magpie, and Crow Family: Corvidae

Ostensibly songbirds by membership in the order Passeriformes, these birds are **not** noted for their singing voices, producing instead a noisy array of caws, cacks, croaks, and raucous yells and screams. Ornithologists consider them among the most intelligent of birds, capable of counting (though not very high), solving puzzles, recalling and applying learning experiences, discriminating among sounds and symbols for food rewards, and the like. Of course, in nature they are actively exploring omnivores, hence predisposed, one might say, to the types of learning we associate with intelligence. Who is to say that a booby or other "bird brain" is any less intelligent just because it won't acknowledge, let alone answer, our questions and puzzles?

The Scrub Jay is common through oak woodlands and chaparral, though magpies and crows tend to avoid the interior of the Buttes, preferring the farmlands and orchards, where they often are abundant.

The Titmouse and Bushtit Families: Paridae and Aegithalidae

Sometimes while leading a group through an oak grove, I call out "titmouse" when I hear the *tsick-a-dee* call or *witt-y witt-y witt-y* song of the little gray, crested bird. I forget that some of my associates at such times are unfamiliar with the birds, and I may see puzzled looks or self-conscious smiles in response to my utterance of the word. "Titmouse" is derived from neither of the roots we Americans might suspect. The Old Icelandic "titr" means something small, and the Anglo-Saxon "mase", for a kind of bird, has been corrupted over the years to "mouse" (Terres 1980), but there is nothing mammalian about these tiny, plain-plumaged birds. In this country, we call those with dark cap and bib "chickadees", but in the Old World there is no embarrassed tittering about calling them "tits".

Year-round residents in the Buttes, the Plain Titmouse is usually seen in pairs, the Bushtit in loose flocks kept in touch by "high, thin, fussing notes" (Robbins *et al* 1966). The titmouse nests in cavities, but the Bushtit builds an impressively large hanging nest, gourd-shaped, with the entrance on one side.

The Wren Family: Troglodytidae

High on the face of an andesite cliff, the song begins. Sharp clear whistles vigorously descend the scale, slowing as if running out of steam, ending softly and anticlimactically with a harsh buzz. Then, as if revived, the singer bursts into song again, the descending notes seeming to bounce down boulder by boulder to the talus jumble below. The singer appears suddenly, creeps along the steep wall, then ducks for an instant into a crevice after a spider. Its white chest makes an immaculately clean bib above a richly rufous belly. The Canyon Wren is a dashing member of its family, a cave-dweller or creeper-into-holes as "troglodyte" implies (Terres 1980). An old cabin or shack and the man-made rock walls are acceptable habitats too.

The Rock Wren likewise likes the feel of gritty rock, speckled with lichens, beneath its toes. Its variable sequences of trills reminds one of the vocal virtuosity of a Mockingbird. Contrary to typical field guide depictions, this wren does not habitually cock up its tail, as many others do.

Shrubby, densely vegetated thickets and streamsides support a good population of Bewick's (pronounced "Buicks") Wrens in the Buttes. House Wrens, which nest in riparian woodlands on the valley floor, stop by in the Buttes on migration in March through May and again in September. Marsh Wrens, ubiquitous among the tules of Gray Lodge, appear in the hills only on migration.

The Old World Warblers and Allies Family: Muscicapidae

The recent taxonomic revisions of the American Ornithologists' Union leave us with a big, rather awkward family instead of the discrete families of kinglets, gnatcatchers, thrushes, wrentit, and others with which we were familiar. There's not even a convenient common name for the disparate group. European and American biologists may lament the subordination of groups that to them seemed so distinct. Yet in the tropics, the former categories fail to suffice; family borders blur into meaninglessness. On a global perspective, these apparently discrete groups clearly are so closely related as to justify being included in one big family.

Still, from our local perspective, a robin and a bluebird have more in common than do a robin and a kinglet, so here I will discuss subfamilies which formerly held familial rank.

The Gnatcatcher and Kinglet Subfamily: Sylviinae

"Little kings" by virtue of jewel-studded crowns, the kinglets fail to act the part. The chunky-bodied little mites twitch their wings nervously and are in continual motion, completely lacking regal bearing. But then it is **we,** not they themselves, who call them kinglets.

Peterson (1961) describes the Blue-gray Gnatcatcher as "like a miniature Mockingbird", though its "thin, squeaky, wheezy" song in no way compares to that of the larger bird. It often cocks its long tail over its back as a wren does, flipping it about erratically. Gaines (1979) found some in April or May of 1978, and I have records of one or two individuals in the Buttes on 2/14/78, 5/3/78, 5/17-19/78, 11/18/78, 4/29/79, 4/27/80, and 5/1-30/82, all in different parts of the range.

American Robin

The Thrush Subfamily: Turdinae

Most of our thrushes winter locally, but in highly varying numbers, depending on food supplies across northern California. Nine years of

Christmas Bird Counts (Appendix I) show this startling variability: American Robin 5 to 471, Varied Thrush 3-47, Hermit Thrush 7 to 127, Western Bluebird 0 (once) to 69, Mountain Bluebird 0 (4 times) to 77. A few robins stay to breed, and Swainson's Thrushes pass through on spring migration. Two Townsend's Solitaires, a mountain species, appeared in the Buttes on January 24, 1982, to my knowledge the first record for Sutter County.

The Hermit Thrush is a virtuoso songster, yet gives us no more than an occasional *chup* or a nasal *pay* when we see one in Buttes woodlands and thickets. Occasionally we hear the tangy, eerie flutings of the Varied Thrush and glimpse the orange-browed bird of northwest coniferous forests. The two bluebirds prefer different habitats, Westerns frequenting oak woodlands and Mountains favoring open and rocky grasslands.

The Mockingbird and Thrasher Family: Mimidae

Those of us who listen to bird songs, identifying the singer by voice rather than by sight, must beware the Northern Mockingbird. These accomplished mimics can copy other sounds so closely that even electronic analysis may not discriminate between songs of model and mimic (Terres 1980). Fortunately, the Mocker tends to sing a series of one song type, then a series of another, then another; we need only listen for the inevitable changes to give them away. Then too, many of the songs are novel to mockingbirds, so no confusion should occur.

So **why** do mockingbirds mimic other birds, barking dogs, yowling cats, screaming sirens, and tooting trains? Some have speculated that competitors of other species (e.g., berry-eaters like robins, waxwings, etc.) are thus excluded from their territories, giving them a fat and easy life when eating between singing bouts. Studies fail to support this, and the hypothesis certainly couldn't account for the variety of non-avian sounds imitated.

Evidence suggests, instead, that mimicry is simply a means of increasing repertoire size — signal variety — which improves success in establishing a territory and attracting a mate (Howard 1974). A large and complex vocal repertoire, then, impresses male Northern Mockingbirds negatively, females positively, and human beings just incidentally!

The largest member of the family in the state is the California Thrasher, a chaparral bird that **ought** to find some of the brush-covered slopes in the Buttes to its liking. **Getting** to the Buttes seems to be the problem, as individuals are sedentary, rather clumsy fliers, loath to leave protective cover. The Buttes might just as well be an island in the ocean as far as these land-lubbers are concerned.

The Pipit Family: Motacillidae

High above, a nondescript brownish bird roller-coasters over, uttering a simple two-note call. A pipit, I declare. Birding novices seem amazed. The brief look offered no way to see the white outer tailfeathers, slender beak, lightly streaked breast, or long hind toenails, yet the flight style, size, and calls made instantaneous identification possible.

Pipits don't mind getting their toes wet, as they walk (not hop!) on soggy pasture or muddy shoreline and snatch up insects and seeds on the way. Their tails wag continually and their heads nod dovelike with each step. A field filled with pipits is a masterpiece of kinetic art.

The Waxwing Family: Bombycillidae

Though it scarcely matters to the birds, the names we apply to them in dignified Latin carry a measure of authority and an implication of erudition. One can excuse lapses in common names (e.g., White-fronted Goose, which seen from below is conspicuous by its white **rear**), since "common folk" can't be expected to be highly accurate and discerning, but we expect the polysyllabic Latinized names to be **right;** the genus and species words form the **scientific** name, after all.

For example, the previous family's name, Motacillidae, comes from "motax" (mover) and "illa" (little), in reference to the wagging, bobbing movement of pipits and wagtails (Gruson 1972). Without bothering to check derivations, some ornithologists assumed the name meant "moving tail", a fairly literal translation of wagtail. From there, the bird scholars took "cilla" and applied it where they meant "tail". Thus the White-tailed Eagle became *Haliaeetus albicilla,* even though that **really** means "little white sea (salt) eagle"! Similarly, *Bombycilla* for the waxwings was intended to mean "silk-tail" but really means "little silky". For very readable accounts of the origins of bird names and the people in that business, I highly recommend the book by Gruson (1972).

Even if the waxwing's scientific name is in error, its common name is appropriate. The tips of the secondary feathers (smaller flight feathers closer to the body than the primaries when the wing is extended) have bright red waxy-looking droplets. No one knows why.

Winter waxwings are gregarious; if you see one, you see a flock. They are nomads, unpredictable except for being absent during our summer months. On August 30, 1977, two appeared in the Buttes in the wake of an exceptional windstorm, the earliest fall returnees to the valley that we know of (Table 5).

That winter of 1977 we found waxwings regularly; there were 103 on our Christmas Bird Count, even though they were missed in four subsequent years (Appendix I).

Waxwings fascinate me. They tend to breed rather late in the season and defend no territory but the nest. Young fledglings stretch themselves up tall, like bitterns, when approached; certainly they look very unlike birds in that pose. Courtship may involve two or more waxwings sitting in a row, passing a cherry or other tidbit back and forth, back and forth. Though their black masks give them a seemingly serious expression, they can become boisterous drunks on fermented berries. Their gypsy traipsings leave me wondering just when and where I'll next see these sleek, handsome birds.

The scientist in me wants more facts, expects a rational explanation for all that a waxwing is and all that a waxwing does. The artist in me thrills in the unknowable, the mysterious essence of the bird.

The Silky Flycatcher Family: Ptilogonatidae

A whistled *"quip?"* from the top of an oak alerts me to the presence of a Phainopepla. Jet black and crested, the male Phainopepla stares at me through bright red eyes, then launches into the air, flashing white wing patches as it labors (or so its slow butterfly-like flight appears) across the clearing to join its gray mate.

Here is a desert bird at the north end of its range. Most of its type live in scrublands throughout Mexico and Arizona. What brings it to the Buttes, apparently, is abundance of mistletoe clumps in oaks and cottonwoods. The pale whitish, sticky berries are irresistible to Phainopeplas, delicacies that sustain bird flesh even as the tiny seeds proceed through the digestive system to be voided elsewhere; some may start new mistletoe clumps.

When its favorite food is unavailable, the Phainopepla may sally out, flycatcher fashion, and seize insects in the air or may seek out berries of Blue Elder, Hollyleaf Redberry, and other woody plants. Resemblance to flycatchers is strictly superficial. Authorities suspect possible relatedness to waxwings, and it has been suggested that solitaires, usually grouped with thrushes, may actually belong to this family.

The Shrike Family: Laniidae

Is it mere coincidence or actual design that our only truly predatory songbirds, frequent killers of other vertebrates, wear black masks? Laniidae means "butcher", alluding to the common habit of impaling prey on thorns, sharp twigs, or barbed wire. The word shrike means "shriek", for these birds may give harsh, grating blats of unpleasant sound. Yet songbirds they are; occasionally I have heard quite a pleasant, rather complicated soft song from the Loggerhead.

Some Loggerhead Shrikes breed in the Buttes, but there are more in winter. They tend to be solitary when not breeding, as befits a predator. Their populations do not depend upon patchy, highly variable food supplies and hence vary little from year to year. Nine years of Christmas Bird Counts give a local average of 58 Loggerhead

Loggerhead Shrike

Shrikes (ranging 47 - 70); considering variables in conducting the count, it is evident that populations fluctuate little.

The Northern Shrike breeds across northern Eurasia as well as northern North America (hence is appropriately named). We occasionally see bold individuals at the southern limit of their winter range, just as other observers in Great Britain, North Africa, Arabia, and India see similar adventurers from lands north of them.

Birds have total disregard for political boundaries, yet invisible territorial lines enforced by members of the same species are as effective as stone walls or iron curtains. Think of this planet as a mosaic of boundaries, patches over patches, properties meaningful for shrike to shrike, eagle to eagle, kinglet to kinglet, person to person. Yet eagle, kinglet, and person ignore the shrikes' boundaries, just as shrikes do ours. If we wish to live according to responsible environmental ethics, we need to recognize the invisible layers of property claims that overlap ours. In our arrogance and ignorance, we often are true claim jumpers, usurpers of lands and resources staked out for countless generations before we appeared. Since our needs are different from those of warbler and wren, our claim **can** overlap their claims and we can still coexist peacefully. But if, instead of adapting to the land, we attempt to reshape it to exclusively human purposes — parking lots, extensive monocultural crops, etc. — the implied overlay of fellow creature lifespace disappears.

At present, though changes have occurred, the Sutter Buttes are one of the few areas in the Great Valley where man and wildlife live in reasonable harmony.

The Starling Family: Sturnidae

Like rats and House Mice, Rock Doves and House Sparrows, medflies and cockroaches, European Starlings have an image problem. "Aliens", we call them, though other introductions, such as pheasants and partridges, are more gently termed "exotics".

Like the sorcerer's apprentice, the person who introduced 100 starlings to New York's Central Park in 1890-1891 had no idea of the force about to be unleashed. The stocky, squeaky-voiced *Sturnus* spread like an epidemic, reaching California in the 1940's, swarming over the entire continent except for the extreme north. Every Christmas Bird Count that includes land in California — the desert, the mountains, the valleys, the coast, even the Farallon Islands — has starlings, some places by the tens of thousands.

Our prejudices are obvious. We consider them "dirty, ugly black birds", when a closer look reveals glossy purples and greens, plus hundreds of star-like spangles of white when they're in winter dress. Their abilities as mimics can provide us with songs and calls of meadowlarks, yellowlegs, killdeer, flickers, quail, and so forth, even in urban and suburban environments where bird diversity is low. We despise them for nabbing a cherry or other fruit now and then, yet fail to credit them for devouring untold numbers of insects destructive to our crops. We abhor their usurpation of nesting holes in which we'd rather see native species, yet forget that it is **our** impact on natural environments that has allowed starlings to succeed so exceedingly well. How can we justify hatred of and sturnicide to (homicide simply doesn't apply) birds that indirectly compliment us by so completely accepting the man-built environment? Perhaps they remind us of the costs that accompany "progress". They may be "avian rubbish" littering the once-unspoiled landscape, feathered unreturnables, yet today European Starlings are as American as Wild Oats and Common Dandelions, indeed as American as we ourselves.

The Vireo Family: Vireonidae

Warbling and Solitary Vireos drift through the Buttes in April and May, leaving snatches of song in return for the insects they remove. How they return to winter haunts in the fall is a mystery to me, as they seem to bypass the Buttes. Similarly, Laymon's Dog Island study near Red Bluff revealed a significant spring migration pulse, with few or no vireos in the fall (Gaines 1977). Whither wanders the vireo?

Bell's Vireos, once abundant in riparian forests in the valley, may be completely extinct there now. Warbling Vireos have similarly declined and have ceased to be local breeders. Implicated in these reductions is the Cowbird, the nest parasite, whose numbers have increased thanks to man's activities (Gaines 1977).

Hutton's Vireos are very rare in the valley. I saw two in the Buttes on March 8, 1980, and Bruce Deuel saw the first for Gray Lodge on August 28, 1980. Another was seen on the 1980 Christmas Bird Count. An obscure little bird, confusingly similar to the Ruby-crowned Kinglet, the Hutton's Vireo was named for William Hutton, "about whom little is known" (Gruson 1972). I have nothing to add.

The Emberizid Family: Emberizidae

Here we are again with a catch-all family, a grouping of subfamilies formerly treated as families. We'd never say, "There goes an Emberizid!" the way we might quickly pick out a passing wood warbler, sparrow, or blackbird. Yet these birds share so many traits and overlap so much in characters in the tropics that we can't in good conscience treat them as separate families.

The formerly large family, Fringillidae, has been reduced to a modest family of finches, goldfinches, crossbills, and redpolls, plus a good representation of endemic Hawaiian birds. Most of the former Fringillids have been shuffled over into the Emberizidae with the orioles, meadowlarks, tanagers, and American warblers, though given recognition as two subfamilies: Emberizinae and Cardinalinae.

The reorganization shows us that in the past we paid too much attention to certain anatomical features that may have evolved through convergence — different lines coming up with similar evolutionary solutions in response to similar ways of life. The Evening Grosbeak, for example, is not a grosbeak at all but belongs in a totally different family. The Lazuli Bunting and the Lark Bunting occupy different subfamilies. And the Yellow Warbler has more in common with the Blue Grosbeak, the Brown Towhee, the White-crowned Sparrow, and the Yellow-headed Blackbird than any of these do with the Purple Finch or Lesser Goldfinch.

It's still convenient to discuss these groups as subfamilies, but keep in mind their roots, their presumed common descent with all other members of the large family.

The Wood Warbler Subfamily: Parulinae

The great American artist, Francis Lee Jacques, preferred to paint the larger birds: the eagles, waterfowl, shore and sea birds that related well to the landscapes in which he placed them. He once suggested that "the difference between warblers and no warblers is very slight." Jacques' bias reflected his vision, his perception of nature as a harmonious interaction of landscape and wildlife on a scale as seen by the unaided human eye.

Just as microbes may be ignored when no microscope exists to make them visible (real?), warblers may catch only casual attention unless seen well through binoculars or spotting scopes. Only then can we appreciate the sparkling eyes, the soft overlap of feathers, the dazzling colors that make warblers the "butterflies of the bird world".

No warblers breed in the Buttes, merely stopping by en route elsewhere or, in the case of the Yellow-rumped Warbler, spending the winter. The Yellow-rumped is a taxonomical merger of the former Audubon's and Myrtle Warblers, demoted to mere races when caught in the act of miscegenation by attentive (voyeuristic?) ornithologists.

The Tanager Subfamily: Thraupinae

Our Western Tanager is a flashy bird, the male dazzling with his yellow body, red head, and black tail and wings, the latter with two wingbars each, one yellow and one white. Yet this is but one of a showy family of more than 200 species, mostly in tropical South America.

We see this classy species in the Buttes only while migrating. They breed in mountain forests throughout our North American West and winter in Mexico and Central America.

Actually, our tanagers are modest in coloration compared to many of the tropical species, which often have numerous colors and highly iridescent feathers. Because of larger size, they compete for our attention very favorably with the dazzling hummingbirds of tropical America. Listen to these names which imply some of the qualities of the tropical tanager: Glistening-green, Multicolored, Opal-rumped, Opal-crowned, Paradise, Seven-colored, Green-headed, Red-necked, Gilt-edged, Brassy-breasted, Emerald, Spotted, Speckled, Dotted, Golden-eared, Silver-throated, Flame-faced, Blue-browed, Purplish-mantled, Yellow-scarfed, Diademed, Moss-backed, Gold-ringed, Azure-shouldered, Golden-chevroned, Flame-rumped, Crimson-collared, Vermilion, Lemon-browed, Ruby-crowned, Black-goggled, Cherry-throated, Cone-billed, Grass-green, Cinnamon, and on and on. Impressive group indeed!

The Grosbeak Subfamily: Cardinalinae

This bunch of heavy-billed, seed-cracking songbirds includes the Cardinal of the East, the typical and appropriately-named grosbeaks, and the showy little Lazuli Bunting, which passes through in highest numbers when the flowers are at their peak in April. Black-headed and Blue Grosbeaks show up in April too and seem to thrive in the summer months when some of us wilt and complain or hide in air-conditioned retreats. The Rose-breasted Grosbeak for the most part summers east of the Mississippi and north of the Mason-Dixon Line. It was astonishing, then, to see a pair of these northeasterners in a Sutter Buttes canyon throughout the summer of 1977.

Rufous-Sided Towhee

The Sparrow Subfamily: Emberizinae

Towhees may be considered overgrown sparrows in a sense, with the Brown as drab as the Rufous-sided is showy. They are masters of the double-footed scratch, somehow tossing loose leaves back with both feet simultaneously without falling on their beaks. A foraging towhee in dried leaf litter makes more noise than a deer.

The Lark Bunting is a prairie bird of the central plains, a rare and irregular visitor to California (Small 1974). The Sutter Buttes may offer the most appealing habitat that a displaced bird can find in the Sacramento Valley, for Laymon and Gaines list six records (from November 10 to February 10) for the Buttes, three records elsewhere. In five years of looking, I have seen a male in striking black-and-white plumage on April 4, 1979 and a female-feathered bird on September 27, 1981, both times in open, rocky grassland far from the nearest tree or shrub.

Twice the Peace Valley bird count has led the nation in numbers of Lark Sparrows, handsome birds with songs as rich as those of the Harz Mountain Canary (Appendix I). A little spindly grass seems to do just fine as a canopy over the grass-lined bowl holding the typical four or five eggs.

Rufous-crowned Sparrows reside year-round near rocky outcrops with scattered brush, often neighbors of Rock Wrens. During the winter I locate them by their calls, a thin rising *tseee* or a descending series of *deeer* notes that I think of as sounding impatient, despite knowing better. Spring brings out the complex melodic song, never overstated, a soft tumbling series suggestive of that of the House Wren.

White-crowned Sparrow

Most other sparrows visit us in winter (Savannah, Vesper, White-crowned, Golden-crowned, Fox, Lincoln's), on migration (Chipping), or as spill-over from valley habitat (Song). A Black-throated Sparrow in December 1980 and a Harris' Sparrow in December 1982 both were well out of normal wintering range.

Few tangles of blackberries or brushy fencelines lack wintering flocks of White- and Golden-crowned Sparrows. Fair days stimulate active singing, even in winter. What allows them to join in apparently convivial chorus when, a few months later, the same songs are interpreted as nasty threats and claims of domain?

Finally there are the juncos, dark-hooded sparrows with pink bills and white outer tailfeathers. A few eastern "Slate-colored" may appear with the common "Oregon" type in the Buttes, both kinds now demoted to mere subspecies of the Dark-eyed Junco. Here they rarely play their role as "snowbirds", leaving the white slopes of the mountains to their hardier brethren.

The Blackbird and Oriole Subfamily: Icterinae

The rising winter sun rim-lines the Buttes as the blackbirds awaken in their roost, stirring and calling and finally rising up in a swarm to fly off to a feeding area. It is an awe-inspiring sight, a long, broad wave undulating just above the trees, thousands of *chek* calls accompanying the Morse code flickering of wings. Each bird gives three or four quick flaps, then a glide with wings folded against the body — dots and dashes, a binary pattern that multiplied by thousands of birds becomes an ever-changing pulsing of plus and minus signs.

Gregarious to an extreme, blackbirds may be the most abundant land birds in North America. In 1978, the Peace Valley Christmas Bird Count had an estimated three million Red-winged Blackbirds, and in 1976 and 1977, the count of the less common Tricolor was the highest in the nation (Appendix I).

Superficially similar, the two showy-winged blackbirds live quite different social lives. The male Redwing, whose shoulder epaulets are scarlet and yellow, defends his territory vigorously against other males; the male Tricolor, with crimson and white epaulets, is gregarious even when breeding, defending a territory no more than a meter or two across within which his several mates may actually have nests in contact with one another. One 60-acre marsh contained an estimated 200,000 nests (Terres 1980 quoting Bent 1958). Obviously Tricolors can't support themselves by foraging on such tiny territories so feed in flocks elsewhere. Adapted to exploiting temporarily abundant food supplies, Tricolors are the only songbirds "known to nest under natural conditions in California regularly in spring and again in autumn" (Payne 1969:79). Flocks of blackbirds working through the uplands of the Buttes in spring or fall, in my experience, are more likely to be Tricolors than Redwings.

Yellow-headed Blackbirds claim the most productive marshlands, hence rarely visit the Buttes proper. Brewer's Blackbirds are quite comfortable in uplands, especially cow pastures, and nest well up in the Buttes interior. Cowbirds, true to their name, frequent livestock areas through the winter, dispersing more in spring to practice their trade as nest parasites. Ornithologists have found their eggs in nests of more than 200 species of birds (Terres 1980), some of which incubate and rear the cowbird young as if their own.

The fiery orange and black orioles follow a lifestyle unlike that of their more somberly garbed relatives. Flocking doesn't appeal to them, nor does hanging around north of the border in winter. Yet each spring they forsake the tropical lands of Central America to return northward, building pendulous nests in the branches of cottonwood, willow, or oak, and feasting on such delicacies as caterpillars, beetles, weevils, ants, grasshoppers, and occasional fruits. How conservative a cottonwood would seem without the flashy colors and garrulous conversations of a pair of orioles!

You could describe a meadowlark as a chunky, robin-sized bird with a yellow breast crossed by a black V, with white outer tailfeathers which are often

Oriole Nest

twitched nervously, with camouflaging bars and streaks of brown on back and central tailfeathers, with black and white head streaking and a bit of yellow before the eye, with a long sharp beak reminiscent of that of a starling, ... and you'd have covered the basic, superficial Western Meadowlark. Yet when one throws its head back and releases its song, the bird becomes more than three-dimensional. It has been described as "a bubbling medley of rich, flutelike phrases ... hints of the Wood Thrush and the Baltimore Oriole, with some of the Bobolink's exuberance added for good measure"(Storer 1964). To me, the meadowlark's song is the distillation of the grassland experience, the spontaneous amplification of the thousands of tiny sounds — grass blade swishing against grass blade, cricket stridulating, spider thrumming the threads of its web, dewdrop sliding off a leaf — that I would listen for if I were a meadowlark.

Lest you think that I am hopelessly romantic about meadowlarks, let me point out that I am aware of the more mundane aspects of their lives. It bothers me not a whit (whatever that is) that meadowlarks may be the champion chip-flippers of the cow pasture. A study at the University of California Sierra Foothills Range Field Station, within view of the Sutter Buttes, revealed that Western Meadowlarks were the only local birds to poke about in "cattle dung pads" (Anderson and Merritt 1977). Throughout the winter, these birds unself-consciously pecked and probed for barley seeds, scattering the scat with flailing beaks and feet. As a result, meadowlark-attacked pads degraded more than a year sooner than untouched pads, promoting nutrient recycling and subsequent growth of grass.

Functionally, then, what we humans might frown on as a rather bad habit certainly results in benefits to man and his domestic animals. All the same, I prefer not to associate the sights or sounds of this scatological scavenging with the sweet, liquid melodies of a singing meadowlark.

The Finch Family: Fringillidae

A special treat on a winter day is to approach a ragged patch of thistles being worked over by a busy flock of chunky little seed-cracking goldfinches. They tolerate your approach just so long, then explode into the air like fireworks, tooting and undulating away. In winter, these birds are gregarious; the pale to lemon-yellow Americans, the greenish-yellow Lessers, and the brown-striped Pine Siskins with yellow wingbars often mingle freely in the same flocks. Even then, however, there are pronounced habitat preferences. Christmas Bird Count totals (Appendix I) show both Lessers and Americans as fairly abundant, though Lessers are the common goldfinch in the upland Buttes, the American more so in the lowlands. Siskins are less predictable, sometimes absent, sometimes abundant, real opportunists linked to food patchiness.

Breeding time in late summer brings greater segregation. Siskins head for the coniferous hills; Americans gravitate toward riverland forest edge, lowland thickets, and woody towns; Lessers take up residence in oak woodlands, orchards, and other semi-open areas.

Lawrence's Goldfinches are rare in the Sacramento Valley, and there are no nesting records (Laymon and Gaines, ms), yet in the Buttes they can be reasonably common in early May, even more than a month later than the late records for the valley floor (Table 5).

The House Finch is one of the most common breeding birds in oak woodland in the Buttes (Table 4) and is abundant in winter also, often in large flocks (Appendix I). Its mountain-breeding cousin, the Purple Finch, is a rare winter wanderer to the range, as is the Evening Grosbeak, not a true grosbeak at all.

The Weaver Finch Family: Passeridae

The House, or English, Sparrow is no sparrow at all but an Old World bird that has been introduced to every continent but Antarctica, thriving among the stables and gutters and docksides of man. Hindsight suggests it was a mistake, but the introductions, beginning around 1850 in New York, were deliberate and persistent, for the bird had its influential human admirers in those days. Marysville and Gridley had sightings as early as 1888, so the Buttes has known the presence of the feisty little birds for almost a century.

One male House Sparrow can single-wingedly destroy an entire Cliff Swallow colony, entering each mud nest to throw out the eggs inside, claiming one of the abandoned nests for its mate and itself. Fortunately, few of the "street urchins" go far from human habitation, so we rarely encounter them in the Sutter Buttes interior.

References

Anderson, J.R. and Merritt, R.W. 1977. The impact of foraging meadow-larks, *Sturnella neglecta*, on the degradation of cattle dung pads. *Journal of Applied Ecology* 14:355-362.

Cogswell, H.L. 1977. *Water Birds of California.* University of California Press, Berkeley.

Gaines, D. 1977. The valley riparian forests of California: their importance to bird populations. In A. Sands, ed. *Riparian forests in California: their ecology and conservation.* Institute of Ecology, Davis, Calif. Publ. No. 15:57-86.

Gaines, D. 1979. Breeding bird census: oak woodland. *American Birds* 33:83.

Grant, K.A. and Grant, V. 1968. *Hummingbirds and Their Flowers.* Columbia University Press, New York.

Gruson, E.S. 1972. *Words for Birds.* Quadrangle Books, New York.

Harrison, C. 1978. *A Field Guide to the Nests, Eggs, and Nestlings of North American Birds.* Collins, Cleveland.

Harrison, H.H. 1979. *A Field Guide to Western Birds' Nests.* Houghton Mifflin Co., Boston.

Howard, R.D. 1974. The influence of sexual selection and interspecific competition on Mockingbird song. *Evolution* 28:428-438.

Koenig, W.D. and Pitelka, F.A. 1981. Ecological factors and kin selection in the evolution of cooperative breeding. Pp. 261-280, in R.D. Alexander and D.W. Tinkle, eds. *Natural Selection and Social Behavior: Recent Research and New Theory.* Chiron Press, New York.

Laymon, S. and Gaines, D. 1st rough draft. Distributional list of the birds of the Sacramento Valley.

MacRoberts, M.H. and MacRoberts, B.R. 1976. Social organization and behavior of the Acorn Woodpecker in central coastal California. *Ornithological Monographs* 21.

Payne, R.B. 1969. Breeding seasons and reproductive physiology of Tricolored Blackbirds and Red-winged Blackbirds. *University of California Publications in Zoology* 90.

Peterson, R.T. 1961. *A Field Guide to Western Birds.* Houghton Mifflin Co., Boston.

Robbins, C.S., Bruun, B., and Zim, H.S. 1966. *Birds of North America: A Guide to Field Identification.* Golden Press, New York.

Simpson, R. 1977. *Ooti: A Maidu Legacy.* Celestial Arts, Millbrae, Calif.

Small, A. 1974. *The Birds of California.* Macmillan Publ. Co., New York.

Stacey, P.B. 1979. Habitat saturation and communal breeding in the Acorn Woodpecker. *Animal Behaviour* 27:1153-1166.

Storer, R.W. 1964. Meadowlarks, blackbirds, and orioles: vocalists of field and wood. Pp. 292-315, in A. Wetmore *et al. Song and Garden Birds of North America.* National Geographic Society, Washington D.C.

Terres, J.K. 1980. *The Audubon Society Encyclopedia of North American Birds.* Alfred A. Knopf, New York.

Udvardy, M.D.F. 1977. *The Audubon Society Field Guide to North American Birds: Western Region.* Alfred A. Knopf, New York.

Verner, J. and Boss, A.S., eds. 1980. *California Wildlife and Their Habitats: Western Sierra Nevada.* U.S. Forest Service Gen. Tech. Rep. PSW-37, U.S. Dept. Agric., Berkeley, Calif.

Wiens, J.A. 1973. Pattern and process in grassland bird communities. *Ecological Monographs* 43:237-270.

11

Class Conflict: Mammals

As mammals ourselves, we ought to be partial to other members of the class which share with us such traits as warm-bloodedness, body hair, mammary glands, a muscular diaphragm, seven neck vertebrae, and so on. Except for the smaller mammals (rodents and bats especially), most general types are in anyone's vocabulary. Yet personal experience with and detailed knowledge of mammals tend to be very limited. There are few mammal-watchers compared to bird-watchers.

Take a typical weekend class that would accompany me to the Buttes and Gray Lodge in winter. Without excessive effort, we would see 80-100 species of birds, literally millions of individuals. By contrast, the only mammals we could expect to see, and in low numbers at that, would be California Ground Squirrel, Black-tailed Jackrabbit, and Black-tailed Deer. With luck at Gray Lodge, we'd find Muskrat. Anything else would be noteworthy enough to make it a special day indeed. In late spring, we could easily locate more reptiles and amphibians (or more butterflies) than mammals (checklist Appendix J).

Mammals tend to be nocturnal, secretive, and quiet. Compared to birds with the freedom and mobility that flight provides, mammals are earth-bound and hence less equipped to defend exclusive territories; we don't find them advertising themselves in the bold and blatant manner of birds. Most mammals are unambiguously predators or prey — stealth and discretion pay off better than does conspicuousness.

So we rejoice in the few direct observations we get but concentrate on looking for sign, the indirect evidence of their existence. We study the ground for tracks, scats or droppings, dens and burrows, browse marks and prey remains (Murie 1954, Burt and Grossenheider 1964, Whitaker 1980). We see where they have been and what they have eaten — then we mentally extrapolate to a feeling for their life styles.

Our empathy with other mammals has never been particularly close, Bambi and Thumper notwithstanding. A century and a half ago, the Sutter Buttes and Butte Sink supported high populations of Tule Elk, Pronghorns, and Grizzly Bears, now gone and nearly forgotten locally. Perhaps every mammal on the species list has had members "controlled" by trap, gun, club, poison bait, gas, drowning, or intentional running-over. Ranchers in the county have reported losses to wildlife of livestock, poultry, pets, bees, fruit trees, nuts, grains, other crops, flowers, buildings, and so on. People fear the spread of such diseases as rabies, bubonic plague, sylvatic plague. They seek some mammals for their fur, their antlers, or their meat and kill others in the name of sport. One could easily conclude from our behaviors that we don't like mammals at all!

Statistics in Sutter County show that vertebrate pest control is a major effort. Sutter County is "the most intensely farmed county in California" (Alfred Perrin, Jr. in the 1978-79 Annual Report of the Sutter County Agricultural Commissioner). Animal control is just one of the ways that the county attempts to protect that resource. County officials merely respond to public demand to reduction of animal depredations, but in recent years, they have heard the loud voices of the preservationist element too. The 1975 Annual Report (p. 4) emphasizes this dilemma: "In the fight to produce more food for mankind the department is caught in the middle between the farmer, who wants to protect or save his crop, and the extremist environmentalist who only believes in natural control".

What is the magnitude of the control effort? Table 6 shows reported totals of removals by the county trapper. Direct reductions by landowners, ranchers, farmers, sportsmen, fur trappers, etc. are not included. In the last 7 years, at least 570 medium to large mammals have been eliminated in the Buttes area. Deer, hares, and squirrels, the animals most often seen by hikers, are not in this category. The control program undoubtedly reinforces the secretive and elusive tendencies of these mammals. These statistics give more of an impression of population densities, even if biased by differential effort, than do direct field observations.

Table 7 shows the converse to the control results, the damages reported by ranchers. Not all the damage is attributable to the controlled animals of

Table 6. Summary of Sutter County Predatory Animal Control (from Agricultural Commissioner Annual Reports).

	1973 -74	1974 -75	1975 -76	1976 -77	1977 -78	1978 -79	1979 -80	7-year totals
Badger	2	—	—	—	—	—	—	2
Beaver	2	5	2	6	2	5	1	23
Bobcat	—	—	1	—	—	—	—	1
Coyote	12	10	17	9	26	28	23	125
Fox	11	7	12	5	2	6	4	47
Muskrat	8	27	1	—	—	—	—	36
Opossum	—	—	1	—	—	—	—	1
Porcupine	—	1	—	1	1	1	1	5
Raccoon	27	16	22	8	2	3	3	81
Skunk	43	50	41	22	14	27	51	248
Spotted Skunk	1	—	—	—	—	—	—	1

Table 7. Total Losses from Predatory Animals Reported by Ranchers (from Agricultural Commissioner Annual Reports).

	1973 -74	1974 -75	1975 -76	1976 -77	1977 -78	1978 -79	1979 -80	7-year totals
Calves	2	1	—	—	—	2	1	6
Goats	—	—	—	—	1	—	3	4
Domestic Rabbits	—	—	—	—	20	15	—	35
Sheep	176	276	102	163	116	82	105	1020
Chickens	153	200	70	45	110	79	42	699
Turkeys	—	—	1	3	5	11	8	28
Pheasants	1500	—	—	—	—	—	—	1500
Bees (hives)	24	10	5	15	7	31	22	114
Almonds (tons of nuts)	—	1	1	3	5	4	20	34
Fruit Trees (tons of fruit)	—	115	6	45	25	28	10	229

Table 6. Of the $37,520 loss reported in 1979-80, a total of $31,000 was to fruit trees and almond nuts destroyed by crows, jays, magpies, ground squirrels, raccoons, and beavers. Skunks are hard on bee hives and chickens. Coyotes and dogs take most of the reported livestock losses. County officials believe the losses would be significantly higher without the "pest management".

Rats, mice, gophers, and squirrels are rarely controlled as directly as the larger mammals, but effort is a function of equipment and products used. The county report for the 1971 fiscal year lists the arsenal employed against troublesome small mammals: poison bait for rodents, strychnine jackrabbit poison, mechanical applicator gopher poison, strychnine gopher poison, anti-coagulant rodent poison, "1080" grain bait, zinc phosphide grain bait, anti-coagulant lollipops, gas cartridges, bait boxes. I'd hate to be a rat!

There have been other, perhaps less obvious impacts on our native mammals. Surely grazing and cultivation have eliminated habitats for some mammals, increased habitat for others. Unfortunately, those which increased were usually the ones we define as pests.

Not only have humans eliminated or depleted the populations of some species, they have added others, sending vibrations throughout the threads of the ecological web. The Common Opossum, Muskrat, and Red Fox were introduced from elsewhere in America, the Old World rats and mice from (where else?) the Old World. Dogs and cats turned out by thoughtless owners have become serious pests. Feral goats have wandered in the Buttes for years. Organized in discrete bands, they stick to the high, rocky areas and have multiplied with unusual (and surely unintentional) restraint. In parts of the world — some islands of California and Baja, Hawaii, the Near East, etc. — goats have become incredible agents of ecological destruction. Pray that they don't suddenly take off here and destroy the Buttes!

The most recent mammalian threat to be introduced to the range is the feral pig. Not the shaggy wild boar introduced here and there from Europe, these pigs are descendants of domesticated stock and retain the varied coat patterns of man-manipulated beasts. Yet they have forsaken any direct dependence on man and have exploded in just a few years time from the original introduction of six pigs to literally hundreds of porcine pests. Their prodigious appetites send them digging for roots, bulbs, acorns, grasses, forbs, worms, grubs, lizards, snakes, carrion, and so forth. With snout and hoof they rip up the ground cover, plowing and tilling the soil in a devastating manner, exposing whole hillsides to erosive forces and invasion by weeds. They root up the springs and compete for water and food with both livestock and native animals. Of course the pigs did not stay on the property to which they were introduced; they ignore property lines and landowner permission alike.

Many owners have been forced to try to control them, so blasts of high-power rifles and barks of tracking dogs now disrupt the peaceful stillness of the range. Control by gun can never be complete, and the pigs are likely a permanent, if unwelcome, addition to the fauna. Sometimes I hope for a pig-specific epidemic. Don't get me wrong — I value pork chops and bacon and like domestic pigs well enough, but the place for a pig is in the barnyard, not in the Buttes.

Come along with me now as I take a closer look at some of the 41 species of 18 families of mammals occurring in and adjacent to the Buttes. There are surprises here, tidbits of natural history that might fascinate or entertain us. Perhaps we can override our natural antipathies and look at these creatures with appreciation for their solutions to survival.

The Opossum Family: Didelphidae

Though not a native Californian, the Common Opossum is the only native marsupial in the eastern United States. The founding population of immigrants to California arrived with man's help in 1910. By 1950 some had shown up at Gray Lodge, and they've shambled around Sutter County in their inimitable way ever since.

People often deride the 'possum as lowly, primitive, and small-brained, as if traits on the opposite end of the spectrum from those of man are worthy only of ridicule. Admittedly, the opposum lacks the "classic beauty" of a fox or squirrel or ringtail; its ashy face, naked ears, scaly tail, grizzled fur, and beady eyes fit our perceptions of a refugee from a horror story. Yet the animal has been biologically successful, despite improbable features, and deserves a bit more respect.

That naked tail, for example, is prehensile — an extra "hand" for hanging around in branches or carrying loads. Its inner hind toe is opposable with all other toes — a superthumb. Its fifty teeth, a record for a North American mammal, can handle 'most anything that this omnivorous creature chooses.

The family life of opossums is anything but conventional. The male has a forked penis, the female a double uterus. From conception to birth takes but a dozen days, culminating in the appearance of bean-sized "living embryos" which must climb blindly from the cloaca of the mother to her pouch or marsupium. There, in a fur-lined chamber, are the teats, thirteen on average, for which the young must compete in those litters having more offspring (the losers starve). In twenty days the survivors weigh four grams, ten times their weight at birth. Around three months of age, the young are weaned, and by six to eight months, they may begin breeding. Two litters per year of five to ten babies each are not unusual. Fecundity is their key to success, enabling the lowly opossum to spread and succeed at a level far beyond that of many "higher" species, "modern" placental creatures with bigger brains but slower birth rates.

The Shrew Family: Soricidae

Shrews are our tiniest mammals, aggressive bundles of nervous energy that must eat almost continuously to maintain themselves. One scientist looked at the increasing metabolic rate with decreasing size among several shrew species and "calculated that a shrew weighing less than about 2 grams would require an infinite amount of oxygen and could never eat enough" (Ingles 1965)! They are the foremost carnivores on a Lilliputian scale, devouring their own weight or more each day in invertebrates and small vertebrates such as mice, which they may incapacitate with poisonous saliva.

Imagine the pressure that a shrew faces! Finding and capturing food must nearly always be foremost in its tiny mind. Any shrew entering its domain is a competitor, a potential threat, and is usually attacked without hesitation. A prolonged courtship is out of the question; the suitors might starve if they overextended the foreplay. Initial aggressiveness must be converted quickly by complex courting signals to brief acceptance for mating.

The shrew is the epitome of hyperactivity. When excited, its heart may beat 1200 times per minute, and it is prone to die from shock when disturbed. Any managing to escape from larger predators may have two to four litters, perhaps twenty offspring, before it expires of old age between one and two years. Whew!

The Mole Family: Talpidae

Those mounds of fresh earth punctuating the grassy hills in the Buttes in spring are most likely not mole hills but those of pocket gophers. Moles prefer the lowlands. At Gray Lodge just north of the Buttes, they tunnel in the moist, yielding loams after earthworms, other small invertebrates, and occasionally parts of plants.

Essentially eyeless and earless, moles apparently use their entire bodies to pick up vibrations through the soil. With equally sensitive nose and tail, plus two-way fur, the mole is equipped to reverse its direction at will. The broad, spadelike hands and powerful muscles make it a most efficient digger.

The world of a mole must be a fairly predictable one, a life sheltered from climatic extremes, a landscape with few surprises. In such a world, a miniscule brain and virtual blindness are not handicaps at all.

The Bat Families: Vespertilionidae and Molossidae

On a summer evening as sunlight retreats higher and higher on the canyon walls, the bat flight begins. Down the wooded canyon and out into open grassland stream the bats, not in great crowds but one by one at a rate such that a hundred or more will pass in thirty minutes. Night after night the ritual is repeated, keyed somehow to light levels. Their return is not so obvious in the darker hours, but we know they are there. We detect an occasional squeek or get a glimpse of a flutter across the face of the moon. The night sky belongs to the bats.

Bats are not rare, perhaps second in abundance in North America only to rodents, yet we know them little. Our list contains "hypotheticals", species which **ought to** be here based on range descriptions but for which firm data are lacking (Verner and Boss 1980; Ingles 1965). We are handicapped by the night, by the speed of these flying mammals, by their superficial similarities, and by our fears and the myths that we link to bats.

The *Fledermaus* (German for "flitter mouse") is marvelously adapted to flight: flexible membranes over elongated fingers, hind legs, and tail; backward-folding knees; a keeled breastbone for flight muscle attachment; and echolocation with high frequency sounds. A high metabolic rate requires high food intake; a bat may eat one-third its weight in insects each night. The cooler months with diminished insect activity can render that feeding rate impossible, so some bats migrate and others hibernate.

The Rabbit and Hare Family: Leporidae

Tucked beneath a shady shrub next to a lichen-smattered boulder, the jackrabbit sits motionless and watches the eagle fly by. Its bulging eyes, improbably long ears, high-jumper legs, and grizzled, camouflaged coat are the equipment of a fugitive. Seemingly everybody is out to get him — eagles, foxes, coyotes, bobcats, men, even mosquitoes, flies, and parasites of several kinds.

The Black-tailed Jackrabbit is a true hare, precocial at birth. The mother spreads her risks by keeping her babies hidden separately and only visiting them at well-spaced meals. The Audubon's Cottontail, as a true rabbit, is naked and helpless at first, raised in a sibling group in a nest and tended to more by the mother.

Black-tailed Jackrabbit

Though the senses of rabbits and hares are keen, many fall prey to predators. Their best defense evolutionarily has been their breeding — no, not their upbringing or manners, but their prolific reproduction. If a rabbit pair produced four litters per year of five young each, there would be 22, including the parents, in just a year. If all survived and bred at the same rate (assuming a normal sex ratio), in five years there would be more than 322,000 descendants of the original pair (Cahalane 1961). Obviously high mortality is a necessary complement of a high birth rate. Few rabbits live to their first birthday, and, the famous White Rabbit notwithstanding, fewer still will celebrate it!

Jackrabbits are successful and adaptable, occurring from the grazed savannahs of the Butte Sink right up into the canyons and peaks of the Buttes, usually preferring fairly open grasslands with running room. The "Audubunny" is more specialized, a brush lover of the lowlands like the Sink, now rare because of habitat loss and disturbance.

The Squirrel Family: Sciuridae

In the Western Sierra, the squirrel family is fairly well-represented: one marmot, eight chipmunks, three ground squirrels, two tree squirrels, and a flying squirrel (Verner and Boss 1980). The Buttes would seem neglected. The big arboreal Gray Squirrel scampers among the Valley Oaks of the Butte Sink and may wander into the Buttes on occasion, but that's speculation. Only the California Ground Squirrel finds the Buttes to be prime real estate.

Ground squirrels like each other's company, up to a point. They live in loose colonies and several may share a burrow complex, but each uses his own entrance hole, regardless of which hole is nearest when danger threatens. Nearly all young males disperse to other colonies during their first year, presumably to reduce inbreeding.

Having close neighbors means higher competition for food (roots, bulbs, shoots, leaves, seeds, fruits, flowers, some insects, etc.), good burrow sites, and perhaps mates. Yet there's safety in numbers — more eyes to detect a raid from land or air, more alternatives to confuse an attacker. A sharp "cheesk" of alarm by one squirrel will send them all to cover.

Predation is a strong force on populations, a pressure seldom seen but effective in promoting survival mechanisms, whether they be body structures or behaviors. One day I stopped with my group for a brief rest along a steep trail. We heard an excited "cheesk" and looked up to see squirrels scattering to their burrows as a Red-tailed Hawk swept

California Ground Squirrel

down the canyon from the north. The hawk missed and cruised south, watched by the squirrels now peeking from their burrows. The rodents emerged from their holes but kept a nervous eye down-canyon where the hawk had disappeared. Meanwhile, the Redtail had ducked behind the ridge, circled back to the top of the canyon, and stooped again, this time snatching a squirrel from behind. We had witnessed one of those rare events that help to define the organisms "squirrel" and "hawk".

Squirrels use their burrows to escape from weather extremes, as well. Moderate temperatures and humidity can be maintained in the underground passages. Individuals vary, but some hibernate in cold weather or estivate in hot conditions. It's not unusual to see a squirrel up in a bush, on a boulder, or atop a fencepost early in the day to bask in the sun's warmth. As always for these succulent rodents, vigilence is a must.

The Pocket Gopher Family: Geomyidae

Moles and pocket gophers are independent solutions to the ecological challenge of living in the dirt. Both have reduced eyes, sensitive tails and whiskers, strong digging front feet, supple cylindrical bodies capable of quick U-turns. Beyond that, they are different. Moles are carnivores with 44 teeth — 12 incisors, 4 canines, 16 premolars, and 12 molars. Gophers are vegetarians

with merely 20 teeth — 4 incisors (the typical "buckies" of a rodent), no
canines, 4 premolars, and 12 molars. Gophers' eyes may be small, but they're
visible at least, and there are external ears. Mole hills tend to be cloddy and
with no sign of a plugged hole; those of pocket gophers consist of more finely
worked soil with a distinct earthen "plug" at the side of the mound (Ingles 1965).

Pocket gophers are named for their capacious fur-lined external cheek
pouches in which they transport food and nest material. Their underground
passages have many feet of simple cylindrical tunnels and numerous chambers
specialized as bedrooms, bathrooms, pantries, and miscellaneous storage areas.
Though plugged entrances discourage most would-be predators, a variety of
tiny creatures find the controlled environment of the tunnels to their liking
and coexist with the gophers. Some arthropods are known only from the nests
of the Mountain Pocket Gopher.

Gopher incisors, as those of other rodents, grow continuously throughout
their lives. Unlike moles, gophers employ their teeth in digging, closing a furry
membrane behind the incisors to keep dirt from the mouth. The rate of wear
closely matches the rate of growth. Yellow enamel coats the front of the incisors
but not the back; differential wear keeps them as razor-sharp chisels. If you
handle a pocket gopher, don't use your fingers to test the efficiency of this
self-sharpening mechanism!

The Pocket Mouse and Kangaroo Rat Family: Heteromyidae

This nocturnal, inconspicuous rodent might well have escaped my attention
in the Buttes if my cat hadn't brought one home alive and alert one evening.
Pocket mice tame almost instantly; this one allowed me to handle it and admire
its soft, slightly buffy coat. I decided not to personally inspect its cheek pouches
or pockets; there are limits to familiarity.

The San Joaquin Pocket Mouse would be better named Central Valley Pocket
Mouse, as that completely defines its range. Its specific name *inornatus* refers to
its lack of ornamental markings, such as the racing stripes on the hips of its
cousins, the kangaroo rats.

Pocket mice forage at night, cramming dozens of weed seeds into fur-lined
pouches and hoarding them in underground pantries. Most are independent of
drinking water, able metabolically to manufacture water from dry seeds with
moisture content as low as 5%. Well-stocked larders enable them to sit out
unfavorable weather periods, not to mention reducing risk to the many
predators willing to dine on pocket mouse.

The San Joaquin Pocket Mouse appears to be found throughout the Buttes,
though perhaps sparsely. Those in the Sutter Buttes and some found at Sites

in western Colusa County define the north end of the species' range (Hall 1981).

Kangaroo Rats prefer well-drained soils, so it's not surprising to find them absent from the Sacramento Valley. The one exception is the Sutter Buttes, somewhat of a desert isle in the lowland sea. Here in April of 1912 a zealous collector captured 24 specimens, which presently reside neatly in drawers in the Museum of Vertebrate Zoology in Berkeley. Another specimen in 1930 joined the collection. To date, these are the only known specimens of an endemic race of the California Kangaroo Rat, *Dipodomys californicus eximius*.

The Sutter Buttes race is small and pale, with extended white markings and reduced dark markings compared to other races. It is found nowhere else in the world and may be rare even here, a population obviously vulnerable to extinction. Any developments in the lower grasslands in the southern and western part of the Buttes should address potential impacts on this unique population.

The Beaver Family: Castoridae

The word "rodent" derives from the Latin *rodere*, which means "to gnaw". Some of us would "gnawminate" the beaver as King of Rodentia, the high point in the evolutionary divergence that has produced more than half the mammal species, easily the majority of individual mammals on earth (Whitaker 1980).

The stocky build and webbed feet which make them look rather awkward on land are well-suited to their aquatic life. Few mammals, save humans and elephants, are as capable of altering the environment as are beavers. They can log a stand of trees and build canals, dams, lodges, and networks of trails. Sometimes the changes which ensue conflict with **our** plans for certain canals or trees or roads or pastures; then the beaver may be forcibly removed. Often though, many other creatures benefit from the changes and watersheds may be better protected against erosion.

Beavers occupy permanent water areas along the Sacramento River, Butte Creek, and Gray Lodge, occasionally venturing up to ponds or spring creeks in the Buttes. Each year Sutter County is forced to control a few animals that take a liking to fruit trees; losses of about 40 fruit trees annually are reported by local farmers.

The New World Mouse and Rat Family: Cricetidae

With 70 species, this family is the largest mammalian group in North America. They range in size from a tiny ¼-ounce mouse to the 4-pound muskrat. They can have significant economic impacts: the consumption of weed seeds and injurious insects by mice and the fur-bearer value of muskrats are favorable to us, while occasional crop, lawn, or levee damages are undesirable. In ecosystem terms, the mice are the base of the great pyramid upon which many "higher species" — snakes, owls, hawks, herons, gulls, weasels, foxes, coyotes, badgers, raccoons, bobcats, skunks, etc. — depend.

The Western Harvest Mouse is a real charmer, building birdlike nests up in marsh grasses or weeds. When romantically inclined, the male sings a high-pitched song, barely audible to human ears. Wolves, loons, and humpback whales have had their songs recorded and distributed as records; why not a record of the chorus of the harvest mouse? It would be inspiring music by which to nibble seeds.

The Deer Mouse is the most abundant native mammal in North America, found in many habitats in all parts of the continent except the extreme north and the southeast. Its range exceeds five million square miles! It is an attractive little animal, immaculately garbed with white paws and belly contrasting with grey to rusty fur above. Its housekeeping, however, doesn't live up to the same standards. It eats rather carelessly in bed and soils its "linens" rather than going off to a separate "bathroom" as a pocket gopher would do. It can't stand its own habits after a week or two and moves on to another nest, rotating among several as they have a chance to air out.

Several times in the Buttes I have lifted a log or board and discovered the tightly woven nest of a Deer Mouse. Once the female scurried off, carrying along the litter of youngsters tightly gripping her nipples. Early maturity and rapid cycling between litters provide the numerical increase necessary to compensate for high losses to predation.

The Pinon Mouse resembles the Deer Mouse but has bigger ears, bigger hind feet, a longer tail. It is an upland mouse, unlike the habitat generalist Deer Mouse found both in the lowlands and in the Buttes. How long has this population been isolated in the Buttes? Do the Sutter Buttes locals differ much from their counterparts in the Sierra?

The California Meadow Mouse or Vole is a stocky, short-eared, grizzled-furred rodent preferring fairly dense grass or sedge cover beneath which it follows a labyrinth of trails. It eats fast, breeds fast, and burns out fast. Its chunky body is a most tempting morsel of protein for a legion of hungry predators. Occasionally its populations erupt spectacularly, then crash as carnivores and diseases take their toll. During the short eruptions, domestic crops may be devastated.

Muskrats were introduced to the Sacramento Valley around 1936 and were found at Gray Lodge by 1940; several thousand are trapped there annually now. The fine, soft underfur that insulates these aquatic beasts makes them our nation's most-sought furbearer; about ten million are trapped each year.

The muskrat's tail is flattened vertically, a rudder and counterbalance as the animal propels itself through the water with its partially webbed hind feet. It is easily told from a swimming beaver by its tail, its smaller size, its whitish muzzle, and its rounded, rather than box-shaped, head.

We look for muskrats in marshes and sluggish canals, but once in a while we'll see one ambling across open country. Don't cross it at this time, for muskrats tend to be jumpy and irritable as they disperse in search of less-crowded habitat. Naturally they are most vulnerable to predators at such times. Even if one reaches a pond or channel after such wandering, it will be driven off by established residents if the place is occupied to capacity. Nature has built-in zoning laws that limit population density.

The Old World Mouse and Rat Family: Muridae

These unwanted exotics have helped to give our native mice a bad name. Their adaptability and tolerance for the environments of man have allowed them to spread around the world along with their enemy/benefactor. They devour or foul with their droppings enormous quantities of grain, destroy chickens and eggs, and transmit such diseases as plague, typhus, and food-poisoning. Diseases spread directly or indirectly by rats have "probably cost more lives in the past 10 centuries than all the wars and revolutions ever fought," (Whitaker 1980).

The Norway Rat is inappropriately named. It was native to Western China, spreading westward into Europe between the sixteenth and eighteenth century A.D. and reaching America around 1776 during the American Revolution. The Black Rat, originally from southeast Asia, beat the Norway Rat to our eastern shores by over 150 years. Tiny cousin to the rats, the House Mouse likewise originated in Asia and spread widely, reaching Florida with the Spanish in the early 1500's and the New England area the next century. They now occupy every state on the continent. In the 1920's, the Central Valley suffered a population explosion of House Mice "*Mus*-calculated" at densities of 82,000 mice per acre!

The murids thrive best around human habitation and disturbed areas, including croplands, but some survive in wild habitats too. The Norway Rat is perhaps most localized around buildings, the House Mouse most widespread. Few of these pests venture far into the interior of the Buttes.

Are there no redeeming features to these creatures? Of course there are. Think how rare and unhappy those disease organisms would be without such capable hosts to spread them! Consider the losses of revenue to rodenticide manufacturers and pest controllers without these prolific and persistent animals. And don't forget that the white rat and white mouse, laboratory-bred descendants of the Norway Rat and House Mouse, have yielded untold benefits as research subjects. I am awed by the countless millions of bar-presses performed by volunteer rats in Skinner boxes, all so that we could better understand our own foibles. Whether we like it or not, the world we have today is a world built hand in paw by rats and mice and men.

The Porcupine Family: Erethizontidae

Usually associated with conifers, the Porcupine nevertheless occurs in the Buttes and apparently does well enough without them. In the daytime we have encountered them up in a bay or oak; at night we have met them on the prowl.

Erethizon means "he who rises in anger", and it is generally a foolish animal that fails to grant one due respect. The hollow quills are barbed with minute projections that expand in contact with warm tissues and work inward. Trimming the end of an embedded quill releases air pressure and facilitates pulling it out (Whitaker 1980).

There has been endless speculation about how a pair of these spiny beasts can manage to mate. Apparently the female must be aroused enough to relax her quills and raise her tail above her back as she presents herself (Whitaker 1980). The male then mounts, very carefully of course, but omits the arm embrace typical of many mammals.

The Dog Family: Canidae

In Maidu legend, Coyote was brought into the world so that Good could know what Evil was and avoid it (Simpson 1977). Coyote, the trickster, played and performed, setting a negative example for people — what he did, they were to do the opposite. When he lied or cheated, he ended up losing, but the people missed the lesson. They failed to do the opposite, and when they reaped their harvest of "troubles, work, sickness, tears, and death" (Simpson 1977:34), they blamed Coyote instead of themselves.

So it has been ever since, even for the settlers who followed the Indians as occupants of *Estawm Yan*, the Middle Hills or Sutter Buttes. The Coyote inspires controversy. To the sheepman, it may seem a scourge, a sheep-killing renegade without respect or restraint. To many a city-dweller, the Coyote appears to be a grinning, innocent-eyed, over-persecuted creature. Realistically viewed, the Coyote does operate without malicious intent but on occasion does kill sheep. The issue would seem to belong in the grays somewhere between black and white, but in talking about Coyotes, both sides see red.

In the sheep-raising industry, killing a sheep is a **capital** offense. From 1977-1980 (fiscal years ending June 30), totals of 26, 28, and 23 Coyotes each year respectively were eliminated in the Buttes (Sutter County Agricultural Commissioner Annual Reports). Those same years, ranchers reported sheep losses (including lambs) of 116, 82, and 105 animals. In the 1976 report (p. 4), the commissioner states: "The County Trapper ... is constantly fighting one of the largest problems in the Buttes, which is coyotes. There is constant influx of new coyotes into the area". Indeed, unlike wolves which declined dramatically as a result of control efforts by humans, the Coyote has shown an incredible resilience to persecution. In response to lower densities because of trapping and shooting, the remaining Coyotes have on occasion bred at an earlier age and had larger litters. Though **individuals** perished, the species thrived.

In 1978, the Commissioner reported (p. 4): "The County Trapper was kept quite busy during the year. It is our belief that livestock and crop losses, without the present protection, would be at least ten times the amount shown as estimated Livestock and Crop Losses from predatory animals in Sutter County". The reported losses were 116 sheep and lambs, valued at $6845.

Of course, losses to predatory animals are often (nearly always) examined after the deed; it is possible various predators were involved or even that Coyotes at times were implicated simply because they showed up to partake in a bit of carrion. Feral dogs are notorious killers of game such as deer and of defenseless stock such as lambs. For the calendar year 1971, the Commissioner commented (1971:8): "Coyotes and dogs cause a large loss to the sheep ranchers each year". For all of 1971, the trapper controlled 8 Coyotes and 43 Wild Dogs (1972 report, p. 17). In subsequent annual reports, "Wild Dogs" are never again mentioned. They are routinely controlled by the sheep herders and quietly buried. The days of advertising trapping prowess by hanging predator carcasses on the fence appear to be gone.

Well, when they're not eating leg of lamb, what do Coyotes eat? Few animals have had their diets analyzed so intensively. They are flexible opportunists, primarily consuming mice, ground squirrels, pocket gophers, rabbits, and other small mammals but also settling for birds, snakes, frogs, toads, insects, carrion, assorted fruits, grasses, and sedges. Group effort may on rare occasion reward them with venison; once in the Buttes we witnessed a dramatic chase in which four coyotes pursued two deer; the outcome, unfortunately from our viewpoint, was ultimately decided behind a rocky peak.

The Gray Fox is the gray ghost of the Buttes, a silent flash of grizzle and rust disappearing among boulders and shrubs. Those times I have surprised one, I've been impressed with its catlike agility, really beyond the skill of a cat, more of a controlled floating. This species is a notable tree-climber; I've found its scats in an abandoned eagle's nest up in a massive oak.

Gray Fox

Hunting mostly at night, the 7-13 pound mammal takes a great variety of foods, but is less carnivorous than might be expected. In a Utah study, primary foods were fruits, insects, and carrion, in that order (Trapp 1978). In the Buttes, partially-digested fruits of Coffeeberry, Toyon, and Large Manzanita are often found in fox scats.

No one seems to be positive how or from where, but the Red Fox appears to have been introduced to the Sacramento Valley around 1880. Though native Red Foxes in the Sierra Nevada prefer upper elevation forests, the valley population prefers the lowlands. Only occasionally does one venture into the Buttes. In the flatlands, Red Foxes may replace the native Grays through competitive effects (John Cowan, Gray Lodge Mammal List, undated).

The Raccoon Family: Procyonidae

These animals tend to evoke sympathetic reactions from people. Big eyes (all the better for their nightlife) peer from broad faces giving a mischievous look to the black-masked Raccoon, an innocent and curious look to the white-spectacled Ringtail. Those tails are the badges of the family — full and bushy with 4-6 complete black rings for the Raccoon, longer and more slender with 7-8 black rings incomplete on the underside for the Ringtail. Cahalane (1961) goes so far as to call the Ringtail "the most appealing of all the furry mammals".

Bassariscus astutus translates "clever little fox", and it's meant as a compliment. *Procyon* refers to a star which arises before the Dog Star, "pre-dog", and perhaps the connotation of "earlier than dog" was then applied to this mammal. *Lotor* means "washer", alluding to the species' almost obsessive tendency to moisten and manipulate objects, especially food items.

Ringtail

Both species are omnivorous, the Ringtail being perhaps more predatory, especially for mice. Its superior rodent-catching abilities earned it the sobriquet "Miner's Cat" during the Gold Rush. Both species enjoy fruits of Toyon, Large Manzanita, and Coffeeberry in season in the Buttes, and the 'coons are wild about Wild Figs. Ringtails often deposit their scat on boulders, 'coons on tree branches and logs. Look for Raccoons or their sign near water — creeks, ponds, springs — and Ringtails around cliffs, talus slopes, boulder jumbles, and riparian forest.

Trapping studies have shown the Ringtail to be one of our most strictly nocturnal species (Trapp 1978). Hence even when they are common, we seldom see them. I've seen several at night, two just after dawn, and one in mid-day, coinciding with a dark but brief thundershower.

Bait used to trap Raccoons may be tin or aluminum foil on the trigger of the trap; the curious animal is like a compulsive shoplifter, unable to resist touching and feeling the trinket. A Ringtail often is vulnerable to its sweet tooth, a sucker for a treat of raisins, honey, or fruit jelly. I've seen captured animals having been subjected to handling, measuring, and marking techniques, hesitate but a moment when released, then return to the bait instead of fleeing!

Part of the appeal of these charming creatures, if I may be so judgmental, derives from their alertness, curiosity, and activity patterns. A mole or rabbit may have its own appeal, but seems a relative bore next to a 'coon or Ringtail. The latter two, being omnivores, must be particularly sensitive to their surroundings. They investigate, explore, handle, examine, speculate, and react to things quickly and decisively; their diet demands it.

The Mustelid Family: Mustelidae

This family is a mixed bunch — some members swimmers (aquatic), climbers (arboreal), diggers (fossorial), and down-to-earth walkers (cursorial). What they have in common is typically low-slung bodies, five-toed feet, thick silky fur (not only valuable to them but also often sought by humans), paired anal scent glands, and a unique combination of molar teeth.

Despite their track record as valuable fur-bearers, they have often suffered a bad press, and some species (e.g., skunks, weasels, wolverines, badgers) may have more detractors than champions. Not that it matters much to them. Being a "good weasel" means doing that which through evolutionary time has paid off in weasel terms — namely, weasel genes. Why should they care if we disapprove of their scents or their predatory habits? I find it amusing that we so readily borrow their names and adapt them as epithets toward fellow people — "sneaky weasel", "dirty skunk", "no-good polecat", etc.

Found across most of the United States, the Long-tailed Weasel is a **likely** resident of the Buttes and Butte Sink. Almost strictly carnivorous, it is seldom abundant, and in low density, would be overlooked fairly easily. Perhaps life-long human residents of the Buttes have seen them. Their reputation as chicken-killers, despite their undoubted value in controlling rats and mice, has marked them as outlaws in many areas. A southern Michigan survey revealed that "seven out of ten weasels seen on farms ... were killed on the spot" (Cahalane 1961:182). I was unable to determine **which** spot.

Minks mingle with Muskrats in marshes, not as peaceful neighbors but as voracious predators. A male Mink may occupy a home range of more than 1100 acres, but one 935-acre marsh supported 30 minks, thanks to the presence of some 9000 Muskrats (Ingles 1965). Crayfish, fish, frogs, snakes, coots, waterfowl, rabbits, mice, and assorted small creatures may fall prey to these active carnivores. Apart from slight risk from foxes, Bobcats, and Great Horned Owls, most Minks have only man, parasites, and diseases to fear. By their very nature, they don't even fear these threats. Minks epitomize raw courage, defiance, pugnacity — or so we interpret it.

The first American furbearer to be "domesticated" was the Mink (Cahalane 1961). Small-scale fur-farming actually began before the Civil War. Locally, a few Mink may be trapped incidentally in Muskrat harvests. Their strong affinity for wetlands keeps them out of the Buttes interior, though riparian habitat and marshlands in the Butte Sink and Sutter Bypass are suitable.

The Badger is best known for its **miner** achievements. Squat, bow-legged, pigeon-toed, it is built to dig. When harassed by a potential predator, it can dig itself out of sight in a few moments, capably defending itself with formidable teeth and claws, if necessary. Even digging specialists — moles, pocket gophers, ground squirrels — are no match for the Badger in an earth-moving competition. This rodent control incidentally benefits humans who more often only notice the negative effects of holes in levees or pastures.

Badger

Badgers prefer open country with loose soils and abundant rodent prey. Cultivation and rodent control by humans has diminished their habitat significantly, and levee-diggers are eliminated even more directly. If Badgers didn't tend to be solitary in the first place, you might expect the local ones to be getting more and more lonely these days.

The bold black-and-white pattern of a skunk flashes a warning recognized by all but the most naive animals. Armed with obnoxious oily musk and a capable delivery system, the skunk can get by with its plodding, rolling gait and a rather indifferent attitude toward large predators. Even bears and Bobcats usually avoid the little beasts, though a Great Horned Owl won't hesitate to pick one off, being blessed with a negligible sense of smell.

Skunks will eat whatever flesh, fruit, eggs, or carrion they can acquire, but insects may be most important. They scratch and poke and snatch up beetles, crickets, grasshoppers, grubs, even bees. Since many apiarists keep hives in the Buttes, they occasionally suffer raids by skunks. Over the last seven years, 114 destroyed hives were reported to Sutter County officials and 248 skunks were destroyed in turn (Tables 6 and 7).

Both skunk species tend to be nocturnal, with the little Spotted Skunk more so. It's daintier and livelier than its larger Striped cousin, able to discharge its defensive (and offensive!) spray from the conservative four-footed stance or the acrobatic hand-stand. *Spilogale* tends to stay close to the cover of brush and boulders on its nightly forays and nimbly ascends trees and shrubs when so inclined. *Mephitis* may be encountered almost anywhere, fearlessly shuffling across open grassland, where we have occasionally crossed paths with one during our own explorations by moonlight.

River Otters frequent the Sacramento River, Butte Creek, and minor waterways around the Buttes. Their mainly carnivorous diet can include crayfish, fishes of many kinds, clams, Muskrats, Beavers, ducks — in short, items for which people often make competing claims. Yet few of us harbor a grudge against the otter, an artless charmer. Look at the adjectives we apply to these creatures, descriptions perhaps lacking scientific basis but with irresistible applicability — delightful, frivolous, high-spirited, graceful, amusing, exuberant, patient, peaceful, affectionate, gentle, intelligent, easily trained, friendly (Cahalane 1961). It seems quite proper in science to avoid anthropomorphism, to ascribe no human traits to animals. Yet how much of this restraint is objectively scientific and how much is subtle racism ("speciesism", if you prefer)? Can we not stand it if "lower" animals display temperaments or behaviors like ours? There is plenty of danger in "Disney-izing" animals, but it may be equally unfair to "objectify" them as mechanistic, stimulus-response products of structure, metabolism, hormones, and instinct.

Watch these animals in action (this valley is as good a place as any in which to find them), and leave your mind open. Then judge as you would be judged.

The Cat Family: Felidae

One day I was prowling around alone atop a rubbly, wooded volcano near North Butte. I had been out all day and had eased into a woodsman's style of movement — slow, quiet, alert. I chanced to look behind myself and barely glimpsed the tawny shape of a Bobcat as it effortlessly leaped a low fence, dodged a manzanita, and disappeared downslope. It was **close,** yet I heard no sound — no rustle of leaf, no impact of paw, no gasp of breath. I felt as awkward as a cow by comparison.

There's no easy way to census Bobcats. In five years of exploring the Buttes, I've seen one live animal (barely that!) and one carcass. The County Trapper knows they're there; he removed one in 1975-76, and he sees their sign. How often do they see me? What crosses their feline minds when they observe a herd of bipedal primates examining flowers and oak galls and peering at birds through binoculars?

A relative newcomer in the Buttes is the feral House Cat (*Felis domestica*), a quick and able predator on small mammals and birds. When you surprise one, it acts as if it knows it doesn't belong there. It exudes an impression of guilt, and yet its stare brings forth guilt in you, for you know that humans are responsible for it being there.

The Deer Family: Cervidae

"Have you seen the white deer?" has been a frequent question addressed to me by Sutter County residents. It occurs with a frequency to place it in a curiosity category along with the nonexistent "central crater", the unverified "robber's cave", and the occasional reports of UFO's. In fact, I have **not** seen a white deer in the Buttes, but that doesn't make it mythical. Albino or partial albino deer have turned up occasionally over the years at the Buttes, Gray Lodge, and up the valley all the way to Chico. Some of these have ended up as specimens on trophy walls. Being conspicuous would seem bad enough, but being unique makes it worse. Probably few white deer live long enough to contribute many genes to the population, but some genes no doubt persist in normal-looking carriers. I've heard no verified reports of white individuals in the past five years, but they may occur again.

Our deer are Black-tailed, technically a recognizable race of the Mule Deer. Black-tails, generally smaller and darker than Mulies, have a flattened tail

entirely dark above; the Mule Deer tail is more rounded and black only at the
tip. Mulies have a metatarsal gland on the hind leg about five inches long,
compared to three inches in the Black-tailed Deer. Black-tails are typical of
coastal regions all the way from south-central California to southeast Alaska,
while Mulies take over in the intermountain west; both types overlap in the
northern Sierra Nevada.

Deer often become tame and approachable in areas where they are protected
and in frequent contact with humans, but those in the Buttes tend to be wild
and skittish. When hunting season begins, even though the Buttes do not
receive heavy hunter pressure, bucks really make themselves scarce. High water
in the valley can force many deer from the lowlands to the
island sanctuary of the Buttes. I've seen up to fifty deer on a single winter day.

Black-tailed Deer

References

Burt, W.H. and Grossenheider, R.P. 1964. *A Field Guide to the Mammals.* Houghton Mifflin Co., Boston.

Cahalane, V.H. 1961. *Mammals of North America.* The Macmillan Co., New York.

Hall, E.R. 1981. *The Mammals of North America.* John Wiley & Sons, New York.

Ingles, L.G. 1965. *Mammals of the Pacific States.* Stanford University Press, Calif.

Murie, O.J. 1954. *A Field Guide to Animal Tracks.* Houghton Mifflin Co., Boston.

Simpson, R. 1977. *Ooti: A Maidu Legacy.* Celestial Arts, Millbrae, Calif.

Trapp, G.R. 1978. Comparative behavioral ecology of the Ringtail and Gray Fox in southwestern Utah. *Carnivore* 1(2):3-32.

Verner, J. and Boss, A.S., eds. 1980. *California Wildlife and their Habitats: Western Sierra Nevada.* U.S. Forest Service Gen. Tech. Rep. PSW-37, U.S. Dept. of Agriculture, Berkeley, Calif.

Whitaker, J.O., Jr. 1980. *The Audubon Society Field Guide to North American Mammals.* Alfred A. Knopf, New York.

12

Land Use and Abuse: The Hand of Man

We who reckon time in hours and days can't fully appreciate the meaning of centuries, let alone millions of years. Geologically, the Sutter Buttes is young — what's two million years on a planet with a five billion year history? The so-called native peoples or Indians have only been in western North America for a few tens of thousands of years. The Spanish didn't even see the Buttes until the 1850's. Yet the changes in the Sacramento Valley landscape in the past 100-150 years have been profound, merely precursors of more changes which seem inevitable.

Flying over the valley at night provides some insight into human impact. Points of light are scattered below, in places concentrated in swarms of illumination marking towns and cities — Chico, Oroville, Gridley, Live Oak, Yuba City, Marysville, Sutter, Colusa, Willows, etc. To the south the metropolitan glow of Sacramento lights the sky. Yet one area is curiously dark, a major blank on an electrical map — the Sutter Buttes and Butte Sink.

Flying over again by day reveals the character of the upland and marshland so little affected by nocturnal lights. Surrounding these relatively natural features is a maze of rectangular fields, highways, buildings, and other human artifacts. Daylight reveals a man-aged land, from which the Buttes rise in peculiar isolation and grandeur. Yet even they show the scars of roadways, power lines, quarries, and the like.

The Maidu Indians called them Estawm Yan or Histum Yani, the Middle Hills. Maidu and Wintun (Colus) people both claimed the region (Jenson 1970) and held the hills sacred. It was here, according to Maidu legend, that the World Maker created man and woman, from whom a great family — a People — descended (Simpson 1977).

Two centuries ago Indians were widespread in California, living close to the land upon which they depended (Heizer and Whipple 1971). A century later white man's diseases, guns, and civilizing influences had reduced them to a tenth of their former numbers, taking with them much of their cultural heritage. In the Buttes they left behind a scattering of sites with bedrock mortars, pestles, arrowheads, a few other artifacts. Many of the artifacts have been taken from the Buttes for private collections, or more often, to become dust-gathering souvenirs forgotten in a shoebox. Only a few sites have been properly catalogued by archeologists (Jensen 1970), and the real significance of the Buttes to the Indians can only be guessed at from tiny scraps of evidence.

Bedrock Mortars

We can visit a site of bedrock mortars, listen to the gurgling winter creek whose waters the Indians used to leach the bitter tannins from the acorns, look up to the same peaks they revered, even feel the shade of some of the same old oaks they knew. One wonders how many rhythmic strikes of the pestle each mortar hole felt. How many generations of Maidu and Wintun lived here in traditional ways before that way of life came to a sudden and irreversible halt?

We know that the Indians defended territorial claims, but this was a defense of group space, a way to maintain an area in which to hunt, fish, gather, and dwell. What a surprise it must have been when white man came, planting flags and declaring ownership, later building fences and moving the surviving

Indians around like pawns on a chessboard, literally brushing many of them off the board of occupiable land. Could they understand the network of fences subdividing the Buttes today, let alone the deeds and papers by which we claim **ownership** of the land and everything thereon?

The history of American settlement and development is far better known to us than that of the Indians, reflecting both cultural and temporal bias (see references in Hendrix 1970 or contact the Sutter County Historical Society or the Community Memorial Museum). It is beyond the scope or intent of this book to summarize the wealth of historical material presently known or yet to be uncovered. Instead I will draw attention to a few examples as they relate to visible impacts upon the natural ecosystems of the Buttes.

Though the Buttes bear his name, Sutter probably had little direct impact on the range. It was merely part of the 48,827-acre land grant, New Helvetia, that he received from the Mexican government in 1841. The Buttes went by a number of names (e.g., Marysville Buttes, Los Tres Picos, Sacramento Buttes) until standardized in 1949 to match the name of the county.

General John Fremont and his U.S. Army troops, primarily engaged in a scientific expedition, were swept up by the current of events in 1846 into activities which finally exploded in the Bear Flag Revolt and ultimately the formation of the state of California. It is surprising to look back at journals and early accounts to see how much the formation of this state depended on seemingly random events, quirks of personality and timing. We so often treat the statistics of history as if they were rational, sequential, perhaps even inevitable. It just wasn't so. That this particular story is written in English rather than Spanish may be just one of the consequences of historical flukes. Who can say?

So chance events brought Fremont and his men back to California in 1846, back from Oregon where they were on their way east. From May 30 - June 8 the group camped in the Sutter Buttes, meeting with settlers worried about rumors of Indian attacks and with men eager to go to war if necessary to create a new republic. The Buttes were chosen deliberately, the logical rendezvous site in the valley. Fremont's men found the Buttes a "happy hunting ground", where a single morning's take of game might number eighty deer, elk, and bear. That abundance seemed inexhaustible, yet the frontier harvest, of which Fremont's camp was typical, in a matter of years eliminated the elk, the pronghorn, and the bear, yes even the symbol of the Bear Flag Revolt. In 1850 a horseback rider in the Buttes experienced what he described in gory detail as an unprovoked attack by a grizzly (Delano 1854). The bear, of course, was killed by the heroic efforts of the narrator (unwitnessed "attacks" made the best stories, after all). It didn't take civilization long to remove the golden grizzly not only from the Buttes but from the entire state of California.

The gold rush of 1849 and after quickly changed the face of northern California. Families and buildings remaining in Sutter County today trace their histories to settlement in the 1850's, 1860's, and later. Ripples of reaction to the Civil War were felt in the area. Slowly at first, then with growing momentum, the land felt the ax, the plow, the wagon wheel. Rock walls still standing remind us of intensive hand and horse labor, the efforts of Chinese, Germans, and others at 10-25 cents per day, to fence properties and clear a little rock from the pastures at the same time. Later came barbed wire, a revolutionary technological change, though erecting fence posts in the rocky land was scarcely easier than building a rock wall. Examples of the early varieties of barbed wire are displayed in the Sutter County Community Memorial Museum. Century-old strands of Buckthorn Ribbon Wire may still be encountered in certain places in the Buttes.

Transportation was a bit of a problem in the early days. Flooding of the valley floor was not infrequent, so several wagon roads were scratched out in the Buttes, well above the threatening waters. Traces remain, narrow winding tracks, often lined by the great stones moved aside in construction.

At one time or another, almost every decent spring was claimed as a homesite. We have found relics of those homesteads — a few orchard trees, rusted stoves and pots — in the most surprising places, far up in the hills where no roads go. Any trip out for supplies and back must have been a major expedition.

As settlement progressed, small communities sprang up — North Butte (later Pennington), West Butte, and South Butte (later Sutter). West Butte at the western end of Pass Road and near the wildlife-rich Butte Sink, was a major stopover on the route between Colusa and Marysville and a pick-up point for the market hunters' take of ducks. South Butte was a loose collection of ranches from 1861 until 1887 or so, a place with agricultural potential but vulnerability to the periodic flooding which swept the valley; at least its residents were close to high ground when evacuation was necessary.

The South Butte community was awakened from its sleepy existence in 1887 when local papers announced a building boom, a plan to make a real town — Sutter City — from the farmland and orchards. A P.D. Gardemeyer stood behind the proposal, setting up a syndicate in San Francisco called the Sutter County Land and Improvement Company (Hendrix 1980). Gardemeyer had been in the area for three years and had met and married a wealthy local widow, whose lands and fortune fueled the land enterprise.

By 1890 Sutter City had some 200 buildings and 800 residents. There was a courthouse, bank, school, two churches, hotel, newspaper office, even a planned college site. Gardemeyer told of plans for railroad and canal connections to the town. Perhaps his most ambitious plan, however, was for the Buttes themselves. He envisioned them as more than a picturesque backdrop to the new Sutter City. He imagined the south face of South Butte, the highest peak in the range, neatly terraced and built up as a luxury resort hotel, where clients could step out into an extensive game reserve for the sport of shooting the elk, deer, antelope, and other animals.

Promises and expectations took the town a long way, but the railroad, the canal, the resort hotel were never to be. Confidence in the syndicate began to erode, and Gardemeyer was sued on a number of mortgage defaults. The zealous promoter staved off conviction for a time through technicalities, then skipped the area, reappearing later in Texas as the instigator of equally bogus land schemes.

The Sutter City boom was over; many investors went broke, some houses were moved to Yuba City, development lots were converted back to orchards. Poor Mrs. Gardemeyer, abandoned by her parasitic husband, was later murdered by one of his irate financial victims. And the Sutter Buttes was spared the defacement of a resort hotel, though more than a half century later, an access road and communication towers scarred the same peak.

Though grazing for cattle and sheep was the primary use of the Sutter Buttes uplands from the start, there was interest in mining. Some coal was extracted from the sedimentary materials predating the Buttes themselves. In 1864, a

Rhyolite Dome

Gas Well

shaft sunk on Davis property near South Butte failed to reach coal, but proved without doubt that natural gas was present. The resultant explosion knocked the miners for a loop. What a disappointment it must have been — nothing but **gas** in their hole! Not until 1932 was that find turned to economic advantage, when the Buttes Oil Fields Company spudded their Buttes No. 1 well. Today the rhythmic pumping, almost like tomtoms softly in the distance, marks the continued extraction of natural gas from what has become an extensive and highly productive field (Thamer 1961).

The search for gold following the 1849 discovery first concentrated in the Sierra, but it was inevitable that the gravels lifted up by the Buttes volcanics should be inspected too. Gold there was, enough to support a few people for a few years of wet-season placer mining from the late 1880's to the early 1900's, but no one ever grew rich from the effort.

The deposits of eroded-down particles of andesite and rhyolite in the rampart of the Buttes made excellent road bed and construction material in a county without any other surface rock. In recent years the utility of that resource has had to be weighed against esthetic considerations, as the gouges left by the mighty machines leave scars visible for miles. The Sutter County General Plan on Conservation and Open Space, 1972-1990, sets standards of landscape restoration for quarries and encourages measures to reduce visual blight caused by other extractive industries, such as gas wells.

Sheep

Grazing of cattle and sheep must have had some significant effects on the Sutter Buttes landscape, especially initially, when the domesticated grazers replaced the mixed community of grazers and browsers. Coincident with the advent of grazing came introduction, intentional or accidental, of many species of plants. Grazing, fire, and introductions changed species compositions, we know. The full extent will never be known, however, because there were no quantitative baseline studies (even few **qualitative** statements) on what was was there initially.

The impact of grazing has not been uniform. Some ranges have been stocked moderately and managed with long-term sustainability in mind; these ranches have good mixed stands of native bunchgrasses and floral patterns that suggest that such grazing is not incompatible with wildlife and scenic values.

Other ranches show years of livestock abuse: eroded gullies, heavy stands of noxious weeds, and dead trees standing with random piles of fallen limbs at their bases. The face of the land displays the worth of the rancher better than does the balance in his checkbook.

Several columns of towers carrying high voltage power lines march across the Buttes, often with access roads beneath them. More have been proposed. One might think that such visual blight in a highly scenic area could be avoided by keeping such corridors in the flat lands, where installation ought to be easier as well. Apparently the lower cost of right-of-way over grazing land as opposed to agricultural land favors cross-Buttes routes. But has the long-range cost to the scenic and recreational resource been assessed?

Similarly, the placement of communication towers atop South Butte, along with the slashing switchbacks of the access road, has created a visual eyesore. When the first tower was proposed, the key landowner even then was ambivalent about the impact of the structure. He decided that the need for the communication link was high enough to justify the damage to the landscape; in recent years, he has admitted to harboring second thoughts. Now we hear that the McClatchy corporation, owner of the summit of North Butte, wishes to erect one or more structures there. Then the two highest peaks of Estawm Yan, the sacred range of the Maidu, would bear the blatant artifacts of twentieth century man (who knows if such structures will even be useful in the next century?). The impact of these towers and roads is not trivial. South Butte a few decades ago was a dramatic, inspirational peak; now it seems a cripple, a domesticated piece of property. If North Butte were lost, the entire range would be diminished. How many intrusions — towers, roads, quarries, buildings — will it take before the Buttes is reduced from a rare and spectacular ecosystem to a hodgepodge of properties varying only in degree of degradation? There are enough people who care about the Buttes that it need not become that way.

I would be interested in knowing the Indian reaction to the placement of the Titan Missile Base in the northwest edge of the Buttes in 1960. Their sacred range was forced to be the repository for incredible weapons of destruction. Ironically, the weapon system was declared obsolete by the time it was finished, and by 1966, the land was back in private ownership. The missiles were gone but the silos remained, naturally stimulating a barrage of ideas of what they could be used for. Even the unthinkable was thought of — why, wouldn't this be a fine place to dump radioactive wastes? Since ground water leaked into (and out of) at least one of the silos, the possibility of ground water contamination must have seemed a bit high. Others have proposed dumping local garbage into the concrete pits. If that were to happen, we might have a world record in the ratio of values of container to contents. It would pose no threat to human life, at least.

Limited access to the private lands to some extent controls deer hunting pressure in the Buttes. The ruggedness of the landscape discourages certain would-be hunters, and locked gates prevent some four-wheelers from practicing the drive, hop out, and shoot tactics. Many landowners minimize hunting impact by restricting it to family and a few friends. Yet there are abuses. Poachers can be so bold as to shoot or cut locks and chains. There are a few who have used old friendships and a variety of leverages to get access to much of the interior, where they know they can get away with pretty much what they please. I wonder if these are among the last of the poachers that the Buttes will know or if there is an outlaw niche that will be filled whenever an opening appears.

Other forms of recreation are non-consumptive: hiking, bird-watching, nature study, photography. The demand has always been there. The presence of the peaks beckons the adventurer in us, draws us upward to see the view or simply what's behind the next bend.

For a long time, the needs of curious outsiders were easily satisfied. Landowners rarely challenged the occasional visitor, who usually was careful in closing gates, avoiding livestock concentrations, and the like. But easy access was abused by the few, those nameless persons who through either carelessness or outright belligerence spooked the animals, drove their vehicles off the established roads, started fires. In the mid-1960's, a number of cases of arson turned the hills into blazing infernos. The trust was badly damaged, and the landowners, certainly with justification, basically sealed off public access. Aerial and road patrols put teeth into the "No Trespassing" words posted conspicuously along the fences. Trespassers caught without permission were often prosecuted. And the damage did diminish. Occasionally some idiot would start a fire along Pass Road or elsewhere around the periphery, but these fires could be more easily contained than ones set far in the interior.

Then the Buttes experienced the "forbidden fruit" or "grass is greener" syndrome. While some school groups, scout troops, and friends of landowners did manage to get in if they had the right connections, the "average" citizen of Sutter County or the Sacramento Valley was denied access. The effectiveness of the owners in protecting the land from public use simply made the land even more desirable to people seeking meaningful outdoor experiences in land that wasn't replete with the scars and symbols of man's use.

In the 1970's the growing demand for attractive recreational land and the beauty of the Buttes drew the attention of the state. Spurred by the activities of a local group called "Save the Sutter Buttes", a movement to create a state park in the range grew. Landowners tended to resent the implications of SSB; after all, they figured with reasonable justification that **they** were already saving the Buttes. Many people questioned the actual fate of the land should the public have fairly free access in a state park. Could the impact be contained completely within park boundaries? It may be somewhat of an oversimplification, but the rising heat from the friction between the increasingly polarized sides led to a backing off by the state, at least a temporary tabling of park plans.

In the meantime, one landowner reasoned that eventually the state would be back. If his land were managed for public access, the state should see no need to acquire property with limited park funds to provide essentially the same function. With consulting help from the National Audubon Society, he set up the West Butte Sanctuary Company and hired Rebecca and me as directors in October of 1976.

On December 26 the first party of people accompanied me on a "Boots in the Buttes" hike. There followed a series of day and weekend outings that provided not only access, but considerable natural history information — an educational and recreational experience. We felt that the opportunities for legal access helped reduce pressure on other landowners, as well; most people interested in the Buttes were willing to pay for the privilege of access with an expert naturalist rather than risk illegal trespass.

Gradually other naturalists became involved. The prototype of public access on private land seemed to be working admirably. Yet growing awareness of philosophical differences between the company owner and us led to the sudden, rather surprising, closure of WBSC in February of 1979.

We felt that the concept of use of private land for public education and enjoyment was too valuable for it to cease. If a valid concept, it should not depend on the patronage of a single landowner. I sat down and drew up three forms — a basic statement of principle, an access agreement, and a liability release — and approached other Sutter Buttes landowners. The response has been most gratifying. By 1982 more than three dozen landowners have granted access to parties under my supervision. More naturalists have shared their enthusiasm and expertise with an appreciative and cooperative public. The rights of landowner and land have been respected and observed, and the Sutter Buttes has become a regional center for learning about the natural world.

The idea of restricted access is not unique to the Sutter Buttes. For example, Stanford University allows certain classes and age groups access to the Jasper Ridge Reserve with docent guides. The **resource,** the very reason for the existence of such reserves, is protected, while a high quality educational experience is provided.

Occasionally conservationists are challenged with the argument that "locking up" the land in reserves means that only an "elite" group — the young and fit, the wealthy — can get in. As presently practiced, the access program in the Buttes is fair and democratic. Daily fees vary according to services provided, but most are quite modest; a full day's hike may cost less than a fine dinner. Classes offered through Yuba College are tuition free, the only requirement a willingness to come and learn. Age and infirmity need not be barriers either. I have been accompanied by tiny children and elderly persons in their mid-80's. By special arrangement, trips can be set up which involve frequent stops by car, with a minimum of walking.

The pioneers moved west to seek opportunity, space and resources that the already crowded east could not provide. Their very migration carried a conservation implication, but they didn't see it. Land and wildlife in the west seemed limitless, yet little by little the game diminished, the soil grew depleted, the water table dropped.

Ducks and geese in the Butte Sink filled the sky, and market hunters shipped their fresh carcasses by the thousands to San Francisco. Gradually the evening

Pintail

flights dropped from unimaginable clouds to countable flocks. Some restraint seemed advisable — perhaps no spring shooting and no more than fifty birds per day in fall and winter (Epperson and Epperson 1978). From 1891 through 1912, those restrictions scarcely handicapped the market hunter, but gradually declining flocks did. By 1913 the bag limit was dropped to 25 ducks per day and the season reduced to October 15 to February 1. Today harvest limits are much lower. It is an inescapable fact that rising human populations with rising demands cannot maintain even the same per capita consumption of a declining resource. We live in an age of limits, and we need to recognize those limits and adjust to them as we go.

The same is true, of course, of the land as an agricultural and recreational resource. The Sutter County General Plan on Conservation and Open Space, 1972-1990, acknowledges this fact (p. 10):

> "The purpose of the plan is to preserve as much open space as is possible whether it be agriculture, flood plain or wildlife habitat. ... the intent of the plan is to confine urbanization and to create no new urban communities."

Later (p. 19), the plan recommends:

> "It is proposed that certain portions of the Buttes be preserved in their natural state and that they not be scarred by roads cut out of mountains and cliffs."

Clearly, the county planners see the Sutter Buttes as a valuable attraction and asset. It remains to be seen whether that recognition will be translated into positive action to protect the integrity of the range or whether planner recommendations will be ignored when economic and political pressures are brought to bear.

Both the Sutter Buttes and Butte Sink are listed as California Natural Areas (Hood 1981). The Buttes are notable for examples of volcanism, Blue Oak woodland, and chaparral. The California Institute of Man in Nature considers the Buttes to be a vital central link in the Across California Land Heritage Corridor. Planning and acquisition teams of the California State Parks system have visited the Buttes several times in recent years; their interest has not died, despite the controversy they discovered in the 1970's.

So what is the future of the Buttes? Here is an ecosystem and geologic masterpiece that has survived intact to date through a fortunate set of circumstances, including ownership by people whose ambitions have so far been compatible with maintenance of the resource. Here is an area increasingly recognized by individuals and organizations for its natural values, a recognition that stirs a desire to maintain and to experience those values. Here are other resources — construction rock, natural gas, desirable building sites, tower locations — that attract interests which may be incompatible with others.

How tempting it would be to stop time if we could. On countless hikes in the past half dozen years I have walked through tall grasses along lichen-spattered rock walls; heard the unrestrained lyrics of Canyon Wrens and the impressive screams of Red-tailed Hawks; watched lizards doing push-ups and Golden Eagles soaring by; felt the wind caroming off a rhyolite dome and back off an oak grove; and met the friendly horseman riding fence or checking for new calves.

I can't imagine this lovely place nicked up piece by piece by developers who capitalize on people's desires to have a "country home". Nor can I see this as a "civilized" park with paved roads, campgrounds, concession stands, campfire talks, signed nature trails.

Our programs of controlled access have worked out well so far. Landowners continue their traditional ranching, outsiders enjoy the environmental experience, and both types coexist in friendship and respect. Private enterprise can be sensitive and still protect the resource base, perhaps more easily than can public agencies which may yield to public demands.

Yet this model of cooperation can persist only with the continued restraint and good intentions of both the naturalist-guide and the landowner. Private enterprise is vulnerable to exploitation, and even if a majority of Sutter Buttes properties were to be managed properly, the improper manipulation of a few key areas could destroy the character of the whole area.

Already, mechanized "tram" rides (carts pulled by a caterpillar tractor over dirt roads as a tram jockey announces points of interest to guests wearing head phones) have been proposed for one property, a golf course for another. One man has speculated that a rock concert might well be accommodated in a natural amphitheater of rounded hills. There has been talk of setting up private hunting preserves, providing lodging and recreation to wealthy clients (shades of P.D. Gardemeyer's South Butte scheme). Of course there are people interested in hang gliding, off-road vehicle races, and who knows what all. If the bottom line reads right, private enterprise can accommodate them. Ironically, a blatant abuse or threat of abuse might again stir the bureaucratic machinery into action toward taking public ownership; either way, the land may change away from its present, relatively natural state.

I tend to lean rather naturally toward continued private ownership of the Buttes, inasmuch as long-term family continuity can foster a feeling of individual responsibility that implies land stewardship. But I realize that tradition may have to be tempered by constraints, that the type of abuses mentioned earlier must be protected against.

Zoning or the purchase of scenic easements or development rights for upland areas without existing buildings might be a feasible approach. Inappropriate construction, development, or activities would be regulated by a board or agency charged with overseeing the ongoing integrity of the range. Planning **must** have a holistic, ecosystem emphasis.

Secondly, public access to private land should continue on a scheduled, guided basis in order to maintain high quality and prevent abuse. Ideally a natural history association would coordinate scheduling and assignment of

Hikers

naturalist guides. Monitoring of the environment should allow protection of sensitive areas (eagle or falcon nesting sites, lambing areas, fragile ground cover locations, etc.).

With proper scheduling, many guided groups can be present in the Buttes simultaneously without direct contact or competition. Most access should be on foot, since the carrying capacity for hikers (in terms of quality of experience) far exceeds that of drivers on designated roads. Edward Abbey (1968:62) points out that "a motorized vehicle, when not at rest, requires a volume of space far out of proportion to its size."

The changes in our country in the past hundred years have been astounding, even staggering to contemplate. We would be foolish to think that the status quo in the Sutter Buttes can be maintained without some planning followed by active management. It **is** possible to see traditional ranching continued while allowing public access for environmental study while protecting the landscape and its biota. It will take close cooperation among the private owners, the land planners, the various friends of the Buttes. May this book be a step in that direction.

References

Abbey, E. 1968. *Desert Solitaire.* Ballantine Books, New York.

Delano, A. 1854. *Life on the Plains and Among the Diggings.* Miller, Orton, and Mulligan, Auburn and Buffalo.

Epperson, M. and Epperson, R. 1978. Hunting waterfowl. *Sutter Co. Historical Soc. News Bulletin* 17(1):9-30.

Heizer, R.F. and Whipple, M.A., eds. 1971. *The California Indians.* University of California Press, Berkeley.

Hendrix, L.B. 1980. *Sutter Buttes: Land of Histum Yani.* Hendrix, Yuba City, Calif.

Hood, L., ed. 1981. *Inventory of California Natural Areas.* California Natural Area Coord. Council, Sonoma, Calif.

Jensen, P. 1970. Notes on the archeology of the Sutter Buttes, California. In *Papers on California and Great Basin Prehistory,* Center for Archeol. Research at Davis, Calif., Publ. #2.

Simpson, R. 1977. *Ooti: A Maidu Legacy.* Celestial Arts, Millbrae, Calif.

Thamer, D.H. 1961. Marysville Buttes. *Geological Society of Sacramento Annual Field Trip Mimeo,* 36-41.

Appendix A. General Rock Types. (after Flint and Skinner 1974, Pough 1976)

A. Sedimentary: rock derived from cementing or natural binding of loose rock particles or mineral grains at ordinary temperatures near or at the earth's surface.

Ex. siltstone   mainly composed of compacted dust-sized particles (silt) plus some clay; slightly gritty surface

sandstone   quartz and other medium-sized grains cemented by a natural glue such as iron oxide, silica, or calcium carbonate

shale   compacted clay, silt, or mud in fine-grained form with a smooth surface and a tendency to break into thin layers

chert   hard, dense rock (often red, green, or yellow) formed primarily of microscopic quartz crystals

conglomerate   mixture of rounded waterworn pebbles cemented in finer-grained materials

breccia   mixture of angular-edged pebbles cemented in finer-grained materials

limestone   fine-grained calcareous rock dominated by calcite (calcium carbonate), formed by chemical precipitation and/or from shells of marine organisms

B. Metamorphic: rock derived within earth's crust by high temperature and/or pressure modifying existent rocks.

Ex. slate   altered shale, harder and more lustrous than the original shale, tending to cleave into thin plates, often across original sedimentary layering

schist   highly metamorphosed shale with distinctly obvious flaky or elongate minerals (mica, chlorite, hornblende)

gneiss   very coarse-grained metamorphic rock with pronounced layering but imperfect cleavage

quartzite   sandstone cemented with quartz so tightly that the grains no longer separate on fracture but break right through

coal   black burnable carbon-based rock (lignite when a softer
                sedimentary rock just slightly metamorphosed)

greenstone   dark, fine-grained rock, often but not always greenish,
                derived from basic igneous rock (e.g., basalt)

C. Igneous: rock derived by cooling and solidifying magma (molten silicate
   material beneath the earth's surface); considered intrusive or plutonic if
   cooled slowly at depth, extrusive or volcanic if erupted at earth's surface.

granite   coarse-grained, light-colored plutonic rock with
                abundant quartz and orthoclase feldspar, micas (mus-
                covite and biotite), and sometimes hornblende

diorite   coarse-grained, medium-colored plutonic rock with
                little or no quartz, abundant plagioclase feldspar,
                micas, and sometimes pyroxene

gabbro   coarse-grained, dark-colored plutonic rock with no
                quartz, plentiful plagioclase feldspar, abundant
                pyroxene, and sometimes olivine

rhyolite   fine-grained, light-colored volcanic rock with abun-
                dant quartz and orthoclase feldspar, commonly with
                biotite

dacite   fine-grained, fairly light-colored volcanic rock with
                amounts of quartz, biotite, and hornblende interme-
                diate between those of rhyolite and andesite

andesite   fine-grained, medium-colored volcanic rock with little
                or no quartz, abundant plagioclase feldspar, and
                usually hornblende more common than biotite

basalt   fine-grained, dark-colored volcanic rock with no
                quartz, abundant plagioclase feldspar, plentiful pyro-
                xene, and sometimes olivine

obsidian   non-granular dense glass formed by sudden chilling of
                (usually rhyolitic) lava

pumice   extremely light-weight, light-colored glassy froth
                blasted out from a volcano, often chemically identical
                to obsidian and rhyolite

tuff   a rock composed of volcanic fragments less than 2 mm in size

porphyritic rocks   any igneous rock with large isolated crystals within the groundmass; andesite from the Sutter Buttes is strongly porphyritic with prominent feldspar crystals

propylites   altered andesites which, in the Buttes, probably were changed by action of carbon dioxide-charged hot water acting so as to replace hornblende crystals with those of the minerals chlorite and calcite

Appendix B. Particles, Sediments, Sedimentary Rocks.
(after Flint and Skinner 1974:table 5.1)

Particle Name	Approximate Diameter (mm)	(inch)	Loose Sediment	Consolidated Rock
clay	$<\dfrac{1}{256}$	<0.00015	clay	claystone mudstone shale
silt	$\dfrac{1}{256}$ - $\dfrac{1}{16}$	0.00015-0.0025	silt	siltstone
sand	$\dfrac{1}{16}$ - 2	0.0025-0.09	sand	sandstone
pebble	2-64	0.09-2.5	gravel	conglomerate (rounded)
cobble	64-256	2.5-10	gravel	or
boulder	>256	>10	gravel	sedimentary breccia (angular)

Appendix C. Checklist of Some Larger Fungi of the Sutter Buttes.

EUMYCOPHYTA DIVISION

Helvellaceae
_____ *Helvella crispa*

Tremellaceae
_____ *Tremella mesenterica*

Clavariaceae
_____ *Clavariadelphus pistillaris*
_____ *Sparassis radicata*

Polyporaceae
_____ *Laetiporus sulphureus*

_____ *Trametes versicolor*
        (*Coriolus v.;Polyporus v.*)

Amanitaceae
_____ *Amanita vaginata*

Bolbitiaceae
_____ *Bolbitius vitellinus*

Boletaceae
_____ *Suillus spp.*

Cortinariaceae
_____ *Inocybe spp.*

Russulaceae
_____ *Lactarius deliciosus*
_____ *Russula spp.*

Tricholomataceae
_____ *Mycena spp.*

Geastraceae
_____ *Geastrum spp.*

Lycoperdaceae
_____ *Bovista pila*
_____ *Calbovista subsculpta*
_____ *Lycoperdon perlatum*

Saddle Fungus Family
_____ Fluted White Helvella

Jelly Fungus Family
_____ Witches' Butter

Coral Fungus Family
_____ Pestle-shaped Coral
_____ Rooting Cauliflower Mushroom

Polypore Family
_____ Chicken Mushroom or Sulphur
        Shelf Fungus
_____ Rainbow Shelf Fungus or
        Turkey-tail

Amanita Family
_____ Grisette

Bolbitius Family
_____ Yellow Bolbitius

Bolete Family
_____ Suillus

Cortinarius Family
_____ Fiber Head

Russula Family
_____ Delicious Milky Cap
_____ Russula

Tricholoma Family
_____ Mycena

Earthstar Family
_____ Earthstar

Puffball Family
_____ Papery or Tumbling Puffball
_____ Sculptured Puffball
_____ Gem-studded Puffball

Appendix D. Checklist of Vascular Plants of the Sutter Buttes.

LEPIDOPHYTA DIVISION

Isoetaceae
____ *Isoetes howellii*
____ *Isoetes nuttallii*

Selaginellaceae
____ *Selaginella hansenii*

Quillwort Family
____ Howell's Quillwort
____ Nuttall's Quillwort

Club Moss Family
____ Hansen's Club Moss or
Resurrection Fern

CALAMOPHYTA DIVISION

Equisetaceae
____ *Equisetum laevigatum*

Horsetail Family
____ California Horsetail or Scouring Rush

PTEROPHYTA DIVISION

Marsileaceae
____ *Marsilea vestita*
(*M. mucronata*)

Polypodiaceae
____ *Adiantum jordanii*
____ *Cheilanthes californica*
(*Aspidotis c.*)
____ *Cheilanthes covillei*
____ *Cystopteris fragilis*
____ *Dryopteris arguta*
____ *Pellaea andromedifolia*
____ *Pellaea mucronata*
____ *Pityrogramma triangularis*
____ *Polypodium californicum*
____ *Woodwardia fimbriata*

Salviniaceae
____ *Azolla mexicana*

Pepperwort Family
____ Clover Fern or
Hairy Pepperwort

Fern Family
____ California Maidenhair Fern
____ California Lace Fern

____ Bead Fern or Coville's Lip Fern
____ Brittle Fern or Bladder Fern
____ Coastal Wood Fern
____ Coffee Fern
____ Bird's-foot Cliff Brake
____ Goldenback Fern
____ California Polypody
____ Giant Chain Fern

Water Fern Family
____ Water Fern or Mexican Duckweed

CONIFEROPHYTA DIVISION

Cupressaceae
____ *Juniperus californica*

Cypress Family
____ California Juniper

ANTHOPHYTA DIVISION

Dicotyledoneae Class

Amaranthaceae
____ *Amaranthus albus*
____ *Amaranthus blitoides*
____ *Amaranthus retroflexus*

Amaranth Family
____ Tumbleweed or Pigweed
____ Prostrate Pigweed
____ Rough or Green Pigweed

Anacardiaceae
_____ *Toxicodendron diversilobum*
(Rhus d.)
_____ *Rhus trilobata*

Apiaceae (Umbelliferae)
_____ *Anthriscus caucalis*
(A. scandicina)
_____ *Conium maculatum*
_____ *Daucus pusillus*
_____ *Eryngium vaseyi*
_____ *Lomatium macrocarpum*

_____ *Lomatium tomentosum*
(L. dasycarpum)
_____ *Lomatium utriculatum*
_____ *Perideridia bolanderi*
_____ *Perideridia kelloggii*
_____ *Sanicula bipinnata*
_____ *Sanicula bipinnatifida*
_____ *Sanicula crassicaulis*
_____ *Sanicula tuberosa*
_____ *Tauschia hartwegii*
_____ *Torilis heterophylla*
_____ *Torilis nodosa*

Aristolochiaceae
_____ *Aristolochia californica*

Asclepiadaceae
_____ *Asclepias cordifolia*
_____ *Asclepias eriocarpa*
_____ *Asclepias fascicularis*

Asteraceae (Compositae)
_____ *Achillea millefolium*
_____ *Achyrachaena mollis*
_____ *Agoseris heterophylla*
_____ *Ambrosia psilostachya*
_____ *Anthemis cotula*
_____ *Arnica discoidea*
_____ *Artemisia douglasiana*
_____ *Aster exilis*
_____ *Baccharis glutinosa*
(B. viminea)
_____ *Baccharis pilularis*
_____ *Balsamorhiza macrolepis*
_____ *Blennosperma nanum*
_____ *Brickellia californica*
_____ *Calycadenia truncata*
_____ *Carduus pycnocephalus*

Sumac Family
_____ Poison Oak

_____ Squaw Bush

Carrot Family
_____ Bur-chervil

_____ Poison Hemlock
_____ Rattlesnake Weed
_____ Vasey's Coyote-thistle
_____ Giant-seeded Lomatium or
Sheep Parsnip
_____ Woolly-fruited Lomatium

_____ Common Lomatium or Bladder Parsnip
_____ Bolander's Yampah
_____ Kellogg's Yampah
_____ Poison Sanicle
_____ Purple Sanicle
_____ Pacific Snakeroot
_____ Tuberous Sanicle
_____ Hartweg's Tauschia
_____ Hedge-parsley
_____ Knotted Hedge-parsley

Birthwort Family
_____ Dutchman's Pipe

Milkweed Family
_____ Purple Milkweed
_____ Woolly-pod or Indian Milkweed
_____ Narrow-leaved Milkweed

Composite or Sunflower Family
_____ Common Yarrow
_____ Blow Wives
_____ Woodland Dandelion
_____ Western Ragweed
_____ Mayweed or Dog Fennel
_____ Rayless Arnica
_____ California Mugwort
_____ Slim Aster
_____ Mulefat

_____ Coyote Brush or Chaparral Broom
_____ California Balsamroot
_____ Yellowfields or Common Blennosperma
_____ California Brickellbush
_____ Rosinweed
_____ Italian Thistle

Asteraceae (Compositae) (continued)

_____ *Centaurea calcitrapa* — Purple Star Thistle
_____ *Centaurea melitensis* — Tocalote or Napa Thistle
_____ *Centaurea solstitialis* — Yellow Star Thistle
_____ *Cichorium intybus* — Chicory or Blue Sailors
_____ *Cirsium occidentale* — Cobweb Thistle
_____ *Cirsium proteanum* — Red, Venus, or Coulter Thistle
_____ *Cirsium vulgare* — Bull Thistle
_____ *Conyza bonariensis* — South American Conyza
_____ *Conyza canadensis* — Horseweed
_____ *Ericameria linearifolius* — Narrowleaf Goldenbush
    (Haplopappus l.)
_____ *Erigeron divergens* — Diffuse Daisy or Spreading Fleabane
_____ *Erigeron inornatus* — California Rayless Daisy
_____ *Eriophyllum lanatum* — Woolly Sunflower
_____ *Euthamnia occidentalis* — Western Goldenrod
    (Solidago o.)
_____ *Filago gallica* — Narrow-leaved Filago
_____ *Gnaphalium californicum* — California Cudweed or Green Everlasting

_____ *Gnaphalium beneolens* — Fragrant Everlasting
_____ *Gnaphalium luteo-album* — Weedy Cudweed
_____ *Gnaphalium palustre* — Lowland Cudweed
_____ *Grindelia camporum* — Great Valley Gumplant
_____ *Helianthus annuus* — Wild Sunflower
_____ *Hemizonia fitchii* — Fitch's Spikeweed
_____ *Hemizonia luzulaefolia* — Hayfield Tarweed
_____ *Hemizonia parryi* — Parry's Spikeweed
_____ *Hypochoeris glabra* — Cat's Ear
_____ *Lactuca serriola* — Prickly Lettuce
_____ *Lagophylla ramosissima* — Common Hareleaf
_____ *Lasthenia californica* — Goldfields
    (L. chrysostoma)
_____ *Lasthenia fremontii* — Fremont's Lasthenia
_____ *Layia platyglossa* — Tidy Tips
_____ *Lessingia virgata* — Virgate Lessingia
_____ *Madia elegans* — Common Madia
_____ *Madia exigua* — Small or Pygmy Madia
_____ *Madia gracilis* — Slender Madia
_____ *Madia subspicata* — Madia
_____ *Malacothrix floccifera* — Woolly Malacothrix or White Dandelion

_____ *Matricaria matricarioides* — Pineapple Weed
_____ *Micropus californicus* — Cottonweed
_____ *Microseris acuminata* — Acuminate Microseris
_____ *Microseris douglasii* — Douglas's Microseris
_____ *Microseris elegans* — Elegant Microseris
_____ *Microseris lindleyi* — Lindley's Microseris
    (M. linearifolia)

_____ *Microseris sylvatica*   _____ Sylvan Microseris
_____ *Psilocarphus oregonus*   _____ Oregon Woolly Marbles
_____ *Rafinesquia californica*   _____ California Plumeseed
_____ *Senecio vulgaris*   _____ Common Groundsel or Common Butterweed

_____ *Silybum marianum*   _____ Milk Thistle
_____ *Solidago californica*   _____ California Goldenrod
_____ *Soliva pterosperma*   _____ South American Soliva
_____ *Sonchus asper*   _____ Prickly Sow Thistle
_____ *Sonchus oleraceus*   _____ Common Sow Thistle
_____ *Stephanomeria virgata*   _____ Twiggy Wreath Plant
_____ *Taraxacum officinale*   _____ Common Dandelion
_____ *Wyethia angustifolia*   _____ Narrowleaf Mule Ears
_____ *Wyethia helenioides*   _____ Gray Mule Ears
_____ *Xanthium spinosum*   _____ Spiny Clotbur
_____ *Xanthium strumarium*   _____ Cocklebur

Aizoaceae — **Carpetweed Family**
_____ *Mollugo verticillata*   _____ Indian Chickweed

Berberidaceae — **Barberry Family**
_____ *Mahonia dictyota* (*Berberis d.*)   _____ California Barberry or Jepson's Mahonia

Boraginaceae — **Borage Family**
_____ *Amsinckia intermedia*   _____ Common Fiddleneck
_____ *Amsinckia menziesii*   _____ Menzies' Fiddleneck
_____ *Amsinckia retrorsa*   _____ Retrorse Fiddleneck
_____ *Cryptantha affinis*   _____ Common Cryptantha
_____ *Cryptantha flaccida*   _____ Flaccid Cryptantha
_____ *Cryptantha hendersonii*   _____ Henderson's Cryptantha
_____ *Cynoglossum grande*   _____ Grand Hound's-tongue
_____ *Heliotropium curassavicum*   _____ Salt Heliotrope
_____ *Heliotropium europaeum*   _____ European Pusley
_____ *Pectocarya penicillata*   _____ Winged Pectocarya
_____ *Plagiobothrys canescens*   _____ Valley Popcorn Flower
_____ *Plagiobothrys nothofulvus*   _____ Common or Rusty Popcorn Flower
_____ *Plagiobothrys stipitatus*   _____ Small or Stipitate Popcorn Flower (2 races)

Brassicaceae (Cruciferae) — **Mustard Family**
_____ *Arabis breweri*   _____ Brewer's Rock Cress
_____ *Athysanus pusillus*   _____ Dwarf Athysanus or Sandweed
_____ *Brassica campestris*   _____ Field Mustard
_____ *Brassica geniculata*   _____ Shortpod or Mediterranean Mustard
_____ *Brassica nigra*   _____ Black Mustard
_____ *Capsella bursa-pastoris*   _____ Shepherd's Purse
_____ *Cardamine oligosperma*   _____ Western Bittercress
_____ *Descurainia sophia*   _____ Tansy Mustard

Brassicaceae (Cruciferae) (continued)
_____ *Erysimum capitatum*   _____ Douglas's Wallflower
_____ *Lepidium nitidum*   _____ Shining Peppergrass
_____ *Lepidium strictum*   _____ Wayside Peppergrass
_____ *Raphanus sativus*   _____ Wild Radish
_____ *Rorippa nasturtium-aquaticum*   _____ White Water Cress
_____ *Sisymbrium officinale*   _____ Hedge Mustard
_____ *Thysanocarpus curvipes*   _____ Fringe Pod or Lace Pod
_____ *Thysanocarpus laciniatus*   _____ Narrow-leaved Fringe Pod
_____ *Tropidocarpum gracile*   _____ Slender Tropidocarpum

Callitrichaceae   **Water-starwort Family**
_____ *Callitriche heterophylla*   _____ Two-leaved Water-starwort
_____ *Callitriche marginata*   _____ California Water-starwort

Campanulaceae   **Bellflower Family**
_____ *Downingia bicornuta*   _____ Two-horned Downingia
_____ *Downingia pulchella*   _____ Valley Downingia
_____ *Githopsis specularioides*   _____ Common Blue Cup
_____ *Heterocodon rariflorum*   _____ Heterocodon
_____ *Triodanis perfoliata*   _____ Venus Looking-glass

Caprifoliaceae   **Honeysuckle Family**
_____ *Lonicera interrupta*   _____ Chaparral Honeysuckle
_____ *Sambucus mexicana*   _____ Mexican Blue or Southwestern
     Elderberry
_____ *Symphoricarpos rivularis*   _____ Common Snowberry

Caryophyllaceae   **Pink Family**
_____ *Arenaria californica*   _____ California Sandwort
_____ *Arenaria douglasii*   _____ Douglas's Sandwort
_____ *Cerastium glomeratum*   _____ Mouse-ear Chickweed
_____ *Petrorhagia velutina*   _____ Wild Carnation or Grass Pink
     (Tunica prolifera)
_____ *Polycarpon tetraphyllum*   _____ Four-leaf Polycarp
_____ *Sagina apetala*   _____ Sticky Pearlwort
_____ *Sagina decumbens*   _____ Western Pearlwort
     (S. occidentalis)
_____ *Silene gallica*   _____ Common Catchfly or Windmill Pink
_____ *Silene pratensis (Lychnis alba)*   _____ Evening Lychnis
_____ *Silene verecunda*   _____ Dolores Campion
_____ *Spergula arvensis*   _____ Spurry
_____ *Spergularia bocconii*   _____ Boccon's Sand Spurry
_____ *Spergularia rubra*   _____ Ruby Sand Spurry
_____ *Stellaria media*   _____ Common Chickweed
_____ *Stellaria nitens*   _____ Shining Chickweed

Chenopodiaceae   **Goosefoot Family**
_____ *Atriplex rosea*   _____ Red Saltbush
_____ *Chenopodium album*   _____ Lamb's Quarter
_____ *Chenopodium californicum*   _____ California Goosefoot

Chenopodiaceae (continued)
_____ *Chenopodium murale*   _____ Nettle-leaved or Wall Goosefoot
_____ *Chenopodium vulvaria*   _____ Stinking Goosefoot
_____ *Salsola australis*   _____ Russian Thistle
          (S. iberica)

Convolvulaceae   **Morning Glory Family**
_____ *Calystegia occidentalis*   _____ Western Morning Glory
_____ *Convolvulus arvensis*   _____ Field Bindweed

Crassulaceae   **Stonecrop Family**
_____ *Crassula aquatica*   _____ Water Pygmyweed
          (Tillaea a.)
_____ *Crassula erecta*   _____ Pygmy Stonecrop
          (Tillaea e.)
_____ *Crassula muscosa*   _____ Pygmyweed
          (Tillaea m.)
_____ *Parvisedum pumilum*   _____ Dwarf Cliff Sedum

Cucurbitaceae   **Gourd Family**
_____ *Cucurbita sp.*   _____ Gourd
_____ *Marah fabaceus*   _____ California Manroot or
                                              Wild Cucumber

Cuscutaceae   **Dodder Family**
_____ *Cuscuta campestris*   _____ Western Field Dodder

Ericaceae   **Heath Family**
_____ *Arctostaphylos manzanita*   _____ Large Manzanita

Euphorbiaceae   **Spurge Family**
_____ *Eremocarpus setigerus*   _____ Turkey Mullein or Dove Weed
_____ *Euphorbia maculata*   _____ Spotted or Milk Spurge
_____ *Euphorbia ocellata*   _____ Valley Spurge
_____ *Euphorbia serpyllifolia*   _____ Thyme-leaf or Ground Spurge
_____ *Euphorbia spathulata*   _____ Reticulate-seeded Spurge

Fabaceae (Leguminosae)   **Pea Family**
_____ *Amorpha californica*   _____ California Indigobush
_____ *Astragalus gambelianus*   _____ Gambel's Dwarf Locoweed
_____ *Cercis occidentalis*   _____ Western Redbud
_____ *Lathyrus sulphureus*   _____ Sulphur or Snub Pea
_____ *Lotus corniculatus*   _____ Bird's Foot Trefoil
_____ *Lotus humistratus*   _____ Hill Lotus
_____ *Lotus micranthus*   _____ Miniature Lotus
_____ *Lotus purshianus*   _____ Spanish Lotus
_____ *Lotus scoparius*   _____ Deerweed
_____ *Lotus strigosus*   _____ Strigose Lotus
_____ *Lotus subpinnatus*   _____ Chile Lotus
_____ *Lupinus albifrons*   _____ Silver or Bush Lupine
_____ *Lupinus bicolor*   _____ Miniature or Bicolored Lupine
_____ *Lupinus densiflorus*   _____ Whitewhorl Lupine
_____ *Lupinus succulentus*   _____ Arroyo Lupine

Fabaceae (Leguminosae) (continued)

_____ *Lupinus vallicola* — Valley Sky Lupine

_____ *Medicago polymorpha* — Bur Clover

_____ *Medicago sativa* — Alfalfa

_____ *Melilotus albus* — White Sweet Clover

_____ *Melilotus indica* — Yellow Sweet Clover

_____ *Trifolium albopurpureum* — Olive or Indian Clover
    (T. olivaceum)

_____ *Trifolium bifidum* — Notch-leaved Clover

_____ *Trifolium ciliolatum* — Tree Clover

_____ *Trifolium columbinum* — Columbia Clover

_____ *Trifolium depauperatum* — Balloon or Cowbags Clover

_____ *Trifolium frageriferum* — Strawberry Clover

_____ *Trifolium fucatum* — Bull or Sour Clover

_____ *Trifolium gracilentum* — Pinpoint Clover

_____ *Trifolium hirtum* — Rose Clover

_____ *Trifolium microcephalum* — Maiden or Small-headed Clover

_____ *Trifolium obtusiflorum* — Clammy or Creek Clover

_____ *Trifolium oliganthum* — Few-flowered Clover

_____ *Trifolium repens* — White or Ladino Clover

_____ *Trifolium subterraneum* — Subterranean Clover

_____ *Trifolium tridentatum* — Tomcat Clover

_____ *Trifolium variegatum* — White-topped Clover

_____ *Trifolium wormskjoldii* — Cow Clover

_____ *Vicia americana* — American Vetch

_____ *Vicia sativa* — Spring Vetch

Fagaceae — **Oak or Beech Family**

_____ *Quercus douglasii* — Blue Oak

_____ *Quercus dumosa* — Scrub Oak

_____ *Quercus x jolonensis* — Jolon Oak (Hybrid: *Q. douglasii x Q. lobata*)

_____ *Quercus lobata* — Valley Oak

_____ *Quercus x morehus* — Oracle Oak (Hybrid: *Q. wislizenii x Q. kelloggii*)

_____ *Quercus x townei* — Town Oak (Hybrid: *Q. dumosa x Q. lobata*)

_____ *Quercus wislizenii* — Interior Live Oak

Garryaceae — **Silktassel Family**

_____ *Garrya fremontii* — Fremont's Silktassel

Gentianaceae — **Gentian Family**

_____ *Centaurium floribundum* — June Centaury

_____ *Centaurium trichanthum* — Alkali Centaury

_____ *Cicendia quadrangularis* — Timwort or American Microcala
    (Microcala q.)

Geraniaceae — **Geranium Family**

_____ *Erodium botrys* — Long-beaked Storksbill

_____ *Erodium brachycarpum* — Screw-seed Filaree or Storksbill
    (E. obtusiplicatum)

Geraniaceae (continued)
____ *Erodium cicutarium* — Redstem Storksbill
____ *Erodium moschatum* — Whitestem Storksbill
____ *Geranium carolinianum* — Carolina Geranium
____ *Geranium dissectum* — Cut-leaved Geranium
____ *Geranium molle* — Dove's-foot Geranium

Hydrophyllaceae / Waterleaf Family
____ *Eriodictyon californicum* — Yerba Santa
____ *Nemophila heterophylla* — Vari-leaf Nemophila
____ *Nemophila menziesii* — Baby Blue Eyes
____ *Nemophila pedunculata* — Meadow Nemophila
____ *Phacelia cicutaria* — Caterpillar Phacelia
____ *Phacelia egena* — White Phacelia
____ *Phacelia imbricata* — Imbricate Phacelia
____ *Phacelia tanacetifolia* — Tansy Phacelia

Juglandaceae / Walnut Family
____ *Juglans hindsii* — Hind's Walnut

Lamiaceae (Labiatae) / Mint Family
____ *Lamium amplexicaule* — Clasping Henbit
____ *Marrubium vulgare* — Horehound
____ *Monardella odoratissima* — Coyote Mint
____ *Pogogyne douglasii* — Douglas's Pogogyne
____ *Pogogyne serpylloides* — Thyme-like Pogogyne
____ *Salvia columbariae* — Chia
____ *Scutellaria tuberosa* — Danny's Skullcap
____ *Stachys palustris* — Rigid Hedgenettle
____ *Stachys stricta* — Sonoma Hedgenettle
____ *Trichostema lanceolatum* — Vinegar Weed, Turpentine Weed, or Blue-curls

Lauraceae / Laurel Family
____ *Umbellularia californica* — California Bay or Laurel, Oregon Myrtle, or Pepperwood

Loasaceae / Loasa Family
____ *Mentzelia laevicaulis* — Stickleaf or Blazing-star

Lythraceae / Loosestrife Family
____ *Ammannia coccinea* — Red-berry or Long-leaved Ammannia
____ *Lythrum hyssopifolia* — Hyssop Loosestrife

Malvaceae / Mallow Family
____ *Abutilon theophrasti* — Velvet Leaf
____ *Malacothamnus fremontii* — Fremont or White-coat Globemallow
____ *Malva neglecta* — Round-leaf or Dwarf Mallow
____ *Malva parviflora* — Cheeseweed
____ *Sidalcea diploscypha* — Fringed Sidalcea
____ *Sidalcea hartwegii* — Hartweg's Sidalcea

Martyniaceae / Martynia Family
____ *Proboscidea louisianica* — Unicorn Plant or Devil's Claw

Moraceae
_____ *Ficus carica*

Oleaceae
_____ *Fraxinus latifolia*

Onagraceae
_____ *Boisduvalia cleistogama*
_____ *Boisduvalia densiflora*
_____ *Boisduvalia glabella*
_____ *Boisduvalia stricta*
_____ *Camissonia campestris*
        (Oenothera dentata)
_____ *Clarkia biloba*
_____ *Clarkia concinna*
_____ *Clarkia gracilis*
_____ *Clarkia purpurea*
_____ *Clarkia unguiculata*
_____ *Epilobium adenocaulon*
_____ *Epilobium paniculatum*
        (E. brachycarpum)

Orobanchaceae
_____ *Orobanche uniflora*

Oxalidaceae
_____ *Oxalis corniculata*

Papaveraceae
_____ *Eschscholzia caespitosa*
_____ *Eschscholzia californica*
_____ *Eschscholzia lobbii*
_____ *Platystemon californicus*

Plantaginaceae
_____ *Plantago bigelovii*
_____ *Plantago coronopus*
_____ *Plantago erecta*
_____ *Plantago lanceolata*

Platanaceae
_____ *Platanus racemosa*

Polemoniaceae
_____ *Gilia achilleaefolia*
_____ *Gilia capitata*
_____ *Gilia tricolor*
_____ *Linanthus androsaceus*
_____ *Linanthus bicolor*
_____ *Linanthus ciliatus*
_____ *Linanthus dichotomus*
_____ *Linanthus filipes*
_____ *Microsteris gracilis*

Mulberry Family
_____ Common Fig

Olive Family
_____ Oregon Ash

Evening Primrose Family
_____ Cleistogamous Boisduvalia
_____ Dense-flowered Boisduvalia
_____ Smooth Boisduvalia
_____ Narrow-leaved Boisduvalia
_____ Field Primrose

_____ Bilobed Clarkia
_____ Lovely Clarkia
_____ Slender Clarkia
_____ Winecup Clarkia
_____ Elegant Clarkia
_____ Northern Willowherb
_____ Parched Fireweed or Panicled
        Willowherb

Broomrape Family
_____ Naked Broomrape

Oxalis or Wood Sorrel Family
_____ Creeping Wood Sorrel

Poppy Family
_____ Tufted Poppy
_____ California Poppy
_____ Lobb's Poppy or Frying Pans
_____ Cream Cups

Plantain Family
_____ Annual Coast Plantain
_____ Cut-leaved Plantain
_____ Dwarf Plantain
_____ English Plantain

Sycamore Family
_____ California Sycamore

Phlox Family
_____ California Gilia
_____ Blue-headed Gilia
_____ Bird's-eye Gilia
_____ False Baby Stars or Common Linanthus
_____ True Baby Stars or Bicolored Linanthus
_____ Whisker Brush or Hairy Linanthus
_____ Evening Snow
_____ Wild Babies' Breath or Small Linanthus
_____ Slender Phlox

Polemoniaceae (continued)

_____ *Navarretia cotulifolia*   _____ Cotula Navarretia
_____ *Navarretia intertexta*   _____ Needle Navarretia
_____ *Navarretia leucocephala*   _____ White-flowered Navarretia
_____ *Navarretia pubescens*   _____ Downy Navarretia
_____ *Navarretia tagetina*   _____ Marigold Navarretia
_____ *Navarretia viscidula*   _____ Sticky Navarretia

Polygonaceae   **Buckwheat Family**

_____ *Chorizanthe membranacea*   _____ Clustered or Pink Spineflower
_____ *Chorizanthe stellulata*   _____ Starry Spineflower
_____ *Eriogonum nudum*   _____ Naked Buckwheat
_____ *Eriogonum roseum*   _____ Virgate Buckwheat
_____ *Eriogonum vimineum*   _____ Wicker-stemmed Buckwheat
_____ *Polygonum aviculare*   _____ Common Knotweed
_____ *Polygonum californicum*   _____ California Smartweed
_____ *Polygonum lapathifolium*   _____ Willow Smartweed
_____ *Polygonum persicaria*   _____ Lady's Thumb
_____ *Pterostegia drymarioides*   _____ Pterostegia
_____ *Rumex californicus*   _____ California Dock
_____ *Rumex conglomeratus*   _____ Green Dock
_____ *Rumex crispus*   _____ Curly Dock
_____ *Rumex pulcher*   _____ Fiddle Dock
_____ *Rumex salicifolius*   _____ Willow-leaved Dock

Portulacaceae   **Purslane Family**

_____ *Calandrinia ciliata*   _____ Red Maids
_____ *Lewisia rediviva*   _____ Bitterroot
_____ *Montia fontana (M. hallii + M. verna)*   _____ Vernal Montia
_____ *Montia perfoliata*   _____ Miner's Lettuce
_____ *Portulaca oleracea*   _____ Purslane

Primulaceae   **Primrose Family**

_____ *Anagallis arvensis*   _____ Scarlet Pimpernel
_____ *Dodecatheon clevelandii*   _____ Padres' Shooting Star
_____ *Dodecatheon hansenii*   _____ Hansen's Shooting Star

Ranunculaceae   **Buttercup Family**

_____ *Clematis lasiantha*   _____ Virgin's Bower or Pipestem Clematis
_____ *Clematis ligusticifolia*   _____ Western Clematis
_____ *Delphinium hesperium*   _____ Foothill Delphinium or
                       Western Larkspur
_____ *Delphinium nudicaule*   _____ Canyon Delphinium or Red Larkspur
_____ *Delphinium patens*   _____ Zigzag Delphinium or
                       Spreading Larkspur
_____ *Delphinium variegatum*   _____ Royal Delphinium or Royal Larkspur
_____ *Ranunculus aquatilis*   _____ Water Buttercup
_____ *Ranunculus californicus*   _____ California Buttercup
_____ *Ranunculus hebecarpus*   _____ Bluntseed Buttercup
_____ *Ranunculus muricatus*   _____ Prickleseed Buttercup
_____ *Ranunculus occidentalis*   _____ Western Buttercup

Rhamnaceae
_____ *Ceanothus cuneatus*
_____ *Rhamnus californica*
_____ *Rhamnus ilicifolia*
    (R. crocea)

Rosaceae
_____ *Alchemilla occidentalis*
_____ *Cercocarpus betuloides*
_____ *Heteromeles arbutifolia*

_____ *Holodiscus boursieri*
_____ *Prunus amygdalus*
_____ *Prunus avium*
_____ *Prunus virginiana*
_____ *Rosa californica*
_____ *Rubus procerus*
_____ *Rubus ulmifolius*
_____ *Rubus ursinus*

Rubiaceae
_____ *Cephalanthus occidentalis*
_____ *Crucianella angustifolia*
_____ *Galum aparine*
_____ *Galium mexicanum*
    (G. asperrimum)
_____ *Galium parisiense*
_____ *Galium porrigens*

Rutaceae
_____ *Ptelea crenulata*

Salicaceae
_____ *Populus fremontii*
_____ *Salix gooddingii*
_____ *Salix laevigata*
_____ *Salix lasiolepis*

Saxifragaceae
_____ *Lithophragma affine*
_____ *Lithophragma parviflorum*
_____ *Lithophragma bolanderi*
    (L. scabrella)
_____ *Lithophragma trifoliatum*
_____ *Ribes quercetorum*
_____ *Saxifraga californica*
_____ *Saxifraga fragosa*

Scrophulariaceae
_____ *Antirrhinum breweri*
_____ *Castilleja affinis*
_____ *Castilleja subinclusa*

Buckthorn Family
_____ Buckbrush
_____ California Coffeeberry
_____ Hollyleaf Redberry

Rose Family
_____ Dew Cup or Western Lady's Mantle
_____ Mountain Mahogany
_____ Toyon, Christmas Berry, or
    California Holly
_____ Cream Bush or Ocean Spray
_____ Almond
_____ Sweet Cherry
_____ Western Choke Cherry
_____ California Wild Rose
_____ Himalaya Blackberry
_____ Wild Blackberry
_____ California Blackberry

Madder Family
_____ Buttonbush or Button Willow
_____ Narrow-leaved Crosswort
_____ Common Bedstraw or Cleavers
_____ Tall Rough Bedstraw

_____ Wall Bedstraw
_____ Nuttall's or Climbing Bedstraw

Rue Family
_____ Western Hop Tree

Willow Family
_____ Fremont or Valley Cottonwood
_____ Goodding's Willow
_____ Red Willow
_____ Arroyo Willow

Saxifrage Family
_____ Woodland Star
_____ Prairie Star
_____ Sierra Star

_____ Threeleaf Woodland Star
_____ Rock or Wood Gooseberry
_____ California Saxifrage
_____ Fleshy-leaved Saxifrage

Figwort Family
_____ Brewer's Snapdragon
_____ Coast Paint Brush
_____ Long-leaved Paint Brush

Scrophulariaceae (continued)
_____ *Collinsia heterophylla* — Purple-and-white Chinese Houses
_____ *Collinsia sparsiflora* — Spinster's Blue-eyed Mary
_____ *Keckiella breviflora* — Bush Beardtongue or Stubflower
     (Penstemon b.)   Penstemon
_____ *Keckiella corymbosa* — Red or Thymeleaf Penstemon
     (Penstemon c.)
_____ *Linaria canadensis* — Blue Toadflax
_____ *Mimulus douglasii* — Chinless or Douglas's Monkeyflower,
     or Purple Mouse Ears
_____ *Mimulus floribundus* — Floriferous Monkeyflower
_____ *Mimulus guttatus* — Common or Seep-spring Monkeyflower
_____ *Mimulus tricolor* — Tricolor Monkeyflower
_____ *Orthocarpus attenuatus* — Narrow-leaved Owlclover
_____ *Orthocarpus erianthus* — Butter-and-eggs or Johnny Tuck
_____ *Orthocarpus purpurascens* — Red Owlclover
_____ *Penstemon heterophyllus* — Foothill Penstemon
_____ *Scrophularia californica* — California Figwort
_____ *Verbascum blattaria* — Moth Mullein
_____ *Verbascum thapsus* — Woolly Mullein
_____ *Veronica peregrina* — Purslane Speedwell
_____ *Veronica persica* — Persian Speedwell

Simarubaceae — **Quassia Family**
_____ *Ailanthus altissima* — Tree of Heaven

Solanaceae — **Nightshade Family**
_____ *Datura meteloides* — Jimsonweed or Tolguacha
_____ *Nicotiana acuminata* — Many-flowered Tobacco
_____ *Nicotiana glauca* — Tree Tobacco
_____ *Physalis acutifolia* — Lance-leaved Ground Cherry
     (P. wrightii)
_____ *Solanum parishii* — Parish's Nightshade

Urticaceae — **Nettle Family**
_____ *Urtica dioica* — Stinging Nettle

Valerianaceae — **Valerian Family**
_____ *Plectritis ciliosa* — Long-spurred Plectritis
_____ *Plectritis congesta* — Short-spurred Plectritis
_____ *Plectritis macrocera* — White Plectritis

Verbenaceae — **Vervain Family**
_____ *Lippia nodiflora* — Garden Lippia
_____ *Verbena lasiostachys* — Western Vervain
_____ *Verbena robusta* — Robust Vervain

Violaceae — **Violet Family**
_____ *Viola douglasii* — Douglas's Violet

Viscaceae (Loranthaceae) — **Mistletoe Family**
_____ *Phoradendron tomentosum* — Greenleaf Mistletoe
_____ *Phoradendron villosum* — Hairy Mistletoe

Vitaceae
_____ *Vitis california*

Grape Family
_____ California Wild Grape

Zygophyllaceae
_____ *Tribulus terrestris*

Caltrop Family
_____ Puncture Vine

Monocotyledoneae Class

Alismataceae
_____ *Alisma triviale*
_____ *Machaerocarpus californicus*
_____ *Sagittaria longiloba*
_____ *Sagittaria montevidensis*

Water Plantain Family
_____ Common or Broadleaf Water Plantain
_____ Fringed Water Plantain
_____ Long-barb Arrowhead
_____ Hooded Arrowhead

Amaryllidaceae
_____ *Allium amplectens*
_____ *Brodiaea elegans*
_____ *Dichelostemma congestum*
_____ *Dichelostemma multiflorum*
_____ *Dichelostemma pulchellum*
_____ *Triteleia hyacinthina*
_____ *Triteleia ixioides*
_____ *Triteleia laxa*

Amaryllis Family
_____ Paper or Narrow-leaved Onion
_____ Elegant or Harvest Brodiaea
_____ Forktooth Ookow
_____ Roundtooth Ookow
_____ Blue Dicks or Wild Hyacinth
_____ White Hyacinth
_____ Foothill Pretty Face or Golden Brodiaea
_____ Ithuriel's Spear or Wally Basket

Cyperaceae
_____ *Carex barbarae*
_____ *Carex densa*
_____ *Cyperus aristatus*
_____ *Cyperus difformis*
_____ *Cyperus eragrostis*
_____ *Cyperus strigosus*
_____ *Eleocharis palustris*
    (E. macrostachya)
_____ *Scirpus acutus*

Sedge Family
_____ Santa Barbara Sedge
_____ Dense Sedge
_____ Awned Cyperus
_____ Obtuse Cyperus
_____ Tall Cyperus
_____ Straw-colored Cyperus
_____ Common or Creeping Spikerush

_____ Common Tule or Hardstem Bulrush

Juncaceae
_____ *Juncus balticus*
_____ *Juncus bufonius*
_____ *Juncus mexicanus*
_____ *Juncus phaeocephalus*
_____ *Juncus xiphioides*
_____ *Luzula subsessilis*

Rush Family
_____ Baltic Rush
_____ Toad Rush
_____ Mexican Rush
_____ Paniculate Rush
_____ Xiphioid Rush
_____ Sessile Wood Rush

Lemnaceae
_____ *Lemna minor*
_____ *Lemna minuta*

Duckweed Family
_____ Lesser Duckweed
_____ Least Duckweed

Liliaceae
_____ *Calochortus luteus*
_____ *Chlorogalum pomeridianum*
_____ *Fritillaria lanceolata*
_____ *Zygadenus fremontii*

Lily Family
_____ Gold Nuggets or Yellow Mariposa
_____ Wavy-leaf Soap Plant or Amole
_____ Mission Bells
_____ Fremont's Camas or Star Lily

Poaceae (Gramineae)

_____ *Agropyron elongatum*
_____ *Agrostis avenacea*
_____ *Agrostis exarata*
_____ *Aira caryophyllea*
_____ *Alopecurus saccatus*
_____ *Andropogon virginicus*
_____ *Aristida hamulosa*
_____ *Aristida oligantha*
_____ *Arundo donax*
_____ *Avena barbata*
_____ *Avena fatua*
_____ *Avena sativa*
_____ *Briza minor*
_____ *Bromus madritensis*
_____ *Bromus mollis*
_____ *Bromus rigidus*
          (B. diandrus)
_____ *Bromus rubens*
_____ *Bromus sterilis*
_____ *Bromus tectorum*
_____ *Crypsis schoenoides*
          (Heleochloa s.)
_____ *Crypsis vaginiflora*
_____ *Cynodon dactylon*
_____ *Cynosurus echinatus*
_____ *Dactylis glomerata*
_____ *Deschampsia danthonioides*
_____ *Digitaria sanguinalis*
_____ *Distichlis spicata*
_____ *Echinochloa colonum*
_____ *Echinochloa crusgalli*

_____ *Echinochloa crus-pavonis*
_____ *Elymus triticoides*
_____ *Eragrostis pectinacea*
          (E. diffusa)
_____ *Eragrostis pilosa*
_____ *Festuca arundinacea*
_____ *Festuca elmeri*
_____ *Gastridium ventricosum*
_____ *Holcus lanatus*
_____ *Hordeum geniculatum*
_____ *Hordeum jubatum*
_____ *Hordeum leporinum*
_____ *Hordeum vulgare*
_____ *Koeleria macrantha*
          (K. cristata)

Grass Family

_____ Tall Wheatgrass
_____ Avens Bentgrass
_____ Western Bentgrass
_____ Silver Hairgrass
_____ Pacific Foxtail
_____ Broomsedge or Yellowsedge Bluestem
_____ Arizona Three-awn
_____ Few-flowered or Prairie Three-awn
_____ Giant Reed
_____ Slender Wild Oat
_____ Wild Oat
_____ Cultivated Oat
_____ Little Quaking Grass
_____ Spanish or Madrid Brome
_____ Soft Chess
_____ Ripgut Grass

_____ Foxtail Chess or Red Brome
_____ Barren or Poverty Brome
_____ Downy Chess or Cheat Grass
_____ Swampgrass

_____ Crypsis
_____ Bermuda Grass
_____ Hedgehog Dogtail
_____ Orchardgrass
_____ Annual Hairgrass
_____ Large Crabgrass
_____ Saltgrass
_____ Jungle Rice
_____ Barnyard Grass, Water Grass, or
          Wild Millet
_____ Mexican Barnyard Grass
_____ Creeping or Beardless Wildrye
_____ Spreading Lovegrass

_____ Pilose Lovegrass
_____ Tall or Reed Fescue
_____ Elmer's Fescue
_____ Nit Grass
_____ Common Velvetgrass
_____ Mediterranean Barley
_____ Farmer's Foxtail or Foxtail Barley
_____ Hare Barley
_____ Common Barley
_____ Prairie Junegrass

Poacea (Gramineae) (continued)

_____ *Koeleria phleoides*	_____ Annual Junegrass
_____ *Lolium multiflorum*	_____ Italian Rye grass
_____ *Lolium perenne*	_____ English or Perennial Ryegrass
_____ *Lolium temulentum*	_____ Darnel Ryegrass
_____ *Melica californica*	_____ California Melic
_____ *Melica torreyana*	_____ Torrey Melic
_____ *Muhlenbergia rigens*	_____ Deer Grass
_____ *Oryzopsis miliacea*	_____ Smilo
_____ *Paspalum dilatatum*	_____ Dallis Grass
_____ *Phalaris aquatica*	_____ Harding Grass
_____ *Phalaris paradoxa*	_____ Hood Canary Grass
_____ *Poa annua*	_____ Annual Bluegrass
_____ *Poa bulbosa*	_____ Bulbous Bluegrass
_____ *Poa scabrella*	_____ Pine Bluegrass
_____ *Polypogon interruptus*	_____ Ditch Beardgrass
_____ *Polypogon maritimus*	_____ Mediterranean Beardgrass
_____ *Polypogon monspeliensis*	_____ Annual Beardgrass or Rabbitfoot Grass
_____ *Scribneria bolanderi*	_____ Scribner's Grass
_____ *Secale cereale*	_____ Cereal Rye
_____ *Sitanion hystrix*	_____ Bottlebrush Squirreltail
_____ *Sitanion jubatum*	_____ Big Squirreltail
_____ *Sorghum halapense*	_____ Johnson Grass
_____ *Stipa cernua*	_____ Nodding Needlegrass
_____ *Stipa pulchra*	_____ Purple Needlegrass
_____ *Taeniatherum caput-medusae* (*Elymus c.*)	_____ Medusahead Rye
_____ *Triticum aestivum*	_____ Common Wheat
_____ *Vulpia bromoides* (*Festuca dertonensis*)	_____ Six-weeks or Brome Fescue
_____ *Vulpia microstachys* (*Festuca m.; F. eastwoodae, F. pacifica*)	_____ Small Fescue
_____ *Vulpia myuros* (*Festuca m.*)	_____ Rattail Fescue

Potamogetonaceae   **Pondweed Family**

_____ *Potamogeton diversifolius*   _____ Snailseed Pondweed

Typhaceae   **Cattail Family**

_____ *Typha angustifolia*	_____ Nail Rod or Narrowleaf Cattail
_____ *Typha domingensis*	_____ Cattail
_____ *Typha latifolia*	_____ Soft Flag or Broadleaf Cattail

Appendix E. Aquatic Insects of the Sutter Buttes:
a sample taken 18 April 1981.*

ORDER EPHEMEROPTERA   **MAYFLIES**

Baetidae   **Small Mayfly Family**
_____ *Callibaetis sp.*
_____ *Centroptilum sp.*

Leptophlebiidae   **Spinner Family**
_____ *Paraleptophlebia placeri*

ORDER ODONATA   **DRAGONFLIES AND DAMSELFLIES**

Coenagrionidae   **Narrow-winged Damselfly Family**
_____ *Argia vivida*

ORDER PLECOPTERA   **STONEFLIES**

Perlodidae   **Stonefly Family**
_____ *Isogenus alameda*

ORDER HEMIPTERA   **TRUE BUGS**

Corixidae   **Water Boatmen Family**
_____ *Corisella decolor*

Notonectidae   **Backswimmer Family**
_____ *Notonecta undulata*
_____ *Buenoa sp.*

Belostomatidae   **Giant Water Bug Family**
_____ *Belostoma flumineum*

Veliidae   **Riffle Bug Family**
_____ *Microvelia sp.*

Gerridae   **Water Strider Family**
_____ *Gerris incurvatus*
_____ *Gerris remigis*
_____ *Limnoporus notablis*

Hebridae   **Velvet Water Bug Family**
_____ *Merragata hebroides*

Macroveliidae   **Giant Riffle Bug Family**
_____ *Macrovelia hornii*

Saldidae   **Shore Bug Family**
_____ *Micracanthia quadrimaculata*

ORDER MEGALOPTERA   **ALDERFLIES AND DOBSONFLIES**

Corydalidae   **Dobsonfly Family**
_____ *Neohermes californicus*

ORDER TRICOPTERA

CADDISFLIES

Sericostomatidae
_____ *Gumaga sp.*

Sericostomatid Caddisfly Family

Limnephilidae
_____ *Limnephilus sp.*

Northern Caddisfly Family

Hydroptilidae
_____ *Ochrotrichia sp.*

Micro-caddisfly Family

Hydropsychidae
_____ *Hydropsyche sp.*

Web-spinning Caddisfly Family

ORDER COLEOPTERA

BEETLES

Dytiscidae
_____ *Laccophilus decipiens*
_____ *Laccophilus sp.*
_____ *Thermonectus basillaris*
_____ *Agabus approximatus*
_____ *Agabus disintegratus*
_____ *Agabus tristis*
_____ *Bidessus affinis*
_____ *Hydroporus vilis*
_____ *Deronectes sp.*

Predaceous Diving Beetle Family

Gyrinidae
_____ *Gyrinus plicifer*

Whirligig Beetle Family

Hydrophilidae
_____ *Hydrophilus triangularis*
_____ *Tropisterus lateralis*
_____ *Tropisterus columbianus*
_____ *Cymbiodyta imbellis*
_____ *Cymbiodyta punctatostriata*
_____ *Enochrus latinsculis*
_____ *Berosus maculosis*

Water Scavenger Beetle Family

ORDER DIPTERA

FLIES

Tipulidae
_____ *Tipula sp.*

Crane Fly Family

Chironomidae
_____ *two species*

Midge Family

Ceratopogonidae
_____ *one species*

No-see-um or Biting Midge Family

Tabanidae
_____ *Tabanus sp.*

Horse and Deer Fly Family

---

*Identifications by Dave Woodward, using the following keys: Edwards, Jensen, and Berner (1976); Menke (1978); Merritt and Cummins (1978); Usinger (1956); Wiggins (1977).

Appendix F. Checklist of Butterflies of the Sutter Buttes (including typical habitats and host plants). *

Papilionidae

Swallowtail Family

Papilio rutulus	___ Western Tiger Swallowtail	Meadows, hilltops	Cottonwood
Papilio multicaudatus	___ Two-tailed Swallowtail	Canyons, fields	Ash
Papilio eurymedon	___ Pale Swallowtail	Meadows, hilltops	Buckthorn
Papilio zelicaon	___ Anise Swallowtail	Edges	Wild Anise
Battus philenor	___ Pipevine Swallowtail	Creek trails	Dutchman's Pipe

Pieridae

Pierid Family

Pieris rapae	___ Cabbage White	Many habitats	Mustards
Colias eurytheme	___ Orange Sulphur	Fields, hilltops	Legumes
Anthocaris sara	___ Sara Orange-tip	Creeks, fencerows	Mustards
Euchloe ausonides	___ Large Marble	Moist areas	Mustards

Danaidae

Milkweed Butterfly Family

Danaus plexippus	___ Monarch	Creek trails	Milkweed

Nymphalidae

Brush-footed Butterfly Family

Phyciodes campestris	___ Field Crescent	Wet meadows	Aster
Phyciodes mylitta	___ Mylitta Crescent	Many habitats	Thistles
Polygonia satyrus	___ Satyr Anglewing	Moist areas	Nettle
Nymphalis antiopa	___ Mourning Cloak	Canyons, treetops	Willows
Nymphalis californica	___ California Tortoise-shell	Transient	Wild Lilac
Vanessa atalanta	___ Red Admiral	Fields	Nettle
Vanessa cardui	___ Painted Lady	Canyon trails	Many plants
Vanessa annabella	___ West Coast Lady	Moist areas	Mallow
Vanessa virginiensis	___ Virginia Lady	Edges	Composites
Precis coenia	___ Buckeye	Many habitats	Plantain
Limenitis lorquini	___ Lorquin's Admiral	Canyon trails	Willow
Limenitis bredowii californica	___ California Sister	Creek trails	Oak

Lycaenidae

Atlides halesus	Great Blue Hairstreak	Fields	Mistletoe
Strymon melinus	Common Hairstreak	Fields	Mallow
Satyrium californica	California Hairstreak	Fields	Oak
Incisalia iroides	Western Elfin	Creek trails	Dodder
Callophrys dumetorum	Bramble Hairstreak	Transient	Lotus
Lycaena xanthoides	Great Copper	Moist areas	Dock
Lycaena helloides	Small Copper	Moist areas	Dock
Everes comyntas	Eastern Tailed Blue	Moist areas	Legumes
Plebejus acmon	Acmon Blue	Many habitats	Legumes

Gossamer-winged Butterfly Family

Hesperiidae

Lerodea eufala	Eufala Skipper	Wet sand, creeksides	Grasses
Paratrytone melane	Umber Skipper	Wet sand, creeksides	Grasses
Ochlodes sylvanoides	Woodland Skipper	Wet sand, creeksides	Grasses
Ochlodes agricola	Rural Skipper	Wet sand, creeksides	Grasses
Atalopedes campestris	Field Skipper	Wet sand, creeksides	Grasses
Hylephila phyleus	Fiery Skipper	Wet sand, creeksides	Grasses
Pholisora catullus	Sootywing	Trailsides	Pigweeds
Heliopetes ericetorum	Large Checkered Skipper	Creek trails	Mallow
Pyrgus communis	Common Checkered Skipper	Fields	Mallow
Erynnis tristis	Mournful Duskywing	Fields, hilltops	Oak
Erynnis propertius	Propertius Duskywing	Fields, uplands	Oak

Skipper Family

---

* Based on personal observations and data from Emmel and Emmel (1973), Peoples (1978), Pyle (1981), Shapiro (1974), Swan and Papp (1972).

Appendix G. Checklist of Amphibians and Reptiles of the Sutter Buttes.

Amphibians

ORDER CAUDATA

Plethodontidae   **Lungless Salamander Family**
_____ *Batrachoseps attenuatus*   _____ California Slender Salamander

ORDER SALIENTIA

Bufonidae   **Toad Family**
_____ *Bufo boreas*   _____ Western Toad

Ranidae   **True Frog Family**
_____ *Rana catesbeiana*   _____ Bullfrog

Hylidae   **Treefrog Family**
_____ *Hyla regilla*   _____ Pacific Treefrog

Reptiles

ORDER TESTUDINES

Emydidae   **Freshwater Turtle Family**
_____ *Clemmys marmorata*   _____ Western Pond Turtle

ORDER SQUAMATA

Iguanidae   **Lizard Family**
_____ *Sceloporus occidentalis*   _____ Western Fence Lizard
_____ *Sceloporus graciosus*   _____ Sagebrush Lizard

Scincidae   **Skink Family**
_____ *Eumeces skiltonianus*   _____ Western Skink

Teiidae   **Whiptail Family**
_____ *Cnemidophorus tigris*   _____ Western Whiptail

Anguidae   **Alligator Lizard Family**
_____ *Gerrhonotus multicarinatus*   _____ Southern Alligator Lizard

Colubridae   **Common Harmless Snake Family**
_____ *Diadophis punctatus*   _____ Ringneck Snake
_____ *Coluber constrictor*   _____ Racer (Western Yellow-bellied Racer)
_____ *Masticophis flagellum*   _____ Coachwhip or Red Racer
_____ *Pituophis melanoleucus*   _____ Gopher Snake
_____ *Lampropeltis getulus*   _____ Common Kingsnake

_____ *Rhinocheilus lecontei*   _____ Long-nosed Snake
_____ *Thamnophis sirtalis*   _____ Common Garter Snake
_____ *Thamnophis couchi*   _____ Western Aquatic (Giant) Garter Snake
Viperidae   **Pit Viper Family**
_____ *Crotalus viridus*   _____ Western (Pacific) Rattlesnake

Appendix H. Checklist of Birds of the Sutter Buttes.

Abundance codes

c = common to abundant
u = uncommon
r = rare or accidental

Seasonal status codes

R = resident year-round; breed
W = winter only; non-breeding
S = spring/summer only; breed
M = migrant, spring or fall
V = visitor from other Sacramento Valley
    habitats during appropriate seasons

ORDER PODICIPEDIFORMES

Podicipedidae
_____ *Podilymbus podiceps*

Grebe Family
_____ Pied-billed Grebe (rV)

ORDER PELECANIFORMES

Pelecanidae
_____ *Pelecanus erythrorhynchos*

Pelican Family
_____ American White Pelican (rV)

ORDER CICONIIFORMES

Ardeidae
_____ *Botaurus lentiginosus*
_____ *Ardea herodias*
_____ *Casmerodius albus*
_____ *Egretta thula*
_____ *Butorides striatus*
_____ *Nycticorax nycticorax*

Heron and Bittern Family
_____ American Bittern (rV)
_____ Great Blue Heron (rV)
_____ Great Egret (rV)
_____ Snowy Egret (rV)
_____ Green-backed Heron (Green H.) (rV)
_____ Black-crowned Night Heron (rV)

ORDER ANSERIFORMES

Anatidae
_____ *Cygnus columbianus*
_____ *Anser albifrons*
_____ *Chen caerulescens*
_____ *Chen rossii*
_____ *Branta canadensis*
_____ *Aix sponsa*
_____ *Anas crecca*
_____ *Anas platyrhynchos*
_____ *Anas acuta*
_____ *Anas cyanoptera*
_____ *Anas clypeata*
_____ *Anas strepera*
_____ *Anas americana*
_____ *Aythya collaris*
_____ *Aythya affinis*
_____ *Bucephala clangula*

Waterfowl Family
_____ Tundra Swan (Whistling S.) (rV)
_____ Greater White-fronted Goose (uV)
_____ Snow Goose (cV)
_____ Ross' Goose (rV)
_____ Canada Goose (uV)
_____ Wood Duck (rV)
_____ Green-winged Teal (rV)
_____ Mallard (uR)
_____ Northern Pintail (cV)
_____ Cinnamon Teal (rV)
_____ Northern Shoveler (rV)
_____ Gadwall (rV)
_____ American Wigeon (rV)
_____ Ring-necked Duck (rV)
_____ Lesser Scaup (rV)
_____ Common Goldeneye (rV)

_____ *Bucephala albeola*   _____ Bufflehead (rV)
_____ *Oxyura jamaicensis*   _____ Ruddy Duck (rV)

ORDER FALCONIFORMES

Cathartidae   **Vulture Family**
_____ *Cathartes aura*   _____ Turkey Vulture (cR)

Accipitridae   **Kite, Hawk, and Eagle Family**
_____ *Elanus caeruleus*   _____ Black-shouldered Kite
    (E. leucurus)   (White-tailed K.) (rV)
_____ *Haliaeetus leucocephalus*   _____ Bald Eagle (rV)
_____ *Circus cyaneus*   _____ Northern Harrier (Marsh Hawk) (uR)
_____ *Accipiter striatus*   _____ Sharp-shinned Hawk (uW)
_____ *Accipiter cooperii*   _____ Cooper's Hawk (uW)
_____ *Buteo lineatus*   _____ Red-shouldered Hawk (rR)
_____ *Buteo swainsoni*   _____ Swainson's Hawk (rV)
_____ *Buteo jamaicensis*   _____ Red-tailed Hawk (cR)
_____ *Buteo regalis*   _____ Ferruginous Hawk (uW)
_____ *Buteo lagopus*   _____ Rough-legged Hawk (uW)
_____ *Aquila chrysaetos*   _____ Golden Eagle (cR)

Falconidae   **Falcon Family**
_____ *Falco sparverius*   _____ American Kestrel (cR)
_____ *Falco columbarius*   _____ Merlin (rV)
_____ *Falco mexicanus*   _____ Prairie Falcon (uR)

ORDER GALLIFORMES

Phasianidae   **Pheasant and Quail Family**
_____ *Phasianus colchicus*   _____ Ring-necked Pheasant (uR)
_____ *Meleagris gallopavo*   _____ Wild Turkey (rR)
_____ *Callipepla californica*   _____ California Quail (cR)
    (Lophortyx c.)

ORDER GRUIFORMES

Rallidae   **Rail Family**
_____ *Gallinula chloropus*   _____ Common Moorhen (C. Gallinule) (rV)
_____ *Fulica americana*   _____ American Coot (uW)

Gruidae   **Crane Family**
_____ *Grus canadensis*   _____ Sandhill Crane (uV)

ORDER CHARADRIIFORMES

Charadriidae   **Plover Family**
_____ *Charadrius vociferus*   _____ Killdeer (uR)

Recurvirostridae   **Stilt and Avocet Family**
_____ *Himantopus mexicanus*   _____ Black-necked Stilt (rV)

Scolopacidae
_____ *Tringa melanoleuca*
_____ *Numenius americanus*
_____ *Limnodromus scolopaceus*
_____ *Gallinago gallinago*
      (Capella g.)

Sandpiper Family
_____ Greater Yellowlegs (uV)
_____ Long-billed Curlew (rV)
_____ Long-billed Dowitcher (rV)
_____ Common Snipe (rV)

Laridae
_____ *Larus delawarensis*
_____ *Larus californicus*

Gull and Tern Family
_____ Ring-billed Gull (rV)
_____ California Gull (rV)

ORDER COLUMBIFORMES

Columbidae
_____ *Columba livia*
_____ *Columba fasciata*
_____ *Zenaida macroura*

Pigeon and Dove Family
_____ Rock Dove (uR)
_____ Band-tailed Pigeon (uW)
_____ Mourning Dove (cR)

ORDER STRIGIFORMES

Tytonidae
_____ *Tyto alba*

Barn-Owl Family
_____ Common Barn-Owl

Strigidae
_____ *Otus kennicottii*
      (O. asio)
_____ *Bubo virginianus*
_____ *Athene cunicularia*
_____ *Asio otus*
_____ *Asio flammeus*

Typical Owl Family
_____ Western Screech-Owl (rR)

_____ Great Horned Owl (cR)
_____ Burrowing Owl (uW)
_____ Long-eared Owl (rW)
_____ Short-eared Owl (rW)

ORDER CAPRIMULGIFORMES

Caprimulgidae
_____ *Chordeiles acutipennis*
_____ *Phalaenoptilus nuttallii*

Goatsucker or Nightjar Family
_____ Lesser Nighthawk (uS)
_____ Common Poorwill (uM)

ORDER APODIFORMES

Apodidae
_____ *Chaetura vauxi*
_____ *Aeronautes saxatalis*

Swift Family
_____ Vaux's Swift (rM)
_____ White-throated Swift (uR)

Trochilidae
_____ *Calypte anna*
_____ *Selasphorus rufus*

Hummingbird Family
_____ Anna's Hummingbird (cR)
_____ Rufous Hummingbird (uM)

ORDER CORACIIFORMES

Alcedinidae
_____ *Ceryle alcyon*
      (Megaceryle a.)

Kingfisher Family
_____ Belted Kingfisher (rV)

ORDER PICIFORMES

Picidae
_____ *Melanerpes lewis*
_____ *Melanerpes formicivorus*
_____ *Sphyrapicus ruber*
    (S. varius)
_____ *Picoides nuttallii*
_____ *Picoides pubescens*
_____ *Colaptes auratus*

Woodpecker Family
_____ Lewis' Woodpecker (uW)
_____ Acorn Woodpecker (cR)
_____ Red-breasted Sapsucker
    (Yellow-bellied S., in part) (uW)
_____ Nuttall's Woodpecker (cR)
_____ Downy Woodpecker (rV)
_____ Northern Flicker (Red-shafted
    F., in part) (cW, rS)

ORDER PASSERIFORMES

Tyrannidae
_____ *Contopus borealis*
    (Nuttallornis b.)
_____ *Contopus sordidulus*
_____ *Empidonax traillii*
_____ *Empidonax difficilis*
_____ *Sayornis nigricans*
_____ *Sayornis saya*
_____ *Myiarchus cinerascens*
_____ *Tyrannus verticalis*

Flycatcher Family
_____ Olive-sided Flycatcher (rM)

_____ Western Wood-Pewee (uS)
_____ Willow Flycatcher (uV)
_____ Western Flycatcher (uM, rS)
_____ Black Phoebe (uV)
_____ Say's Phoebe (uW)
_____ Ash-throated Flycatcher (cS)
_____ Western Kingbird (cS)

Alaudidae
_____ *Eremophila alpestris*

Lark Family
_____ Horned Lark (uR)

Hirundinidae
_____ *Tachycineta bicolor*
    (Iridoprocne b.)
_____ *Tachycineta thalassina*
_____ *Stelgidopteryx serripennis*
    (S. ruficollis)
_____ *Riparia riparia*
_____ *Hirundo pyrrhonota*
    (Petrochelidon p.)
_____ *Hirundo rustica*

Swallow Family
_____ Tree Swallow (uV)

_____ Violet-green Swallow (uS)
_____ Northern Rough-winged Swallow (rV)

_____ Bank Swallow (rV)
_____ Cliff Swallow (cS)

_____ Barn Swallow (uS)

Corvidae
_____ *Aphelocoma coerulescens*
_____ *Pica nuttalli*
_____ *Corvus brachyrhynchos*

Jay and Crow Family
_____ Scrub Jay (cR)
_____ Yellow-billed Magpie (uR)
_____ American Crow (Common C.) (uR)

Paridae
_____ *Parus inornatus*

Titmouse Family
_____ Plain Titmouse (cR)

Aegithalidae
_____ *Psaltriparus minimus*

Bushtit Family
_____ Bushtit (cR)

Sittidae
_____ *Sitta carolinensis*

Nuthatch Family
_____ White-breasted Nuthatch (uR)

Certhiidae
_____ *Certhia americana*
        (C. familiaris)

Troglodytidae
_____ *Salpinctes obsoletus*
_____ *Catherpes mexicanus*
_____ *Thryomanes bewickii*
_____ *Troglodytes aedon*
_____ *Cistothorus palustris*

Muscicapidae
   Sylviinae
_____ *Regulus satrapa*
_____ *Regulus calendula*
_____ *Polioptila caerulea*

   Turdinae
_____ *Sialia mexicana*
_____ *Sialia currucoides*
_____ *Myadestes townsendi*
_____ *Catharus ustulatus*
_____ *Catharus guttatus*
_____ *Turdus migratorius*
_____ *Ixoreus naevius*

Mimidae
_____ *Mimus polyglottos*

Motacillidae
_____ *Anthus spinoletta*

Bombycillidae
_____ *Bombycilla cedrorum*

Ptilogonatidae
_____ *Phainopepla nitens*

Laniidae
_____ *Lanius excubitor*
_____ *Lanius ludovicianus*

Sturnidae
_____ *Sturnus vulgaris*

Vireonidae
_____ *Vireo solitarius*
_____ *Vireo huttoni*
_____ *Vireo gilvus*

Emberizidae
   Parulinae
_____ *Vermivora celata*
_____ *Vermivora ruficapilla*

Creeper Family
_____ Brown Creeper (rV)

Wren Family
_____ Rock Wren (uR)
_____ Canyon Wren (uR)
_____ Bewick's Wren (cR)
_____ House Wren (uM)
_____ Marsh Wren (Long-billed M.W.) (uV)

Old World Warblers and Allies Family
   Kinglet and Gnatcatcher Subfamily
_____ Golden-crowned Kinglet (uW)
_____ Ruby-crowned Kinglet (cW)
_____ Blue-gray Gnatcatcher (uM)

   Thrush Subfamily
_____ Western Bluebird (uW)
_____ Mountain Bluebird (rW)
_____ Townsend's Solitaire (rW)
_____ Swainson's Thrush (rM)
_____ Hermit Thrush (uW)
_____ American Robin (cW, uR)
_____ Varied Thrush (uW)

Mockingbird Family
_____ Northern Mockingbird (cR)

Pipit Family
_____ Water Pipit (cW)

Waxwing Family
_____ Cedar Waxwing (uW)

Silky Flycatcher Family
_____ Phainopepla (uR)

Shrike Family
_____ Northern Shrike (rW)
_____ Loggerhead Shrike (cW, uR)

Starling Family
_____ European Starling (cR)

Vireo Family
_____ Solitary Vireo (uM)
_____ Hutton's Vireo (rV)
_____ Warbling Vireo (uM)

Emberizid Family
   Wood Warbler Subfamily
_____ Orange-crowned Warbler (uM)
_____ Nashville Warbler (rM)

_____ *Dendroica petechia*
_____ *Dendroica coronata*

_____ *Dendroica nigrescens*
_____ *Dendroica townsendi*
_____ *Dendroica occidentalis*
_____ *Oporornis tolmiei*
_____ *Wilsonia pusilla*
_____ *Icteria virens*

Thraupinae
_____ *Piranga ludoviciana*

Cardinalinae
_____ *Pheucticus ludovicianus*
_____ *Pheucticus melanocephalus*
_____ *Guiraca caerulea*
_____ *Passerina amoena*

Emberizinae
_____ *Pipilo erythropthalmus*
_____ *Pipilo fuscus*
_____ *Aimophila ruficeps*
_____ *Spizella passerina*
_____ *Pooecetes gramineus*
_____ *Chondestes grammacus*
_____ *Amphispiza bilineata*
_____ *Calamospiza melanocorys*
_____ *Passerculus sandwichensis*
_____ *Passerella iliaca*
_____ *Melospiza melodia*
_____ *Melospiza lincolnii*
_____ *Zonotrichia atricapilla*
_____ *Zonotrichia leucophrys*
_____ *Zonotrichia querula*
_____ *Junco hyemalis*

Icterinae
_____ *Agelaius phoeniceus*
_____ *Agelaius tricolor*
_____ *Sturnella neglecta*
_____ *Xanthocephalus xanthocephalus*
_____ *Euphagus cyanocephalus*
_____ *Molothrus ater*
_____ *Icterus galbula*

Fringillidae
_____ *Carpodacus purpureus*
_____ *Carpodacus mexicanus*

_____ Yellow Warbler (rM)
_____ Yellow-rumped Warbler
      (Audubon's + Myrtle) (uW)
_____ Black-throated Gray Warbler (rM)
_____ Townsend's Warbler (rM)
_____ Hermit Warbler (rM)
_____ MacGillivray's Warbler (rM)
_____ Wilson's Warbler (uM)
_____ Yellow-breasted Chat (rM)

Tanager Subfamily
_____ Western Tanager (uM)

Grosbeak Subfamily
_____ Rose-breasted Grosbeak (rS)
_____ Black-headed Grosbeak (cS)
_____ Blue Grosbeak (rV)
_____ Lazuli Bunting (cM)

Sparrow Subfamily
_____ Rufous-sided Towhee (cW, uR)
_____ Brown Towhee (cR)
_____ Rufous-crowned Sparrow (cR)
_____ Chipping Sparrow (uM)
_____ Vesper Sparrow (uW)
_____ Lark Sparrow (cR)
_____ Black-throated Sparrow (rV)
_____ Lark Bunting (rV)
_____ Savannah Sparrow (cW)
_____ Fox Sparrow (uW)
_____ Song Sparrow (rV)
_____ Lincoln's Sparrow (uW)
_____ Golden-crowned Sparrow (cW)
_____ White-crowned Sparrow (cW)
_____ Harris' Sparrow (rW)
_____ Dark-eyed Junco (Oregon J.) (cW)

Blackbird and Oriole Subfamily
_____ Red-winged Blackbird (cR)
_____ Tricolored Blackbird (uR)
_____ Western Meadowlark (cR)
_____ Yellow-headed Blackbird (uV)
_____ Brewer's Blackbird (cR)
_____ Brown-headed Cowbird (uR)
_____ Northern Oriole (Bullock's O.) (cS)

Finch Family
_____ Purple Finch (uW)
_____ House Finch (cR)

_____ *Carduelis pinus*   _____ Pine Siskin (uW)
_____ *Carduelis psaltria*   _____ Lesser Goldfinch (cR)
_____ *Carduelis lawrencei*   _____ Lawrence's Goldfinch (uM)
_____ *Carduelis tristis*   _____ American Goldfinch (uR)
_____ *Coccothraustes vespertinus*   _____ Evening Grosbeak (rW)
       (Hesperiphona v.)

Passeridae (Ploceidae)   **Weaver Finch Family**
_____ *Passer domesticus*   _____ House Sparrow (uR)

Appendix I. Summary of Results of Peace Valley Christmas Bird Counts, 1973-1981.

(Boldface indicates highest total nationally, asterisked numbers established national record for highest CBC count since 1900, CP means seen count period (date ± 2 days) but not on count date.

	1973	1974	1975	1976	1977	1978	1979	1980	1981
Eared Grebe	5	4	2	1		1	1	26	
Western Grebe			1						3
Pied-billed Grebe	56	56	89	82	60	45	41	94	98
American White Pelican	1		4	29	74	47	21	61	
Double-crested Cormorant	3	2	4	5	3	4	5	10	102
Great Blue Heron	33	25	52	82	58	53	42	61	55
Green-backed Heron		CP	1	3		2	1		
Cattle Egret							4	6	8
Great Egret	40	32	66	63	45	85	46	73	46
Snowy Egret	28	40	60	32	26	12	4	2	178
Blk-crowned Night Heron	**614**	200	115	295	22	73	327	183	408
Least Bittern				1			1		1
American Bittern	8	34	51	**69**	**53**	53	38	48	28
Tundra (Whistling) Swan	1,952	235	200	166	394	635	106	554	219
Canada Goose	1,117	500	6,653	1,246	10,427	39,036	703	1,608	779
Greater White-fronted Goose	801	1,500	20,000	8,000	3,729	1,986	3,032	5,451	1,404
blue form		1	2		1	1	1		2
Snow Goose	5,079	35,000	124,000	30,000	122,322	**106,499**	64,854	89,370	145,051
Ross' Goose	212	**5,000***	**25,000***	**10,000**	1,951	3,500	**8,157**	753	**3,000**
Mallard	7,674	40,000	130,000	99,360	106,055	34,519	27,666	64,589	133,524
Gadwall	1,652	6,000	2,000	260	533	16,325*	1,570	2,067	3,169
Northern Pintail	**114,196**	**80,000**	**1,034,000**	**600,000**	**671,368**	**313,109**	**1,108,022**	**330,310**	**598,896**
Green-winged Teal	70	2,500	16,000	42,000	30,370	9,844	6,786	31,885	49,917

Species	1	2	3	4	5	6	7	8	9
Blue-winged Teal	1			1			10	"teal" 50	
Cinnamon Teal	151	200	25	17	6	12	13	23	188
Eurasian Wigeon	18*	2	3	1	1	2	2	2	9
American Wigeon	80,201	60,000	106,000	125,000	128,000	50,000	455,000*	115,313	420,315
Northern Shoveler	2,704	15,000	29,000	63,450	27,405	9,926	6,333	24,055	89,329*
Wood Duck	21	11	255	122	91	156	47	29	6
Redhead	4	CP	2	5	5	2		1	8
Ring-necked Duck	18	63	34	74	1,032	3,097	45	19	366
Canvasback	7	29		14	62	42	3	26	1
Lesser Scaup	1	6	7	12	12	12	1		2
scaup spp.	3								
Common Goldeneye	14			CP	4	1	1		1
Bufflehead	26	11	16	12	2	7	9	12	40
Ruddy Duck	420	175	114	402	1,367	8,984	4,404	571	3,915
Hooded Merganser			1						2
Common Merganser		20							
Turkey Vulture	187	409	464	753	806	342	358	418	205
Black-shouldered (White-tailed) Kite	34	63	70	87	30	32	27	64	46
Goshawk			CP						
Sharp-shinned Hawk	10	10	10	14	6	6	7	3	11
Cooper's Hawk	10	7	9	12	12	9	6	7	11
Red-tailed Hawk	127	136	132	208	174	169	176	183	153
Red-shouldered Hawk	6	2	1	5	4	5	5	7	2
Rough-legged Hawk	13	6		2	3	3	1	2	4
Ferruginous Hawk	1	2	5	3	2	1	2	2	2
Golden Eagle	1	1	1	5	7	3	2	2	2

	1973	1974	1975	1976	1977	1978	1979	1980	1981
Bald Eagle				2	3	5	2		
Northern Harrier (Marsh Hawk)	67	88	56	60	73	60	54	78	93
Prairie Falcon	2	4	2	3	3	4	1	4	5
Merlin						1			
American Kestrel	119	83	93	128	80	108	151	119	135
California Quail	33	149	94	195	365	206	355	310	335
Ring-necked Pheasant	122	204	155	131	135	224	182	101	54
Sandhill Crane	346	594	829	923	629	692	822	1,243	811
Virginia Rail	10	7	8	58	40	53	16	14	24
Sora	3	3	3	8	11	12	5	8	3
Common Moorhen (Gallinule)	20	64	96	56	32	27	69	42	39
American Coot	13,578	2,749	25,000	4,296	3,497	7,816	6,520	21,101	22,180
Killdeer	393	386	368	237	239	264	246	246	402
Common Snipe	59	29	66	89	21	32	46	5	25
Long-billed Curlew			66	17	6	15	2	2	
Spotted Sandpiper				1	1	1			1
Greater Yellowlegs	7	9	11	11	20	13	22	4	1
Lesser Yellowlegs		2			1	3	3		
Least Sandpiper	CP	185	141	47	228	180	167	98	15
Dunlin	8	393	170	473	221	237	197		
Long-billed Dowitcher	451	370	699	582	228	172	452	255	74
Western Sandpiper		2	1	7	2				
American Avocet				CP	CP				
Glaucous-winged Gull				2					
Herring Gull	5	5	10	7	4	6	7	17	24

Species									
California Gull	19		5		7	2	2		9
Ring-billed Gull	7	20	100	124	115	48	27	28	24
gull spp.					9	9			27
Band-tailed Pigeon	35			20		9			30
Rock Dove	72	56	75	157	94	132	145	88	89
Mourning Dove	128	156	133	111	112	85	171	82	27
Barn-Owl	2	6	12	4	2	5	7	8	4
Western Screech-Owl	1	2	1						
Great Horned Owl	4	4	13	19	15	9	14	26	16
Burrowing Owl	14	1	1	9	3	3	6	1	3
Long-eared Owl	1								1
Short-eared Owl	2	1	2	7	1				2
White-throated Swift			12	12		7		30	
swift spp.				6					
Anna's Hummingbird	2	9	23	1	4	2	3	26	7
Belted Kingfisher	22	10	15	27	16	18	23	21	10
Northern Flicker (R-s)	193	134	251	292	366	251	210	280	169
Acorn Woodpecker	56	39	42	55	66	36	10	52	68
Lewis' Woodpecker			2	2	19	**148**		4	
Red-breasted Sapsucker	3	3	4	7	31	6	3	4	2
Downy Woodpecker	10	13	18	23	22	7	5	3	9
Nuttall's Woodpecker	33	76	79	69	55	79	90	101	64
Black Phoebe	22	34	35	62	47	73	67	43	61
Say's Phoebe	4	12	11	17	10	9	9	21	14
Horned Lark		990	136	42	1,058	76	304	112	556
Tree Swallow	1	3	12	2	2	2	25	17	
Scrub Jay	227	176	165	164	145	227	185	261	250

	1973	1974	1975	1976	1977	1978	1979	1980	1981
Yellow-billed Magpie	297	535	400	611	452	257	247	259	452
Common Raven		2	1		1 h.				
American Crow	272	1,922	2,960	1,695	3,329	1,193	1,521	543	2,231
Plain Titmouse	73	155	119	140	155	188	150	290	192
Bushtit	33	168	118	273	168	163	182	458	413
White-breasted Nuthatch		4	15	4	7	1	3	19	18
Brown Creeper		4	4	4	2	1	1		12
House Wren	6		2	6	1	9	9	2	1
Winter Wren	1						1		
Bewick's Wren	26	42	57	81	40	52	39	89	36
Marsh Wren	63	74	132	212	152	329	86	86	169
Canyon Wren		10	14	22	24	4	5	10	7
Rock Wren	9	17	18	50	55	71	42	41	41
Northern Mockingbird	39	26	71	39	72	61	48	100	44
American Robin	14	115	471	116	120	5	43	100	42
Varied Thrush	2	3	23	7	43	3	4	47	18
Hermit Thrush	7	76	127	23	44	33	41	81	45
Western Bluebird	55	6	54	65	66	2 CP	20	24	69
Mountain Bluebird	10	2				23		16	77
Blue-gray Gnatcatcher	CP	CP		1					
Golden-crowned Kinglet	43	61	19	4	16	5		15	147
Ruby-crowned Kinglet	230	297	276	392	289	523	290	379	338
Water Pipit	386	357	1,488	795	679	416	690	304	673
Cedar Waxwing	72	36	44		103				
Phainopepla	3	1	1	3	4	2	4	6	14
Northern Shrike	1		2	1	6				

Loggerhead Shrike	69	54	67	64	47	70	48	51	48
European Starling	2,687	3,170	9,573	5,776	5,379	3,342	1,473	10,513	1,065
Hutton's Vireo								1	
Orange-crowned Warbler	3	2	6	5		2	3	16	6
Northern Parula	1								
Yellow Warbler			1					1	
Yellow-rumped (Myrtle) Warbler	48	1	2	27	43	19	28	5	
Yellow-rumped (Audubon's) Warbler	100	123	284	408	461	342	371	300	417
both races				211				162	
Common Yellowthroat	9	6	14	28	16	13	5	22	10
Green-tailed Towhee	1								
Rufous-sided Towhee	107	82	94	79	216	210	201	245	339
Brown Towhee	108	77	121	111	116	150	174	161	155
Savannah Sparrow	1,660	1,439	617	924	476	157	518		531
Vesper Sparrow	71	28	38	27	40	19	20	29	18
Lark Sparrow	1,642	807	523	575	537	529	459	611	638
Rufous-crowned Sparrow		1	7	11	44	12	42	34	17
Black-throated Sparrow								1	
Dark-eyed (Slate-col.) Junco	1							CP	
Dark-eyed (Oregon) Junco	632	508	675	701	954	729	903	521	2
Tree Sparrow	4			1					
Chipping Sparrow	5	1	3						
White-crowned Sparrow	7,306	3,300	3,784	8,101	9,057	4,362	4,352	4,173	3,928
Golden-crowned Sparrow	1,006	338	701	990	2,760	675	742	956	646
White-throated Sparrow		1		1				1	

	1973	1974	1975	1976	1977	1978	1979	1980	1981
Fox Sparrow	7	12	12	31	12	24	20	13	19
Lincoln's Sparrow	30	30	41	52	85	65	24	34	19
Swamp Sparrow	1				1				
Song Sparrow	93	23	110	92	82	126	78	185	71
Western Meadowlark	3,317	1,194	1,670	2,049	1,965	2,576	1,934	2,499	3,441
Yellow-headed Blackbird		27	451	106	2,524	24	21	68	29
Red-winged Blackbird	4,640	4,095	11,287	211,627	44,543	3,000,000	1,087,428	55,767	267,877
Tricolored Blackbird	273	534	2,300	44,560*	15,487	73	262	181	408
Northern Oriole (Bullock's)	1								
Brewer's Blackbird	15,070	10,141	9,409	10,123	12,445	2,060	6,480	7,773	2,465
Brown-headed Cowbird	22	35	5,136	73	4,055	411	529	187	108
blackbird spp.		20,000		160,035	115,700			3,200	800
Evening Grosbeak					3				
Purple Finch	6	9	13	8	24	2		10	10
House Finch	1,262	3,716	1,316	1,730	414	811	1,981	1,601	1,504
Pine Siskin	41		769		254	4	10	2	153
Amer. Goldfinch	762	1,696	346	1,215	1,118	158	153	189	101
Lesser Goldfinch	164	297	618	1,170	790	206	988	238	644
House Sparrow	440	572	287	237	204	239	215	229	189

Appendix J. Checklist of Mammals of the Sutter Buttes.

ORDER MARSUPIALIA

Didelphidae
_____ *Didelphis marsupialis*

Opossum Family
_____ Common Opossum

ORDER INSECTIVORA

Soricidae
_____ *Sorex ornatus*

Shrew Family
_____ Ornate Shrew

Talpidae
_____ *Scapanus latimanus*

Mole Family
_____ Broad-handed or Western Mole

ORDER CHIROPTERA

Vespertilionidae
_____ *Myotis yumanensis*
_____ *Myotis californicus*
_____ *Pipistrellus hesperus*
_____ *Eptesicus fuscus*
_____ *Lasiurus borealis*
_____ *Lasiurus cinereus*
_____ *Plecotus townsendii*

_____ *Antrozous pallidus*

Evening Bat Family
* _____ Yuma Myotis
_____ California Myotis
* _____ Western Pipistrelle
* _____ Big Brown Bat
_____ Red Bat
* _____ Hoary Bat
* _____ Lump-nosed or Townsend's
Big-eared Bat
_____ Pallid Bat

Molossidae
_____ *Tadarida brasiliensis*

Free-tailed Bat Family
_____ Brazilian Free-tailed Bat

ORDER LAGOMORPHA

Leporidae
_____ *Sylvilagus audubonii*
_____ *Lepus californicus*

Rabbit and Hare Family
_____ Audubon's or Desert Cottontail
_____ Black-tailed Hare or Jackrabbit

ORDER RODENTIA

Sciuridae
_____ *Spermophilus beecheyi*
_____ *Sciurus griseus*

Squirrel Family
_____ California Ground Squirrel
* _____ Western Gray Squirrel

Geomyidae
_____ *Thomomys bottae*

Pocket Gopher Family
_____ Botta's Pocket Gopher

Heteromyidae
_____ *Perognathus inornatus*
_____ *Dipodomys californicus*

Pocket Mouse and Kangaroo Rat Family
_____ San Joaquin Pocket Mouse
_____ California Kangaroo Rat

Castoridae
_____ *Castor canadensis*

Beaver Family
_____ Beaver

Cricetidae
_____ *Reithrodontomys megalotis*
_____ *Peromyscus maniculatus*
_____ *Peromyscus truei*
_____ *Microtus californicus*
_____ *Ondatra zibethica*

New World Mouse and Rat Family
_____ Western Harvest Mouse
_____ Deer Mouse
_____ Pinon Mouse
_____ California Vole or Meadow Mouse
_____ Muskrat

Muridae
_____ *Rattus norvegicus*
_____ *Rattus rattus*
_____ *Mus musculus*

Old World Mouse and Rat Family
_____ Norway Rat
_____ Black Rat
_____ House Mouse

Erethizontidae
_____ *Erethizon dorsatum*

Porcupine Family
_____ Porcupine

ORDER CARNIVORA

Canidae
_____ *Canis latrans*
_____ *Vulpes vulpes*
_____ *Urocyon cinereoargenteus*

Dog Family
_____ Coyote
_____ Red Fox
_____ Gray Fox

Procyonidae
_____ *Procyon lotor*
_____ *Bassariscus astutus*

Raccoon Family
_____ Raccoon
_____ Ringtail

Mustelidae
_____ *Mustela frenata*
_____ *Mustela vison*
_____ *Taxidea taxus*
_____ *Spilogale gracilis*
_____ *Mephitis mephitis*
_____ *Lutra canadensis*

Mustelid Family
* _____ Long-tailed Weasel
_____ Mink
_____ Badger
_____ Spotted Skunk
_____ Striped Skunk
_____ River Otter

Felidae
_____ *Felis rufus*

Cat Family
_____ Bobcat

Cervidae
_____ *Odocoileus hemionus*

Deer Family
_____ Mule (Black-tailed) Deer

---

* Presence implied by range maps (Ingles 1965; Verner and Boss 1980).

INDEX

Additional information about individual species can be found in the species lists, pages 276 - 314, and on geographical places in locational maps, pages xviii, xix, and 3.

Acacia Avenue, 4
Acarina, 158
Accipitridae, 12, 205
Achillea, 73
Achyrachaena, 71
Across California Land Heritage Corridor, 269
Adenostoma, 55
Admiral, Lorquin's, 139, 146; Red, 139, 145
Aedes, 136
Aegithalidae, 217
Aesculus, 55
Agelinopsis, 156
Agoseris, 74
Ahart, Lowell, 56, 91
Ailanthus, 107
Alameda County, 54
Alcedinidae, 213
Algae, 38, 41, 48-49, 56, 127, 131, 165
Alisma, Alismataceae, 111-12
Alligator Lizard, 177-78
Almond Orchard Road, 6
Almonds, 4, 6, 237-38
Amanita, 45
Amaryllidaceae, Amaryllis, 112
Amorpha, 55
Amsinckia, 55
Anacardiaceae, 67
Anagallis, 98
Anatidae, 203
Andesite, 20, 23-28, 30-34, 264
Andricus, 152-53
Anglewing, 139, 144-45
Anguidae, 177
Anopheles, 136
Ants, 120
Anthemis, 73
Anthocaris, 143
Antron, 152-53
Apiaceae, 15, 68
Aphids, 151
Aphodius, 149
Apodidae, 212
Arachnid, 155-58
Argiope, 156
Aristida, 54, 115

Aristolochia, 70, 140; Aristolochiaceae, 68
Arrowhead, 111-12
Artemisia, 73
Asclepiadaceae, 71
Ash, Oregon, 94
Ash, volcanic, 20-21, 23-26, 28, 31
Aster, 72, 144
Asteraceae, 15, 71
Asterella, 57-58
Atlides, 147
Atypoides, 157
Avena, 115, 117
Avocet, 197, 209
Azolla, 64

Baby Blue Eyes, 88
Baccharis, 73
Backswimmer, 130-31
Bacteria, 37-41, 151-52
Badger, 237, 253-54
Balsamorhiza, Balsamroot, 71
Barbed wire, 262
Barberry, California, 75
Barley, 116-17
Barnyard Grass, 116
Basalt, 19. 21, 31
Bassariscus, 251
Bat, 84, 241
Battus, 140
Bay, California, 90-91, 188, 190
Bear, Grizzly, 236, 261
Beardgrass, 116-17
Beardtongue, 105
Beaver, 237-38, 245, 247
Bedstraw, 103
Bees, 77, 81, 88, 97, 99, 102, 105, 109, 157, 164, 215, 237-38, 254
Beetles, 95, 133-34, 149; Dung, 149; Predaceous Diving, 133; Water Scavenger, 134; Whirligig, 134
Bellflower, 77
Berberidaceae, 75
Bermuda Grass, 115, 119
Bindweed, 79
Biotite, 30

Walt Anderson

In an era of specialists, it is surprising but refreshing to find someone like WALT ANDERSON, "the naturalist of old cast in modern times, the next generation of a proud and ancient lineage". While the Sutter Buttes has been a major focal point for the past seven years, Walt has managed to develop a global perspective on ecosystems, serving as expedition guide throughout the American West, Baja, Alaska, East Africa, and South America. Trained as a scientist and experienced as a wildlife biologist on federal refuges, Walt also has the eye and sensitivity of an artist. His award-winning photographs and wildlife paintings attest to the breadth of his interests and talents.